Cesáreo Hernández · Marta Posada
Adolfo López-Paredes
Editors

Artificial Economics

The Generative Method in Economics

Dr. Cesáreo Hernández
Dr. Marta Posada
Dr. Adolfo López-Paredes
Valladolid University
InSiSoc. E.T.S.I. Industriales
Paseo del Cauce, 59
47011 Valladolid
Spain
cesareo@eis.uva.es
posada@eis.uva.es
adolfo@insisoc.org

ISSN 0075-8442
ISBN 978-3-642-02955-4   e-ISBN 978-3-642-02956-1
DOI 10.1007/978-3-642-02956-1
Springer Dordrecht Heidelberg London New York

Library of Congress Control Number: 2009931062

© Springer-Verlag Berlin Heidelberg 2009
This work is subject to copyright. All rights are reserved, whether the whole or part of the material is concerned, specifically the rights of translation, reprinting, reuse of illustrations, recitation, broadcasting, reproduction on microfilm or in any other way, and storage in data banks. Duplication of this publication or parts thereof is permitted only under the provisions of the German Copyright Law of September 9, 1965, in its current version, and permission for use must always be obtained from Springer. Violations are liable to prosecution under the German Copyright Law.
The use of general descriptive names, registered names, trademarks, etc. in this publication does not imply, even in the absence of a specific statement, that such names are exempt from the relevant protective laws and regulations and therefore free for general use.

Cover design: SPi Publisher Services

Printed on acid-free paper

Springer is part of Springer Science+Business Media (www.springer.com)

Acknowledgements

Our thanks go to the members of the Scientific Committee who reviewed the submitted papers and gave most valuable comments to the authors:

- Frédéric Amblard - Université de Toulouse 1, France
- Luis Antunes - Universidade de Lisboa, Portugal
- Robert Axtell - Brookings Institution, George Mason University, USA
- Bruno Beaufils - Université of Lille 1, France
- Olivier Brandouy - Université de Lille 1, France
- Charlotte Bruun - Aalborg Universitet, Denmark
- Alessandro Cappellini - Università degli Studi di Torino, Italy
- Silvano Cincotti - Università degli Studi di Genova, Italy
- Andrea Consiglio - Università degli Studi di Palermo, Italy
- Christophe Deissenberg - Université de la Méditerranée, France
- Giorgo Fagiolo - LEM, Scuola Superiore Sant'Anna, Pisa, Italy
- José Manuel Galán - Universidad de Burgos, Spain
- Florian Hauser - Universität Innsbruck, Austria
- Wander Jager - Rijksuniversiteit Groningen, The Netherlands
- Marco Janssen - Arizona State University, USA
- Alan Kirman - GREQAM, France
- Philippe Lamarre - LINA, Université de Nantes, France
- Thomas Lux - Universität zu Kiel, Germany
- Marco Licalzi - Università "Ca' Foscari" di Venezia, Italy
- Luigi Marengo - LEM, Scuola Superiore Sant'Anna, Pisa, Italy
- Philippe Mathieu - Université de Lille 1, France
- Akira Namatame - National Defense Academy, Japan
- Javier Pajares - Universidad de Valladolid, Spain
- Juan Pavón - Universidad Complutense de Madrid, Spain
- Paolo Pellizzari - Università "Ca' Foscari" di Venezia, Italy
- Denis Phan - Université de Rennes I, France
- Juliette Rouchier - GREQAM, France
- Annalisa Russino - Università degli Studi di Palermo, Italy
- Leigh Tesfatsion - Iowa State University, USA
- Elpida Tzafestas - National Technical University of Athens, Greece
- Murat Yildizoglu - Université Paul Cézanne, GREQAM, France

Thanks as well to the authors and to the Springer-Verlag editors. They made it possible to publish this volume in time for the Conference.

We acknowledge financial support for the conference and the book by the Spanish Ministry of Science and Education TIN2008-06464-C03-02, to the Council of Education of Castilla y León and to the University of Valladolid. Thanks as well to our colleague Pablo Martín for producing the manuscript.

Preface

The organizers of the Artificial Economics Conference 2009 (AE09) are pleased to present this book that gathers the accepted papers. The Conference is the fifth regular meeting of researchers interested in the Agent Based Approach to Economics and Managerial Applications, this year in Valladolid (Spain) September 10-11th, 2009. The main aim of the event is to favour the meeting of people and ideas from both, the Computer Science community and the Economics and Finance community, in order to be able to construct a much structured multi-disciplinary approach to the complexity of Economics. Since this is a book about Artificial Economics, we should briefly describe what it means for the Editors.

Artificial Economics (AE) is Experimental Economics using Software Agents. Econometrics was founded as a bridge between Statistics and Mathematics in Economics. AE can be thought of, as a bridging discipline between Economics and Agent Based Modelling (ABM) and Distributed Artificial Intelligence (DAI). Today we are in the early stages of AE but there is a solid and growing stream of ABM applications, both practical and focused on the development of better explanations of economic observed facts. The proceedings of the Conferences published in the Lecture Notes in Economics and Mathematical Systems Springer series, sum up more than 100 papers and are a good sample of the state of the art in AE.

Simulation is used in Economics to solve large econometric models, large scale micro simulations and obtaining numerical solutions for policy design from a top down established model. But these uses fail to take advantage of the facilities offer by Artificial Intelligence and Distributed Computing. AE can leverage these facilities. AE should not be considered a chapter of Computational Economics, the main difference being the bottom-up approach of ABM and the generative nature of the method. We should be grateful to the promoters of the first AE Conference in September 2005 at Lille, France, P. Mathieu, O. Brandouy and B. Beaufils for coining the AE name just avoiding the confusion going on in the field. In fact even in this Conference we had to reject some papers because of their computational top-down approach.

As pointed out by Axtell (2008), ABM simulation in Economics, from now on AE, can be viewed as a very elegant and general class of modelling techniques that generalize numerical economics, mathematical programming and micro simulation approaches. When agent models are populated by non autonomous agents whose behaviour is pre-specified and neither adaptive nor strategic, they become microsimulations. When individual agents are optimizers and there is a social planning agent that can be viewed as coordinating or aggregating these individual decisions, then we have ABM behaving as general mathematical programming models. But AE models with agents that are systematically heterogeneous, purposeful, bounded rational and interacting over networks, away from equilibrium, do not generally correspond to the accepted Economic Theory models. In Axtell (2008) words, so general is the agent approach to Economics, and so prodigious has computing technology become, that it is tempting to call this new approach computational enabled Economics.

Economics is a social science. Being social inherits complexity and being a science calls for experimentation. The complexity in Economics is not only due to the fact that we observe just real aggregated data from simple agents with myriad interactions: a hard computational problem. A higher and different kind of complexity comes from the personal exchange where perhaps there are few agents but they are bounded rational, they learn from other agents behaviour and they are adaptive, purposeful and strategic (López-Paredes *et al.*, 2002). In both cases experimentation is necessary to explore and discover the emerging macro behaviour. Historical records are not enough to discover or test economic theories. Experimental Economics with humans has provided a replicable Lab that provides further empirical data and it has been recently welcome by the economist profession. But human behaviour in the experiment is not directly controllable and the question of what the agent's behaviour is, remains open. AE has broadened the scope of Experimental Economics, allowing the modeller to check alternative individual behaviour. In this sense ABM simulation in feedback, when this is possible, with Experimental Economics with humans, is a "killer approach" to Economic Theory.

There are three dimensions that are essential when modelling any economic issue: the institution (I) (the exchange rules, the way the contracts are closed, and the information network), the environment (E) (the agent's endowments, values, resources and knowledge) and the agent behaviour (A). By mapping different arrangements of the elements of this triplet (IxExA) into generated outcomes a host of experimental results can be obtained and explored. Experimental Economists have been doing that for the last 30 years and they have gained very valuable insight in many difficult and unsolved economic issues. AE can go even further in this direction. Exporting Economic Theory to other fields including natural resources management has proved forced labour. With ABM, we can export the AE methods to any physical landscape populated by social agents such as in the management and economics of natural resources (Galán *et al.*, 2009).

The neoclassical conception of Economics, the "value window", is not capable to explain dynamics and evolution, a fact widely acknowledged: "For the real dynamics, which investigates the precise motions, usually far away from equilibria, a much deeper knowledge...is required" (Von Neumann and Morgenstern, 1944: 44-45). In the last 20 years a lot of research has been done using biologically inspired analogies to extend the "value window" in evolutionary and behavioural economics. But as Schredelseker and Hauser (2008) pointed out (although not exactly in this terms) AE can provide socially inspired analogies to solve complex problems in Economics with a full behavioural focus.

The shocking prediction accuracy of "Prediction Markets" (Arrow *et al.*, 2008) is an experimental proof of the spontaneous capacity of ABM for computing equilibriums (when there are) in a generative way: the "exchange window"; the spontaneous and emerging order of Hayek. AE can thus contribute to get deeper insights in this fascinating "exchange window" approach to solve the complexity of Economics: how can the autonomous local exchange of heterogeneous, bounded rational and purposeful agents generate the observed economic behaviour? AE is a generative approach to Economics. The purpose of AE is to grow explanations and when there exist, to generate the equilibriums, not just assuming their existence to force the economic models (Epstein, 2006).

Two prestigious invited speakers have contributed to the Conference with topics not included in the book. As in previous meetings they represent some of the interdisciplinary fields that sustain AE: in this case Artificial Intelligence and Econophysics. *Agents, Information and Negotiation* is the talk of Carles Sierra, Professor at the Institute of Research on Artificial Intelligence of the Spanish Council for Scientific Research at Barcelona. Successful negotiators fix up by their position along five dimensions: Legitimacy, Options, Goals, Independence, and Commitment, (LOGIC). He introduces a negotiation model based on these dimensions and on two primitive concepts: intimacy (degree of closeness) and balance (degree of fairness). The intimacy is a pair of matrices that evaluate both an agent's contribution to the relationship and its opponent's contribution. Each matrix includes an information view and from a utilitarian view across the five LOGIC dimensions. The balance is the difference between these matrices. The negotiation strategy maintains a set of Options that are in-line with the current intimacy level. The tactics wrap the Options in argumentation with the aim of attaining a successful deal and manipulating the successive negotiation balances towards the target intimacy. Summary measures of trust and reputation are also discussed.

How do Micro-Economic Simple Rules Generate Complex Macro-Economic Behavior? An Agent Based Modelling Approach for Connecting Empirical Facts with Theoretical Predictions is the talk by Sorin Solomon, Professor at the Racah Institute of Physics at the Hebrew University of Jerusalem. For a very long while it was customary in Economics to formalize mathematically a collection of many similar objects in terms of "representative agents" or "mean field": a continuous functions in space and time representing the local average of their individual properties. In fact, this "mean field", is what kept the various scientific domains apart. When "More Is Different" (the title of the article published 35 years ago by Nobel Laureate Phil Anderson) the singular, extreme, and very rare events become crucial. One can think about the "elementary" objects belonging to the "simpler" level (say firms in microeconomics) as the nodes of a network and about the "elementary" interactions between them as the links of the network. The dynamics of the entire system is then emerging from the interactions of the individual links and nodes. The global features of the resulting network correspond to the collective properties of the emerging system: (quasi-)disconnected network components correspond to (almost-)independent emergent economic branches; scaling properties of the network correspond to power laws in the firms distribution, long-lived (meta-stable) network features correspond to critical slowing down activity. The knowledge of the collective emerging features of the network allows one to devise methods to expedite by orders of magnitude desired processes (or to delay or stop un-wanted ones). S. Solomon describes the application of this approach to Macroeconomics and confronts the results to empirical data.

The AE Conferences are a two-day meeting without parallel sessions to promote a full participation in the discussions. The disadvantage of this choice is the limitation in the number of accepted papers. 21 papers were selected from 56 submitted extended abstracts after a blind reviewing process. We are grateful to all the submitters. The contributions are arranged in seven chapters: Macroeconomics, Industrial Organization, Market Dynamics and Auctions, Finance, Financial Markets, Information and Learning, and Methodological Issues

Valladolid, Spain
May 2009

Cesáreo Hernández
Marta Posada
Adolfo López-Paredes

References

Axtell, R. (2008). The Rise of Computationally Enabled Economics. Eastern Economic Journal, 34, pp. 423–428.

Arrow, K.J., *et al.* (2008). The Promise of Prediction Markets. Science vol 320 16 may 2008.

Epstein, J.M. (2006). Generative Social Science: Studies in Agent-Based Computational Modeling. Princeton University Press.

Galán, J. M., López-Paredes, A., and del Olmo, R. (2009), An agent based model for domestic water management in Valladolid metropolitan area, Water Resource Research, 45, W05401.

López-Paredes, A. Hernández, C. and Pajares, J. (2002) Towards a New Experimental Socio-Economics. Complex Behavior in Bargaining. Journal of Socio-economics. Vol.: 31, pp. 423–429. Elsevier.

Schredelseker, K., and Hauser, F. (2008). Complexity and Artificial Markets. Lecture Notes in Economics and Mathematical Systems. N° 614.Springer. Berlin.

Von Neumann, J., and Morgenstern, O. (1944). Theory of Games and Economic Behavior. Princeton University Press, Princeton, NJ.

Contents

Part I Macroeconomics

1   A Potential Disadvantage of a Low Interest Rate Policy: the Instability of Banks Liquidity 3
Gianfranco Giulioni
  1.1   Introduction 3
  1.2   The Bank 5
    1.2.1   Profitability and Liquidity 6
    1.2.2   An Idealization of the Bank Activity 6
    1.2.3   The Lending Activity 7
  1.3   Simulations 9
  1.4   Comparative Static, Dynamics and Credit Rationing 11
  1.5   Conclusions 12
  References 13

2   Keynes in the Computer Laboratory. An Agent-Based Model with MEC, MPC, LP 15
Giulia Canzian, Edoardo Gaffeo and Roberto Tamborini
  2.1   Introduction 15
  2.2   The Model 17
    2.2.1   Methodological Premises 17
    2.2.2   Modelling the Market Sentiment 18
    2.2.3   The Marginal Efficiency of Capital 19
    2.2.4   The Marginal Propensity to Consume 20
    2.2.5   The Liquidity Preference 21
    2.2.6   Aggregate Supply 22
  2.3   Simulations Results 23
    2.3.1   GDP Series 23
    2.3.2   GDP and its Components 25
  2.4   Conclusions 26
  References 27

3 Pride and Prejudice on a Centralized Academic Labor Market 29
Philippe Caillou and Michele Sebag
- 3.1 Introduction 29
- 3.2 Related Work 30
- 3.3 The French Academic Labor Market 31
  - 3.3.1 The Hiring Process 31
  - 3.3.2 Empirical Evidence 31
- 3.4 Academic Labor Market Modelling 32
  - 3.4.1 Agent Preferences 32
  - 3.4.2 Multi-Agent Based Model 32
- 3.5 Simulation Results 34
  - 3.5.1 Methodology and Experimental Settings 34
  - 3.5.2 No Learning Setting 35
  - 3.5.3 Learning Universities Setting 36
- 3.6 Conclusion 39
- References 39

Part II Industrial Organization

4 U. S. Defense Market Concentration: An Analysis of the Period 1996–2006 43
Wayne Zandbergen
- 4.1 Introduction 43
- 4.2 Analysis of U. S. Defense Market Structure 1996–2006 44
  - 4.2.1 Data Sources 44
  - 4.2.2 Market Description & Unique Factors 44
  - 4.2.3 Results and Findings 46
- 4.3 Two Simple Computational Models 49
- 4.4 Conclusion and Further Research 51
- References 52

5 Operator's Bidding Strategies in the Liberalized Italian Power Market 53
Eric Guerci, Mohammad Ali Rastegar and Silvano Cincotti
- 5.1 Introduction 53
- 5.2 ACE Model 55
  - 5.2.1 Market Model 55
  - 5.2.2 Grid Model 57
  - 5.2.3 Agent Model 57
  - 5.2.4 Learning Model 59
- 5.3 Results 60
- 5.4 Conclusions 64
- References 65

6 Selection Processes in a Monopolistic Competition Market 67
Jose I. Santos, Ricardo del Olmo and Javier Pajares
- 6.1 Motivation 67
- 6.2 A Formal Model of a Differentiated Industry 68
  - 6.2.1 Consumer Behavior 68
  - 6.2.2 Evolutionary Firm Behavior 69
- 6.3 Selection and Monopolistic Competition 71
  - 6.3.1 Homogeneous Product Competition 71
  - 6.3.2 Differentiated Product Competition 72
  - 6.3.3 Heterogeneity and Other Model Parameters 74
- 6.4 Conclusions 77
- References 77

Part III Market Dynamics and Auctions

7 Symmetric Equilibria in Double Auctions with Markdown Buyers and Markup Sellers 81
Roberto Cervone, Stefano Galavotti and Marco LiCalzi
- 7.1 Introduction 81
- 7.2 The Model 82
  - 7.2.1 The Environment 83
- 7.3 Call Market 83
  - 7.3.1 General Markup and Markdown Coefficients 84
  - 7.3.2 Ex Ante Equilibria 85
- 7.4 Bilateral Trading 86
- 7.5 Continuous Double Auction 87
- 7.6 Conclusions 92
- References 92

8 Multi-Unit Auction Analysis by Means of Agent-Based Computational Economics 93
Asuncion Mochon, Yago Saez, David Quintana and Pedro Isasi
- 8.1 Introduction 93
- 8.2 The Ausubel Auction 95
- 8.3 The Agent-Based Model 96
- 8.4 The Experimental Results 97
  - 8.4.1 Decreasing Marginal Values 97
  - 8.4.2 Increasing Marginal Values 98
- 8.5 Conclusions 100
- References 101

9 Social Learning and Pricing Obfuscation 103
Maciej Latek and Bogumil Kaminski
- 9.1 Introduction 103
- 9.2 Model Architecture 105
  - 9.2.1 Obfuscation Game and Dimensions of Intervention 105

		9.2.2 Recursive Companies 106

    9.2.2   Recursive Companies 106
    9.2.3   Adaptive Customers 107
9.3 Experiments... 108
    9.3.1   Baseline Behaviors 109
    9.3.2   Efficiency of Market Intervention 110
9.4 Conclusions... 112
References 113

Part IV Finance

10 Mutual Funds Flows and the "Sheriff of Nottingham" Effect 117
Lucia Milone and Paolo Pellizzari
10.1 Introduction 117
10.2 A Simple Example and One Analytical Result 119
10.3 A Computational Model.................................... 122
     10.3.1 Results 123
10.4 Conclusion.. 127
References 128

11 Foundations for a Framework for Multiagent-Based Simulation of Macrohistorical Episodes in Financial Markets 129
Bàrbara Llacay and Gilbert Peffer
11.1 Introduction 129
11.2 What is Wrong with MABS?................................ 130
     11.2.1 Barriers to MABS for Macrohistorical Research in Finance... 131
11.3 Proposal for a MABS Framework........................... 135
     11.3.1 A Bird's Eye View of the Framework 136
     11.3.2 The Modelling Process 139
11.4 Conclusions... 142
References 143

12 Explaining Equity Excess Return by Means of an Agent-Based Financial Market... 145
Andrea Teglio, Marco Raberto and Silvano Cincotti
12.1 Introduction 146
12.2 The Model 147
     12.2.1 Firms... 147
     12.2.2 Households.. 148
     12.2.3 The Banking Sector................................ 150
     12.2.4 The Government 151
12.3 Simulation Results 151
12.4 Conclusions... 154
References 156

Part V Financial Markets

13 Bubble and Crash in the Artificial Financial Market 159
Yuji Karino and Toshiji Kawagoe
- 13.1 Introduction 159
- 13.2 An Artificial Financial Market 160
  - 13.2.1 Market Settings 160
  - 13.2.2 Trading Agents 162
  - 13.2.3 Transaction System 164
- 13.3 Results 165
  - 13.3.1 Simulation Results 165
  - 13.3.2 Definition of Price Bubble 166
  - 13.3.3 Sensibility Analysis 169
- 13.4 Conclusion 169
- References 170

14 Computation of the Ex-Post Optimal Strategy for the Trading of a Single Financial Asset 171
Olivier Brandouy, Philippe Mathieu and Iryna Veryzhenko
- 14.1 Introduction 171
- 14.2 Elements of the Game and Formalizations 173
  - 14.2.1 Initial Simplification 174
  - 14.2.2 A Linear Programming Method For the Identification of $S*$ 176
  - 14.2.3 Embedding the Identification of $S*$ in a Graph Structure 177
  - 14.2.4 The $S*-determination$ Algorithm 179
- 14.3 Numerical Illustrations and Conclusive Remarks 181
- References 184

15 A Generative Approach on the Relationship between Trading Volume, Prices, Returns and Volatility of Financial Assets 185
José Antonio Pascual and Javier Pajares
- 15.1 Introduction 185
- 15.2 Historical Precedents and Motivation 186
- 15.3 Methodology 187
  - 15.3.1 The ISS-ASM Model 188
  - 15.3.2 Dataset 189
  - 15.3.3 Cross-Correlations and Causal Relation 189
- 15.4 Conclusions - Results 189
  - 15.4.1 Price-Volume Relationship 190
  - 15.4.2 Return-Volume Relationship 191
  - 15.4.3 Volatility-Volume Relationship 192
  - 15.4.4 Causal Relationship 193
- 15.5 Summary 195
- References 195

Part VI Information and Learning

16 Comparing Laboratory Experiments and Agent-Based Simulations: The Value of Information and Market Efficiency in a Market with Asymmetric Information 199
Florian Hauser, Jürgen Huber and Michael Kirchler
16.1   Introduction 199
16.2   Market Model 200
16.3   Experimental Implementation and Simulation 201
16.4   Results 203
       16.4.1   Distribution of Returns 203
       16.4.2   Market Efficiency 207
16.5   Conclusion 209
References 209

17 Asset Return Dynamics under Alternative Learning Schemes 211
Elena Catanese, Andrea Consiglio, Valerio Lacagnina and Annalisa Russino
17.1   Introduction 211
17.2   The Model 213
       17.2.1   The Market Setting 213
       17.2.2   The Portfolio Model 214
       17.2.3   The Learning Process 214
       17.2.4   Statistical Measures of Population Heterogeneity 216
17.3   Calibration and Results 217
       17.3.1   Simulation Parameters 217
       17.3.2   Comparison between the Learning Models 218
References 222

18 An Attempt to Integrate Path-Dependency in a Learning Model 223
Narine Udumyan, Juliette Rouchier and Dominique Ami
18.1   Introduction 223
18.2   Study of CPR Based on Information Issue 225
       18.2.1   Lack of Information and Over-Exploitation 225
       18.2.2   Dealing with Scarce Information in ABM 225
18.3   The Model 227
       18.3.1   Main Assumptions and General Framework 227
       18.3.2   Resource Dynamics and Probabilistic Choice of Effort .. 227
18.4   Simulations 229
18.5   Results 230
18.6   Discussions 231
18.7   Conclusion 232
References 233

Part VII Methodological Issues

19 A Model-to-Model Analysis of the Repeated Prisoners' Dilemma: Genetic Algorithms *vs*. Evolutionary Dynamics 237
Xavier Vilà
19.1 Introduction 237
19.2 The Analytical Model 238
  19.2.1 The Replicator Dynamics Analysis 239
19.3 The Computational Model 241
19.4 Conclusions 243
References 244

20 Impact of Tag Recognition in Economic Decisions 245
David Poza, Félix Villafáñez and Javier Pajares
20.1 Introduction 245
20.2 Cognitive Foundations 246
20.3 The Model 247
20.4 The Model with One Agent Type 248
  20.4.1 Replication 248
  20.4.2 Introduction of a New Decision Rule 251
  20.4.3 Introduction of a Variable Payoff Matrix 251
20.5 The Model with Two Agent Types (the "Tag" Model) 254
20.6 Conclusions 255
References 255

21 Simulation of Effects of Culture on Trade Partner Selection 257
Gert Jan Hofstede, Catholijn M. Jonker and Tim Verwaart
21.1 Introduction 257
21.2 Hofstede's Dimensions and Trade Partner Selection 259
21.3 Representation in Agents 260
21.4 Simulation Results 263
21.5 Conclusion 265
References 267

List of Contributors

Dominique Ami
IDEP DESMID, 2, rue de la Charité 13002 Marseille - France, e-mail: dominique.ami@univmed.fr

Olivier Brandouy
LEM, UMR CNRS-USTL 8179, Université de Lille 1, France, e-mail: olivier.brandouy@univ-lille1.fr

Philippe Caillou
LRI, Université Paris Sud, F-91405 Orsay, France, e-mail: caillou@lri.fr

Giulia Canzian
Dept. of Economics, University of Trento, and OPES-Trento, Italy, e-mail: giulia.canzian.1@email.unitn.it

Elena Catanese
Dip. di Scienze Statistiche e Matematiche "Silvio Vianelli", University of Palermo, Italy, e-mail: elena_catanese@hotmail.com

Roberto Cervone
Dept. Applied Math., University of Venice, Italy, e-mail: roberto.cervone@stud.unive.it

Silvano Cincotti
DIBE-CINEF, University of Genova, Via Opera Pia 11a, 16145, Italy, e-mail: cincotti@i2.unige.it

Andrea Consiglio
Dip. di Scienze Statistiche e Matematiche "Silvio Vianelli", University of Palermo, Italy, e-mail: consiglio@unipa.it

Edoardo Gaffeo
Dept. of Economics, University of Trento, Italy, e-mail: edoardo.gaffeo@unitn.it

Stefano Galavotti
Dept. Decision Sciences, University of Florence, Italy, e-mail:
stefano.galavotti@unifi.it

Gianfranco Giulioni
Department of Quantitative Methods and Economic Theory,
University of Chieti-Pescara, Viale Pindaro 42, 65127 Pescara, Italy,
e-mail: g.giulioni@unich.it

Eric Guerci
GREQAM, 2, rue de la Charité, 13236, Marseille, France, e-mail:
eric.guerci@univmed.fr

Florian Hauser
Department of Department of Banking and Finance, Innsbruck University School
of Management, Universitaetsstrasse 15, A-6020 Innsbruck, Austria, e-mail:
Florian.Hauser@uibk.ac.at

Gert Jan Hofstede
Wageningen University, Hollandseweg 1, 6706 KN Wageningen, The Netherlands,
e-mail: gertjan.hofstede@wur.nl

Jürgen Huber
Department of Department of Banking and Finance, Innsbruck University School
of Management, Universitaetsstrasse 15, A-6020 Innsbruck, Austria, e-mail:
Juergen.Huber@uibk.ac.at

Pedro Isasi
Universidad Carlos III de Madrid, Avenida de la Universidad 30, Madrid, Spain,
e-mail: pedro.isasi@uc3m.es

Catholijn M. Jonker
Delft University of Technology, Mekelweg 4, 2628 CD Delft, The Netherlands,
e-mail: c.m.jonker@tudelft.nl

Bogumil Kaminski
Decision Analysis and Support Division, Warsaw School of Economics, Poland,
e-mail: bkamins@sgh.waw.pl

Yuji Karino
Future University - Hakodate, 116-2 Kameda Nakano cho, Hakodate, Hokkaido,
041-8655 Japan, e-mail: g2108012@fun.ac.jp

Toshiji Kawagoe
Future University - Hakodate, 116-2 Kameda Nakano cho, Hakodate, Hokkaido,
041-8655 Japan, e-mail: kawagoe@fun.ac.jp

Michael Kirchler
Department of Department of Banking and Finance, Innsbruck University School
of Management, Universitaetsstrasse 15, A-6020 Innsbruck, Austria, e-mail:
Michael.Kirchler@uibk.ac.at

List of Contributors

Valerio Lacagnina
Dip. di Scienze Statistiche e Matematiche "Silvio Vianelli", University of Palermo, Italy, e-mail: ricopa@unipa.it

Maciej Latek
Department of Computational Social Science, George Mason University, U.S.A, e-mail: mlatek@gmu.edu

Marco LiCalzi
SSE and Dept. Applied Mathematics, University of Venice, Italy, e-mail: licalzi@unive.it

Barbara Llacay
Dept. for Economic, Financial, and Actuarial Mathematics, University of Barcelona, Av. Diagonal 690, 08034 Barcelona, Spain, e-mail: bllacay@ub.edu

Philippe Mathieu
LIFL, UMR CNRS-USTL 8022, Université de Lille 1,France, e-mail: philippe.mathieu@lifl.fr

Lucia Milone
Dept. of Applied Mathematics, University Ca' Foscari of Venice, Italy, e-mail: lucia.milone@unive.it

Asuncion Mochon
UNED, Paseo Senda del Rey 11, Madrid, Spain, e-mail: amochon@cee.uned.es

Ricardo del Olmo
University of Burgos (c/ Villadiego s/n, Burgos, Spain) and INSISOC, e-mail: rdelolmo@ubu.es

Javier Pajares
Grupo InSiSoc, Departamento de Organización de Empresas y C.I.M., Universidad de Valladolid, Paseo del Cauce 59, 47011 Valladolid, Spain, e-mail: javier@insisoc.org

José Antonio Pascual
Grupo InSiSoc, Departamento de Organización de Empresas y C.I.M., Universidad de Valladolid, Paseo del Cauce 59, 47011 Valladolid, Spain, e-mail: pascual@eis.uva.es

Gilbert Peffer
Dept. for Economic, Financial, and Actuarial Mathematics, University of Barcelona, Av. Diagonal 690, 08034 Barcelona, Spain, e-mail: g.peffer@ub.edu

Paolo Pellizzari
Dept. of Applied Mathematics and SSE, University Ca' Foscari of Venice, Italy, e-mail: paolop@unive.it

David Poza
INSISOC, Valladolid University, Paseo del Cauce 59, 47011 Valladolid, Spain, e-mail: e-mail: djpoza@gmail.com

David Quintana
Universidad Carlos III de Madrid, Avenida de la Universidad 30, Madrid, Spain, e-mail: david.quintana@uc3m.es

Marco Raberto
School of Science and Engineering, Reykjavik University, Kringlan 1, 103 Reykjavik, Iceland, e-mail: raberto@ru.is

Mohammad Ali Rastegar
DIBE-CINEF, Unversity of Genova, Via Opera Pia 11a, 16145, Italy, e-mail: rastegar@dibe.unige.it

Juliette Rouchier
GREQAM, 2, rue de la Charité 13002 Marseille, France, e-mail: juliette.rouchier@univmed.fr

Annalisa Russino
Dip. di Scienze Statistiche e Matematiche "Silvio Vianelli", University of Palermo, Italy, e-mail: russino@unipa.it

Yago Saez
Universidad Carlos III de Madrid, Avenida de la Universidad 30, Madrid, Spain, e-mail: yago.saez@uc3m.es

Jose I. Santos
University of Burgos (c/ Villadiego s/n, Burgos, Spain) and INSISOC, e-mail: jisantos@ubu.es

Michele Sebag
LRI, Universite Paris Sud, F-91405 Orsay, France, e-mail: sebag@lri.fr

Roberto Tamborini
Dept. of Economics, University of Trento, Italy, e-mail: roberto.tamborini@unitn.it

Andrea Teglio
DIBE-CINEF, University of Genova, Via Opera Pia 11a, 16145, Italy, e-mail: teglio@i2.unige.it

Narine Udumyan
GREQAM, 2, rue de la Charité 13002 Marseille, France, e-mail: narine.udumyan@univmed.fr

Iryna Verizhenko
LIFL & LEM, Université de Lille 1,France, e-mail: iryna.verizhenko@univ-lille1.fr

Tim Verwaart
LEI Wageningen UR, Postbus 29703, 2502 LS Den Haag, The Netherlands, e-mail: `tim.verwaart@wur.nl`

Xavier Vilà
Universitat Autònoma de Barcelona, Spain, e-mail: `Xavier.Vila@uab.cat`

Félix Villafáñez
INSISOC, Valladolid University, Paseo del Cauce 59, 47011 Valladolid, Spain, e-mail: `villafafelix@yahoo.es`

Wayne Zandbergen
Center for Complexity Analysis, LLC, 2111 Wilson Blvd, Suite 700, Arlington, Virginia 22201,U.S.A., e-mail: `wayne@groupw.com`

Part I
Macroeconomics

Chapter 1
A Potential Disadvantage of a Low Interest Rate Policy: the Instability of Banks Liquidity

Gianfranco Giulioni

Abstract This paper joins the strands of literature supporting the idea that monetary policy should consider seriously the behavior of financial institutions. In a number of recent episodes, lowering the interest rate has been ineffective in bringing economies out of unfavorable conditions. We show how a low interest rate policy could have adverse effects that oppose the positive ones for which they are adopted. In particular, banks may choose to finance more risky borrowers who have an higher average return to cancel out the negative effects triggered by a low interest rate on their revenues. This behavior could seriously endanger macroeconomic performances.

1.1 Introduction

Although the economic effects of financial conditions in general, and those of credit in particular have been a topic in macroeconomic theory (see Gertler, 1988, and Bernanke, 1993, for surveys; Bhattacharya *et al.*, 2004, for a recent book), their importance seems to be underestimated in the frameworks currently used to conduct monetary policy. Differently from the usual view to which the majority of central bankers seems to refer (the so called "money view"), a number of economists have been stressing the importance of banks decisions in modifying the impulses given by the central bank. This is the so called "credit view". One of the most recent updates of this view is contained in a book by Stiglitz and Greenwald (2003) to which this paper is particularly related as it will become clear below. As one can imagine, the crucial point is whether credit is special for firms, or in other words if it is difficult to substitute it with other form of finance. A large number of microeconomic

G. Giulioni
Department of Quantitative Methods and Economic Theory, University of Chieti-Pescara, Italy,
e-mail: g.giulioni@unich.it

investigations, especially those which recognize the relevance of information imperfections, provide reasons for the special nature of credit.

The special nature of credit implies that macroeconomic performances are affected by the state of the credit market. The further natural step in the reasoning is that the central bank can affect the real part of the economy by modifying the conditions of the credit market. To this aim, a number of mechanisms have been identified. The first one is the effects of changes of the credit market interest rate (a simple and well known model incorporating this effect is presented in Bernanke and Blinder, 1988). Other models highlight the potential amplification of financial factors due to the fact that the financial condition of a firm affects its ability to obtain credit that in turn affects its financial condition (Bernanke and Gertler, 1989, Greenwald and Stiglitz, 1993, Kiyotaki and Moore, 1997, Kiyotaki and Moore, 2002). When the banks themselves cannot resolve the asymmetric information problem another mechanism can be identified. In these situations the interest rate and the amount of credit observed in the credit market could not be determined as the intersection point between credit demand and supply. A situation of equilibrium credit rationing (see Stiglitz and Weiss, 1981, among others) where the interest rate is "sticky" and it is the amount of extended credit that changes, can prevail. The models presented in Stiglitz and Greenwald (2003)'s book also discuss the potential macroeconomic effects of this phenomenon.

The need for the adoption of a more comprehensive framework in monetary policy making is also signaled by a particular aspect of the real world. It is a task of central banks to keep the banking system healthy to avoid the negative real effects of credit crunches (see Bernanke, 1993, p.60 for the macroeconomic role of credit crunches). Recently, a new database on systemic banking crisis has been put forward by Laeven and Valencia (2008). They identify 124 systemic banking crises in the period of 1970 to 2007. The recurrent appearance of systemic banking crises shows a wanting in the theoretical understanding of the phenomenon. Experiences in getting out of such situations are well documented even in Laeven and Valencia (2008)'s work, but the most important point is how to prevent them (see Kaufman, 1999, for example).

Thus far we have maintained that the initial impulses of monetary policy (as well as exogenous shocks) have to pass through a medium represented by the banking system. However, our knowledge on what happens to the input signal when it passes through this medium is perhaps yet incomplete (more incomplete for example than our knowledge of what happens to a shaft of light when it passes through a prism). It is evident that, if credit is special for firms, a detailed knowledge of how the banking system reacts to external stimuli is needed. Experience teaches us that this process can lead to unexpected outcomes. Blum and Hellwig (1995) for example highlight how the adoption of capital adequacy ratios can enhance macroeconomic fluctuations.

In this paper we concentrate in particular on the effects of downward movements of the discount rate. A low interest rate policy is commonly viewed as a remedy able to foster investments and consumption in difficult economic conditions. It is however important to check whether a remedy is beneficial for all the components of a system. In this work we aim to discuss how a low level interest rate impacts on the banking system. The point is that, by lowering banks profits, a low interest rate might pose banks difficulties while improving the demand for credit from entrepreneurs and consumers. This could create a bottleneck to the positive effects of the policy we are talking about. In the worst case, a low interest rate policy can ease the development of systemic banking crisis that could seriously endanger macroeconomic performances. Hints for this statement can be found in real life. Three commonly known events involving the banking sector (the Great Depression, the prolonged Japanese depression of the '90s, and the worldwide financial crisis started in 2007) have been preceded by a low interest rate period (Friedman and Schwartz, 1963, Bernanke, 2000, Powell, 2002).

Before going to the model it is perhaps useful to highlight a point. As our focus is on what happens when the interest rate reaches low levels, the constraints a bank has to deal with become protagonists of our investigation.[1] In performing their activity, banks have to satisfy two constraints. Firstly, they have a liquidity constraint in the very short run and secondly, being mainly private enterprises, they have to match a profitability constraint. Our aim is to investigate how banks behave to meet the profitability constraint when economic conditions change and how this affects the liquidity constraint.

The paper is organized as follows. In the next section we present our model of the banking activity. The profitability and liquidity constraints are defined. How the lending activity is conducted to meet the profitability constraint (section 1.2.3) is the main outcome of this paper. In section 1.3 we simulate a bank who manage using the result obtained in the previous section. We point our attention on what happens to the liquidity of a bank who wants to avoid the shut down of its activity due to low profitability. In section 1.4 we briefly discuss a number of possible implications of the model. Section 1.5 concludes the paper.

1.2 The Bank

We investigate here a setting in which the sole activity of a bank is that of lending to firms that implement a production investment. There is no asymmetric information between the bank and the entrepreneur, so that the bank knows the features of the project the entrepreneur is going to implement.[2] The exchanges of funds are regulated by standard debt contracts of fixed period (say a quarter) that allows the projects to be implemented and to come to maturity.

---

[1] In our framework, banks decide their strategies by profit maximization when the policy interest rate is sufficiently high. For example, we can obtain credit rationing as the outcome of profit maximization. These aspects are not treated here because they are already well known in the literature (Stiglitz and Greenwald, 2003).

[2] The presence of asymmetric information is crucial to equilibrium credit rationing. In the present model, liquidity problems can arise even with perfect information.

1.2.1 Profitability and Liquidity

Let us start with the bank balance sheet

$$L + C = D + E, \qquad (1.1)$$

where L is liquidity, C credit, D deposits and E the bank equity. We assume for the sake of simplicity that the interest rate on liquidity and on deposits is zero. Under these assumptions, the profit for a bank can be expressed as

$$\Phi = \phi C - wC - eE, \qquad (1.2)$$

where ϕ is the average interest rate gained on loans, w the cost for each unit of credit and e are dividends. We further assume that capital is proportional to lending $E = \gamma C$ as required for example by the Basel accords (Basel Committee on Banking Supervision, 2003). In this context a profitability constraint can be identified by imposing $\Phi \geq 0$. This bring us to

$$\phi \geq s, \qquad (1.3)$$

where $s = w + \gamma e$ is assumed to be a constant.

As is usual, the interplay between new deposits and withdrawing of old ones generates fluctuations in D and the bank must have enough cash to face the troughs of this variable. As usual we require $L \geq \hat{L} = kD$. Using the balance sheet equation the liquidity constraint can be expressed as:

$$\hat{L} = lC, \qquad (1.4)$$

where $l = k(1-\gamma)/(1-k)$.[3] In our model, cash arrives to the bank as interest rate payments from borrowers.

Of course both liquidity and profitability must be satisfied. Now we describe the interplay of these two aspects with the following idealization of the banks activity.

1.2.2 An Idealization of the Bank Activity

Our idealization of the bank activity in a working day is the following. The opening hours are organized in four parts. The first part is dedicated to borrowers. Those whose debt comes to maturity refund the bank according to the content of the contract (principal and interest if their projects were successful and the whole outcome of their activity if not). The refunded can be lent again to those who sign new contracts.[4] Now the bank computes its liquidity and is ready to operate in the second part of the day when the interbank market is open. The aim of this phase is of course

---

[3] Making substitutions we have $kD + C = D + \gamma C \Rightarrow (1-k)D = (1-\gamma)C \Rightarrow D = [(1-\gamma)/(1-k)]C$.

[4] In the following we concentrate on a situation where the whole principal is lent again.

to reach (or to get as close as possible to) the liquidity target level lC by lending to or borrowing from other banks. In the third phase only depositors are allowed in the bank offices: they adjust their liquidity position. In the final part of the day, the cash resulting from the previous three phases is used to pay bank expenditures (w) and dividends (e).

In this paper we focus on the lending activity because it determines the cash influx on which the bank activity relies (that is the liquidity at the end of the first phase).

1.2.3 The Lending Activity

The bank finances investment projects. To be realized they require the same amount of funds, but the result obtained differs among projects. Each project has a return made up of two parts. The first one is equal for all and it depends on the macroeconomic conditions. We denote it with c_ω where ω signals the general state of the economy. The second is specific to the project and it is represented by a random variable Π_i. This is a Bernoulli random variable which takes the two values $\{\pi_i, 0\}$ with probabilities $\{p_i, 1-p_i\}$. Under these assumptions the mean and variance of the projects are $\mu_i = c_\omega + p_i \pi_i$ and $\sigma_i^2 = \pi_i^2 p_i (1-p_i)$. We require the probability of the success to decrease with the result in the case of success (π_i) so that good results are realized more rarely. We also require that these probabilities are such that a higher revenue is associated with a higher level of risk in accordance with one of the general principles of finance. This requirement is satisfied if the derivatives of the mean and variance with respect to π_i are both positive. A functional form that satisfies these requirements is $p_i = (1+\pi_i)^{-\alpha}$ provided that $0 < \alpha \leq 1$.

In this case we have

$$\mu_i = c_\omega + \pi_i(1+\pi_i)^{-\alpha}. \tag{1.5}$$

The derivative is

$$\frac{d\mu_i}{d\pi_i} = (1+\pi_i)^{-\alpha} - \alpha\pi_i(1+\pi_i)^{-\alpha-1} = (1+\pi_i)^{-\alpha}[1 - \alpha\pi_i(1+\pi_i)^{-1}], \tag{1.6}$$

that is positive as long as $\alpha \leq 1$.

The variance is

$$\begin{aligned}\sigma_i^2 &= \pi_i^2(1+\pi_i)^{-\alpha}[1-(1+\pi_i)^{-\alpha}] \\ &= \pi_i^2(1+\pi_i)^{-\alpha} - \pi_i^2(1+\pi_i)^{-2\alpha} \\ &= (\mu_i - c_\omega)^2[(1+\pi_i)^\alpha - 1].\end{aligned} \tag{1.7}$$

The derivative is

$$\frac{d\sigma_i^2}{d\pi_i} = 2(\mu_i - c_\omega)\frac{d\mu_i}{d\pi_i}[(1+\pi_i)^\alpha - 1] + (\mu_i - c_\omega)^2 \alpha(1+\pi_i)^{\alpha-1}, \tag{1.8}$$

that is positive for $\alpha > 0$.

We will use this functional form in our numerical investigations.

The central bank sets the discount rate r. According to portfolio theory, the market determines a risk premium β. The existence of such a premium affects the banks ability to set the interest rate. We analyze a situation where the bank is able to detect the risk of each project. When bargaining the rate for a new loan the bank must take into account that the interest rate an entrepreneur is willing to pay takes the risk premium into account. As a consequence the interest rate on loans is determined by

$$r_i = r + \beta \sigma_i. \tag{1.9}$$

The bank lends to a number of entrepreneurs each implementing a project. As mentioned above, all the projects have a minimum revenue c_ω, so that the bank is always refunded by borrowers whose interest rate is lower than this value. Imposing the condition $c_\omega = r_i$ and solving σ one obtains the threshold

$$(c_\omega - r)\frac{1}{\beta} := \sigma^c \tag{1.10}$$

above which the bank has a positive probability to loose the amount $r_i - c_\omega$. It is why in the following we label as "subprimes" the entrepreneurs implementing a project whose $\sigma_i > \sigma^c$ and we will refer to σ^c as the "subprime" threshold.

Let us give the following definition

$$R(\sigma_i) = \begin{cases} r_i & \text{if } \sigma_i \leq \sigma^c, \\ c_\omega + \Pi_i & \text{if } \sigma_i > \sigma^c, \end{cases} \tag{1.11}$$

so that the expected value ($E[.]$) is:

$$E[R(\sigma_i)] = \begin{cases} r_i & \text{if } \sigma_i \leq \sigma^c, \\ r_i p_i + c_\omega(1 - p_i) & \text{if } \sigma_i > \sigma^c. \end{cases} \tag{1.12}$$

For a bank financing a large number of heterogeneous projects the average amount of interest received is

$$\phi(\sigma) = \int_0^\sigma p_{\sigma_i} E[R(\sigma_i)] d\sigma_i, \tag{1.13}$$

where p_{σ_i} is the probability of financing a project with a risk equal to σ_i.

Using the profitability constraint (equation 1.3) we identify in the value σ^s that satisfies the equation

$$\phi(\sigma^s) = s \tag{1.14}$$

a second threshold at which we will refer to as the profitability threshold. This value depends directly on s and inversely on r, it is equal to zero as long as $r > s$ and it is higher than the value of σ that satisfies $r_i = s$ (that we denote with d).

The relative position of the two identified thresholds depends on the parameters c_ω, s and r. This relative position is important because it determines the composition

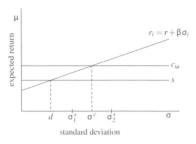 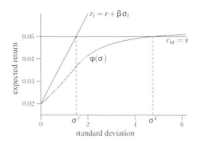

Fig. 1.1 The thresholds in a graph usually used for portfolio analysis.

Fig. 1.2 Numerical computation of σ^s.

of the bank customers. In particular the share of prime customer (those whose $r_i \leq c_\omega$) is given by $\frac{\sigma^c}{\max(\sigma^c, \sigma^s)}$. Figure 1.1 shows two alternative situations. In one of them $\sigma^s = \sigma_1^s$ so that $\sigma^s < \sigma^c$ and the bank, by lending to customers with $\sigma_i < \sigma^c$ can satisfy the profitability constraint lending exclusively to prime customers. In the other one ($\sigma^s = \sigma_2^s$) we have $\sigma^s > \sigma^c$ so that the bank must lend also to a number of subprime customers to match the profitability constraint.

The final objective of this work is to analyze how changes in the above identified thresholds due to movements in the the policy interest rate affect the bank liquidity. We do this in the following section.

1.3 Simulations

In this section we investigate numerically the model presented above. First of all we compute the profitability threshold. Figure 1.2 reproduces figure 1.1 in the benchmark case $c_\omega = s$ with these variables equal to 5%. We set the risk premium parameter β to 0.02, $\alpha = 1$ and the discount rate to 2%. The figure shows how ϕ rises slowly with the riskiness of the projects.

A more general exercise is presented in figure 1.3 which is obtained using the same parameters, but we allow the discount rate to change. In this figure one can see how, differently from the subprime threshold, the profitability threshold rises in a non linear way when the discount rate is lowered.

In the remainder of this section we present the results of simulations. The results are obtained under the condition $c_\omega = s = l$. It is because this represents a neutral case in the sense that it is not favorable nor penalizing to the bank. To see this, let us take up again the idealization presented in section 1.2.2. Let us assume further the central bank set r at the same level of c_ω, s and l. In this setting all the lent funds where used to implement projects whose revenue is obtained with certainty (see figure 1.3). When the contracts comes to maturity, entrepreneurs go to the bank

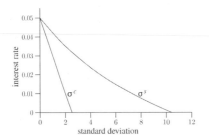
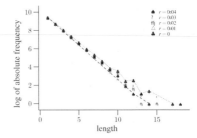

Fig. 1.3 σ^c and σ^s as a function of r.

Fig. 1.4 Length of liquidity shortages.

in the first part of the day bringing with them the principal and the interest rate payments. The principal is lent again to implement new projects, and at the end of this first part of the day the bank has enough liquidity because $r = l$. No exchanges take place on the interbank market. Now it is depositors' turn. Suppose this third phase ends up as expected: new deposits and withdrawals balance exactly and the money in the banker's hand is still equal to r. When passing to the last phase, we see that also the profitability constraint is met being $r = s$. Of course this is a special case and the profitability constraint normally is not satisfied each day. However this does not matter because bank suppliers and shareholder are more patient than depositors. Indeed, the profitability constraint will be satisfied in a longer time span.

The above model is implemented in our simulations as follows. We consider a time interval (say a quarter). Each simulation step represents a day. In Each day a fixed number (N) of standard debt contracts comes to maturity. Each customer always pays back the principal, but the refunding of the interest amount is not obtained with certainty. The bank obtains r_i if $c_\omega > r_i$. When $r_i > c_\omega$, the bank obtains r_i if the project is successful and c_ω otherwise. In any case the principal is lent to another customer whose π_i is randomly drawn from a uniform distribution with boundaries 0 and $\max(\pi(\sigma^c), \pi(\sigma^s))$.

From the simulations we collect data on the cash the bank has at the end of phase one of our idealization. Even in these simulations the parameters are $c_\omega = s = l = 5\%$, $\beta = 0.02$, $\alpha = 1$. We set N (the number of contracts that come to maturity each day) to 1000. As explained above, if the discount rate is 5% the time series of cash influxes is constant at a level which satisfies the liquidity constraint. The performed simulations start with this level of the discount rate, than we move it to a lower level in a given point in time. At the same time, we allow the bank to lend to more risky customers as indicated in figure 1.3 so that the profitability constraint can be met. We hold this situation for 10000 simulation time steps. Table 1.1 reports summary variables for the time series of the liquidity (L) obtained at different values of the discount rate.

The figures in the table show how in correspondence with lower discount rates, the standard deviation of the liquidity time series increases. Furthermore, the maximum ($\min(L) - \hat{L}$) and the mean ($\langle L^- \rangle - \hat{L}$) of liquidity shortages increase. In other words, other thing being equal, the liquidity conditions of the bank gradually worsen

1 A Potential Disadvantage of a Low Interest Rate Policy

Table 1.1 Summary variables from simulations with $N = 1000$ and 10000 time steps. L is the realized liquidity; L^+ and L^- denote liquidity excess and shortage; $\hat{L}$ is the required liquidity; $\langle . \rangle$ denotes the average.

r	standard deviation of L	$\frac{\sigma^s - \sigma^c}{\sigma^s}$	number of L^-	$\min(L) - \hat{L}$	$\langle L^- \rangle - \hat{L}$	$\max(L) - \hat{L}$	$\langle L^- \rangle - \hat{L}$
0.05	0	0	0	0	0	0	0
0.04	0.175	0.614	4909	-0.68	-0.137	0.736	0.143
0.03	0.279	0.646	4919	-1.137	-0.223	1.157	0.224
0.02	0.35	0.686	5003	-1.286	-0.275	1.207	0.281
0.01	0.398	0.724	5129	-1.374	-0.314	1.577	0.322
0	0.434	0.76	5117	-1.422	-0.341	1.834	0.350

in correspondence with lower discount rates. The explanation for this phenomenon is that banks change the compositions of their customers in reply to interest rate movements. When the interest rate is lowered, banks lend more to more risky borrowers ($(\sigma^s - \sigma^c)/\sigma^s$ increases). The latter pay more, but less frequently and consequently banks run into liquidity problems more often.

As a second exercise, we build the frequency distribution of the length of liquidity shortages, that is the number of simulation ticks between an occurrence of $L \geq \hat{L}$ and the next one. The distributions for different levels of the discount rate are reported in Figure 1.4. Although a systematic pattern cannot be clearly detected, figure 1.4 hints at an increase of the frequency for longer liquidity shortages in correspondence with lower discount rates. The dashed line one can see in the figure is the downward part of the convex hull obtained using data from the distribution for the higher discount rate considered ($r = 0.04$). This hints to the fact that the shortest liquidity shortage periods are in general, realized for this level of the interest rate. The dotted line connects the frequencies for the lowest discount rate ($r = 0$). Apart from one exception, longer periods of liquidity shortage are more frequent for this level of the discount rate.

1.4 Comparative Static, Dynamics and Credit Rationing

Till now, we have analyzed in detail the case where all the relevant parameters (c_ω, s and l) are at the same value. Now we comment on comparative static exercises to see what happens to the bank liquidity when these parameters change. Improved economic conditions (an increase in c_ω), for example, increases the "subprime" threshold leaving the profitability threshold unchanged. As a consequence, the banking system moves towards a safer situation.

A first evaluation of monetary policy measures can be attempted. When economic conditions worsen and there are no other reasons for upward pressure on inflation, the central bank may decrease the discount rate to help improving the economic performances. More precisely, we are thinking of a situation where the discount rate is decided according to $r = r(c_\omega)$ with $0 < dr/dc_\omega < 1$. When c_ω decreases, the adoption of the described rule moves the two thresholds in opposite directions. In particular, the "subprime" threshold decreases while the profitability threshold increases. In other words, a "side effect" of this policy is that of increasing the average riskiness of bank customers that, as discussed above, in turn increases the fluctuations of banks liquidity.

The comparative static exercises could continue, however, we want to briefly discuss dynamic aspects. In particular, the response function of s and l should be investigated. In the presented framework, shocks, including discount rate changes, have no effects as long as there is perfect synchronization, that is if the condition $c_\omega = s = l$ holds even though their value changes in time and if $c_\omega - r$ is kept constant over time. These two conditions imply that the two thresholds keep constant over time. As one can imagine these are very special conditions. It might be the case that when economic conditions worsen, households have to rely on their deposits so that l increases; another possibility is that a decrease of the risk free interest rate could induce a "bullish" period in the stock market so that bank shareholders will expect a higher dividend so that s increases. In other words, the asynchronous motion of the thresholds affects the composition of bank customers over time. Our message is that these aspects should gain importance in policy makers decision processes.

Another topic is that of capital adequacy standards at which we hinted above. We have shown that a decrease of the discount rate (other things being equal) increases σ^s, so that the average riskiness of bank activity increases. Capital adequacy rules require an increasing relationship between banks capital and the riskiness of their assets. In the notation of section 1.2.1 we can write $\gamma(\sigma^s)$ with $d\gamma/d\sigma^s > 0$. There we have also defined $s = w + \gamma e$, so that a decrease in the discount rate causes an increase in s, that in turn brings to an increase in σ^s.

Let us make a final comment on the possibility to have credit rationing in the presented framework. Of course the rationing that can arise is different from that caused by asymmetric information at high levels of the interest rate. Note that in our framework "subprime" customers always refund a higher amount than "primes" ($\sigma_i < \sigma^c \Rightarrow r_i < c_\omega$). It follows that a low level interest rate motivates banks to avoid lending to "prime" customers. In the benchmark case presented in section 1.3, for example, both profitability and liquidity can be met by excluding "prime" customers from credit and using all the available funds to finance "subprimes".

1.5 Conclusions

The commonly (traditional) accepted view of macro-economic policy is in favor of putting the economy under the wings of central banks during bad periods, but "It is precisely when monetary policy becomes of crucial importance that the traditional models fail most dramatically" (Stiglitz and Greenwald, 2003, p. 4). Stiglitz and Greenwald (2003) maintain that the failure of monetary policy in recent episodes like the 1991 US recession and East Asia recessions started in 1997 were due to the low relevance given by the models currently used to conduct monetary policy to financial institutions. In particular the authors attribute a central role to the amount of credit the banking system is willing to extend. They write that banks "may decide to hold government bonds rather than loans ... Some would argue that this is precisely what happened to Japan in the 1990s" (Stiglitz and Greenwald, 2003, p. 189).

The aim of this paper is to take a closer look at how a monetary expansion can affect a bank behavior. We concentrate in particular on the lending activity of depository banks in a situation where they are not allowed to buy government bonds or other financial activities. We claim that a low discount rate, although beneficial to most of the economic agents, could have negative effects on the banking system. If it is true, the large potential benefits of such a policy cannot be fully harvested because the banking, and more generally the financial system represents a bottleneck through which these advantages have to pass.

We start from the observation that a low interest rate reduces the revenue from the lending activity. On the other hand, banks must meet a profitability constraint to survive. A way to satisfy the profitability constraint is lending to entrepreneurs that are willing to pay a higher interest rate. But a basic principle of finance tell us that a higher expected return is necessarily associated with a higher risk. In our framework, a higher risk means that a borrower pays back the interest less often. We show, by using numerical simulations, that the recomposition of banks customers after a reduction of the discount rate lead the cash influx of a bank to be more volatile. This could bring the banking system liquidity problems. More serious consequences could be involved if a high risk causes an increase of the average delay in refunding both the interest and the principal, but this case in not discussed here.

Our results go in the direction of Stiglitz and Greenwald (2003)'s claim that an expansive monetary policy can fail to improve macroeconomic conditions in recessions or depressions. Truly, something more can be ventured. In the worst case, prolonged periods of low discount rates could create the conditions in which systemic events develop more easily even in healthy economies.

The model presented here is simple and several extensions are possible. Some of them have already been sketched out in section 1.4, others could be that of building a model with several banks to see to what extent the modified liquidity needs can be resolved in the interbank market, or to build a more general model in which the macroeconomic effects can be evaluated.

References

Basel Committee on Banking Supervision (April, 2003). The New Basel Capital Accord. Consultative Document. Bank for International Settlements.

Bernanke, B. and A. S. Blinder (1988). Credit, Money and Aggregate Demand. *American Economic Review, Papers and Proceedings 78*, 435–439.

Bernanke, B. S. (1993). Credit in the macroeconomy. *Federal Reserve Bank of New York Quarterly Review*, 50–70.

Bernanke, B. S. (Ed.) (2000). *Essays on the Great Depression*. Princeton University Press.

Bernanke, B. S. and M. Gertler (1989). Agency Costs, Net Worth and Business Fluctuations. *American Economic Review 79*, 14–31.

Bhattacharya, S., A. Boot, and A. Thakor (Eds.) (2004). *Credit, Intermediation, and the Macroeconomy*. Oxford University Press.

Blum, J. and M. Hellwig (1995). The macroeconomic implications of capital adequacy requirements for banks. *European Economic Review 39*, 739–749.

Friedman, M. and A. J. Schwartz (1963). *A Monetary History of the United States, 1867–1960*. Princeton University Press.

Gertler, M. (1988). Financial Structure and Aggregate Economic Activity: an Overview. *Journal of Money, Credit and Banking 20*, 559–88.

Greenwald, B. C. and J. E. Stiglitz (1993). Financial Market imperfections and Business Cycles. *Quarterly Journal of Economics 108*, 77–114.

Kaufman, G. G. (Ed.) (1999). *Bank Crises. Causes, Analysis and Prevention*. Elsevier.

Kiyotaki, N. and G. Moore (1997). Credit Cycles. *Journal of Political Economy 105*, 211–248.

Kiyotaki, N. and G. Moore (2002). Balance-Sheet Contagion. *American Economic Review Paper and Proceedings 92*, 46–50.

Laeven, L. and F. Valencia (2008). Systemic banking crises: A new database. IMF working paper, WP/08/224.

Powell, B. (2002). Explaining Japan's Recession. *The Quarterly Journal of Austrian Economics 5*, 35–50.

Stiglitz, J. E. and B. Greenwald (2003). *Towards a New Paradigm in Monetary Economics*. Cambridge University Press.

Stiglitz, J. E. and A. Weiss (1981). Credit Rationing in Markets with Imperfect Information. *American Economic Review 71*, 393–410.

Chapter 2
Keynes in the Computer Laboratory. An Agent-Based Model with MEC, MPC, LP

Giulia Canzian, Edoardo Gaffeo and Roberto Tamborini

Abstract The present paper aims at taking the core of Keynes's macroeconomics - as it is portrayed in the 1937's *QJE* paper - into the computer laboratory, in the spirit of a *counterfactual history of economic thought*. We design an agent-based model in which the principal role in determining economic dynamics is played by the three pillars of Keynesian economics, namely the Marginal Efficiency of Capital, the Marginal Propensity to Consume and the Liquidity Preference. The latter magnitudes are modelled with particular attention to their behavioural foundations. Indeed, in Keynes's thought, such behavioural foundations result greatly important in determining the development of the business cycle. Simulation results endorse this view, with our model being able to recreate economic fluctuations with interesting statistical properties.

2.1 Introduction

Supply of an *authentic* interpretation of Keynes's ideas by means of more or less conventional tools and languages is extremely vast. Why add one more?

Keynes's thought, after many ups and downs, successes and reversals, continues to exert influence on macroeconomics either as a cornerstone for followers or as a stumbling block for advocates of different views and theories. Recurrent booms and slumps of modern capitalism - the ongoing world financial turmoil is a dramatic example - keep the idea alive that there is more in the General Theory (GT, Keynes, 1936) about the economic system we live in than it has been caught by

---

G. Canzian
Dept. of Economics, University of Trento, and OPES-Trento, Italy, e-mail: `giulia.canzian.1@email.unitn.it`

E. Gaffeo · R. Tamborini
Dept. of Economics, University of Trento, Italy, e-mail: `edoardo.gaffeo;roberto.tamborini@unitn.it`

subsequent "technical developments" (to paraphrase Blanchard, 2000), whether in the same Keynesian inspiration or pointing to alternative directions (Leijonhufvud, 2008). Thus, better understanding of Keynes's theory is not an issue of mere historical interest.

Nonetheless, it is not - and it has not been - simple to study the GT main intuitions since what Keynes presented was a literary model describing the functioning of a complex economic environment, quite difficult to reconcile with mathematical formalism. Neoclassical economics tackled the question by claiming that Keynes's work was not suitable for explaining economic systems because it lacked any microfoundation (namely, agents solving constrained optimization problems) and was not amenable to rigorous formal treatment. Although a tentative reconciliation of Keynesian macro with microfoundations has been carried out by New Keynesianism (Blanchard, 2000), it seems to us that such an attempt has not succeeded in incorporating one of the most important features of Keynes's economy, that is, the behavioural background that characterizes agents in the GT.

Indeed, Keynes (see in particular the 1937 QJE article, Keynes, 1937, pp. 112-115) clearly refused the perfect rationality hypothesis because he claimed that there is no scientific basis for probabilistic computation of future states of the world, so that there exists "true uncertainty" about the latter. Instead, he claimed that people cope with uncertainty resorting on heuristics, sentiment, chance and that in particular they give much importance to others' opinions to take economic decisions. These intrinsic features of economic decisions render them flimsy, prone to sudden changes and open to mass conditioning through social interaction (e.g. Keynes, 1937, p. 118). Recent authoritative contributions (e.g. Akerlof and Shiller, 2009) have revived the long-standing argument that this kind of behavioural microfoundations cannot be eradicated from the search of consistent interpretations of the sources of economic fluctuations. On the other hand, refusal of any formal and quantitative language has turned out to be a blind alley, more harmful than beneficial to the Keynesian cause.

Our contribution moves in this direction. Our aim is to seriously take Keynes's behavioural foundations into consideration, taking stock of more recent advances in the field and in available modelling techniques. Among the latter, we have chosen Agent-Based Modelling (ABM) (e.g. Colander *et al.*, 2008). A first motivation is that we subscribe to the idea that Keynes's view of the macreconomy is best understood as one populated by many heterogeneous, interacting, "simple" agents giving rise to a complex adaptive system (Leijonhufvud, 1993). Advances in computational theories and applications are rendering ABM methodology a rigorous and reliable platform to deal with the formidable constructive and interpretative problems posed by complex adaptive systems. Second, ABM permits to overcome the difficulties encountered at Keynes's time and after until very recently in translating his ideas into a computable, quantitative model (recent examples include Bruun, 1999, 2008, Fontana and Marchionatti, 2007).

In our research programme, the present exercise represents a first step that we may dub a "counterfactual history of economic thought". That is to say, we have first tried to identify the core of Keynes's macroeconomics in Keynes's own (in our view) best self-portrait, namely the 1937 QJE paper. Drawing on textual evidence, we have identified three analytical building blocks: the Marginal Efficiency of Capital (MEC), the Marginal Propensity to Consume (MPC) and Liquidity Preference (LP)[1]. It is easy to see that these are indeed the same building blocks that Hicks (1937) sorted out from the GT in order to construct his IS-LM model of Keynes's theory. The subsequent story is well known. The relevant point here is that these concepts were translated into ad hoc fixed parameters that were neither grounded into classical decision theory nor in Keynes's own view of the underlying behaviours. This ingenious, but devious, shortcut conditioned profoundly the subsequent development of Keynesian macroeconomics. Hence, we have sought to recast MEC, MPC and LC in Keynes's original framework, and then to take this restored IS-LM model of the business cycle to the computer laboratory and analyze how the outcome looks like. If our reconstruction does capture the so-far least tractable features of Keynes's economics, then its results can suggest how different Keynesian economics could have been if these results had been available from the beginning.

2.2 The Model

2.2.1 Methodological Premises

The common trait of MEC, MPC and LP in Keynes's writings is that they reflect human decision making under non-probabilistic uncertainty regarding, respectively, investment in physical capital, consumption and saving, portfolio selection. In the first place, we have focused on this common trait, though Keynes also gave relevance to other different nuances arising from different characterization of the motivations of entrepreneurs with respect to consumers, asset holders, etc.

In the second place, we have sought for a unifying characterization of Keynes's treatment of non-probabilistic uncertainty across MEC, MPC and LP, and we have opted for "Market Sentiment", or the "disobedient psychology of the market" in Keynes's words[2]. Market Sentiment conditions the way agents project their present

---

[1] "The theory can be summed up by saying that, given the psychology of the public, the level of output and employment as a whole depends on the amount of investment. I put it in this way, not because this is the only factor on which aggregate output depends, but because it is usual in a complex system to regard as the causa causans that factor which is most prone to sudden and wide fluctuations. More comprehensively, aggregate output depends on the propensity to hoard, on the policy of the monetary authority as it affects the quantity of money, on the state of confidence concerning the prospective yield of capital-assets, on the propensity to spend and on the social factors which influence the level of the money-wage. But of these several factors it is those which determine the rate of investment which are most unreliable, since it is they which are influenced by our views of the future about which we know so little." (Keynes, 1937, p.121)

[2] Keynes's treatment of uncertain decision-making about investment is generally associated with the popular idea of "Animal Spirits". Animal Spirits have come to denote almost everything is not fully rational, or is even irrational, in entrepreneurial decision making. This roughly irrationalist use of the term is not appropriate, nor is it appropriate its exclusive association to entrepreneurs.

state into a better or worse future state. This is clearly an aggregative concept, that results from an individual and a social-interactive dimension. The individual dimension hinges on the important point that decision making under uncertainty is not to be meant as a purely irrational activity, but an activity where the lack of the "scientific basis" indicated by probability theory is supplemented by other practices and tools that human beings do associate with rationality (see in particular Keynes, 1936, p. 114, GT, p. 163). In a Keynesian world, optimism can be defined as non-probabilistic confidence in a favourable or better future state. By contrast, pessimism is the same mechanism applied to an unfavourable or worse future state. Since agents know very little about the future, individual optimism/pessimism is filtered through a social interaction process whereby it can be enhanced or corrected (Keynes, 1937, p. 114). In our model, the interaction process is the one proposed by Kirman (1993) of random meetings among optimistic or pessimistic individuals resulting in change or non-change of the initial mood of the single agent. It is also worth recalling that Market Sentiment, measured for both entrepreneurs and consumers has become a rather common tool for conjunctural analysis. (e.g. Taylor and McNabb, 2007; Throop, 1992).

The theoretical structure of the model resembles the traditional Keynesian framework in which the IS function is derived from an aggregate investment function and an aggregate consumption function, and the LM curve results from money demand and money supply controlled by the central bank. The model is further completed by an aggregate supply function. The aggregate functions are to be interpreted as the emergent characteristics of a population of interacting agents in the meaning proposed by Colander *et al.* (2008) and Delli Gatti *et al.* (2008), though in our model the role of "bottom-up" interaction is restricted to the determination of the MEC, MPC, and LP drivers of, respectively, the investment, consumption and money demand functions that are instead directly treated as aggregate variables

In the following, the three protagonist on stage will described in details, and their relationship with the Market Sentiment will be clarified.

2.2.2 Modelling the Market Sentiment

Market Sentiment in this model is the result of repeated social interactions between optimists and pessimists. An effective model of this opinion formation mechanism has been put forward by Kirman (1993). At any point in time there are O_t optimistic agents out of a population of N agents. Agents meet randomly pair-wise and exchange their opinions. If the two agents have the same opinion, nothing happens. If they have different opinions, there is a fixed probability $(1 - \delta)$ that one of the two

---

As recently stressed also by Fontana and Marchionatti (2007), by evoking Animal Spirits Keynes seeks to denote, not a sort of irrational optimism of entrepreneurs, but the fact that human beings in general feel urged to act not perceiving, or overcoming, their lack of "scientific basis" for decision making as a limitation to action. For this, and other reasons explained in the text, we have opted for the more general, and less compromised, concept of *Market Sentiment*.

changes opinion. There is also a (small) fixed probability ε that an agents changes his/her opinion independently.

Extending the interaction mechanism to the whole population, the social dynamics of optimists will be completely described by

$$O_t = O_{t-1} + \begin{cases} 1 \text{ with probability } p_{t-1}^1 = \left(N - \frac{O_{t-1}}{N}\right)\left(\varepsilon + (1-\delta)\frac{O_{t-1}}{N-1}\right), \\ -1 \text{ with probability } p_{t-1}^2 = \frac{O_{t-1}}{N}\left(\varepsilon + (1-\delta)\frac{N-O_{t-1}}{N-1}\right), \\ 0 \text{ with probability } p_{t-1}^3 = 1 - p_{t-1}^1 - p_{t-1}^2. \end{cases}$$

Note that the probability of a pessimist becoming an optimist, and viceversa, depends on the share of optimists and pessimist respectively, so that the more numerous the social group the more social power it has. Nonetheless, the dynamics is completely determined by ε and δ.

The algorithm results particularly suitable to represent the Market Sentiment since it displays perpetual change, that is, O_t does not reach a steady state value, rather its evolution is characterized by sudden changes. Moreover, these sudden changes are solely driven by the endogenous interaction between agents rather than some exogenous shocks.

2.2.3 The Marginal Efficiency of Capital

According to Keynes, in each time period an entrepreneur decides to invest if her/his MEC is greater than the real interest rate (Keynes, 1936, p. 135). The MEC is also known in corporate finance as "internal rate of return", the rate of discount that equates the net present value of the future profit streams to unit capital cost. Hence the MEC is fundamentally related to entrepreneurs' expectations on future profit streams, and it is this dependence "which renders the Marginal Efficiency of Capital subject to the somewhat violent fluctuations which are the explanation of the trade cycle" (Keynes, 1936, p.118). Operationally, we translate the former into an aggregate investment function in which investment is determined by the relative value of the MEC with respect to the interest rate. With simple manipulations, this ratio is also equivalent to "Tobin's q" (Tobin, 1969). Therefore, aggregate investment is described by

$$I_t = \phi I_{t-1} + \lambda (q_t - 1), \qquad (2.1)$$

where $q_t = \overline{\rho}_t / \hat{r}_t$. In the latter, $\overline{\rho}$ is the aggregate MEC which in turn results from the linear combination of optimists' and pessimists' expectations:

$$\overline{\rho}_t = \frac{O_t}{N}(1+\eta)\hat{\rho}_{t-1} + \left(1 - \frac{O_t}{N}\right)(1-\eta)\hat{\rho}_{t-1}, \qquad (2.2)$$

where $\hat{\rho}_{t-1} = \alpha Y_{t-1}/K_{t-1}$ is a measure of the economy's rate of return to capital in the previous period, αY_{t-1} represents a proxy for previous period aggregate profits as a share of GDP, while K_{t-1} represents the aggregate capital stock measured with the Perpetual Inventory Method.

Accordingly, all entrepreneurs observe the latest realization of the rate of return to capital in the economy, $\hat{\rho}_{t-1}$[3]. Then an optimist believes it will rise by $\eta > 0$ in next period, whereas a pessimist believes the opposite. Consequently, optimists make $\bar{\rho}$ rise, and pessimists make it fall, with respect to the given real interest rate. Depending on overall Market Sentiment, investment is driven up or down. The investment function also includes a first-order delayed term to capture inertial factors that tend to peter out over time.

2.2.4 The Marginal Propensity to Consume

In chapter 8 of the GT Keynes identified the factors determining consumption, that is, current disposable income, objective factors and subjective factors, the latter consisting in "the subjective needs and the psychological propensities and habits of the individuals composing [the community]" (Keynes, 1936, p. 91). In his view, the relationship between consumption and income follows a psychological law stating that people are willing to increase/decrease consumption when income increases/decreases, but not by the same amount, that is, the variations in the consumption level and in the income level have the same sign but not the same magnitude. Keynes also asserted that the subjective factors controlling consumption are relatively stable over time; though, they still play an important role in the development of the theory, mostly because they represent a way to cope with the uncertainty that characterizes consumption decisions. In devising our consumption function, however, we have also sought to take into account the fact that, though to a lesser extent than investment, consumption, too, is a volatile variable. Past studies as well as more recent ones (Taylor and McNabb, 2007; Throop, 1992), indicate that changes in the consumer confidence indicators, such as the University of Michigan's Consumer Sentiment Index, cause changes in GDP both for Europe and US and that these indicators perform well in explaining GDP's variability.

To this end, we have designed aggregate consumption in such a way that income dynamics determines consumption increases and decreases, while the Market Sentiment determines the quantitative impact of the latter over consumption. We have taken inspiration from the early Permanent Income theories[4] in that, given a

---

[3] The rate of return to capital coincides with the MEC of the marginal investing firm.

[4] Modigliani and Brunberg (1954), Friedman (1957). This may at first sight appear inappropriate, since these authors are generally associated with "neoclassical" reformulations of the consumption function. However, this interpretation is not entirely correct. In particular with regard to Modigliani, his original aim was to test and enhance empirically Keynes's intuition about consumption smoothing a well-known empirical regularity. In fact, the key idea of Modigliani and Friedman, that households compare their present income with future prospects, as well as the idea

constant normal level of consumption $\overline{C}$, optimistic agents are those who, in a situation of increasing income, believe it to be permanent, and hence raise their normal consumption by the same amount. The same agents, in a situation of decreasing income, believe it to be transitory, and hence they do not change their normal consumption by dissaving. Pessimistic agents behave symmetrically, judging income gains transitory, and hence saving them, while judging losses permanent and thus reducing normal consumption. Summarizing,

- If $Y_t - Y_{t-1} > 0$

    Optimists consume $C_t^O = \overline{C} + (Y_t - Y_{t-1})$
    Pessimists consume $C_t^P = \overline{C}$ and save $S_t^P = (Y_t - Y_{t-1})$

- If $Y_t - Y_{t-1} < 0$

    Optimists consume $C_t^O = \overline{C}$ and save $S_t^O = (Y_t - Y_{t-1}) < 0$
    Pessimists consume $C_t^P = \overline{C} - (Y_t - Y_{t-1})$

Hence, aggregate consumption results to be the linear combination of pessimists' and optimists' consumption,

$$C_t = \begin{cases} \overline{C} + \dfrac{O_t}{N}(Y_t - Y_{t-1}) & \text{if } Y_t - Y_{t-1} > 0, \\ \overline{C} + \left(N - \dfrac{O_t}{N}\right)(Y_t - Y_{t-1}) & \text{if } Y_t - Y_{t-1} < 0. \end{cases} \quad (2.3)$$

Note that the MPC is not constant but depends on the degree of optimism among consumers. In particular, it results that the effect of optimism or pessimism is asymmetric during booms or slumps. If say optimism prevails during booms and pessimism during slumps, then Market Sentiment acts as cyclical amplifier; if instead consumers happen to change their mood in a counter cyclical manner, then Market Sentiment helps smooth the cycle.

2.2.5 The Liquidity Preference

Finally, in order to design the LM curve we have relied on Keynes's intuition about the psychological way in which people treat money. In particular, he asserted that pessimistic people who are more doubtful about the future feel the possession of actual money as reassuring (Keynes, 1937, p. 116), and for this reason they will be more willing to use money as a store of wealth, while optimistic people will behave the opposite. This behaviour has effects on the determination of the interest rate, so

---

of saving in good times to sustain consumption in bad times, were already in Keynes. The neoclassical twist of the theory occurred when it was assumed that households have perfect information or Rational Expectations about their future income streams, and on this basis they engage in lifetime expected utility maximization In the present model, these two assumptions are (re)dropped, whereas Market Sentiments about future prospects are reinstated.

that Keynes argued that "the rate of interest is a highly psychological phenomenon" (Keynes, 1936, p. 202).

In terms of our model, these intuitions translate into an LM curve depending on the Market Sentiment. In particular, we have assumed that in a money market dominated by pessimists money demand receives a positive shock, which then impacts positively upon the interest rate, whereas the opposite occurs when the market is dominated by optimists. Thus, we introduce into the standard LM function a shock term that account for the relative impact of optimists or pessimists over money demand:

$$r_t = \frac{\mu}{\theta} y_t - \frac{1}{\theta}(m - p_t) + v_t, \tag{2.4}$$

where r_t is the nominal interest rate, m is the nominal money stock, p_t is the general price level, μ and θ are the income and interest elasticity of money demand, and v_t a shock driven by the Market Sentiment. The shock is given by:

$$v_t = \left(\frac{O_t}{N}\right) v^O + \left(1 - \frac{O_t}{N}\right) v^P \quad \text{with} \quad v^O < 0 \text{ and } v^P > 0. \tag{2.5}$$

2.2.6 Aggregate Supply

The model is closed by the introduction of an aggregate supply function which takes the form:

$$\pi_t = \beta \pi_t^e + \varphi(Y_t - Y_{t-1}), \tag{2.6}$$

where $\pi_t = p_t - p_{t-1}$.

This function has been designed in a Marshallian fashion since it encapsulates the idea of quantifying by how much the actual general price level should rise in order to induce firms to increase supply from Y_{t-1} to Y_t. Indeed, underlying the supply curve there is the idea of the price surprise, which if positive, that is, if prices grow more than expected, leads to a decrease in actual real wages and hence into an increase in firms' supply. If the price surprise is negative the opposite happens[5].

Accordingly, inflation expectations are assumed to be adaptive, such that $\pi_t^e = \overline{\pi}_{t-5}$, i.e., expected inflation is equal to the average inflation of the last five periods.

Finally, the simple market clearing condition for output is:

$$Y_t = C_t + I_t. \tag{2.7}$$

---

[5] Indeed, the basic principle which characterizes supply theory in the GT is the distinction drawn in chapter 19 between contractual wages, which are in money terms, and actual real wages, which result from the general price level, the latter being out of control of single firms and workers. As a consequence, money wage bargaining takes place with a view to the general price level that will prevail afterwards, which paves to way to unexpected changes in actual real wages.

2.3 Simulations Results

The implementation of our ABM is aimed at assessing what kind of dynamics the designed system produces once we introduce the influence of Market Sentiment on economic decision making. This paper presents simulations that do not want to quantitatively account for economic fluctuations. Instead their scope is to qualitatively analyze the dynamics of the system, in the spirit of "counterfactual history of thought" expressed at the beginning: What are the macro-characteristics of this economy? Does it behave as Keynes thought of it? Does it display critical states, such as prolonged depression? What is the role of money supply?

Therefore, we have not calibrated the model, and parameters have not been set so as to have the ambition of replicating real magnitudes (this exercise is left for further research). Nor have we performed any kind of robustness analysis in terms of analyzing the whole range of possible parameters' values. This because, as already pointed out, our final aim is to take into the computer laboratory the original Keynesian set up and to check for its dynamic properties. That is, we want to assess whether the model Keynes presented produces the dynamics he had in mind, with particular attention to the intuition that the main source of economic instability resides in the Market Sentiment dynamics (through its influence on the three pillars).

Upon these considerations, in the simulations presented below, we have borrowed the LM parameters from the basic inventory model of money demand (e.g. Tobin, 1956). The remaining parameter configuration reflects a single criterion: they have been chosen in order to ensure that the economic system possesses a steady state, that is, we have ruled out parametric sources of instability, so as to reserve the prominent role in determining volatility to Market Sentiment.

As to Kirman's exogenous probabilities, we have chosen the combination in which agents rarely change their mind autonomously (low $^\varepsilon$), and instead they require to interact with others to be willing to change (high $^{1-\delta}$). This is the combination that in our opinion better reproduces the optimism/pessimism waves Keynes was pointing at.

The parameter set up is shown in Table 2.1.

2.3.1 GDP Series

To get rid of long run dynamics, we have filtered the series with the Hodrick-Prescott method, setting the smoothing parameters equal to 100 for annual data, since in our framework, one period corresponds to one year. Figure 2.1 shows the detrended GDP series.

Given the initial parameters set up, the model generates irregular fluctuations of different amplitudes and frequencies, resembling the business cycle ones. Irregular fluctuations appear to be set off by the underlying social dynamics (Figure 2.2). Indeed, the simple correlation between the proportion of optimists in the economy in a given period and the related GDP is high (corr$(Y_t, O_t) = 0.6$).

Table 2.1 Parameters set up

Variable	Description	Value
T	Number of periods	400
N	Number of agents	1000
S	Nr. of intraperiod interactions for Kirman's algorithm	150
$\bar{C} = \bar{Y}$	Steady state values for consumption and output	100
ϕ	Persistence coefficient in the investment function	0.7
λ	Tobin's q weight	10
P	Price index	1
v^O	Optimistic Liquidity Preference momentum	-0.1
v^P	Pessimistic Liquidity Preference momentum	0.1
θ	Interest rate elasticity	0.5
μ	Income elasticity of money	0.5
$1-\delta$	Pr. of changing opinion when meeting someone in Kirman's algorithm	0.9
ε	Pr. of changing opinion autonomously	0.000325
β	Inflation expectations' coefficient	0.9
φ	Output gap coefficient	0.2

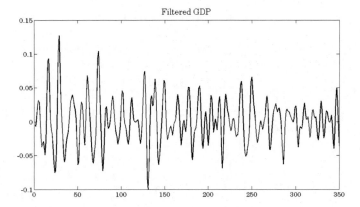

Fig. 2.1 Detrended GDP series (filtered with Hodrick-Prescott method)

Not only, analyzing the cross correlation structure between the proportion of optimists and output at various leads and lags (see also Table 2.3), the social dynamics appears to lead the business cycle, so that we can think of Market Sentiment driven cycles, as also seems to be the case in the real-world data recalled above.

It should be noted, however, that simulations display no tendency to persistent stagnation, nor even in spells with high rates of pessimists. This results signals a major point of departure from Keynes's concern with long-lasting low-level activity that is worth of further investigation in subsequent research

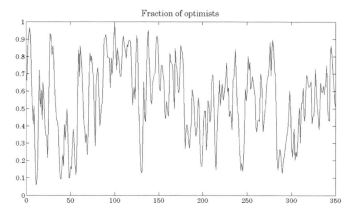

Fig. 2.2 Model results

2.3.2 GDP and its Components

At this stage, it is interesting to analyze the relations among the key series, that is, GDP, consumption and investment (Figure 2.3).

The empirical literature about business cycle[6] recognizes some regularities concerning the ratio between series' standard deviations, with consumption being nearly as volatile as output and investment being two/three times more volatile than GDP. Our model seems to endorse this evidence.

Comparing detrended series' standard deviations, consumption is less volatile than GDP while investment's volatility is much bigger than GDP's one.

Also the cross correlation structure between variables and output leads/lags presents some interesting results:

- Both consumption and investment are procyclical with respect to the cycle, but contrary to the empirical evidence and contrary to Keynes' supposition too, consumption leads the cycle while investment tends to lag it.
- The nominal interest rate as well as the real one are procyclical reflecting a positive relationship between output increases and rates' increases. Moreover, both

Table 2.2 Detrended series, standard deviations' ratio

	Absolute	wrt GDP
Output	0,018	1
Investment	0,091	5,03
Consumption	0,009	0,52

---

[6] See for example Agresti and Mojon, 2001, Stadler, 1994, Stock and Watson, 1999.

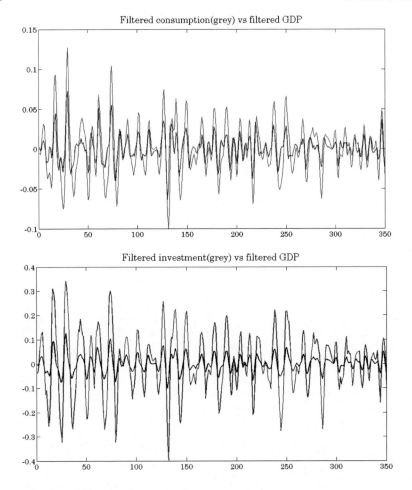

Fig. 2.3 Relationship between GDP, consumption and investment

the rates lead output downturns by approximately one period time since they display the highest negative correlation with output at one period lag.
- Along with the empirical literature, inflation is strongly procyclical.

2.4 Conclusions

The scope of this paper has been to present the preliminary results of a project aiming at "taking Keynes in the computer laboratory", that is to say, construct an ABM

Table 2.3 Variables' correlation with output at different k leads and lags

k	-3	-2	-1	0	1	2	3
Consumption	-0,72	-0,32	0,39	0,85	0,72	0,28	-0,1
Investment	-0,02	0,4	0,8	0,93	0,58	-0,01	-0,46
Nominal rate	0,02	0,31	0,54	0,33	-0,29	-0,68	-0,49
Real rate	-0,01	0,26	0,48	0,3	-0,3	-0,68	-0,46
Inflation	-0,44	-0,25	0,26	0,79	0,88	0,5	0
Mkt Sent	-0,01	0,02	0,08	0,15	0,2	0,14	0,01

model in the IS-LM style capable of complementing Keynes's macro-framework and his behavioural microfoundations of MEC, MPC and LP.

In the spirit of "counterfactual history of thought" of this paper, we deem the results presented above encouraging in that Market Sentiment as a social-interactive phenomenon arising from boundedly rational (though not irrational) behaviour concerning uncertainty, and embedded into a traditional Keynesian macroeconomic framework, proves able to generate business cycles as envisaged by Keynes, and with sensible statistical properties.

Of course, as said above, these results are very preliminary and the agenda for further research is quite extensive. First of all, it is important that we have also found that one of Keynes's key predictions persistent low-level activity is not an emergent property of the economic system we have designed. This indicates that some additional factor(s), beyond the basic ones used here, has to be introduced. A second area of research concerns the empirical validation of the model and its comparative fit with alternative business cycle theories. A third line of development of the model should include policy instruments, and the use of the model for policy analysis and prescription.

References

Agresti A-M., Mojon B. (2001), "Some stylized facts on the Euro area business cycle". European Central Bank Working paper nø95.

Akerlof G., Shiller R. (2009), Animal Spirits: How Human Psychology Drives the Economy, and Why It Matters for Global Capitalism, Princeton, Princeton University Press.

Blanchard O. J. (2000), "What Do We Know about Macroeconomics that Fisher and Wicksell Did Not Know?", Quarterly Journal of Economics, vol. 115, pp. 1375–1409.

Bruun C. (1999), "Agent-based Keynesian economics: simulating a monetary production system bottom-up".

Bruun C. (2008), "Rediscovering the Economics of Keynes in an Agent- Based Computational Setting". Forthcoming in "Eastern Economic Journal".

Colander D., Howitt P., Kirman A., Leijonhufvud A. Meherling P. (2008), "Beyond DSGE Models: Toward an Empirically Based Macroeconomics, Papers and Proceedings of the American Economic Association, American Economic Review, 98, 236–240.

Delli Gatti D., Gaffeo E., Gallegati M., Giulioni F., Palestrini M. (2008), Emergent Macroeconomics, Wien, Springer.

Fontana M., Marchionatti R. (2007), "Endogenous Animal Spirits and Investment: an Agent Based Model". Department of Economics "Cognetti de Martiis"- CESMEP Working Paper 09/2007.

Friedman M. (1957), A Theory of the Consumption Function, Princeton, Princeton University Press.

Keynes J.M. (1936), The General Theory of Employment, Interest and Money, London, Macmillan

Keynes J.M. (1937), "The General Theory of Employment", Quarterly Journals of Economics, vol.51 n.2 209–223; in The Collected Writings of John Maynard Keynes, ed. by E. Moggridge, London, Macmillan, 1973, vol. XIV.

Kirman A. (1993), "Ants, rationality and recruitment", Quarterly Journal of Economics, vol.108, 137–156

Hicks J.R. (1937), "Mr. Keynes and the Classics: A Suggested Interpretation", Econometrica, vol. 5.

Leijonhufvud A. (1993), "Towards a Not-Too Rational Macroeconomics", Southern Economic Journal, vol.60, pp.1–13

Leijonhufvud A. (2008), "Keynes and the Crisis", CEPR Policy Insight, n. 23.

Modigliani F., Brunberg R. (1954), "Utility Analysis and the Consumption Function. An Interpretation of Cross-Section Data", in Kurihara K.K. (ed.), Post Keynesian Economics, New Brunswick N.J., Rutgers University Press.

Stadler G.W. (1994), "Real Business Cycle". Journal of Economic Litera-ture, vol. XXXII.

Stock J.H., Watson M.W. (1999), "Business cycle fluctuations in US macroeconomic time series". In J.B. Taylor, M. Woodford (ed.), "Handbook of Macroeconomics", vol. 1, 3–64, Elsevier.

Taylor K., McNabb B. (2007), "Business cycle and the role of confidence: evidence from Europe". Oxford Bulletin of Economics and Statistics vol. 69, n. 2, 185–208.

Throop A.W. (1992), "Consumer sentiment: its causes and effect". Economic Review Federal reserve Bank of San Francisco, n.1.

Tobin J. (1956), "The Interest Elasticity of the Transactions Demand for Cash", Review of Economics and Statistics, 38, pp. 241–247.

Tobin J. (1969), "A General Equilibrium Approach to Monetary Theory", Journal of Money Credit and Banking, vol.I, n.1, pp. 15–29.

Chapter 3
Pride and Prejudice on a Centralized Academic Labor Market

Philippe Caillou and Michele Sebag

Abstract The Academic Labor Market in France can be viewed as a constrained Stable Marriage problem, pairing universities and candidates according to their (elitist) preferences. A Multi-Agent based model, calibrated after the empirical evidence, is used to investigate how universities can recruit the best candidates with high confidence. Extensive simulations suggest that universities can be divided in four categories: top and medium universities have no difficulty in attracting the candidates they have selected, contrarily to good and bad universities. In this paper, a learning mechanism is presented: universities are allowed to tune their expectations depending on whether they did succeed to attract candidates in the previous recruitment rounds. The impact of over/under estimations is analyzed with respect to the hiring efficiency and quality.

3.1 Introduction

National academic labor markets (ALMs) are strongly influenced by the culture and history of the country (Musselin, 2005). The French system examined in this paper reflects an egalitarian tradition; the hiring process globally aggregates the preferences of universities and candidates using a Stable Marriage-like algorithm (Gale and Shapley, 1962). Due to administrative constraints (limited size of the short list), this centralized procedure might entail some hiring inefficiencies, where good universities might select top candidates, who will ultimately prefer better universities. Universities might therefore use less elitist and more secure recruitment strategies. The goal of this paper is to examine how strategies based on raising/lowering the university expectations might improve their hiring efficiency. In an earlier study of the French ALM (Caillou and Sebag, 2008), a Multi-Agent (MA) simulation framework has been proposed to assess the hiring rate and the quality of the recruitment

P. Caillou · M. Sebag
LRI, Universite Paris Sud, F-91405 Orsay, France, e-mail: caillou;sebag@lri.fr

process. In this paper, this framework is extended, allowing universities to adjust their selectivity depending on their hiring success in the previous steps. The efficiency of the considered strategies is discussed with respect to the university position (relatively to the set of universities).

The paper is organized as follows. Section 3.2 briefly reviews and discusses relevant work. The French academic labor market (ALM) is presented in section 3.3. Section 3.4 describes the MA-based model. Section 3.5 discusses the lessons learned from extensive simulations conducted with this model, and the paper concludes with some perspectives for further research.

3.2 Related Work

Centralized (labor) markets are based on the preferences of sellers (here, the candidates) and buyers (the universities). The combinatorial optimization problem of building an optimal pairing, referred to as *Stable Marriage* problem, has been extensively investigated since Gale & Shapley pioneering work (1962). The French ministry actually uses a variant of the Stable Marriage algorithm (akin, Baiou and Balinski, 2004) to compute an optimal assignment of candidates to universities. Importantly, the procedure is shown to be *truthful*, in the sense that no agent could improve its outcome by lying about its preferences (Ito and Parkes, 2006). The optimality and truthfulness properties however only hold in an idealized setting (rational agents, unbounded shortlists).

The French academic labor market has more specifically been studied by Musselin (2005) in a sociological perspective. This work focuses on organizational, societal and cognitive aspects; the professional efficiency, the university organization and department cohesiveness, and the quality assessment are related to the hiring process. The Local Hiring phenomenon has been investigated in a specific area by Combes *et al.* (2008), empirically measuring how the proximity between the PhD jury of a candidate and the jury of highly competitive national examinations, is correlated with the probability of success of the candidate.

On the computational side, a variety of social and economical problems have been investigated using multi-agent systems (MAs) (Axelrod, 2004; Tesfatsion, 2006). MAs have demonstrated their ability to both represent (cognitive) agents and constrained interaction rules, and provide insights into the dynamics of the system. More generally, MAs are increasingly being considered as a flexible and versatile modelling framework, enabling positive and normative investigations of phenomena out of reach of analytical studies, and supported by efficient programming environments (e.g., ModulEco (Phan, 2004) and RePast (North *et al.*, 2006)). In an earlier work (Caillou and Sebag, 2008), a MAS has been proposed to model the French ALM and study the local hiring problem; interestingly, local hiring (see below) was shown to be an efficient hiring strategy (as opposed to, a "bad university habit") in some settings.

3.3 The French Academic Labor Market

This section describes the French academic hiring process and the available ground truth.

3.3.1 The Hiring Process

- The list of all open positions in all universities is published by the State department. Every PhD[1] is free to apply to any such position; the number of applications is not restricted.
- In each university, for each position, a jury is designated, selects candidates and interviews the selected candidates.
- Every selected candidate goes to every interview (except for conflicting schedules or if he has been formerly top-listed in a University he prefers).
- For each position, the jury publishes a shortlist of at most five names, selected among the interviewed candidates.
- Each candidate is informed of the positions he has been shortlisted for, together with his rank; he symmetrically ranks all positions (no length constraint) according to his preferences.
- All university shortlists and candidate ranking lists are sent to the ministry; a stable marriage like algorithm is used to compute the actual matching.

3.3.2 Empirical Evidence

In 2007, the number of open positions, the number of candidates and the number of applications in every discipline were published by the State department (Table 3.1). Three main categories were distinguished. In the first category, including Law, Economics & Management (L&M) disciplines, each candidate applies on average to 50% of the opened positions. In the other categories, including Science on the one hand and Literature and Humanities on the other hand (H&S), the number of candidates per position (pressure) is significantly higher and the number of applications per candidate is significantly lesser. Globally, the hiring process is efficient in the sense that the recruitment rate is 98%. The local hiring rate, that is the percentage of universities recruiting candidates who passed their PhD in this same university, is circa 28% (37% in L&M, 24% in Humanities and 28% in Science).

---

[1] A pre-filter referred to as "qualification" is used to reject PhDs with no teaching experience. This step is left out of the study for the sake of simplicity.

Table 3.1 The French academic labor market in 2007.

2007	Total	L&M	Hum.	Science
Positions	2110	324	695	1000
Candidates	9318	555	3135	5540
Applications/candidate	8,3	26,8	8,8	6,0
HiringRate	98%	94%	99%	99%
LocalHiring rate	28%	37%	24%	28%
nbSections	57	6	25	23
Avg. nbJobs / sect.	37,0	54,0	27,8	43,5

3.4 Academic Labor Market Modelling

This section describes the Multi-Agent model proposed for the French academic labor market, together with the assumptions made regarding university and candidate preferences.

3.4.1 Agent Preferences

It might be safely assumed that universities aim at recruiting the best candidates while candidates aim at being recruited in the best universities. Usually each agent has however different quality criteria; and, would it exist, the "true quality" ordering is unknown.

The proposed modelling will thus proceed in a backward manner, assuming that there exists such a "true ordering", of which each agent preference ordering is a perturbed variant. Only two types of perturbations are considered at the moment, respectively based on locality preferences and on random noise (see below).

Formally, letting U denote the number of universities, it is assumed with no loss of generality that the set of universities $\{u_1,\ldots,u_U\}$ is ordered according to the "true ordering". Symmetrically, C denotes the number of candidates and $\{c_1,\ldots c_C\}$ the set of candidates ordered after the "true ordering".

3.4.2 Multi-Agent Based Model

The MAS involves two types of agents, candidates $\{c_1,\ldots,c_C\}$ and universities $\{u_1,\ldots,u_U\}$, where an agent index stands for its rank after the (unknown) "true ordering". Furthermore the model is spatialized, that is, to each agent are associated 2D coordinates (in $[0,1]$). The home University of an candidate is the nearest one after the Euclidean distance.

3.4.2.1 Candidates

Candidate c_i is characterized from five parameters. The first two parameters (in $[0,1]$) govern his preference ordering: i) elitism e_i stands for his bias toward the best universities; ii) locality ℓ_i stands for his bias toward the nearest universities. A random perturbation, modelled as $(1 - e_i - \ell_i)V$ with V uniformly drawn in $[0,1]$, accounts for his subjective preferences. Overall, the quality $q(i,t)$ of university u_t for candidate c_i is computed as (the lower the better):

$$q(i,t) = e_i \times \frac{t}{U} + \ell_i \times d(c_i, u_t) + (1 - e_i - \ell_i) \times V. \tag{3.1}$$

Three more parameters are used to model the application strategy of candidate c_i. A risk-propensity parameter r_i determines whether he rather applies to the top-ranked universities (according to the preference ordering $q(i,\cdot)$), or to the universities best matching his own rank. Precisely, the strategic ordering of c_i is defined as (the lower the better):

$$s(i,t) = r_i q(i,t) + (1 - r_i) \frac{|i - t|}{C}. \tag{3.2}$$

His application strategy is finally defined from the number N_i of positions he will apply to; c_i applies to the top N_i universities after the ordering $s(i,t)$. Independently, c_i applies to his home University with probability h_i (empirically, candidates always apply to their home university).

3.4.2.2 Universities

Likewise, university u_t is characterized from four parameters. The first two parameters (in $[0,1]$) govern his preference ordering: i) elitism e_t stands for its bias toward the best candidates; ii) locality ℓ_t stands for its bias toward local candidates. Lastly, a random perturbation modeled as $(1 - e_t)V$ with V uniformly drawn in $[0,1]$, accounts for the "subjective" preferences of university u_t. Overall, the quality $r(i,t)$ of candidate c_i for university u_t is:

$$r(i,t) = (e_t \times \frac{i}{C} + (1 - e_t)V)(1 - \ell_t . \delta_{i,t}), \tag{3.3}$$

where $\delta_{i,t}$ is 1 iff c_i is local to u_t and 0 otherwise.

University u_t selects the candidates to be interviewed after its risk propensity r_t and a *SelfAssessment* parameter o_t, where o_t is positive (respectively negative) if university u_t tends to consider itself less attractive (respectively more attractive) than it is after the "true" university ordering. More precisely, its strategic ordering is defined as:

$$s'(i,t) = r_t \times r(i,t) + (1 - r_t) \times \frac{|i - (t + o_t)|}{C}. \tag{3.4}$$

Two settings, referred to as *NoLearning* and *Learning*, are distinguished in the following. In the *NoLearning* setting, o_t is set to 0. In the *Learning* setting, o_t is adjusted after each "move" (yearly recruitment). In the case the university did not recruit its candidate, it lowers its expectation and o_t is incremented. Otherwise o_t is decremented with probability α, where α is computed after the empirical hiring rate[2].

3.4.2.3 Interaction Rules

Every candidate c_i applies for the top N_i positions after ordering $s(i,\cdot)$, where N_i is uniformly selected in $[1, Max.Application]$, and he applies to his home university with probability h_i.

Every university u_t produces a shortlist of 5 names, the top 5 candidates after ordering $s'(\cdot, t)$[3].

Every candidate c_i thereafter ranks the universities having shortlisted him after the $q(i, \cdot)$ ordering. Eventually, the candidates and universities preferences are aggregated by a variant of Stable Marriage algorithm (Baiou and Balinski, 2004), an optimal matching is derived, and the recruitment decisions are made accordingly.

3.5 Simulation Results

3.5.1 Methodology and Experimental Settings

The main two efficiency indicators of an ALM are the *HiringRate* (fraction of positions fulfilled) and the *LocalHiring* rate (fraction of positions fulfilled by local candidates). We further consider the *FameLoss* of each university, defined as the difference between the rank of the recruited candidate and its own rank (not fulfilled positions are not considered).

The key parameters of the MA-based model (number of positions, of candidates and maximal number of applications per candidate, size of the shortlist) are calibrated after the empirical evidence presented for the H&S disciplines[4] (section 3.4). The behavioral parameters (elitism, localism, risk-propensity) are set to the

---

[2] Formally, α is such that the average hiring rate converges toward the empiric rate ω. At the equilibrium, the expected increase equals the expected decrease:

$$1 - \omega = \omega \times \alpha \Rightarrow \alpha = \frac{1-\omega}{\omega}. \qquad (3.5)$$

[3] For the sake of simplicity, the impact of the live interviews is not accounted for in the model.

[4] The L&M setting corresponds to a saturated market, where almost 50% of the candidates apply to every job; in this situation a high locality bias is needed to enforce a reasonable hiring rate, as shown in Caillou and Sebag (2008).

Table 3.2 Parameter Values in the Simulations

General				Candidates				Universities			
Positions	Candidates	Max.Application	ω	e_i	ℓ_i	r_i	h_i	e_t	ℓ_t	r_t	o_t
50	200	20	.97	.7	.1	U[.1; 1]	1	.7	U[0, .2]	U[.1;1]	0

so-called elitist settings (Table 3.2), studied and validated in Caillou and Sebag (2008). The simulations were performed using the RePast Framework (North *et al.*, 2006). All reported results are averaged over 1,000 independent simulations with same parameter setting.

3.5.2 No Learning Setting

In the *NoLearning* case ($o_t = 0$), the results closely match the available ground truth: *HiringRate* rate is 97% (vs 94% in empirical data) and Local Hiring rate is 28% (vs 28%). Interestingly, the *HiringRate* and the average number of received applications do not vary linearly w.r.t. the university rank. More precisely, four categories of universities can be distinguished (Fig. 3.1):

- The *Best* (Top 8 universities) have a high *HiringRate* and receive many applications. The *Best* universities choose the best candidates, who come. The *Local-Hiring* rate is the lowest one (Fig. 3.2).
- The *Good* (rank between 9 and 21) have a low *HiringRate* although they receive a high number of applications. These universities, in the shadow of the *Best* ones, particularly suffer from the limited size of the short list to select the best candidates. While many good candidates apply to the *Good* universities, if they are selected they seldom come; they go to the *Best* universities.

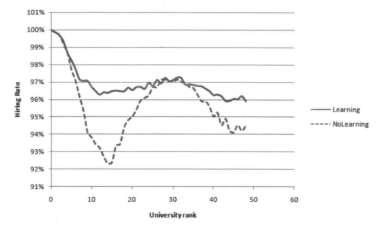

Fig. 3.1 *HiringRate* versus University Rank in the *NoLearning* and *Learning* cases

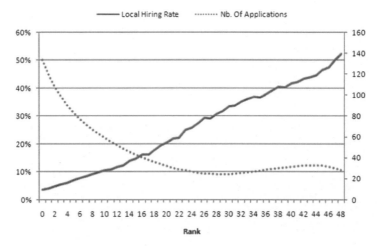

Fig. 3.2 Local Hiring Rate and Nb. of applications vs. university rank in the No-Learning case

- The *Medium* (between 22 and 39) have a high *HiringRate*, despite the fact that they receive few applications. They interview good risk-adverse candidates and local candidates. The short-listed candidates (including local candidates) come, as the *Medium* universities is the best they can pretend to. Both *HiringRate* and *LocalHiring* rate are high.
- The *Bad* (between 40 and 50) also receive few applications; they have a low *HiringRate* and a very high *LocalHiring* rate. Like *Medium* universities, they interview good risk-adverse and local candidates; however their top-listed candidates are more likely to defect if they can, and the *HiringRate* therefore decreases.

With respect to the *FameLoss* criteria, Fig 3.3 shows two groups of universities with significantly different behaviors: *Best* and *Good* universities recruit the best candidates they can attract whereas *Medium* and *Bad* universities recruit candidates with a disappointingly low rank. Furthermore, the *FameLoss* increases with the risk propensity (Fig. 3.3). This unexpected phenomena is blamed on the "subjectivity" effect involved in the preference $r(\cdot, t)$. The more risk-taker the university, the more it follows its own preference ranking, possibly selecting candidates with low rank due to subjective or local preferences.

3.5.3 Learning Universities Setting

In the *Learning* case, universities are allowed to increase/decrease their *SelfAssessment* depending on the success of the past hiring rounds. The results (averaged over 1000 independent runs) are measured after stabilization (1000 time steps). As could have been expected, learning makes universities more efficient: the *HiringRate*

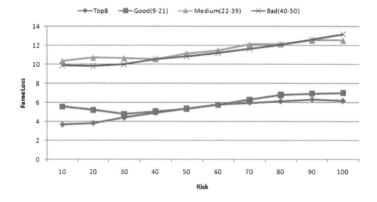

Fig. 3.3 Impact of risk-propensity on *FameLoss*, for Top, Good, Medium and Bad universities in the NoLearning case

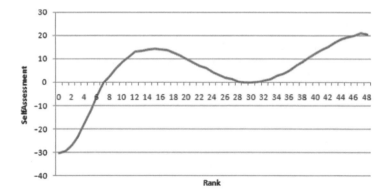

Fig. 3.4 Over and Under assessment of Universities vs Rank (learning setting). Top universities tend to over-estimate themselves; good and bad universities tend to under-estimate themselves; medium universities show no bias.

increases compared to the *NoLearning* case (Fig. 3.1). The *SelfAssessment* curve (Fig. 3.4) displays contrasted situations, mirroring the *HiringRate* curve (Fig. 3.1 - *NoLearning* case). Roughly speaking, the *Best* universities tend to overestimate themselves, the *Good* ones, to depreciate themselves (in order to anticipate the defection of their candidates), the *Medium* ones seemingly have no bias, and the *Bad* ones underestimate themselves.

The impact of the risk propensity is analyzed wrt the *FameLoss*, as the *HiringRate* does not discriminate among good and bad universities in the *Learning* case. Fig. 3.5 suggests that the risk propensity has no impact on the *FameLoss* except for the *Best* universities, that should rather have a conservative strategy (low risk propensity).

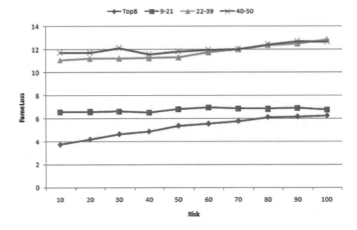

Fig. 3.5 Impact of risk-propensity on *FameLoss*, for Top, Good, Medium and Bad universities in the Learning setting

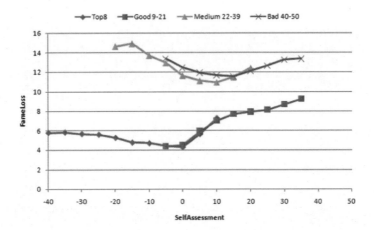

Fig. 3.6 *FameLoss* vs. university *SelfAssessment* for Top, Good, Medium and Bad universities in the Learning setting

In the meanwhile, the *SelfAssessment* parameter features a high impact on the *FameLoss* (Fig. 3.6). If *Best* universities overestimate themselves, the weight of their subjective preferences increases, which results in recruiting lower-ranked candidates everything else being equal. Inversely, *Good* universities should not deprecate themselves in order to minimize the Fame loss. Quite the contrary, the *Medium* and *Bad* universities optimize their *FameLoss* by underestimating themselves.

3.6 Conclusion

This paper, resuming an earlier work devoted to the inefficiencies of Centralized Academic Labor Market (Caillou and Sebag, 2008), investigates how universities can increase their hiring rate. The proposed mechanism, relying on the self evaluation of the universities expectations, duly addresses the market inefficiencies regarding the Hiring rate. Extensive empirical investigations however suggest that this way of increasing the hiring rate can entail some undesirable Fame Loss. Specifically, Best and Good universities should not underestimate (respectively overestimate) themselves in order to recruit best or good candidates. Quite the contrary, Medium and Bad universities should deliberately underestimate themselves to secure the recruitment of acceptable candidates.

Further research will consider more comprehensive learning/optimizing setting for universities and candidates, allowing them to fine tune their behavioral parameters in order to maximize their consolidated Fame for universities, and their job quality for candidates.

References

Axelrod, R.: Advancing the art of simulation in the social sciences. Advances in Complex Systems **7**(1) (2004) 77–92

Baiou, M., Balinski, M.: Student admissions and faculty recruitment. Theor. Comput. Sci. **322**(2) (2004) 245–265

Caillou, P., Sebag, M.: Modelling a centralized academic labour market: Efficiency and fairness. In: ECCS 2008. (2008)

Combes, P., Linnemer, L., Visser, M.: Publish or peer-rich? the role of skills and networks in hiring economics professors. Labour Economics **15**(3) (2008) 423–441

Gale, D., Shapley, L.S.: College admissions and the stability of marriage. American Mathematical Monthly **69** (1962) 9–14

Ito, T., Parkes, D.: Instantiating the contingent bids model of truthful interdependent value auctions. In: 5th Int. Joint Conf. on Autonomous Agents and Multiagent Systems. (2006) 1151–1158

Musselin, C.: European academic labor markets in transition. Higher Education **49**(1-2) (2005) 135–154

North, M., Collier, N., Vos, J.: Experiences creating three implementations of the repast agent modeling toolkit. ACM Transactions on Modeling and Computer Simulation **16**(1) (2006) 1–25

Phan, D.: From agent-based computational economics towards cognitive economics. In: Cognitive Economics. Handbook of Computational Economics. Springer (2004) 371–398

Tesfatsion, L.S.: A constructive approach to economic theory. In: Handbook of Computational Economics. Volume 2 Agent-Based Computational Economics of Handbooks in Economic Series. North-Holland (2006)

Part II
Industrial Organization

Chapter 4
U. S. Defense Market Concentration: An Analysis of the Period 1996–2006

Wayne Zandbergen

Abstract The defense market in the United States has undergone a significant amount of merger activity over the past 20 years. Several sources claim an increasing level of market concentration to be occurring. This paper examines several measures of the structure of the U. S. defense market from 1996–2006. Firm size is established as being Zipf distributed with exponent stable during this period. Other measures also show that significant market concentration has not resulted from these mergers. Simple computational approaches used to generate similar distributions methods do not explain this observation, suggesting that market entry conditions, firm growth rates, and diffusion of sales associated with purchased firms may be a factor in maintaining market structure.

4.1 Introduction

Since Gibrat's groundbreaking work in 1931, researchers have been analyzing empirical data searching for patterns in market structure. It has been shown that firm size distributions exhibit regular patterns, with firm sizes approximating a power-law distribution. Specifically, it has been shown that U. S. firms are Zipf distributed (Axtell, 2001). Generative methods have been developed that result in these distributions (see DeWit, 2003, for an overview of these processes). One would expect market structure to be significantly altered as a result of the merger of firms dominant in a given market yet the processes suggested as generating the appropriately observed distributions do not account for the impact of mergers amongst firms of significant size. Ijiri and Simon (1971) point out the counterintuitive empirical finding that mergers and acquisitions (M&A) do not appear to impact firm size distribution or market concentration. Ijiri and Simon suggest a mathematical treatment as a possible explanation for this observed phenomena.

W. Zandbergen
Center for Complexity Analysis, LLC, 2111 Wilson Blvd, Suite 700, Arlington, Virginia 22201, U.S.A., e-mail: wayne@groupw.com

Other efforts have been made to find regularity in firm growth rates. In general it is agreed that firm growth rates are heavy tailed, but the specific distribution observed empirically is still contested. Bottazi, in several works, has argued that the growth rates are Laplace, or more generally Subottin, distributed (Bottazi and Secchi, 2006; Bottazi et al., 2002). Perline et al. (2006) argue that growth rate patterns, although being better described by a Subottin distribution than other possible forms, are asymetric and, at least in the case of small firms assessed by Perline, do not conform to Laplace or Subottin distributions. In each of these studies addressing M & A is either not appropriate, as in Perline's small business concerns, or is rendered computational neutral by combining merged, and spun off, firms into "super firms", as in Bottazi.

4.2 Analysis of U. S. Defense Market Structure 1996–2006

Little empirical research exists on the impact of M&A on dynamic market structure. The U. S. defense market provides an interesting target to begin to remedy this deficiency. During the period of 1996–2006 a significant level of M&A activity occurred, often between major firms as both buyer and seller. Also, detailed data for this market is publicly available. This paper shows that the United States defense market structure, as expressed in annual value of prime contract awards from the U. S. government to the 100 largest firms, has not changed significantly during the study period. This evidence provides support for Ijiri and Simon's 1971 empirical claim regarding structural invariance to M & A. This suggests that in some real sense an acquired firm's market share is eventually distributed across the collection of surviving firms, a condition cited by Ijiri and Simon (1971) as being necessary for firm concentration to remain stable in an M & A environment.

4.2.1 Data Sources

Data on prime contract awards is publicly available through the United States Department of Defense. Summary data, providing the value of prime contract awards for the 100 largest firms for each company and its subsidiaries is compiled and available for each of the years from 1996 through 2006. Additional data is available for years previous to 1996, but the data is not easily compiled into the requisite summary statistics. Data for all firms is also available, though not in an eassy to process format, hence was not included in this study.

4.2.2 Market Description & Unique Factors

Procurement in the U. S. defense market includes purchases of products ranging from multibillion dollar weapons systems such as aircraft carriers to small purchases of basic supplies such as toilet paper, as well as services ranging from long term contracts for hundreds of semi-skilled personnel to manage and operate cafeterias to single short-term purchases of highly skilled professional consultants. In Fiscal Year 2006 (October 2005 - September 2006) 3,681,301 seperate procurement awards were made for a total of almost $295 billion.

The United States defense market has undergone significant changes during the past 20 years. In 1993, during an event later referred to as "The Last Supper", senior members of the Department of Defense indicated to industry that a significant contraction in major platform procurements resulting from the collapse of the Soviet Union would lead to many of the independent firms within given manufacturing subsectors being overly redundant and unable to survive. Policies were instituted to encourage firms to merge, allowing certain merger and acquisition costs to be recovered under Defense Contract Audit Agency (DCAA) cost-reimbursement policies. The result of these policies was a wave of major and minor mergers in the defense market (Watts, 2008, Chao *et al.*, 2007).

U. S. responses to the attacks of September 11, 2001 demonstrated that predictions of a long-term contraction in procurement activities within the defense sector were inaccurate. In fact, the market for defense procurements almost doubled between 2001 ($154 billion) and 2006 ($295 billion), an increase of 67% even after adjusting for inflation.

As compared with other commercial markets firms doing business with the U. S. government have several regulatory restrictions in place that can significantly influence the market structure. For purposes of this study, perhaps the most important is documented in Federal Acquisition Regulation (FAR) Section 19, Small Business Programs. The overall intent of this policy is contained in FAR 19.201 "It is the policy of the Government to provide maximum practicable opportunities in its acquisitions to small business, veteran-owned small business, service-disabled veteran-owned small business, HUBZone small business, small disadvantaged business, and women-owned small business concerns". For the period 1997 through 2006 the percentage, by value, of prime contracts awarded to small businesses, as defined by the Small business Administration, was stable, ranging from between 19.9% and 21.9%. As small businesses grow beyond the set limits or are acquired by larger firms, the value of the prime contracts held by the previously small businesses must be shifted to other firms that remain classified as small. This encourages the creation of new small businesses. Therefore, although the regulatory and cost accounting environment for defense firms may be more stringent than many other markets, entry conditions are relatively easy.

An additional factor influencing firm size and composition are regulations concerning Conflict of Interest (COI). Firms may be prohibited from bidding on certain contracts due to conflicting business interests. For example, a firm with a contract to manufacture a fighter aircraft would have a potential conflict bidding on a contract to provide technical support to an organization tasked with testing the delivered fighter. The limits imposed by this type of regulation can sometimes be organizationally mitigated, but it is not uncommon for firms to be prohibited from bidding on contracts as a result of COI regulations. The impact on the market of these types of regulations is unclear, but it would be expected that this would result in some limitations on expansion into some submarkets within the Defense community.

4.2.3 Results and Findings

There were two specific objectives of the empirical data analysis presented. First, to develop an understanding of market level of concentration and structure for the subject time period and second, to begin to develop an understanding of specific firm growth rates for the larger firms active in the U. S. defense market.

Firm Concentration - Market concentration was evaluated using several techniques. The 5, 10, and 100 firm concentration values, Gini Index and the Herfindahl-Hirschman Index were computed for each year using published data on the prime contract value awards by firm. Firm Concentration values were computed as a percentage of the total U. S. defense market. As the values for all firms in the market were not readily available the Gini and Herfindahl-Hirschman indeces were computed using the 100 largest firms.

Figure 4.1 shows the Five, Ten, and 100 Firm concentration ratios over the study period. The Five Firm ratio ranges from a low of 23.3% in 1996 to a high of 33.0% in 2001, a range of almost 41%. In 1998 an observable increase in the Five Firm concentraiton level occurred, corresponding to the purchase of McDonnell-Douglas Aircraft by Boeing. From the high in 2001, Five Firm concentration levels have decreased to the level of 27-28%. The Ten Firm concentration level presents a similar form, from 30.1% in 1996 to 39.9% in 2001, a range of 22.8%. Consistent with the Five Firm ratio, the level of concentration has decreased from the 2001 high. The percentage of prime contracts won by the Top 100 firms showed a reasonable steady increase during the first half of the study period, climbing from 52.8% to 59.8% in 2001, an increase of 13%. Since 2001, however, the 100 Firm share of the market has again stabilized. Finally, the Five Firm ratio as a function of the top 100 firms,

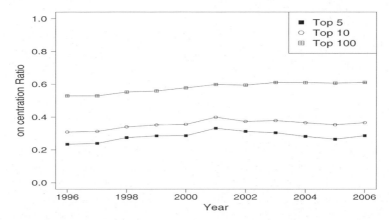

Fig. 4.1 Firm Concentration Ratio

4 U. S. Defense Market Concentration   47

Table 4.1 Gini and Herfindahl-Hirschman Concentration Indices

	1996	1997	1998	1999	2000	2001	2002	2003	2004	2005	2006
Gini	0.64	0.63	0.66	0.66	0.66	0.65	0.68	0.67	0.66	0.64	0.65
HHI	625	627	695	697	702	753	687	635	552	486	559

vice the entire market, was computed (not shown in Figure 4.1). A similar pattern emerges, with a peak at 2001. In this case the levels of concentration return to 1996 levels by 2005.

Although some concentration resulted in the late 1990's, the levels of increase were surprisingly small, with the Five Firm concentration trending back towards levels found in the late 90s. Despite continued merger activity, the 10 and 100 Firm levels, after peaking in 2001, have either decreased or stabilized.

Table 4.1 presents the Gini and Herfindahl-Hirschman Indices. Computed based using the Top 100 firms as the market, these indices provide an additional measure of the level of inequality in the given market. The Gini index is clearly quite stable of the study period. The Herfindahl-Hirschman Index remains quite low, signifying a low level of market concentration. Given the number and size of mergers during this period, it is again apparent that little structural change has occured, at least as reflected in the Top 100 firms.

In conclusion, with the exception of one large merger event, that of the purchase of McDonnell-Douglas Aircraft by Boeing, there are few significant changes in the levels of inequality in this market. Certainly variance occurs, but the market appears to be trending toward a reasonably stable structure, with the relationship between the very largest firms (largest 5 or 10), the large firms (largest 100), and the total market being stable. In light of the number and size of mergers occurring during this period, as well as the significant growth of the market in the last five years of the study period, this result is somewhat surprising.

Market Structure - There are several methods that are commonly used to analyze data that appear to display power law characteristics. The current analysis utilizes two specific methods - Least-squares linear fit to the rank log-log data and Hill's method (Hill, 1975). Firms are ranked from largest to smallest annual prime contract awards. The index of the rank is compared with the value of prime contract awards for the associated firm. A linear least-squares fit of the logarithm of each data sequence is then performed. The linear least squares fit is a common and simple approach used to determine whether the data conforms to a power law but does suffer from limitations, not the least of which is that all values in the data sequence have equal weight in the linear fit. Figure 4.2 presents the log-log graph for 1996, 2001 and 2006 showing the strong linear character of the ranked data. Exponents for all 11 years range from 0.996 to 1.085. R^2 values range from 0.976 to 0.993, suggesting a strong linear fit and conformance to a Zipf distribution with exponent near the critical value of 1.0.

Using Hill's method to approximate the tail distribution parameter require selecting a cut-off on the sample size. There is some debate over the number of values, or

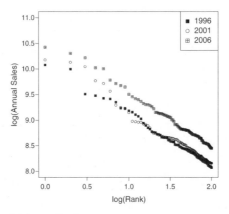

Fig. 4.2 Log-Log Annual Sales vs. Rank

size of the tail, that should be used in Hill's method. Conservative estimates range from 1-5% of the total sequence values. With more than 500,000 seperate corporate entities receiving some form of work from the U. S. Department of Defense, we can reasonably consider the Top 100 firms ($N = 100$) to be an appropriately small sample set. Table 4.2 shows the associated distribution statistics for the computed Hill estimation parameter α_0, for the years 1996, 2001, and 2006 and a 95% confidence interval.

The statistics suggest all three years fit a Pareto distribution, with a μ value surprisingly close to 1.0, i.e., the classic Zipf distribution where firm size is closely approximated by $x_i = x_1/i$ where the x_i are the rank order firm size values. All methods presented suggest a stable market structure for the 100 largest firms in the U. S. defense market and a near-Zipf distributed value of prime contract awards.

Firm Growth Rate - As previously mentioned, firm growth rates have been scrutinized extensively. In the referenced studies Bottazi and Secchi (2006), Bottazi et al. (2002), and Perline et al. (2006) the impact of M&A is neither the focus, nor a finding. Preliminary empirical analysis has begun on the publicly available data, however much remains to be done. As of this study the three largest firms, as of 2006, have been analyzed.

Lockheed Martin (LMI): During the study period LMI had no significant M&A activity. Market share in 2006 (9.1%) was almost identical to 1996 (9.0%). Year to year change in market share varied widely from -15.9% (2005) to 24.9% (2006).

Table 4.2 Hill Estimation Parameter Statistics for $\hat{\alpha}_0$

Year	$\hat{\mu}_\alpha$	$\hat{\sigma}_\alpha$	$\hat{\mu}_{Lower}$	$\hat{\mu}_{Upper}$
1996	1.074	0.443	0.985	1.162
2001	1.117	0.893	0.939	1.295
2006	1.040	0.353	0.970	1.110

Boeing: Boeing engaged in one significant acquisition, that of McDonnell Douglas (MDD) in 1997. In 1996 Boeing and MDD combined had 8.8% of the market. In 2006, the combined companies captured 6.9% of the market, a decrease of 28.3%.

Northrop Grumman (NG): NG began the study period with 1.97% of market share and ended with a 5.64% share. It was one of the more active firms, engaging in at least 9 acquisitions during the study period with four being considered significant. In chronological order (year of acquisition, market share of last reporting year) Logicon (1997, 0.26%), Litton (2000, 1.91%), Newport New Shipbuilding (2001, 3.82%) and TRW (2002, 1.12%). Newport News Shipbuilding had very erratic market share as a result of large, single item awards for major ship construction. However, considering an average share over the five reporting years in the source data yields a 1.31% market share. Summing these shares yields an expected market share of 6.57%, suggesting that without considering other smaller acquisitions, NG's market share decreased by 16.5%.

This brief description of the expected versus actual market shares of the three largest firms supports the contention that acquisitions have yielded negative overall growth rates, in terms of market share, as compared with the market share of the individual firms before being acquired. This would be a requirement if the market presents the claimed stable structure in an environment of significant M&A activity.

4.3 Two Simple Computational Models

Given the regular nature of the market structure discussed in the empirical analysis it is desired to develop a simple simulation that replicates this structure while also representing merger activity. Gulden (2004) provides a starting point by defining a "Jars and Beans" model. A set of jars contain integer beans. Two jars are randomly selected to play a simple game, betting half of the beans in the smallest jar. A coin is flipped, and the winner receives the beans from the loser. A simple boundary condition also holds, that a jar with only one bean can participate in a bet but cannot lose the last bean. Over a large enough number of games the distribution of beans in the jars is consistent with a Zipf distribution. The number of beans and jars remain constant throughout Gulden's model.

In the case of modeling the U. S. defense market, the number of firms is too large to represent completely and would assume one had a quantitative description of those firms. Starting from Gulden, two experiments were conducted to gather further insight into simulation mechanisms that would reproduce the dynamics and the structure of the market comprising the largest 100 firms in an M&A environment. First, a simple model of mergers was developed to examine the implcations of merger activity on an originally Zipf distributed market. The second model is a small modification to the first model where total market size is kept constant.

Model 1 uses a preset initial largest firm size, S_{max}, and number of firms, N. For this analysis $S_{max} = 100$ and $N = 100$. Initial firm size x_i is constructed assuming a Zipf distribution with exponent 1. The list $\{x_i\}$ represents the largest firms in the defense sector, ranked largest to smallest. It is assumed that a wide array of smaller

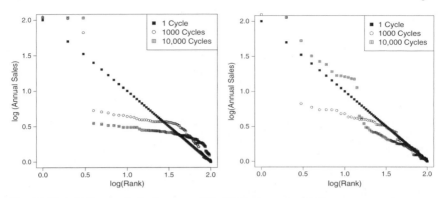

Fig. 4.3 Model 1 Results. Left: $frac_{max} = 40\%$. Right: $frac_{max} = 70\%$

firms exist, but are not explicitly modeled. It is also assumed that there is no firm growth other than through acquisition and that the total size of the 100 firms be reasonably bounded (see Step 6). For a fixed number of cycles the following actions are performed.

1. Select an acquiring firm using an integer uniform draw $i = U[1, N]$.
2. Select the size of firm to be acquired as $S = x_i * U[0.0, frac_{max}]$, where $frac_{max}$ is a global parameter.
3. If $S < x_{100}$, the firm to be acquired is not in the Top 100 list, so increment x_i by S.
4. If $S \geq x_{100}$, select the firm j most closely matching the desired size. The size of the acquiring firm is set to the sum of the two firms, and the bought firm is removed from the distribution. A replacement firm is created of size $x_1/100$.
5. Reorder firms
6. Divide all firm sizes by the size of the smallest firm.

Figure 4.3 shows the results of two runs of Model 1. Each graph shows the log-log rank vs. size plot at three points in the model run, at initialization (1 Cycle), after 1000 mergers (1000 Cycles), and after 10,000 mergers (10,000 cycles). Comparing Figure 4.3 (left) with Figure 4.3 (right) shows that the market quickly diverges from the initial Zipf distribution of firm sizes. It is also apparent that the larger value of $frac_{max}$, as shown in Figure 4.3 (right), appears after 10,000 cycles to be closer in form to Zipf than the other results shown. Although interesting this extreme in the model run space would map to the case where firms can acquire firms up to 70% of their own size. This does not corrsponde to any of the empirical data gathered, but does offer possible insight into generative methods to obtain a near Zipf distribution from this type of model.

The second, slightly more complex, model adjusts firm sizes after every aquisition in order to maintain a fixed market size for the firms x_i. This more accurately reflects the empirical findings that would result from normalizing the market share of the top 100 firms, thus resulting in no overall market growth. To achieve this objective Step 6 in Model 1 is modified as follows.

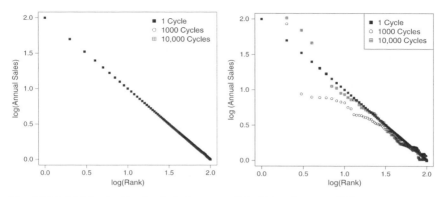

Fig. 4.4 Model 2 log-log Results. Left: $frac_{max} = 40\%$. Right: $frac_{max} = 70\%$

6. Generate a Zipf distributed array y_i with $\Sigma y_i = 1$.
7. Compute new firm sizes as $x_i = x_i - \Delta M * y_i \; \forall i$ where ΔM is the increase in market size as a result of the most recent merger.

Figure 4.4 shows the results of two runs of Model 2. Again, each graph shows the log-log rank vs. size plot at three points in the model run, at initialization (1 Cycle), after 1000 mergers (1000 Cycles), and after 10,000 mergers (10,000 cycles). A comparison of Figure 4.4 (left) with Figure 4.4 (right) again shows that the market quickly diverges from the initial Zipf distribution of firm sizes. And again it also appears that for the larger value of $frac_{max}$, as shown in Figure 4.4 (right), after 10,000 cycles to be closer in form to Zipf than the other results shown, but appears to be a less consistent fit to Zipf than given in Model 1.

Neither Model 1 nor Model 2 provide the ability to generate the observed structure with dynamic merger activity. It is planned that further simulation enhancement will be executed in order to capture several other features of the market, including differing propensities for firms to engage in acquisition, distributed mean zero firm growth rates, and extending the market size to include a set of firms that would reasonably reflect a larger market as an approximation of the entire defense market.

4.4 Conclusion and Further Research

Early attempts to find a simple computational method to generate a stable Zipf distributed market within an environment of firm mergers have been unsatisfactory. Further analysis of the underlying data for the Top 100 firms, as well as the complete market, is necessary in order to develop appropriate extensions to the models presented. Empirical analysis and description of rates and sizes of merger, rates of firm growth, and detailed analysis of firms of size below the 100 largest firms is necessary in order to provide parameters for more complete modeling of the U. S. defense market.

However, the empirical findings clearly suggest that in the wake of significant M&A activity and significant market growth, US defense market structure, analysed for the top 100 firms, has remained surprisingly stable. Although not demonstrated by this research, it is conjectured that the intentional policy of mandating that a significant market share be awarded to smaller firms is a significant factor in easing market entry. Within the well defined market of defense procurements, this suggests that larger firms will find it difficult to maintain market share that is achieved through acquisition. Based upon preliminary analysis of the three largest firms, this indeed proves to be the case. This is an important finding for policy making regarding U. S. governemnt procurement and runs contrary to beliefs held by many in both government and industry regarding the impact of mergers on this market.

References

Axtell, R. (2001). "Zipf Distribution of U. S. Firm Sizes". Science. 293:5536 [1818-1820].

Bottazi, G. and Secchi, A. (2006). "Explaining the distribution of firm growth rates". RAND Journal of Economics. 37:2 [235–256].

Bottazi, G., Sefis, E. and Dosi, G. (2002). "Corporate growth and industrial structures: Some evidence from the Italian manufacturing industry". Industrial and Corporate Change. 11:4 [705–723].

Chao, P., Ben Ari, G., Sanders, G., Scruggs, D. & Wilson, N. (2007). "Structure and Dynamics of the U. S. Federal Professional Services Industrial Base 1995–2005". Center for Strategic and International Studies. Washington.

DeWit, G. (2003). "Firm Size Distributions: An overview of steady-state distributions resulting from firm dynamics models". Scientific Analyses of Entrepreneurship and SMEs, Zoetermeer, NE.

Gibrat, R. (1931). "Les Inegalites Economiques". Librairie du Recueil Sirey. Paris.

Gulden, T. (2004) "Adaptive Agent Modelling in a Policy Context". Doctoral Dissertation. http://www.cissm.umd.edu/papers/display.php?id=93.

Hill, B. (1975) "A Simple General Approach to Inference About the Tail of a Distribution". The Annals of Statistics, 3:5, [1163–1174].

Ijiri, Y. and Simon, H. (1971). "Effects of Mergers and Acquisitions on Business Firm Concentration". The Journal of Political Economy. 79:2 [314–322]. Chicago.

Perline, R., Axtell, R. and Teitelbaum, D. (2006). "Volatility and Assymetry of Small Firm Growth Rates Over Increasing Time Frames". Small business Administration. Washington, DC.

Watts, B. (2008). "The U.S. Defense Industrial Base: Past, Present, and Future". Center for Strategic and Budgetary Assessments, Washington, DC.

http://siadapp.dmdc.osd.mil/procurement/historical_reports/statistics/procstat.html.

Chapter 5
Operator's Bidding Strategies in the Liberalized Italian Power Market

Eric Guerci, Mohammad Ali Rastegar and Silvano Cincotti

Abstract This paper studies the Italian wholesale electricity market by means of a realistic agent-based computational model of the day-ahead market session, of the thermal-power production pool and of the Italian high-voltage transmission network. The aim of the paper is twofold. Firstly, it studies how the strategic behavior of the thermal power plants can influence the level of price at a national level. Secondly, it performs an empirical validation of the computational model over a period of one month which enables to assess the validity of the proposed model. In particular, three scenarios are studied and compared, i.e., the historical performance, a marginal cost based case and a strategic case where generation companies learn according to a reinforcement learning algorithm their best strategy. Results show that the strategic model reproduces real price dynamic during low- and medium-demand periods, whereas during peak-hours the strategic model tends to underestimate historical performances.

5.1 Introduction

In the last decade, several countries in the world have been obliged to intensively regulate the electric sector, either for starting and supporting the liberalization process (e.g., Directives 96/92/EC and 2003/54/EC of the European Commission recommended all European countries to switch to market-based prices) or for amending

---

E. Guerci
GREQAM, 2, rue de la Charité, 13236, Marseille, France, e-mail: eric.guerci@univmed.fr

M.A. Rastegar
DIBE-CINEF, University of Genova, Via Opera Pia 11a, 16145, Italy, e-mail: rastegar@dibe.unige.it

S. Cincotti
DIBE-CINEF, University of Genova, Via Opera Pia 11a, 16145, Italy, e-mail: cincotti@i2.unige.it

and improving proposed regulations because of shortcomings in the market design or market failures (e.g., the 2001 California crisis has motivated U.S. Federal Energy Regulatory Commission to propose a common wholesale power market for adoption by all United States). In all cases, common restructuring proposals are to adopt complex market structures, where several interrelated market places are envisaged and where the integration of the national markets towards an interregional/continental perspective is encouraged (e.g., European Union and U.S.A.). The appealing perspective of modeling complex market models from a bottom-up perspective motivates the adoption of a computational approach in economics and in particular in the study of wholesale electricity markets (Guerci *et al.*, 2009). In these artificial modeling environments, autonomous, self-interested, adaptive and heterogeneous market agents may interact repeatedly among each other, thus reproducing a realistic economic dynamic system (Tesfatsion and Judd, 2006). Several works in the literature, such as (Bower *et al.*, 2001; Bunn and Martoccia, 2005; Bunn and Day, 2009; Conzelmann *et al.*, 2005; Genoese *et al.*, 2005; Rastegar *et al.*, 2009; Sun and Tesfatsion, 2007; Veit *et al.*, 2006; Weidlich and Veit, 2008), have proposed detailed model of national wholesale electricity markets, but only some of them addressed the issue of an empirical validation at least at an aggregate level. This paper belongs to this strand of research and proposes a realistic agent-based computational model of the Italian wholesale electricity market where simulation results at an aggregate level are compared to historical market results.

In Italy, the liberalization process was late if compared to other European countries. The Italian power exchange (IPEX) started on the 1st April of 2004 run by the Gestore Mercato Elettrico (GME), i.e., the Italian market operator. IPEX market structure has been conceived according to common practice guidelines adopted in the different European electricity market restructuring proposals. Several subsequent market sessions for both trading energy and managing critical services such as reserves and real-time balancing are run daily. These are the Day-Ahead Market session - (DAM), (*Mercato del Giorno Prima* - MGP), the Adjustment Market sessions and the Ancillary Services Market. The most important (liquid) session is the day-ahead market which is organized as a double-auction market where approximately 60 percent of national production is traded. This paper focuses on the modeling of the DAM session. In particular, we aim to study the impacts on MGP prices of the strategic behavior of the thermal power-plants with respect to different demand levels, i.e., a representative daily load profile. This paper extends a previous work (Rastegar *et al.*, 2009), aiming to empirically validate simulation results over a larger period of time i.e., November 2006. In order to better replicate the real features of the market, we similarly adopt a data-driven computational model where historical data of the IPEX at year 2006 are used to build the artificial economic environment. The proposed Italian wholesale electricity market model implements a realistic MGP clearing procedure, entailing the zonal market structure and the relevant transmission network, and is populated with the real zonal loads and the set of all major Italian thermal power-plants at year 2006, i.e., 158 generating units. It is worth noting that electricity generation in Italy is mainly characterized by fossil fuel generation, i.e., coal, natural gas, oil, gasoline, which covered at year 2006 almost 74 percent of the national gross generation capacity. Renewable generation is almost irrelevant except for hydro generation which corresponds to approximately 24 percent of the total gross generation capacity. In our model, the historical bids associated to renewable generation are realistically included at zero price. On the other hand, bilateral contracts, which in reality are included in the market clearing procedure at zero price on the supply side and at price cap on the demand side and which are exactly balanced in terms of quantity in both supply and demand curves, have been modeled differently. In particular, the demand quantity has been considered analogously inelastic, thus reproducing exactly the contribution of the bilateral contracts. Conversely, as far as concerns the supply side, each generator is assumed to have not sold capacity in forward markets. All their capacity is sold directly as an offer in the DAM. Finally, import and export has been taken into account in our simulation model by considering the exact historical values. As a final remark, the oligopolistic structure of the market at year 2006 presented ENEL S.p.A. as the incumbent operator owning the 34.8 percent of national gross production, while the three biggest operators owning the 54 percent.

The paper is organized as follows. Section 5.2 presents the physical constrained market model, the Italian grid model, the agent based computational model and the learning algorithm employed. Section 5.3 describes the computational experiment settings and it presents and discusses results. The concluding remarks are pointed out in Section 5.4.

5.2 ACE Model

5.2.1 Market Model

In the following, the market clearing procedure adopted for the MGP (DAM) is detailed.

Each ith generator ($i = 1, 2, ..., N$) submits to the DAM a bid consisting of a pair of values corresponding to the limit price $\hat{P}_i$ ([€/MWh]) and the maximum quantity of power $\hat{Q}_i$ ([MW]) that he is willing to be paid and to produce, respectively[1]. We assume that each generation unit has lower $\underline{Q}_i$ and upper $\overline{Q}_i$ production limits, that define the feasible production interval for its hourly real-power production level $\underline{Q}_i \leq \hat{Q}_i \leq \overline{Q}_i$ ([MW]).

The total cost function of ith generator is given by

$$TC_i(Q_i) = FP_l \cdot (a_i \cdot Q_i + b_i), \quad [\text{€/h}], \tag{5.1}$$

---

[1] The supply bidding format in MGP is a step-wise function defined by a maximum of four points (P_i, Q_i). However, a simple statistical analysis performed on 2006 historical data shows that almost 75 percent of the offers are composed by a single point bid.

Table 5.1 Fuel prices (FP_t) at year 2005 [€/GJ]. These values have been used in the computational experiments

Coal	Gasoline	Gas	Oil
2.3	10.5	6.3	5.3

where FP_l ([€/GJ]) is the price of the fuel (l) which is used by the ith generator. The coefficients a_i ([GJ/MWh]) and b_i ([GJ/h]) are assumed constants. This pair of coefficients (a_i, b_i) vary with respect to the efficiency and technology of the power plant. The constant term $FP_l \cdot b_i$ corresponds to no-load costs (Kirschen and Strbac, 2004), i.e., quasi-fixed costs that generators have if they keep running at zero output. However, these costs vanish once shut-down occurs. Finally, Table 5.1 reports the fuel prices (FP_t) considered in the simulation which corresponds at the year 2005, thus assuming that generation companies sign yearly contracts for the provision of such fuels.

The constant marginal costs MC_i for the ith generator can be easily derived from the associated total cost function $TC_i(Q_i)$:

$$MC_i = FP_l \cdot a_i, \ [\text{€/MWh}]. \tag{5.2}$$

After receiving all generators' bids the DAM clears the market by performing a social welfare maximization subject to the following constraints: the zonal energy balance (Kirchhoff's laws), the maximum and minimum capacity of each power plant and the inter-zonal transmission limits. The objective function takes into account only the supply side of the market, because the demand is assumed price-inelastic. Therefore, the social welfare maximization can be transformed into a minimization of the total production costs (see eq. 3). This clearing mechanism is also standardly named as DC optimal power flow (DCOPF) procedure for determining both the unit commitment for each generator and the Locational Marginal Price (LMP) for each bus. However, the Italian market introduces two slight modifications. Firstly, sellers are paid at the zonal prices, i.e., LMP, whereas buyers pay a unique national price (PUN, Prezzo Unico Nazionale) common for the whole market and computed as a weighted average of the zonal prices with respect to the zonal loads. Secondly, transmission power-flow constraints differ according to the flow direction. In the following the formulation adopted in the paper is detailed.

$$\min \sum_{i=1}^{N} \hat{P}_i \cdot Q_i, \ [\text{MW}], \tag{5.3}$$

subject to the following constraints:

- Active power generation limits:
  $\underline{Q}_i \leq Q_i \leq \hat{Q}_i, \ [\text{MW}]$.
- Active power balance equations for each zone z:
  $\sum_{i \in z} Q_i - Q_{z,load} = Q_{z,inject}, \ [\text{MW}]$,

being $Q_{z,load}$ the load demand and $Q_{z,inject}$ the net power injection in the network at zone z. $Q_{z,inject}$ are calculated with the standard DC Power flow model.
- Real power flow limits of lines:
$Q_{l,st} \leq \overline{Q}_{l,st}$, [MW],
$Q_{l,ts} \leq \overline{Q}_{l,ts}$, [MW],
being $Q_{l,st}$ the power flowing from zone s to zone t of line l and $\overline{Q}_{l,st}$ the maximum transmission capacity of line l in the same direction, i.e., from zone s to zone t. $Q_{l,st}$ are calculated with the standard DC Power flow model.

The solution consists of the set of the active powers Q_i^* generated by each power plant and the set of zonal prices ZP_k (LMPs) for each zone $k \in \{1,2,...,K\}$.

The profit per hour R_i for the ith generator belonging to zone k is obtained as follows:

$$R_i = ZP_k \cdot Q_i^* - TC_i(Q_i^*) \quad [\text{€}/\text{h}]. \tag{5.4}$$

5.2.2 Grid Model

The market clearing procedure above described requires the definition of a transmission network. The grid model considered in this paper (Figure 5.1) reproduces the zonal market structure and the relative maximum transmission capacities between neighboring zones of the Italian grid model. The grid comprises 11 zones and 10 transmission lines depicting a chained shape which connects the North to the South of Italy. The different values of maximum transmission capacities for both directions of all transmission lines are also reported. Figure 5.1 further shows also the distribution of generators and representative load serving entities (LSE) at a zonal level. Generally speaking, it corresponds at the grid model defined by the Italian transmission system operator, i.e., TERNA S.p.A., at the end of the year 2006. To be precise Calabria zone, two national virtual zones (TBRV and PBNF) and neighbouring country's virtual zones[2] have been neglected in the definition of the grid model, but their contributions to national loads or production capacities have been adequately included in our simulations.

5.2.3 Agent Model

In our model, buyers are considered as representative LSEs aggregated at a zonal level. Their quantity bids are assumed price-inelastic and corresponds to the values realized in November 2006 (Gestore Mercato Elettrico). We consider historical accepted demand values because in reality the demand exhibits almost always a pure

---
[2] National Virtual Zone are "Point of Limited Production". Neighbouring Country's Virtual Zone are point of interconnection with neighbouring countries. Please refers to www.mercatoelettrico.org

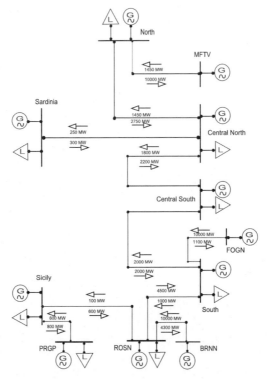

Fig. 5.1 The Italian grid model adopted for the computational experiments comprising 11 zones (buses) and 10 transmission lines. Circles define the presence of generators located in the zone, whereas triangles highlight the load serving entities (LSE) considered for each zone. The numbers above and below of the lines correspond to the lines' maximum transmission capacity constraints for both directions. Arrows indicate the power-flow direction relative to each transmission capacity constraints

inelastic behavior for a wide range of prices and the market clearing price occurs in between.

The supply side of the market is composed by generation companies submitting bids for each of their power plants. In this paper we focus on thermal power plants strategic behavior, because the remaining national production (hydro, geothermal, solar, wind) and imported production can be easily modeled as quantity bids at zero price. Import corresponds in general to power generated abroad by cheap technologies such as hydro or nuclear power plants coming mainly from France and Switzerland. In any case, exact historical values have been assumed for determining all these latter contributions.

The considered set of thermal power plants consists of 158 generating units comprising five different technologies, i.e., Coal-Fired (CF), Oil-Fired (OF), Combined Cycle (CC), Turbogas (TG) and Repower (RP). These power plants were independently or jointly owned at year 2006 by 16 different generation companies (Gencos).

However, in our simulation, the power plant's ownership has been assumed unique for each power-plant by assigning to each power-plant the Genco with the largest share. In order to reduce the number of agents, we have defined 53 agents by grouping thermal power-plants according to the zone in which they inject power, to the technology of production and to the owner, that is, Genco. In particular, the gth Genco owns $N_{g,z,f}$ thermal power plants in zone z with technology f. We group all $N_{g,z,f}$ thermal power plants in 53 different autonomous, self-interested, adaptive and heterogeneous agents.

Each jth agent ($j = 1, 2, ..., 53$) bids to the DAM a pair of values corresponding to a limit price $\hat{P}_{j,i}$ ([€/MWh]) and a quantity of power $\overline{Q}_{j,i}$ [MW] (they are assumed to bid the maximum capacity of their power-plants) that is willing to produce for each agent-owned power plant $i \in \{1, ..., N_j\}$. N_j is the number of agent-owned power plants and if agent j is owned by g^{th} Genco and has its power plants located in zone z with technologies f, then $N_j = N_{g,z,f}$. Furthermore, $\hat{P}_{j,i} = m_j \cdot MC_{j,i}$, where $m_j \in \mathscr{A}_j$ (action space of agent j) is a mark-up value common to all power-plants owned by agent j and $MC_{j,i}$ is the marginal cost of the ith power plant owned by agent j. Finally, $\hat{Q}_{j,i}$ corresponds to the maximum production capacity for each ith power plant owned by agent j. Thus, agents are assumed to bid always the maximum production capacities and a common mark-up value for all their power-plants. In the computational experiments we have assumed $\mathscr{A}_j = \{1.00, 1.05, 1.10, ..., 3.00\}$ corresponding to a mark-up increase value of five percent and a maximum mark-up value of 300 percent with respect to the marginal cost. Therefore the cardinality of agents' action space is equal, i.e., $|\mathscr{A}_j| = M = 60$ for all j.

Accordingly, we define the profit R_j of each jth as follows:

$$R_j = \sum_{i \in 1,...,N_j} ZP_k \cdot Q^*_{j,i} - TC_{j,i}(Q^*_{j,i}), \quad [\text{€/h}], \quad (5.5)$$

being k the zone of the ith power plant.

5.2.4 Learning Model

Agents submit simultaneously 24 bids one for each hourly DAM session. We assume that they learn independently to bid strategically on each hourly market. No interrelationship is considered among such markets, this is an adequate assumption also because in reality the hourly bids are submitted simultaneously and furthermore, in Italy, no block bidding is enabled. Agents are modeled as adaptive agents by implementing a classical reinforcement learning algorithm originally proposed by Roth and Erev (1995). In this learning model, three psychological aspects of human learning are considered: the power law of practice, i.e., learning curves are initially steep and tend to progressively flatten out, the recency effect, i.e., forgetting effect, and an experimentation effect, i.e., not only experimented action but also similar strategies are reinforced. Nicolaisen *et al.* (2001) proposed some modifications to the original algorithm in order to play a game with zero and negative payoffs. In this paper we consider the modified formulation.

For each strategy $a_j \in \mathscr{A}_j$, a propensity value $S_{j,t}(a_j)$ is defined. At every round t, propensities $S_{j,t-1}(a_j)$ are updated according to equation 5.6 to a new vector of propensities $S_{j,t}(a_j)$.

$$S_{j,t}(a_j) = (1-r) \cdot S_{j,t-1}(a_j) + E_{j,t}(a_j), \tag{5.6}$$

where $r \in [0,1]$ is the recency parameters which contributes to decrease exponentially the effect of past results. The second term of equation 5.6 is called the experimentation function.

$$E_{j,t}(a_j) = \begin{cases} \Pi_{j,t}(\hat{a}_j) \cdot (1-e) & a_j = \hat{a}_j \\ S_{j,t-1}(a_j) \cdot \dfrac{e}{M-1} & a_j \neq \hat{a}_j \end{cases} \tag{5.7}$$

where $e \in [0,1]$ is an experimentation parameter which assigns different weights between the played action and the non played actions, M is the number of actions and $\Pi_{j,t}(\hat{a}_j)$ is the reward obtained by playing action $(\hat{a}_j)$ at round t. Rewards are computed as the profits per unit of power ([MW]):

$$\Pi_{j,t}(\hat{a}_j) = R_j(\hat{a}_j)/\overline{R}_j, \tag{5.8}$$

where $\overline{R}_j$ is the maximum profit achievable by agent j, i.e., when ZP_k is equal to price cap and $Q^*_{j,i} = \overline{Q}_{j,i}$ in equation 5.5. The rationale is for uniforming convergence times among the agents due to their heterogeneity in power plants' capacities and technological efficiency.

Propensities are then normalized to determine the probabilistic action selection policy $\pi_{j,t+1}(a_j)$ for the next auction round according to equation 5.9.

$$\pi_{j,t+1}(a_j) = \frac{e^{S_{j,t}(a_j)/\lambda_t}}{\sum_{a_j} e^{S_{j,t}(a_j)/\lambda_t)}}. \tag{5.9}$$

where $\lambda_t = c \cdot t^{-d}$. The time varying parameter λ_t is a cooling parameter that affects the degree to which j^{th} agent makes use of propensity values in determining its probabilistic action selection policy. $\lambda_t \to 0$ entails that the probabilistic action selection policy become increasingly peaked over the particular action (a_j) having the highest propensity values $\pi_{j,t+1}(a_j)$, thereby increasing the probability that these action will be chosen.

5.3 Results

In this study, we explore the potential usefulness of ACE tools for simulating the Italian wholesale power market in November 2006 and, in particular, we aim to

5 Operator's Bidding Strategies in the Liberalized Italian Power Market

Table 5.2 Parameters' values of the adopted learning model

$S_{j,0}$	r	e	c	d
0.6	0.97	0.04	0.00005	0.05

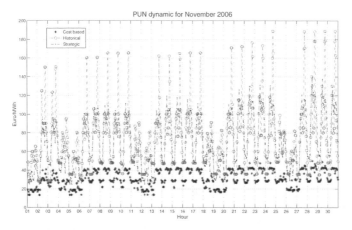

Fig. 5.2 PUN for the 720 hours corresponding to real and simulated values for November, 2006. The x-ticks correspond to the first hour of the numbered days. The line with circles is the historical performance. The line with stars shows the cost based model. The line with dots corresponds to strategic model

investigate to what extent the realistic agent-based computational model implemented is able to reproduce the real price dynamic. The empirical validation is performed only at an aggregate level. We consider the dynamic of the PUN. Two simulation settings are run. The first one is a cost based model used as a benchmark, where all agents are assumed to bid the marginal costs of their power plants. The second one is the strategic model where agents learn their optimal strategy by considering their total cost function. In the latter setting, a computational experiment is defined by 1000 iterations. Moreover, 15 computational experiments have been carried out independently and ensemble averages have been computed to estimate all market outcomes. In each iteration, the profit-seeking agents learn over time what price to report to the IPEX using the classical reinforcement learning algorithm described in previous section. Learning parameters, and in particular the lambda-related parameter c and d, have been calibrated so as to guarantee the convergence within the 1000 iterations of the action selection policies of all 53 agents towards peaked distributions, i.e., the probability associated to one action is greater than 99.9 percent. Table 5.2 reports the values of the constant parameters adopted for all simulations. Agents are homogeneous with respect to the learning model.

Figure 5.2 compares the 720 PUNs, i.e., 24 hours times 30 days, for the two simulation frameworks to the historical performance of November 2006. It is evident that the strategic model fits better than the cost based model historical values. Taking into account the total cost function of each seller and the strategic context improves the simulation performance. This is true in particular when the demand is low, i.e., off-peak hours and weekends. During peak hours, in particular at 18 p.m. and 19 p.m., the simulated PUNs are significantly lower. A reasonable rationale for such tendency concerns the fact that in our simulation all power plants bid throughout the entire computational experiment, but in reality planned or accidental plant outages are common. Thus, power plants, which in reality were off, in the simulation always bid. In peak hours, PUN is more sensitive to plant outages because marginal power plants are less dense. Furthermore, the proposed model is not adequate to reproduce neither collusive behavior among agents nor capacity withholding bidding behavior (power plants bid always their maximum capacity). The latter behavior can raise PUN by increasing zonal market prices when transmission constraints between neighboring zones are satisfied. Finally, it is worth considering how supplier agents are defined (see section 5.2.3), that is, by grouping thermal power-plants according to the zone in which they inject power, to the technology of production and to the owner (Genco). A Genco owns both power-plants in different zones and power-plants of different technology in the same zone. These two aspects are neglected in our current modeling framework. Table 5.3 enables to understand to what extent our assumption may be unrealistic. Each reported value indicates the number of technologies installed for each Genco in each zone, thus the sum of all numbers equals the number of agents, that is, 53. Several ones are present for many Gencos, thus confirming the validity of our assumption. However the incumbent operator "Enel Produzione" (ENELP) and other few big market player may play strategically on the basis of their heterogenous pools of production installed in the different zones. On this purpose, to better evaluate the market power opportunities for the Gencos, we plot the estimated value for a standard index for measuring market power, i.e., the Herfindahl-Hirschman Index(HHI).

In particular, Figure 5.3 reports the Herfindahl-Hirschman Index(HHI) relative to the production levels in each market zone comprising the whole Italy for 19 p.m. of Wednesday 15 November 2006. By definition, larger HHI values indicate a higher degree of market concentration. This figure shows the high degree of market concentration achieved by certain market zones during this hour. This outcome may therefore contribute to explain both the highest historical PUN values and the big discrepancy between simulation and historical values in such peak hours.

Finally, we report in Figure 5.4 the daily and weekly average profits per MW for the five technologies considered by aggregating power plants of all market zones. TG results the most profitable technology in average for all 24 hours and for all days of the week. CF technology power plants is most profitable after TG in particular in hours or days where the demand is lower. CC technology is also highly profitable, but mainly in peak-hours. Conversely, OF and RP technologies are the less profitable, in particular, the former has poor performance during off-peak demand hours but repower technology gets more profits in comparison CC and even if CF during some peak demand hours. These outcomes reflect the characteristics of the Italian electricity production pool, e.g., TG power plants have parameter b in the total cost function and minimum capacity production almost equal to zero.

5 Operator's Bidding Strategies in the Liberalized Italian Power Market   63

Table 5.3 The sum of all numbers is equal to 53 that is the number of agents. Each cell indicates the number of technologies installed for each Genco in each zone zone. Zones are BRNN (BR), Central North (CN), Central South (CS), FOGN (FG), MFTV, North (NO), PRGP (PR), ROSN (RS), Sardinia (SA), Sicily (SI), South (SO)

	BR	CN	CS	FG	MF	NO	PR	RS	SA	SI	SO
A2A	0	0	0	0	2	2	0	0	0	0	0
ACEA	0	0	2	0	0	0	0	0	0	0	0
ACEGAS	0	0	1	0	0	1	0	0	0	0	0
AES	0	0	0	0	0	0	0	0	1	0	0
ATELACTV	0	0	0	0	0	1	0	0	0	0	0
AbruzzoEN	0	0	0	0	0	0	0	0	0	0	0
EDIPOWER	1	0	0	0	0	2	0	0	0	1	0
EDISON	0	1	0	1	0	1	0	0	0	0	1
EGL	0	0	0	0	0	0	0	0	0	0	0
ELECTRAB	0	0	0	0	0	1	0	0	0	0	0
ENELP	1	4	2	0	0	4	1	1	3	1	2
ENERGIA	0	0	0	0	0	0	0	0	0	0	1
ENIPOWER	1	0	0	0	0	1	0	0	0	0	0
EON	0	0	0	0	0	2	0	0	3	1	0
ERG	0	0	0	0	0	0	0	0	0	1	0
EnPlus	0	0	0	0	0	0	0	0	0	0	0
IRIDE	0	0	0	0	0	2	0	0	0	0	0
PiemonteEn	0	0	0	0	0	0	0	0	0	0	0
SARPOM	0	0	0	0	0	1	0	0	0	0	0
SET	0	0	0	0	0	0	0	0	0	0	0
TIRRENOP	0	0	1	0	0	1	0	0	0	0	0

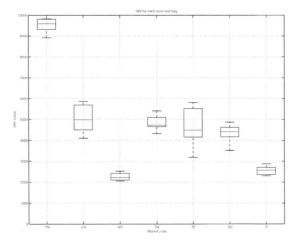

Fig. 5.3 Herfindahl-Hirschman Index relative to the production levels in the most important Italian market zone and in Italy (last x-axis value). The considered hour is 19 p.m. of Wednesday 15 November 2006

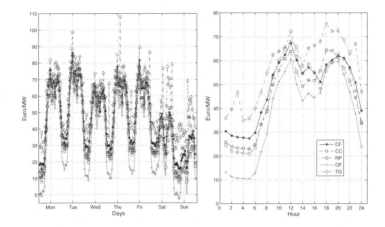

Fig. 5.4 Weekly (left axis) and daily (right axis) average profits per MW for the five technologies considered, i.e., Coal-Fired (CF), Oil-Fired (OF), Combined Cycle (CC), Turbogas (TG) and Repower (RP)

5.4 Conclusions

This paper models realistically the Italian wholesale electricity market by means of an agent-based computational model. Computational experiments show that the adopted market model is able to simulate real market performances. The good level of prices achieved by the strategic simulation, in the majority of the 24 hours, stresses the importance of considering no-load costs in the decision-making process of generation companies. The remarkable difference in the level of PUNs between the cost based and the strategic case, the latter is more than twice the level of the former, is determined thus by both the competitive environment and a correct estimation of total cost functions of each power plant.

However, for some peak hours simulated prices are significantly lower than historical values. The rationale, as previously noted, may be found in the features of the agent's model. In fact, in the current framework agents do not represent exactly Gencos, but each agent represent only a subset of Genco's power plants grouped by technologies. Thus, some strategic decision are discarded in our modeling framework. Furthermore the agent's capability to exercise collusive behavior or capacity withholding bidding behavior has not been implemented. The enhancement of current Genco's decision making process will be certainly addressed in future extension of current setting. Another important discarded aspect regards the fact that in our simulation all power plants have been considered to bid throughout the entire simulation, but in reality planned or accidental outages are common. An arbitrary random process taking into account power plants unavailability according to some standard percentage values could have been considered. But we aim to address in a future extension a more detailed analysis concerning the exact identification of power plants unavailability on the basis of historical values. Finally, as far as concerns profit per MW for the five technologies, simulation results highlight that combined cycle, coal-fired and turbogas technologies are the more profitable. However, a more detailed analysis at a zonal level addressing also the issue of power plants working hours is required to discriminate better among profitability of the different technologies.

References

J. Bower, D. W. Bunn, and C. Wattendrup. A model-based analysis of strategic consolidation in the german electricity industry. *Energy Policy*, 29(12):987–1005, 2001.

D. W. Bunn and C.J. Day. Computational modelling of price formationin the electricity pool of England and Wales. *Journal of Economic Dynamics & Control*, 33:363–376, 2009. URL www.elsevier.com/locate/jedc.

D. W. Bunn and M. Martoccia. Unilateral and collusive market power in the electricity pool of England and Wales. *Energy Economics*, 27:305–315, 2005.

Guenter Conzelmann, Gale Boyd, Vladimir Koritarov, and Tom Veselka. Multi-agent power market simulation using EMCAS. *IEEE Power Engineering Society General Meeting*, 3:2829–2834, 2005.

M. Genoese, F. Sensfuß, A. Weidlich, D. Möst, and O. Rentz. Development of an agent-based model to analyse the effect of renewable energy on electricity markets. In *Proceedings of the 19th Conference 'Informatics for Environmental Protection' (EnviroInfo). Brno*, 2005.

Gestore Mercato Elettrico. Results of GME's markets in 2006. URL http://www.mercatoelettrico.org/En/.

Eric Guerci, Mohammad Ali Rastegar, and Silvano Cincotti. Agent-based modeling and simulation of competitive wholesale electricity markets. In *Handbook of Power Systems*. Springer, 2009.

D. Kirschen and G. Strbac, editors. *Fundamentals of Power System Economics*. John Wiley & Sons, 2004.

J. Nicolaisen, V. Petrov, and L. Tesfatsion. Market power and efficiency in a computational electricity market with discriminatory double-auction pricing. *IEEE Transactions on Evolutionary Computation*, 5(5):504–523, October 2001.

Mohammad Ali Rastegar, Eric Guerci, and Silvano Cincotti. Agent-based model of the Italian wholesale electricity market. In *Proceedings of EEM09 - 6Th International Conference On The European Electricity Market*, 2009.

A. E. Roth and I. Erev. Learning in extensive form games: Experimental data and simple dynamic models in the intermediate term. *Games Econ Behav*, 8(1):164–212, January 1995.

Junjie Sun and Leigh Tesfatsion. Dynamic testing of wholesale power market designs: An open-source agent-based framework. *Comput Econ*, 30:291–327, October 2007.

L. Tesfatsion and K. Judd. *Handbook of Computational Economics: Agent-Based Computational Economics*, volume 2 of *Handbook in Economics Series*. North Holland, 2006.

D. J. Veit, A. Weidlich, J. Yao, and S. S. Oren. Simulating the dynamics in two-settlement electricity markets via an agent-based approach. *International Journal of Management Science and Engineering Management 1 (2)*, pages 83–97, 2006.

A. Weidlich and D. J. Veit. Analyzing interrelated markets in the electricity sector - the case of wholesale power trading in Germany. *IEEE Power Engineering Society General Meeting*, pages 1–8, 2008.

Chapter 6
Selection Processes in a Monopolistic Competition Market

Jose I. Santos, Ricardo del Olmo and Javier Pajares

Abstract In this paper, we extend the traditional evolutionary model of homogeneous product market by incorporating a particular abstraction of imperfect monopolistic competition borrowed from Dixit and Stiglitz. Specifically, we analyze a formal model of an industry in which a set of heterogeneous firms produce differentiated products; consumers have a preference for variety, and therefore firms enjoy an imperfect monopolistic position in the market. We explore the system dynamics, focusing on how selection processes operate depending on the monopolistic intensity of the market and the heterogeneity of firms.

6.1 Motivation

Traditionally, Evolutionary Economics literature on industrial dynamics has been primarily focused on models of homogeneous product markets. However, this assumption does not generally apply in real industries. Firms are not only different in their capacities, knowledge and routines (Nelson and Winter, 1982), but they also produce differentiated products which are perceived as dissimilar by consumers.

Monopolistic competition is a central matter in new Economic Geography (Frenken and Boschma, 2007), which in general terms tries to explain agglomeration phenomena as a consequence of product differentiation dynamics and growth of

---

J.I. Santos
University of Burgos (c/ Villadiego s/n, Burgos, Spain) and INSISOC, e-mail: jisantos@ubu.es

R. del Olmo
University of Burgos (c/ Villadiego s/n, Burgos, Spain) and INSISOC, e-mail: rdelolmo@ubu.es

J. Pajares
University of Valladolid (Paseo del Cauce 59, Valladolid, Spain) and INSISOC, e-mail: pajares@eis.uva.es

varieties. New insights in Evolutionary Economic Geography (Fujita et al., 2001) make used of monopolistic competition arguments too. Hence, there is no doubt of the interest of proposing new formal evolutionary models that face these issues in terms of diversity, selection and development processes.

Kaniovski (2005) points out this idea and proposes a mathematical analysis of the monopoly and duopoly problem using the evolutionary approach. Sharing the same scientific curiosity as Kaniovsky, here we explore the relation between selection and monopolistic competition using a different and more general approach to monopolistic competition.

We propose an evolutionary model of a differentiated industry. In particular, we focus on the selection process and its relation with the level of monopolistic competition in the market. In this paper we intentionally leave aside more complex features of real-world markets, such as innovation processes, which can certainly play a role in market dynamics, but they may also obscure fundamental insights about the interplay of selection pressures and monopolistic competition. Thus, with the aim of understanding the simple before moving to the complex, we reduce the scope of this work to the dynamic analysis of how the degree of monopolistic competition in a market interweaves with the evolutionary pressures that select some firms over others to generate (sufficiently complex) market dynamics.

6.2 A Formal Model of a Differentiated Industry

We combine the well-known model of monopolistic competition by Dixit and Stiglitz (1977) with a deterministic version of the evolutionary model proposed by Winter et al. (2003). For simplicity, in order to focus on the selection processes, we do not consider mechanisms that could create new diversity in the system, such as firms' innovative activities or random experimentation.

6.2.1 Consumer Behavior

We model monopolistic competition as a market of heterogeneous consumption goods which are similar but not perfectly substitutable, i.e. imperfect substitutes. Following Dixit and Stiglitz (1977)'s approach, consumers' behavior is fully described by an aggregate utility function U (Eq. 6.1) with constant elasticity of substitution (CES) between products $j \in \{1, 2, \ldots, n\}$:

$$U = \sum_{j=1}^{n} (w_j q_j^\theta)^{1/\theta}, \ \theta \in (0,1), \qquad (6.1)$$

where q_j denotes the quantity of good j. The parameter $\theta \in (0,1)$ governs consumers' preference for variety, and therefore the degree of monopolistic competition in the market. Higher values of θ denote weaker preferences for diversity. In particular, $\theta = 1$ represents the situation where consumers do not distinguish between products, and the competition is similar to a homogeneous product market. Moreover, consumers exhibit different predilections for each product measured by the corresponding weights w_i.

The specific shape of the aggregate utility function in Eq. 6.1 facilitates the derivation of the demand curve for each product j. We face a usual optimization problem, i.e., the maximization of the utility U (Eq. 6.1) subject to the budget constraint $Y = \sum q_j p_j$, where p_j is the price of product j and Y denotes consumers' aggregate income. Applying the first-order optimality condition, we obtain the following relation for any pair of prices p_i and p_j:

$$p_j = p_i \frac{w_j q_j^{\theta-1}}{w_i q_i^{\theta-1}}. \tag{6.2}$$

Applying the budget constraint, we finally obtain the downward-slop demand curve for product i:

$$p_i = \phi w_i q_i^{\theta-1}, \quad \phi = \frac{Y}{\sum\limits_{j=1}^{n} w_j q_j^{\theta}}. \tag{6.3}$$

Let us briefly look at how the demand for each product is affected by the total number of products n in the industry (Fig. 6.1). New commodities in the market push down demand curves of all products, and this competitive pressure is higher as consumers' preference for variety declines, i.e., as $\theta \to 1$. It is useful to keep in mind this special feature of the family of CES demand curves when analyzing the system from an evolutionary point of view.

6.2.2 Evolutionary Firm Behavior

We complete the monopolistic competition hypothesis assuming that each commodity is produced only by one firm. Firms' behavior is modeled following Winter *et al.* (2003), which is a representative of the family of evolutionary models proposed by Nelson and Winter (1982). Firm behavior does not follow the classical approach of profit maximization (otherwise every firm would enter a race for capital accumulation, as we explain below).

Let index i denotes firms and their corresponding product in the market. At time period t, the firm i produces $q_i(t) = ak_i(t)$ units of product i, according to its stock of physical capital $k_i(t)$ and the global productivity of capital in the industry $a > 0$. We assume that the total production of firm i, $q_i(t)$ is sold at price $p_i(t)$, which is determined by Eq. 6.3. Firm i's profits $\pi_i = (p_i(t) - m_i)q_i(t)$ are the difference between the price $p_i(t)$ and the variable cost per unit of output, $m_i > 0$. Whenever firm i obtains positive earnings, it decides to invest a part of them in new stock of

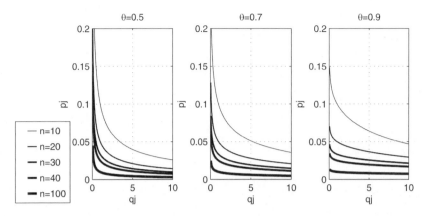

Fig. 6.1 A simplified version of the monopolistic competition market shows the impact of the number of products n on demand curves: $Y = 1$, $w_j = 1 \,\forall j$ and $q_j = 1 \,\forall j \neq i$. The three subgraphs correspond to particular cases of $\theta = (0.5, 0.75, 0.9)$. In every one, the demand curve of the product i (Eq. 6.3) has been drawn for different values of the number of products n in the market. We observe that the sensitivity of the demand curve to changes in the number n is modulated by consumers' preference for variety θ.

capital according to the market global propensity to inves $\lambda \in (0,1)$ and the cost of capital $r > 0$, which are considered identical for all firms. Furthermore, firm i's physical capital depreciates over time at a constant rate $\delta \in (0,1)$. Thus, the change in the stock of capital for firm i is described by the following differential equation:

$$\dot{k}_i(t) = \left(\frac{\lambda a}{r} \max(p_i(t) - m_i) - \delta\right) k_i(t). \tag{6.4}$$

Capital dynamics (Eq. 6.4) are equivalent to a set of replicator equations that govern the selection process. If we define the market share of firm i as $s_i(t) = q_i(t)/\sum q_j(t)$, the corresponding replicator equation is easily derived:

$$\dot{s}_i(t) = s_i(t)(f_i(t) - \bar{f}(t)), \tag{6.5}$$

where $f_i(t)$ is the firm i's fitness function, and $\bar{f}(t)$ denotes the average fitness in the population (Eq. 6.5).

$$f_i(t) = \frac{\lambda a}{r} \max((p_i(t) - m_i) - \delta,$$

$$\bar{f}(t) = \sum_{j=1}^{n} f_j(t) s_j(t). \tag{6.6}$$

With the hypothesis of the proposed model, selection dynamics are deterministic and depend only on the heterogeneity of firms. Note that Eq. 6.4 and Eq. 6.5 are equivalent, and they can both be used to simulate the system behavior over time.

In short, the model describes an industry composed by a population of n heterogeneous firms which differ in their efficiency in the use of production factors (measured by the variable cost m_i), and in consumers' predilection for their product (measured by the weight w_i), competing in an monopolistic economic environment characterized by consumers' preference for variety θ.

In the following section we shall study the long-run behavior of the model for different sets of parameterizations, focusing on steady states and their characteristics.

6.3 Selection and Monopolistic Competition

The main purpose of this paper is to analyze selection processes when markets exhibit imperfect competition between differentiated products. The proposed formal model facilitates studying this issue using only one parameter: consumers' preference for variety θ. However, we will see that CES utility function introduces a very specific demand structure that gives every firm their own market niche as a result of consumers love for variety, and which restricts selection forces as they are commonly understood in evolutionary models.

For simplicity, we have removed any process of diversity creation, so the only evolutionary forces that operate in the industry are strictly selective. We can summarize the industry dynamics as a process in which selection leads the system through different states (Eq. 6.4), destroying diversity in the course, to the point that it is not possible to increase the average population fitness anymore. It is clear that the characteristics of this final steady state will be highly conditioned by the particular value of θ.

6.3.1 Homogeneous Product Competition

The simplest scenario in our model is an industry producing a homogeneous product $\theta = 1$. With this assumption, firms face different prices according to consumers' predilections for each individual product w_i.

$$p_i(t) = \frac{w_i Y}{\sum_{j=1}^{n} w_j q_j(t)}. \tag{6.7}$$

Using Eq. 6.4, we can easily infer that in any steady state (where $\dot{k}_i(t_s) = 0$ for every firm i), surviving firms in the market (for which $k_i(t_s)$) must be making just enough profits to pay for capital depreciation. In other words, we could talk about a critical price p_i^o for each firm that makes $\dot{k}_i(t_s) = 0$, and that is defined as:

$$p_i^o = \frac{\rho r}{\lambda a} + m_i = M_o + m_i. \tag{6.8}$$

Note that firm i's critical price can be written as the sum of its own variable cost m_i and a sort of constant margin M_o of the industry that depends on the capital cost r, the capital depreciation δ, the capital productivity a and the global propensity to invest λ. The evolution of firm i in this market environment can be understood using its critical price: $p_i(t) < m_i$ the firm is unprofitable and its value of its capital depreciates at a constant rate δ; if $m_i < p_i(t) < p_i^o$ the firm, although profitable, sees the value of its capital being reduced at a positive rate lower than δ; and if $p_i(t) > p_i^o$ then the firm increases its value of its stock of capital.

The equilibrium in the industry depends on the selective characteristics of firms (m_i, w_i). In spite of homogeneous product competition, we can expect to observe both monopoly and oligopoly equilibrium states. In the situation where $w_i = 1 \forall i$, monopoly always emerges whenever there is only one firm with the lowest variable cost m_i, but oligopoly is likely if two o more firms are identically efficient because they share the minimum variable cost.

Note that we have supposed that $M_o = \delta r / \lambda a$ is equal for all firms in the industry, but if, for instance, firms differed on their propensity to invest ($\lambda_i \neq \lambda_j \forall i, j$), then evolutionary pressures would not necessarily select the most efficient firms; selection forces would select the firm(s) with the lowest critical prices. Hence, although the industry faces a homogeneous product competition, it is possible to reach steady states where heterogeneous firms coexist. Metcalfe (2002) highlights this selection property.

For a more general case with $w_i \neq w_j \forall i, j$, which is in fact a type of non-homogeneous product market, the oligopoly condition entails the coexistence of n_s firms that simultaneously satisfy $p_i(t_s) = p_i^o$. From Eq. 6.7 and Eq. 6.8, the last condition can be described in terms of firms' selective characteristics and consumers' income as a system of equations (Eq. 6.9) which has multiple solutions.

$$\frac{Y}{\sum_{k=1}^{n_s} w_k q_k} = \frac{M_o + m_i}{w_i} = \frac{M_o + m_j}{w_j}, \forall i, j \in n_s. \tag{6.9}$$

6.3.2 Differentiated Product Competition

We now study the case where the industry comprises a set of heterogeneous firms that produce differentiated products and enjoy an imperfect monopolistic position in the market as a result of consumers' preference for variety $0 < \theta < 1$. The analysis of the system is similar to the homogeneous product competition. Firms deal with different but interrelated demand curves (Eq. 6.3), and evolve over time according to the capital dynamics (Eq. 6.4). Thus, a steady state is defined as:

$$(q_1(t_s), ..., q_{ns}(t_s)) \text{ such that } p_i(t_s) = p_i^o = M_o + m_i, \forall i \in n_s. \tag{6.10}$$

6 Selection Processes in a Monopolistic Competition Market

Some steady states[1] of the Eq. 6.10 contain a solution $q_i(t_s) = 0$ for one or more firms, but these states are not stable. The reason is that once a firm enters the industry it continues indefinitely. Note that demand functions for each product are, in essence, similar to those ones drawn in Fig. 6.1; hence there is always a positive production level that ensures that every firm is making enough profit to remain in the market. We conclude that with the hypothesis of the model and considering a differentiated product competition, $0 < \theta < 1$, stable equilibrium states are always monopolistically competitive, i.e., all firms in the industry are owners of a significant market space or niche.

However, market concentration is also possible in the industry. This is the case where one or more firms monopolize an important part of the total production. In order to study this issue, we express steady state conditions of Eq. 6.10 in terms of firms' output $q_i(t_s)$. To do that, we use Eq. 6.2 to substitute the firm j's output q_j into the budget constraint, and derive the corresponding critical output for firm i:

$$q_i^o = \frac{Y}{\sum_{j}^{n_s} w_j^{1/(1-\theta)} p_j^{o\theta/(\theta-1)}} w_i^{1/(1-\theta)} p_i^{o\theta/(\theta-1)}, \qquad (6.11)$$

where critical prices p_i^o are defined in Eq. 6.8. The firm i's output in any equilibrium state q_i^o depends on the level of monopolistic competition θ and the selective characteristics of firm i, (m_i, w_i). To be more precise, q_i^o depends on the relative differences of these characteristics over the rest of the population. Since $(\theta - 1)^{-1} < 0$, it is clear that firm i's critical output q_i^o increases with w_i (consumers' predilection for firm i's product) and decreases with m_i (firm i's variable cost). This property can be seen more clearly studying firm i's market share equation, which is obtained directly from Eq. 6.11:

$$s_i^o = \frac{q_i^o}{\sum_{j}^{n_s} q_j^o} = \frac{w_i^{1/(1-\theta)} p_i^{o\theta/(\theta-1)}}{\sum_{j}^{n_s} w_j^{1/(1-\theta)} p_j^{o\theta/(\theta-1)}}. \qquad (6.12)$$

Although innovation has been removed from our analysis, the model could easily include two sorts of dynamics: (1) process innovations, associated with efficiency improvements that cause reductions in the variable cost m_i, and (2) product innovations, associated with any product novelty that reinforces consumers' predilection w_i for the product. Since $m_i > 0$, there is a growth limit for market share s_i by cost reductions. On the contrary, there is no growth limit when consumers' predilection rises. In fact, Eq. 6.12 shows that monopoly is an asymptotic solution as consumers' predilection for one product tends to infinity.

Finally, we show that firms in our model do not produce at their product maximizing outputs, as classical economic theory would predict in monopolistic competition markets. Suppose that the firm i's output q_i is small compared to the total industry

---

[1] There could be multiple solutions for the system of non-linear equations (Eq. 6.10).

output. With this assumption, in Eq. 6.3, we can assume that ϕ is a constant given for firm i, and then, obtain the firm i's marginal revenue as θp_i. Profit maximization implies that firm i produces an amount of output q_i^* such that marginal revenue is equal to marginal cost, m_i. Hence, we get that the optimal price p_i^*, which maximizes profits, does not coincide with the critical price p_i^o that firm i faces at the steady state:

$$p_i^* = \frac{m_i}{\theta} \neq p_i^o = M_o + m_i. \tag{6.13}$$

In our model, firms do not pursue profit maximization. Instead, the assumption is that firms update their production according to a simple rule of reinvesting profits. Consequently, the long-run equilibrium differs from the one that classical theory predicts. This model feature of non-profit maximizing firms is in agreement with some evolutionary works (Dutta and Radner, 1999).

6.3.3 Heterogeneity and Other Model Parameters

In this section, we complement the previous analytical study with computer simulations[2] in order to explore the transient behavior of the model and its sensitivity to some of the parameters.

Any complete formal evolutionary model does not only implement a heterogeneous population (diversity) and some sort of selection process, such as the ones proposed in our model, but also development processes of new diversity. The problem is that innovation in economic models, unlike selection, is a complex phenomenon which is very difficult to formalize into a model because one has to make a great number of hypotheses. Here we model innovation processes using an exogenous probability distribution that determines the possible appearance of experimentation in firm behavior at each time period. Admittedly, note that this particular diversity-generating mechanism implies no direct interplay between the processes of innovation and selection. We now study the industry dynamics that emerge from a particular state of heterogeneity in the population of firms, considering this statistical dimension of diversity generation in our model.

We use the Herfindahl index, H, as a measure of market concentration, i.e., the sum of squared market shares of every firm in the market. H approaches zero when a market consists of a large number of firms of relatively equal size, otherwise it approaches to 1. It is commonly accepted that markets in which the H is between 0.10 and 0.18 are moderately concentrated, and those ones in which the H exceeds of 0.18 are concentrated. A set of diverse scenarios, corresponding to different parameterizations of the model, have been simulated in order to show the effect of the

---

[2] The model has been implemented in Netlogo, although any other computational application can be utilized to do simulations. We have included an applet that can be used to replicate all the simulations presented in this paper, and to get a complete description of the model proposed: http://nacho.santos.name/netlogo

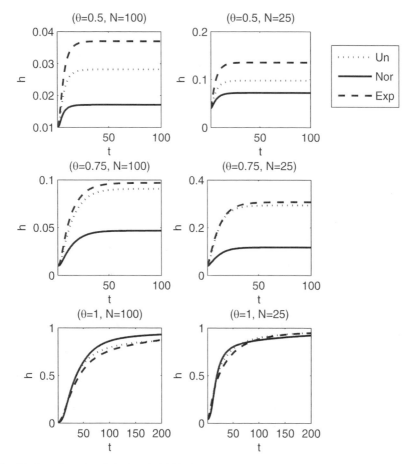

Fig. 6.2 Set of graphs of the Herfindahl index temporal evolution for diverse combinations of consumers' preference for variety θ, and the initial number of firms in the industry n. Each one shows three time series of H corresponding to three different probability distribution of firms' selective characteristics (m_i, w_i): uniform, normal and exponential. Every distribution has a mean of 0.5 and a range of 1. In the case of consumers' predilection for individual products w_i, after setting the corresponding random values for each firm, all values are normalized just as $w'_i = w_i / \sum w_j$. The rest of the parameterization is $Y = 100, a = 1, r = 1, \lambda = 0.75, \delta = 0.3, k_j(0) = 1 \, \forall j \in n$

distribution of firms' selective characteristics. Fig. 6.2 shows the Herfindahl index evolution for every case.

Naturally, simulation results confirm our previous analysis of the model. The level of concentration in the industry depends highly on the monopolistic characteristic of the market. Thus, when consumers' preference for variety decreases as $\theta \to 1$, the fierce competition between firms makes possible the emergence of a monopoly of the fittest firm in terms of selective characteristics (m_i, w_i).

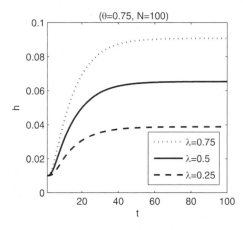

Fig. 6.3 The graph shows the Herfindahl index evolution when we vary the propensity to invest λ. The rest of the parameterization is $\theta = 0.75, n = 100, Y = 100, a = 1, r = 1, \delta = 0.3, k_j(0) = 1 \, \forall j \in n$, and firms' selective characteristics (m_i, w_i) follow a uniform distribution $U(0, 1)$.

Simulations also show the impact of the initial size of population on the final level of concentration H. Obviously, the number of firms is irrelevant for $\theta \approx 1$ because as we have proved monopoly is the most probable state. However, for more differentiated markets, $\theta < 1$, a less number of firms in initial states favor higher concentration levels. The reason is the special nature of the CES utility function that governs consumers' behavior, which can be described as a "love for variety" force that assures always market space for any entrant at the expense of the rest of firms. With these conditions, it is more difficult for any firm to exploit its advantages and hence get more market power in the industry.

Moreover, we explore three particular probability distributions of firms' selective characteristics: uniform $U(0, 1)$, exponential $Exp(0.5)$ and normal $N(0.5, 1/6)$[3]. We observe that the more dispersion -note that with the conditions of simulations the exponential and the uniform distribution have higher variance than the normal distribution-, the more level of concentration. Without any intention of demonstrating a principle, it seems clear that a scattered distribution favor the existence of some firms more differentiated, in terms of lower variable cost and better consumers' predilection for their products, which take advantage of their difference.

Finally, we study the sensitivity of the system behavior to the propensity to invest λ (Fig. 6.3). Note that the effect of other model parameters (see the Eq. 6.4), such as the capital productivity a and the capital cost r, which are supposed identical for all firms in the industry, will be similar. It is clear that λ modulates the effect of firms' selective characteristics. In particular, monopolistic competition is less sensitive to firms' differences for lower values of λ, and therefore industry tends to less concentration levels in those cases.

---

[3] We actually use a trimmed version of the exponential and normal distributions in order to assure that the range of the random variable belongs to (0,1).

6.4 Conclusions

We have proposed a formal model of a differentiated industry making use of the evolutionary approach to industry dynamics and the monopolistic competition abstraction by Dixit and Stiglitz. The industry is characterized by a set of heterogeneous firms which produce differentiated products and enjoy an imperfect monopolistic position in the market. We have explored the system dynamics, focusing on how selection processes operate depending on the monopolistic intensity of the market, which is governed by consumers' preference for variety, and the heterogeneity of firms in terms of two selective characteristics related to efficiency and consumers' predilection for individual products.

The analysis and interpretation of the model is highly conditioned by the special properties of the CES utility function that describes consumers' behavior. Consumers "love for variety" acts as an invisible brake on selection forces that assures a market space or niche for any entrant at the expense of the rest of firms in the industry. Although the equilibrium state is generally monopolistically competitive, market concentration is possible when a few firms take advantage of their better selective characteristics. The level of concentration depends mainly on the monopolistic competition intensity and the heterogeneity of firms in the industry.

Acknowledgements This work has been supported by Junta de Castilla y León (Spain), research project VA006A09.

References

Dixit AK, Stiglitz JE (1977) Monopolistic Competition and Optimum Product Diversity American Economic Review 67(3): 297–308
Dutta PK, Radner R. (1999) Profit maximization and the market selection hypothesis Review of Economic Studies 66(4): 769–798
Frenken K, Boschma RA. (2007) A theoretical framework for evolutionary economic geography: industrial dynamics and urban growth as a branching process Journal of Economic Geography 7(5): 635–649
Fujita M, Krugman PR, Venables A. (2001) The Spatial Economy The MIT Press
Kaniovski S (2005) Product differentiation and competitive selection Journal of Evolutionary Economics 15: 567–580
Metcalfe J (2002) On the Optimality of the Competitive Process: Kimura's Theorem and Market Dynamics Journal of Bioeconomics 4: 109–133
Nelson RR, Winter S (1982) An evolutionary theory of economical change Harvard University Press, Cambridge
Winter SG, Kaniovski YM, Dosi G (2003) A baseline model of industry evolution Journal of Evolutionary Economics 13: 355–383

Part III
Market Dynamics and Auctions

Chapter 7
Symmetric Equilibria in Double Auctions with Markdown Buyers and Markup Sellers

Roberto Cervone, Stefano Galavotti and Marco LiCalzi

Abstract Zhan and Friedman (2007) study double auctions where buyers and sellers are constrained to using simple markdown and markup rules. In spite of the alleged symmetry in roles and assumptions, buyers are shown to have the upper hand both in the call market and in the continuous double auction. We replicate the study and show that their formulation of the sellers' markup strategies, while seemingly natural, exhibits a hidden asymmetry. We introduce a symmetric set of markup strategies for the sellers and show how it explains away the paradox of buyers' advantage in three different double-sided market protocols.

7.1 Introduction

In a recent paper, Zhan and Friedman (2007) study the continuous double auction protocol for a standard exchange market in an environment populated by simulated traders that follow a simple markup (and markdown) rule. As stated by the authors themselves, the goal of the paper is not to approximate human behavior, but rather to gain insight into how traders' profit motives influence the performance of the protocol.

For simplicity, traders' strategies are reduced to a single dimension, called markup for the sellers and markdown for the buyers. (We occasionally encompass the two terms under the single heading of *markup* strategy.) Each seller uses a

---

R. Cervone
Dept. Applied Math., University of Venice, Italy, e-mail: `roberto.cervone@stud.unive.it`

S. Galavotti
Dept. Decision Sciences, University of Florence, Italy, e-mail: `stefano.galavotti@unifi.it`

M. LiCalzi
SSE and Dept. Applied Mathematics, University of Venice, Italy, e-mail: `licalzi@unive.it`

markup m_u over his cost c to post an ask price a; analogously, each buyer adopts a markdown m_d from his value v to issue a bid price b.

The leading case postulated in Zhan and Friedman (from now on, ZF) is the *standard markup* formulation according to which a seller i and a buyer k decide their offers using the rules

$$a_i = c_i(1+m_u) \quad \text{and} \quad b_k = v_k(1-m_d), \qquad (7.1)$$

where $m_u, m_d \geq 0$. ZF assume $m_u = m_d$ and describe the effects of this standard markup rule on allocative efficiency and traders' surpluses in a simple call market and (in much greater detail) in a continuous double auction.

Our curiosity was picked upon reading that their results run against the symmetry inherent in the $m_u = m_d$ assumption of their model, prompting them to "consider two alternative markup specifications" (p. 2990). The *exponential markup* posits $a_i = c_i e^{m_u}$ and $b_k = v_k e^{-m_d}$. The *shift markup* prescribes

$$a_i = \min\{c_i + m_u, 1\} \quad \text{and} \quad b_k = \max\{v_k - m_d, 0\}. \qquad (7.2)$$

Note that ZF omit the truncation in the formulation of the seller's ask for the shift markup rule, but this is irrelevant for their and our results. Kirchamp and Reiss (2008) rename "absolute" the shift markdown in their study of markdown bidders in first-price auctions.

We present the following results. We replicate ZF's study for call markets and continuous double auction and extend it to the bilateral trading model by Chatterjee and Samuelson (1983). We explain the source of the bias in the standard formulation[1] and propose a fourth markup rule that is linear and symmetric but, differently from the three ZF's formulations, also satisfies obvious constraints of incentive compatibility and weak dominance. Finally, we examine in detail ZF's methodology for finding the equilibria of the continuous double auction and show that refining the search space may expand the set of equilibria, affecting some of their results.

The structure of the paper is the following. Section 7.2 describes ZF's model. Section 7.3 studies the call market. Section 7.4 analyzes the bilateral trading model. Section 7.5 examines the continuous double auction. Section 7.6 draws our conclusions.

7.2 The Model

We use the same setup as ZF (2007). Following Smith (1982), we identify three distinct components for our exchange markets. The environment in Section 2.1 describes the general characteristics of the economy, including agents' preferences and endowments. The protocols provide the institutional details that regulate the functioning of an exchange. We study three protocols associated respectively with the

---

[1] The asymmetry applies also to the exponential case; we disregard it for lack of space.

call market, the bilateral trading model, and the continuous double auction: each is described at the beginning of its dedicated Section.

Finally, the behavioral assumptions specify how agents make decisions and take actions. We assume that, whenever requested to do so, sellers (respectively, buyers) utter their asks (bids) deterministically according to one of the markup (markdown) strategies. Contrary to other behavioral assumptions such as zero-intelligence, a trader shouts always the same offer. Following ZF, we assume that all traders in the same market obey the same family of strategies; however, we do not impose $m_u = m_d$.

7.2.1 The Environment

There is an exchange economy with an equal number n of buyers and sellers, who can each exchange a single unit of a generic good. The market is *thick* for $n = 100$, *medium* for $n = 10$ and *thin* for $n = 4$. (Following ZF, we adopt the thick market as baseline.) Valuations and costs are drawn from stochastically independent uniform distributions on the same interval, which we normalize to $[0,1]$. (ZF use the interval $[0,200]$.) An obvious constraint of individual rationality requires that each seller i must sell his unit at a price $p \geq c_i$ and each buyer k must buy one unit at a price $p \leq v_k$. Hence, it is assumed throughout the paper that $m_u, m_d \geq 0$.

7.3 Call Market

In a call market, each trader simultaneously issues a price offer for a single unit. The protocol collects bids and asks from traders, derives supply and demand functions, chooses a market-clearing price p^* that maximizes trade, and executes all feasible trades at p^*.

ZF assume $m_u = m_d = m$ and obtain the following results. Overall efficiency is decreasing in m: a larger markup implies a reduction in the effective demand and supply. Sellers' surplus is also decreasing in m but, surprisingly, buyers' surplus is initially increasing in m. The intuition provided by ZF for this "buyer bias" asymmetry is the observation that for a high m most bids are near zero while asks spread over the interval $[0,2]$. (ZF fail to remark that asks above 1 never trade.)

We find this explanation wanting. ZF do not offer an explicit argument for the choice of the standard markup rule, except for its intuitive appeal and the plausible requirement of individual rationality associated with $m \geq 0$. The theory of mechanism design offers more specific suggestions; see f.i. part II in Nisan *et al.* (2007). Namely, by incentive compatibility and weak dominance, a trading rule should satisfy three constraints: 1) it should be strictly increasing in the cost (or valuation) of the trader; 2) a buyer with $v = 0$ should bid $b = 0$; 3) and a seller with $c = 1$ should ask $a = 1$. It is immediate to check that the sellers' standard markup strategy does not satisfy the latter constraint unless $m_u = 0$. Hence, the "buyer bias" asymmetry originates in an implausible choice of the markup strategies. A similar argument disqualifies the exponential markup, while the shift markup fails the requirement of strict monotonicity.

We formalize the requirement of symmetry with respect to traders' role as follows. Define the strength of a buyer with valuation v as the distance $|v-0|$ from the valuation of the weakest buyer (who has $v = 0$) and the strength of a seller with cost c as the distance $|1-c|$ from the valuation of the weakest seller (who has $c = 1$). Analogously, define the strength of a bid b as the distance $|b-0|$ from the weakest bid (that is $b = 0$) and the strength of an ask a as the distance $|1-a|$ from the weakest ask (that is $a = 1$). Symmetry holds when the strengths of the bid and the ask issued by traders of equal strength x are the same; formally, we require $b(x) = 1 - a(1-x)$.

Among the many rules that satisfy the three constraints, there is only one that is both linear and symmetric with respect to the traders' role for $m_u = m_d$. This unique choice is described by the formulas

$$a_i = c_i + m_u(1 - c_i) \quad \text{and} \quad b_k = v_k(1 - m_d), \tag{7.3}$$

and we call it *convex markup*; see Galavotti (2008). Rewriting them as $a_i = (1 - m_u)c_i + m_u \cdot 1$ and $b_k = (1 - m_d)v_k + m_d \cdot 0$ makes the role-based symmetry and the origin of the name transparent. Note that the original standard markdown rule is unchanged.

Differently from the standard markup rule, in a call market the convex (or the shift) markup formulations with $m_u = m_d = m$ imply that both allocative efficiency and the two traders' surpluses are decreasing in m; moreover, they yield a ratio of buyers' surplus to sellers' surplus constant in m (and equal to 1). The proof follows as a corollary of the analysis below for general coefficients $m_u, m_d \geq 0$.

7.3.1 General Markup and Markdown Coefficients

We repeat ZF's analysis of the call market under the more general assumption that m_u and m_d may be different. Normalize the price p and the quantity q to the interval $[0, 1]$. Consider first the special case of *truthtelling* or price-taking behavior, when $m_u = m_d = 0$. Assuming away sampling variation, the demand function is $p = 1 - q$ and the supply function is $p = q$ so that the competitive equilibrium has $p^* = q^* = 1/2$. Correspondingly, the (realized) traders' surplus is TS$^* = 1/4 = .25$, equally split between buyers' surplus BS$^* = .125$ and sellers' surplus SS$^* = .125$. This allocation is efficient and symmetric, so we adopt it as benchmark.

Assume now that traders adopt the standard markup rules described in (7.1). The demand function is $p = (1 - m_d) - q$ and the supply function is $p = (1 + m_u)q$ so that the market-clearing price and quantity are $p^s = (1 + m_u)(1 - m_d)/(2 + m_u - m_d)$ and $q^s = (1 - m_d)/(2 + m_u - m_d)$. The allocative efficiency is AE^s = TS^s/TS* = $[4(1 + m_u)(1 - m_d)]/(2 + m_u - m_d)^2$ which is respectively split between buyers and sellers as follows:

$$\frac{BS^s}{TS^*} = \frac{2(1-m_d)(1+m_d+2m_u m_d)}{(2+m_u-m_d)^2}, \qquad (7.4)$$

$$\frac{SS^s}{TS^*} = \frac{2(1+2m_u)(1-m_d)^2}{(2+m_u-m_d)^2}. \qquad (7.5)$$

The buyer bias asymmetry is apparent because $BS^s \geq SS^s$ if and only if $m_d \geq m_u/(1+2m_u)$; in particular, for $m_d = m_u$ the buyers' surplus is always bigger than the sellers'.

Assume now that traders adopt the convex markup rules described in (7.3). The demand function is again $p = (1-m_d)-q$ but the supply function becomes $p = m_u + (1-m_u)q$. To ensure that trade can take place, assume $m_u + m_d \leq 1$. Then the market-clearing price and quantity are $p^c = (1-m_d)/(2-m_u-m_d)$ and $q^c = (1-m_u-m_d)(2-m_u-m_d)$. The allocative efficiency is $AE^c = TS^s/TS^* = [4(1-m_u-m_d)]/(2-m_u-m_d)^2$ which is respectively split between buyers and sellers as follows:

$$\frac{BS^c}{TS^*} = \frac{2(1-m_u-m_d)(1-m_u+m_d)}{(2-m_u-m_d)^2}, \qquad (7.6)$$

$$\frac{SS^c}{TS^*} = \frac{2(1-m_u-m_d)(1+m_u-m_d)}{(2-m_u-m_d)^2}. \qquad (7.7)$$

The buyer bias asymmetry disappears because $BS^c \geq SS^c$ if and only if $m_d \geq m_u$. In particular, for $m_d = m_u$ the ratio between buyers' and sellers' surplus is constant and equal to 1.

Finally, consider the shift markup rule in (7.2). Under the assumption $m_u + m_d \leq 1$, the market-clearing price and quantity are $p^{sh} = (1+m_u-m_d)/2$ and $q^{sh} = (1-m_u-m_d)/2$. The allocative efficiency is $AE^{sh} = (1-m_u-m_d)^2$, which is equally split between buyers' and sellers' surplus.

7.3.2 Ex Ante Equilibria

Truthtelling assumes that traders are price-takers: there is no reference to a notion of strategic equilibrium. For large n, it is possible to justify the price-taking assumption as an approximation for the Bayesian Nash equilibrium of a large game with private values and incomplete information; see f.i. Rustichini *et al.* (1994), where it is shown that in any equilibrium the allocative inefficiency is $O(1/n^2)$.

Similarly, ZF's and our analysis have so far assumed that all traders follow the same rule and use the same markup coefficient. While it may be reasonable to justify the commonality of a specific rule on grounds of bounded rationality, it is far less clear that traders would not act strategically in their choice of the coefficients m_u, m_d.

Intuitively, even if each trader has learned to use a given markup rule, it is still up to him to choose the best coefficient.

ZF suggest to account for at least some strategizing by looking at a notion of strategic equilibrium. They restrict all buyers to choose the same m_d and all sellers to the same m_u. In ZF's words, this leads to a two-cartel game for which "a fanciful interpretation is that all buyers belong to a cartel, and all sellers belong to a second cartel, and the members of each cartel agree on a common markup." (p. 2995) We use here the same solution concept, although we prefer to interpret it as an *ex ante* equilibrium where traders must choose a coefficient before learning their types (but knowing which side of the market they will be on). Section 7.5 illustrates a second richer notion of equilibrium and the technical difficulties involved in its calculation.

The unique ex ante equilibrium of the call market under the standard markup rule is $m_u^s = m_d^s = 1/2$. (We do not assume $m_u = m_d$: equality turns out to hold in equilibrium.) The symmetry in coefficients belies an asymmetry in payoffs because the buyers' cartel gets an equilibrium surplus $BS^s = 1/8$ while the sellers obtain $SS^s = 1/16$. On the other hand, the unique ex ante equilibrium under the convex markup rule is $m_u^c = m_d^c = 1 - \sqrt{2}/2 \approx .293$. The symmetry in coefficients persists over the equilibrium payoffs: $BS^c = SS^c = (\sqrt{2}-1)/4 \approx .104$. Not only the convex markup rule restores the symmetry, but it also improves the allocative efficiency of the *ex ante* equilibrium in the call market. Similar comments apply under the shift markup rule. The unique ex ante equilibrium is in weakly dominant strategies and prescribes truthtelling ($m_u^{sh} = m_d^{sh} = 0$): this maximizes allocative efficiency and preserves symmetry.

7.4 Bilateral Trading

The bilateral trading model by Chatterjee and Samuelson (1983) is a workhorse for the study of how strategic incentives affect the allocative efficiency of a trading protocol. It is not studied in ZF, who concentrate most of their attention on the continuous double auction. However, it is similar to ZF's setup for $n = 1$. The buyer shouts a bid b and simultaneously the seller names an ask a. If $b \geq a$, trade takes place at the price $p = (a+b)/2$. Viewed as a game with incomplete information, this provides a perfect example of an environment where the market power of the sides of the market is exactly balanced. Its large set of equilibria is widely studied under general assumptions, but for consistency we concentrate on the special case where both seller's cost and buyer's valuation are uniformly distributed on $[0,1]$.

The bilateral trading model has several Bayesian Nash equilibria. However, there is only one[2] that is symmetric and based on linear bidding functions similar to the markup rules we are interested in. As shown in Chatterjee and Samuelson (1983), a buyer with valuation v bids $b = (2/3)v + (1/12)$ and a seller with cost c asks $a = (2/3)c + (1/4)$. Consequently, the probability of trading is $9/32 \approx .281$ and the

---

[2] We leave it understood that uniqueness refers to offers with nonzero probability to be accepted.

allocative efficiency is $(9/64)/(1/6) = .84375$, which on average is equally shared between buyer's and seller's surplus.

We study what happens when traders play an *ex ante* equilibrium where they are constrained to follow a rule but can choose the markup coefficient. Under the standard markup rule used in ZF, the unique equilibrium is at $m_u^s = m_d^s = 1/3$. Once again, the symmetry is only formal: in equilibrium, any buyer with valuation v in $(0,1]$ has a nonzero probability to trade but for a seller this is the case if and only if he has cost $c < 1/2$. Similarly to what happens in a call market, the standard markup rule favors the buyer over the seller. Correspondingly, the probability of trading is $1/4 = .25$ and the expected allocative efficiency is .750, which is split between the buyer's and seller's surplus in the ratio 2:1.

A similar analysis using the convex markup rule gives a unique equilibrium $m_u^c = m_d^c \approx 0.23$. The symmetry is complete: in equilibrium, a seller (respectively, buyer) trades with nonzero probability if and only if he has cost $c < \bar{k} \approx 0.71$ (valuation $v > 1 - \bar{k} \approx 0.29$). Correspondingly, the probability of trading is about .249 and the expected allocative efficiency is about .792, which is equally shared between buyer's and seller's surplus. A direct comparison with the case of standard markup reveals immediately that the probability of trade is almost the same, the allocative efficiency is higher, and the surpluses are equally distributed.

Finally, a shift markup yields symmetric results analogous to the convex rule. The unique equilibrium is $m_u^{sh} = m_d^{sh} = 1/6$. In equilibrium, a seller (respectively, buyer) trades with nonzero probability if and only if he has cost $c < 2/3$ (valuation $v > 1/3$). The probability of trading is $2/9 \approx .222$ and the expected allocative efficiency is $20/27 \approx .741$, which is equally shared between buyer's and seller's surplus. Like convex markups, the shift rule is symmetric but its overall allocative performance is the worst of the three rules.

7.5 Continuous Double Auction

There are many different implementations of the continuous double auction (from now on, CDA). However, the common theme is that traders arrive sequentially and can place limit orders. An order that is marketable is immediately executed; otherwise, it is stored in a book until execution or cancellation. Differently from the double auctions discussed above, the complexity of the CDA makes analytic results remain elusive even under markup trading. Therefore, ZF (2007) suggests to search for the symmetric equilibria by means of simulation techniques.

Using the conventions set up in LiCalzi *et al.* (2008), our simulations assume a market protocol based on the following rules: 1) single unit trading; 2) price-time priority; 3) no retrading; 4) no resampling; 5) uniform sequencing; 6) halting by queue exhaustion (the market closes down when there are no more traders waiting to place an order). The complete set of conventions used by ZF in their implementation is not made explicit, but we found no reason to expect significant differences in practice; see Cervone (2009).

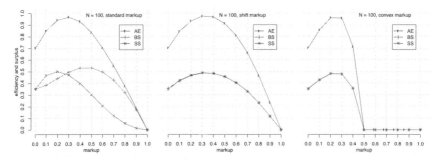

Fig. 7.1 Allocative efficiency and surpluses in the call market under three markup rules.

The left-hand side in Figure 7.1 is the analog of Figure 4 in ZF (2007) and is derived from our independent simulations with $n = 100$. Under the assumption that all traders use the standard rule and the same markup coefficient, it shows allocative efficiency as well as buyers' and sellers' surplus. Data are averaged over $t = 2500$ simulations for each $m_u = m_d = m$ over the grid $\{0, 0.1, \ldots, 0.9, 1\}$. There are two sharp conclusions. First, overall efficiency is initially increasing and then decreasing in m: hence, a larger markup is not necessarily harmful. Second, both sellers' and buyers' surplus are hump-shaped while the ratio between the two favors sellers for low values of m and buyers for high values.

The center and the right-hand side in Figure 7.1 mirror the left-hand side respectively with a shift markup and a convex markup, assuming $m_u = m_d = m$. The general humped shape persists for both the allocative efficiency and the two traders' surpluses, but symmetry is restored because the ratio of buyers' surplus to sellers' surplus is (this being a simulation, virtually) constant in m and equal to 1. The maximum allocative efficiency (computed over the grid $\{0, 0.01, 0.02, \ldots, 0.99, 1\}$) of each rule is .9683 for the standard markup at $m = .29$, .9779 for the shift markup at $m = .34$, and .9778 for the convex markup at $m = .25$. The two symmetric rules (convex and shift) exhibit superior allocative performances.

These results assume that each trader uses the same markup rule and the same coefficient $m_u = m_d = m$. We grant the first assumption for the scope of this paper, but there is no reason to expect that traders on different sides of the market should use the same markup coefficients. This is especially clear for the standard rule, where the asymmetry obviously points buyers and sellers towards different m's. ZF are well aware of this issue and for this reason they suggest taking into account the strategic behavior of traders in the choice of their markup coefficients.

They consider two formulations: the *two-cartel* game leads to equilibria where all the traders on the same side of the market are constrained to use the same markup (or markdown) coefficient; and the *2n-player* game allows for individual deviations from a single trader. We examine the two-cartel game first.

ZF search for the equilibria in pure strategies[3] of the two-cartel game by restricting the choice of m_u and m_d to the 11-point grid $\{0, 0.1, 0.2, \ldots, 0.9, 1\}$. In the

---

[3] Likewise, we ignore equilibria in mixed strategies throughout this section of the paper.

7 Symmetric Markups

Table 7.1 Equilibria in the two-cartel and $2n$-player games for the CDA; from ZF (2007)

parameters	two-cartel standard m_d, m_u	two-cartel shift m_d, m_u	$2n$-player standard m_d, m_u	$2n$-player shift m_d, m_u
$n=100, t=2500$	0.6, 0.5	0.6, 0.6	0.4, 0.3	0.4, 0.4[a]
$n=10, t=5000$	0.5, 0.6	0.5, 0.5	0.3, 0.3	0.4[b], 0.4[c]
$n=4, t=25000$	0.4, 0.5	0.4, 0.4	0.3, 0.3	0.3, 0.3

[a] $\varepsilon = .0012$; [b] $\varepsilon = .00044$; [c] $\varepsilon = .001$

baseline case with $n = 100$ (thick market), they compute the average realized surplus for each side of the market over $t = 2500$ simulations. Using these data, they construct a finite bimatrix game between the buyers' coalition and the sellers' coalition with payoffs equal to their average realized gains. Their main findings for the baseline with standard markup can be read on the left-hand side of Table 7.1.

There is a unique equilibrium for each of three markets and for both standard and shift markup formulation. The equilibrium markup coefficients are increasing in n, but they are symmetric only under the shift rule. Moreover, ZF claim that $m_d = 0.6$ is a weakly dominant strategy for the buyers in the baseline under the standard markup rule.

We replicate and improve on ZF's study using the same grid for the choice of the coefficients. Our results are summarized in Table 7.2 that lists also the sample averages for buyers' and sellers' surplus as well as their sample standard deviations. (These additional pieces of information are not provided in ZF.) The average realized surplus is dependent on the sample and on the precision chosen. For instance, using exactly the same parameters as ZF, we find that $m_d = 0.5$ (ZF has 0.6) is a weakly dominant strategy for the buyers only if we truncate the average realized surplus to the third decimal digit. (Otherwise, $m_d = 0.5$ is less profitable than 0.6 against $m_u = 0$.) This accounts also for slight differences in the equilibrium values under standard markup.

Table 7.2 Equilibria, allocative efficiency and surpluses in the CDA for the two-cartel game

	standard	shift	convex 1st eq.	convex 2nd eq.	convex 3rd eq.
$n=100, t=2500$					
m_d, m_u	0.5, 0.6	0.6, 0.6	0.3, 0.4	0.4, 0.3	
BS, SS	.50384, .30223	.40499, .40350	.39215, .48144	.48310, .39289	
std. dev.	.04283, .02625	.03619, .03489	.02559, .02953	.02923, .02541	
$n=10, t=5000$					
m_d, m_u	0.5, 0.4	0.5, 0.5	0.2, 0.4	0.3, 0.3	0.4, 0.2
BS, SS	.49412, .22781	.37903, .37514	.32217, .50071	.41331, .41389	.50281, .32361
std. dev.	.15585, .09228	.11788, .11732	.08947, .11592	.10151, .10284	.11450, .08915
$n=4, t=25000$					
m_d, m_u	0.4, 0.5	0.4, 0.4	0.2, 0.3	0.3, 0.2	
BS, SS	.38533, .22729	.33786, .33910	.32730, .41307	.41589, .32662	
std. dev.	.25262, .17352	.20701, .20714	.18015, .20905	.20893, .17981	

More interestingly, the equilibrium surplus is split into unequal ratios (favoring the buyers) under the standard rule and symmetrically under the shift rule. But, above all, equilibrium is not unique under the convex rule. However, its allocative efficiency is pretty much the same in each of the equilibria and consistently higher than for the other markup rules. Moreover, for each equilibrium favoring buyers under a convex rule there is a specular equilibrium favoring sellers; hence, symmetry still holds over the set of equilibria. Higher allocative efficiency and set-symmetry of the equilibria suggest that the convex markup rule performs better when traders act strategically.

From a computational viewpoint, the mild discrepancy between ZF's and our results prompted us to refine the grid to a mesh of 0.01 around the equilibrium values found above. This made clear that the weak dominance of the buyers' strategy under the standard markup rule is an artifact due to the limited number of strategies considered. More importantly, we find different sets of equilibria. We illustrate the point with reference to the baseline case of a thick market ($n = 100, t = 2500$). The results for the other two cases are qualitatively similar.[4]

Using a grid with mesh 0.1, the unique equilibrium under standard markup is $(m_d = .5, m_u = .6)$ with allocative efficiency .806. Refining the analysis to a grid with mesh 0.01, we find two equilibria: $(m_d = 0.54, m_u = 0.5)$ and $(m_d = 0.55, m_u = 0.52)$, respectively with average efficiency .801 and .785. The difference in the equilibrium markups is smaller, but both of them still exhibit the usual 2:1 ratio among traders' surpluses in favor of the buyers.

When we repeat the analysis for the convex markup rule, symmetry is restored (up to the inevitable sampling errors and computational approximations). Using a grid with mesh 0.1, we find two equilibria with coefficients lying in the interval [0.3, 0.4]. A blow-up based on a grid with mesh 0.01 reveals three equilibria: $(m_d = 0.32, m_u = 0.34)$, $(m_d = 0.34, m_u = 0.33)$ and $(m_d = 0.36, m_u = 0.32)$, respectively with average realized efficiencies .917, .910, and .900. All three equilibria are consistently more efficient than those under standard markup. They slightly favor the side with higher markup attributing a surplus that is respectively about 4%, 2%, and 9% higher than the other side.

For the shift markup rule, using a grid with mesh 0.01 leads to the unique equilibrium $(m_d = 0.58, m_u = 0.59)$ with an overall allocative efficiency of .828. The sellers' surplus is just 1.6% higher than buyers'. Similarly to the case of bilateral trading, both the convex rule and the shift rule are symmetric but the latter one yields a worse allocative efficiency under strategic behavior.

Turning now to the case of $2n$-player game, ZF search for symmetric equilibria where no single trader has individually profitable deviations before learning his type. That is, the markdown coefficient m_d^* for a buyer must be *ex ante* optimal assuming that all other buyers use m_d^* and all sellers use m_u^*; and similarly for the optimal seller's m_u^*. (Clearly, m_d^* may differ from m_u^*.) Imposing that all traders on the same

---

[4] For $n = 4$ and $n = 10$, in some of several simulations with the shift markup rule we found also spurious equilibria attributable to sampling errors and computational approximations.

side of the market use the same markup coefficient makes their notion of symmetric Nash equilibrium quite restrictive, but we stick with it for ease of comparison.

ZF's results over the 11-point grid $\{0, 0.1, 0.2, \ldots, 0.9, 1\}$ can be read on the right-hand side of Table 7.1. The general picture is similar to the two-cartel game. There is a unique equilibrium for each of three markets and for both standard and shift markup; the equilibrium coefficients are increasing in n and symmetric (except for the baseline with standard markup). However, this formulation leads to equilibria where traders are less aggressive and make offers close to their values or costs.

Our results are summarized in Table 7.3 using the same conventions as in Table 7.2, in particular for the ε-equilibria. We obtain similar values for the equilibrium coefficients, but the explicit computation of traders' surpluses reveals additional information. Under standard markup, the allocation of surplus is skewed in favor of buyers. Symmetry is restored under convex markup: there is either a unique equilibrium with identical surpluses, or two asymmetric equilibria that are symmetric up to a role reversal between traders. A similar situation occurs using the shift markup. The allocative efficiency is decreasing in n for each markup rule. However, for a given n, the overall realized efficiencies are quite close and hence no markup rule emerges as a clear winner from this point of view.

When we repeat the analysis over a grid with mesh 0.01, the following conclusions emerge. First, while the simulations are affected by sampling errors and computational approximations, the qualitative results are similar. Second, the number of equilibria tends to drop and, in many cases, it goes down to one; this pruning follows because a 10% reduction of the mesh induces a 10-fold increase in the number of strategies tested for a trader. Third, the minor differences in the overall allocative efficiency (notwithstanding the asymmetry in the distribution under standard markup) are further reduced.

Table 7.3 Equilibria, allocative efficiency and surpluses in the CDA for the $2n$-player game

	standard	shift		convex	
		1st eq.	2nd eq	1st eq.	2nd eq.
$n=100, t=2500$					
m_d, m_u	$0.4, 0.4^a$	0.4, 0.4		0.3, 0.3	
BS, SS	.53049, .39874	.48408, .48307		.47824, .47848	
std. dev.	.03589, .03160	.04621, .04638		.02950, .02116	
$n=10, t=5000$					
m_d, m_u	0.3, 0.3	$0.4, 0.4^b$		0.2, 0.3	0.3, 0.2
BS, SS	.48348, .38273	.42633, .42581		.39485, .49490	.50196, .39136
std. dev.	.13495, .13355	.12262, .12123		.10678, .11171	.11003, .10144
$n=4, t=25000$					
m_d, m_u	$0.3, 0.3^c$	0.3, 0.4	0.4, 0.3	$0.2, 0.3^d$	0.3, 0.2
BS, SS	.43503, .29794	.32783, .39542	.39613, .32750	.32730, .41307	.41589, .32662
std. dev.	.23875, .20020	.19969, .22117	.22176, .19985	.18015, .20905	.20893, .17981

[a] $\varepsilon = .00111$; [b] $\varepsilon = .00078$; [c] $\varepsilon = .00042$; [d] $\varepsilon = .00100$

7.6 Conclusions

Zhan and Friedman (2007) study three simple families of markup (and markdown) strategies for the continuous double auction. Their main goal is to gain insight into how traders' profit motives influence the performance of the protocol. Our main conclusion is that the standard formulation starring as leading example in their paper is not an appropriate choice, because it fails an elementary test of symmetry in its treatment of buyers and sellers.

We suggest an alternative convex markup rule that is in accordance with the general prescriptions from mechanism design. We test ZF's standard rule, their shift formulation and our convex rule over three different double auction protocols (call market, bilateral trading, and continuous). The standard markup consistently fail the test of symmetry, which is instead passed by the two other formulations. The shift markup rule leads to a higher allocative efficiency only in the call market (and in the baseline for the $2n$-player game), where the strategic interactions are dampened out by the simultaneous aggregation of demand and supply and all nontrivial equilibria are asymptotically efficient under reasonably weak conditions; see Cripps and Swinkels (2006). Therefore, our convex rule seems to offer a more promising route to accommodate strategic behavior while preserving symmetry in a simple behavioral model.

References

Cervone R (2009), Asta doppia continua e strategie di markup. Master's dissertation, University of Venice

Chatterjee K, Samuelson W (1983), Bargaining under incomplete information. Operations Research 31:835–851

Cripps MW, Swinkels JM (2006), Efficiency of large double auctions. Econometrica 74:47–92

Galavotti S (2008), Essays on Bilateral Trade with Incomplete Information. Ph.D. dissertation, University of Venice

Kirchamp O, Reiss J.P. (2008), Heterogenous bids in auctions with rational and markdown bidders: Theory and experiment. August, Jena Economic Research Papers 2008-066

LiCalzi M, Milone L, Pellizzari P (2008), Allocative efficiency and traders' protection under zero intelligence behavior, October, Dept. Applied Mathematics WP 168, University of Venice

Nisan N, Roughgarden T, Tardos E, Vazirani VV (2007), Algorithmic Game Theory. Cambridge University Press

Rustichini A, Satterthwaite MA, Williams SR (1994), Convergence to efficiency in a simple market with incomplete information. Econometrica 62:1041–1063

Smith VL (1982), Microeconomic systems as an experimental science. American Economic Review 72:923–955

Zhan W, Friedman D (2007), Markups in double auction markets. Journal of Economic Dynamics and Control 31:2984–3005

Chapter 8
Multi-Unit Auction Analysis by Means of Agent-Based Computational Economics

Asuncion Mochon, Yago Saez, David Quintana and Pedro Isasi

Abstract In this paper an agent-based computational economics (ACE) model has been developed in order to test the bidding behavior in a multi-unit auction, the Ausubel auction. The model has been studied in two scenarios. In the first one, bidders have weakly decreasing marginal values and the theory predicts that bidding sincerely is a weakly dominant strategy. The ACE model corroborates this finding. In the second scenario, agents present synergies among their valuations. This scenario has been tested for two environments. In the first one, bidders have the same synergy value, but it differs from one experiment to another. In the second one, bidders within the same experiment exhibit different synergy values. The ACE model finds that underbidding is the most frequent strategy to avoid the exposure problem and maximize bidders' payoff in the presence of synergies.

8.1 Introduction

Multi-unit auctions are widely used in different markets for selling goods such as Personal Communications Services (PCS) licenses, treasury bills, electricity, emission permits, etc. This paper is focused on a specific multi-unit auction: the Ausubel auction. With substitute consumptions, where marginal values are weakly decreasing, Ausubel demonstrated that sincere bidding by all bidders is an equilibrium, yielding to an efficient outcome (Ausubel, 2004). Nevertheless, when this auction involves synergies or complementarities (when the value of multiple objects exceeds the sum of the objects' values separately), the theoretical equilibrium has yet to be found.

A. Mochon
UNED, Paseo Senda del Rey 11, Madrid, Spain, e-mail: `amochon@cee.uned.es`

Y. Saez · D. Quintana · P. Isasi
Universidad Carlos III de Madrid, Avenida de la Universidad 30, Madrid, Spain, e-mail: `yago.saez@uc3m.es, david.quintana@uc3m.es, pedro.isasi@uc3m.es`

The challenge addressed in this research is the study of the bidders' behavior for both preference structures using an Agent-based Computational Economics (ACE) approach. The flexibility of this paradigm allows us to work without assuming the existence of fully rational optimizing agents with homogenous beliefs. We have the possibility of modelling the auction with heterogeneous agents and asymmetric information. In this work, two scenarios are simulated: agents interacting having weakly decreasing marginal values and agents with synergies. The presence of synergies has been analyzed for two environments. In the first one, all bidders have the same synergy value but which changes from one experiment to another. In the second one, the synergy value is different among bidders in the same experiment.

There are several markets where synergies can be found. Probably the best known is Personal Communications Services (PCS) spectrum license sales in most countries (USA, UK, Germany, etc), see Ausubel *et al.* (1997). Another market in which synergies play an important role is in procuring transportation services. Usually it is better to have a group of continuous lanes or specific lanes that complement possible networks. Cantillon and Pesendorfer (2004) studied the combinatorial auctions done for the bus routes in London, and found that geographic synergies appear when routes are offered at the same time. Similar synergies can be found in many other markets, such as cable television licenses (Gandal, 1997) or road construction procurement auctions (De Silva, 2005). In the presence of synergies or complementarities, bidders are interested in acquiring more lots in order to obtain their super additive values. This fact can lead to aggressive bidding among participants. However, if bidders only win some of the demanded lots (instead of all of them) they can earn negative profits. This risk might keep bidders away from overbidding to avoid exposure to such loss, i.e., to avoid the "exposure problem".

There is some previous work in auctions with synergies. In Krishna and Rosenthal (1996) the authors analyzed situations where multiple objects are auctioned simultaneously by means of a second-price sealed bid auction. These authors included the presence of complementarities in at least some of the bidders' preferences and showed that the addition of bidders that exhibit complementarities often leads to less aggressive bidding. Rosenthal and Wang (1996) analyze a model that is related to the one developed in Krishna and Rosenthal (1996) but assumes common values in a simultaneous first-price sealed bid auction. Branco (1997) presented the equilibrium behaviour in sequential auctions when some bidders exhibit superadditive values for the objects. In this model, the presence of complementarities leads to intense competition in the earlier auctions, while the price tends to decline over the sequence of auctions. Other authors (Albano *et al.*, 2001) described the equilibria of a simultaneous ascending auction within the framework of Krishna and Rosenthal (1996). They compared the revenue and efficiency generated with those obtained by the sequential, the one-shot simultaneous, and the Vickrey-Clarke-Groves auctions for several values of the synergy parameter. Katok and Roth (2004) compared the descending-price auction and the ascending uniform-price auction of multiple homogeneous objects in a set of environments which include synergies and potentially subject bidders to the exposure problem. Kagel and Levin (2005) experimentally compared the outcomes of sealed-bid and ascending-bid uniform price auctions in the presence of synergies for one of the bidders competing against a number of rivals demanding a single unit. The equilibrium of this model yields to the following behaviour: (1) at lower synergy valuations, the demand reduction force dominates and bidders shave their bids; (2) at the highest valuations the synergy force dominates, so bidders bid high enough to guarantee winning the items; and (3) at middle valuations the two forces counteract each other. The experiment results show that bidding outcomes are closer to equilibrium in clock compared to sealed-bid auctions (although there are considerable and systematic deviations from equilibrium). The research presented in De Silva (2005) investigated the impact of synergies in sequential auctions by examining data on auctions conducted by the Oklahoma Department of Transportation. These authors support theoretical considerations which indicate that winners in the earlier auctions are more likely to participate and win in later auctions. Finally in De Silva et al. (2005), the impact of synergies on bidders' behavior in recurring road construction procurement auctions is analyzed. The results reveal that when bidders with potential synergies participate, their probability of bidding and winning increases and they bid more aggressively.

The remainder of this article is structured in the following manner: the auction model is described in section 8.2. Section 8.3 deals with the agent-based model and the experimental environments. Section 8.4 evaluates the experimental results for both scenarios tested: decreasing marginal values and increasing marginal values (synergies). Finally, in section 8.5 the main conclusions and future work are presented.

8.2 The Ausubel Auction

The multi-unit Ausubel auction (Ausubel, 2004) is an ascending clock auction that sequentially implements the Vickrey rule. Each bidder pays the amount of the kth highest rejected bid, other than his own, for the kth object won. The description of the auction format is the following:

In this auction format, the price increases continuously and for each price, p^l, each bidder i simultaneously indicates the quantity x_i^l he desires (demands are non-incremental in price). Bidders choose at what price to drop out of the bidding, with dropping out being irrevocable. When the price p^* is reached, such that aggregate demand no longer exceeds supply, the auction is over. When the auction is over, each bidder i is assigned the quantity x_i^* and is charged the standing prices at which the respective objects were "clinched": With m object for sale at a price p^l, bidder i clinches an object when the aggregate demand of all other bidders drops, at least, from m to m-1, but bidder i still demands two units or more, that is, when the demand of all bidders except him is smaller than the total supply but the total demand exceeds the total supply. In this situation bidder i is guaranteed at least one object no matter how the auction proceeds.

In this paper, the model is presented for an independent-private-value (IPV) framework and bidders' value for each unit by itself is $(v_{i,1})$, which is drawn independently and identically distributed from an uniform distribution with support $[0, V]$, being $V = 100$. In the presence of synergies, we have used a valuation function extended from the model proposed by Krishna and Rosenthal (1996). The value for bidder i of winning x_i units is equal to:

$$v_{i,x_i} = x_i v_{i,1} + \sum_{z=1}^{x_i-1} \alpha v_{i,z}, \qquad (8.1)$$

$\alpha > 0$ being the synergy parameter.

In each auction participants must decide how many items to demand at the standing price. Each bidder privately knows his personal value for earning one object ($v_{i,1}$) or multiple items (v_{i,x_i}) so he will choose among three global strategies: underbid, overbid or bid sincerely. In order to simulate a wide range of strategies, agents determine their bidding value using a bidding parameter named a, which is a real value between 0 and 1.5. This range allows bidders to test the three global strategies (overbid ($a > 1$), underbid ($a < 1$) or bid their true value ($a = 1$)) with different intensities. All these strategies have an upper bound that is the lowest of either the number of units being auctioned or, alternatively, the units demanded in the previous round (as demand is required to be non increasing). The lower bound is the number of units that the agent has already clinched.

8.3 The Agent-Based Model

We have modelled two types of agents, 4 buyers and 1 seller. Due to the flexibility of the agent-based paradigm, we do not have to assume the existence of fully rational agents with homogenous beliefs. Therefore, we implemented heterogeneous agents with asymmetric information trying to maximize their payoff. The first thing we do in each simulation is to initialize all buyer agents with random strategies and different private values. After that moment, they are free to make any bid based on their own experience gathered interacting with the others. The interaction of the agents take place when the seller agent finishes the auction. Then, agents who fared well in the previous round will transmit this experience to the other agents for the next round. Those who fared poorly will observe which bidding strategies succeeded better and will develop alternatives based on them (mutation). The agents store their experiences in the last 4 rounds in order to decide what the next strategy will be. If the strategy played by the winner agent improves their results, then they update their strategies with part of the winners' strategy.

These interactions are developed in a way similar to the genetic algorithms. Each bidder has been developed as an agent that has a vector made of 4 bits to encode the 16 possible strategies. The best agent is selected in each round, and the rest of the agents mix their strategies with the one played by the winner (with a likelihood of 90%). The mutation is done just after the crossover (10%). Then, the following

8 Multi-Unit Auction Analysis by Means of Agent-Based Computational Economics

Table 8.1 The parameter settings.

Parameter	Value
Number Agents	5
Memory	4
Mutation % (one agent)	10%
Number of strategies	16
Number of auctions	10,000
Number of simulations	100

auction takes place, and when it is over, the memory of the agents is updated with the new outcomes and the interaction starts again.

Each simulation consists of 10,000 successive auctions, and the simulations are executed 100 times per experiment. See table 8.1 for the agent-based used parameter settings.

8.4 The Experimental Results

The aim of this research is to make a what-if analysis of the agents' behavior in different scenarios. In the scenarios studied so far, agents can have decreasing marginal values or additive valuations. In the second scenario, the synergies have been analyzed with homogeneous and heterogeneous synergy parameters.

8.4.1 Decreasing Marginal Values

This scenario has been analyzed in order to test the agent-based model developed. Ausubel established that sincere bidding is a weakly dominant strategy in the auction with no bid information and weakly decreasing marginal values, yielding to an efficient outcome of the auction (Ausubel, 2004). This result has been evidenced in several experimental researches: Kagel and Levin (2001), Kagel et al. (2004) and Dirk and Grimm (2004). We ran 50 experiments with different private values, and the agents found the sincere bidding strategy ($a = 1$) to be the most stable behavior in all of them. These results confirm that the ACE model shows the same behavior as stated in the theoretical model. The bidders' strategies for the first 2,700 auctions of 10,000 for one experiment have been mapped in Figure 8.1. The figures exhibit that, at the beginning of the experiment, bidders test all candidate strategies randomly. Nevertheless, they learn that bidding sincerely ($a = 1$) is their best alternative. The 10,000 iterations have not been included in order to have a better understanding of the figure, but bidding sincerely continues to be the most frequent strategy until the last auction. For these iterations, $a = 1$ is the strategy where bidders outperform 76.07% of the times.

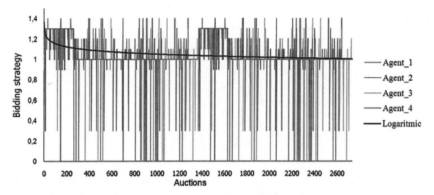

Fig. 8.1 Detail of agents' behaviour (first 2,700 auctions of 10,000).

8.4.2 Increasing Marginal Values

There is no theoretical nor experimental work done with the Ausubel auction in the presence of synergies. The ACE allows us to study this possible scenario and to analyze the auction outcome and the behaviour of the bidders. To this end, agents' valuations change from one experiment to another and different synergy parameters were tested, ranging from 0.2 to 1.0. The simulations with synergies have been done for two experimental environments. In the first one, all bidders have the same synergy parameter but it differs from one experiment to another (experiments I to V). In the second experimental environment, the synergy values are different among bidders and experiments (experiments VI to X). The synergy parameters selected for each environment are reported in table 8.2 and table 8.3 respectively.

A large set of simulations were conducted (500 per environment), and all of them yielded underbidding ($a < 1$) as the most frequent strategy for both environments. Table 8.4 shows the average of the strategies followed by the agents when all bidders have the same synergy parameter. Table 8.5 reports the same information when the synergy parameters differ among bidders. As can be seen, no great differences were found when testing homogeneous and heterogeneous synergy parameters among bidders.

These results reveal that when agents have additive values, bidding sincerely can yield to losses (exposure problem). Hence, agents learn to underbid from their past

Table 8.2 Experimental environment tested when all bidders have the same synergy parameters.

Experiment	Synergy parameter (α) for all bidders
I	0.2
II	0.4
III	0.6
IV	0.8
V	1.0

Table 8.3 Experimental environment tested when bidders have different synergy parameters.

Experiment	Synergy parameter per bidder (α_i)			
	Bidder 1	Bidder 2	Bidder 3	Bidder 4
VI	0.2	0.2	0.4	0.4
VII	0.2	0.2	0.6	0.6
VIII	0.2	0.2	0.8	0.8
IX	0.2	0.2	1.0	1.0
X	0.2	0.4	0.6	0.8

Table 8.4 Frequency of each bidding strategy per experiment when bidders have the same synergy parameter.

Experiment	Underbidding ($a < 1$)	Sincere Bidding ($a = 1$)	Overbidding ($a < 1$)
I($\alpha = 0.2$)	83.39%	8.08%	8.53%
II($\alpha = 0.4$)	86.31%	8.49%	5.20%
III($\alpha = 0.6$)	85.22%	7.16%	7.62%
IV($\alpha = 0.8$)	88.66%	6.17%	5.17%
V($\alpha = 1.0$)	86.64%	4.77%	8.59%

Table 8.5 Frequency of each bidding strategy per experiment when bidders have different synergy parameter.

Experiment	Underbidding ($a < 1$)	Sincere Bidding ($a = 1$)	Overbidding ($a < 1$)
VI	86.09%	8.17%	5.74%
VII	88.23%	6.06%	5.71%
VIII	85.87%	6.82%	7.31%
IX	87.85%	6.10%	6.05%
X	85.42%	8.54%	6.05%

experiences in order to reduce the exposure problem and maximize payoffs. As bidders tend to shade their bids, the auction outcome is no longer efficient and the seller agent obtains lower revenues (tables 8.6 and 8.7 exhibit the sellers' revenues for both experimental environments compared with the one obtained as if all bidders bid sincerely). The intuition for the success of underbidding when preferences involve complementarities rests on the following. If bidders overbid ($a > 1$), they will probably incur losses. Bidding sincerely ($a = 1$) is a safer strategy, although it can also yield to losses because bidders are affected by the exposure problem. Hence, bidders learn from their past experiences that, by underbidding ($a < 1$), they reduce the exposure problem and maximize payoffs. Therefore, bidders tend to shade their bids. This fact makes the Ausubel auction not recommendable for selling goods in the presence of synergies.

Table 8.6 Sellers' revenues per experiment when bidders have the same synergy parameter (standard error means in brackets).

Experiment	Average Compared Revenues
I($\alpha = 0.2$)	0.641(0.162)
II($\alpha = 0.4$)	0.572(0.150)
III($\alpha = 0.6$)	0.560(0.187)
IV($\alpha = 0.8$)	0.518(0.168)
V($\alpha = 1.0$)	0.535(0.196)

Table 8.7 Sellers' revenues per experiment when bidders have different synergy parameter (standard error means in brackets).

Experiment	Average Compared Revenues
VI	0.583(0.166)
VII	0.555(0.159)
VIII	0.573(0.177)
IX	0.527(0.176)
X	0.583(0.172)

8.5 Conclusions

This paper investigates a complex setting where agents are involved in an Ausubel auction and try to maximize their payoff based on past experiences. To this end, an agent-based computational model has been developed for two scenarios. In the first one, bidders have weakly decreasing marginal values and the theory predicts that sincere bidding is a weakly dominant strategy. The second one involves synergies among bidders' valuations which therefore are affected by the exposure problem. The presence of synergies has been tested for two environments. In the first one, all bidders have the same synergy parameter but it changes from one experiment to another. In the second one, the synergy parameter is different among bidders. For this scenario there is no theoretical or experimental work done. In order to simulate a wide range of strategies, agents determine their bidding value using a bidding parameter named a, which is a real value between 0 and 1.5. This parameter allows agents to overbid ($a > 1$), underbid ($a < 1$) or bid their true value ($a = 1$). In the first scenario, when bidders have decreasing marginal values, agents found the sincere bidding strategy ($a = 1$) to be the most stable behavior. These results confirm that the ACE shows the same behavior as stated in the theoretical model. The results obtained in the second scenario reveal that the most frequent strategies that maximize the bidders' payoff are for $a < 1$. In this auction, shading bids is the strategy that yields the highest profits to the bidders and reduces the exposure problem, i.e., the probability of earning negative profits. According to these results, in the presence of synergies, it is not recommendable to use the Ausubel auction as it can yield to demand reduction and inefficient allocation.

Acknowledgements This article has been financed by the Spanish funded research MCyT project MSTAR, Ref: TIN2008-06491-C04-03/TIN.

References

Albano G.L., Germano F., Lovo S. (2001) A comparison of standard multi-unit auctions with synergies. Economics Letters, 71:55–60

Ausubel L.M. (2004) An efficient ascending-bid auction for multiple objects. American Economic Review, 94:1452–1475

Ausubel L.M., Cramton, P., McAfee, P. and McMillan, J. (1997) Synergies in Wireless Telephony: Evidence from the Broadband PCS Auctions. Journal of Economics and Management Strategy, 6(3):497–527

Branco F. (1997) Sequential auctions with synergies: an example. Economics Letters, 54:159–163

Cantillon E., Pesendorfer M. (2004) Combination bidding in multi-unit auctions, mimeo. London School of Economics

De Silva D.G. (2005) Synergies in recurring procurement auctions: an empirical investigation. Economic Inquiry, 43(1):55–66

De Silva D.G., Jeitschko T.D., Kosmopoulou G. (2005) Stochastic synergies in sequential auctions. Internacional, Journal of Industrial Organization, 23(3-4): 183–01

Dirk E., Grimm V. (2004) Bidding Behavior in Multi-Uni Auctions: An Experimental Investigation, IVIE Working Paper WP AD-12

Gandal N. (1997) Sequential auctions of interdependent auctions: Israeli cable television licenses, Journal of Industrial Economics 45(3):227–244

Kagel J.H., Kinross S. and Levin D. (2004) Implementing efficient multi-object auctions institutions: an experimental study of the performance of boundedly rational agents. OSU Working paper 11/04.

Kagel J.H., Levin, D. (2001) Behaviour in multi-unit demand auctions: experiments with uniform price and dynamic Vickrey auctions, Econometrica, 69(2):413–454.

Kagel J.H., Levin D. (2005) Multi-unit demand auctions with synergies: behavior in sealed-bid versus ascending-bid uniform-price auctions. Games and Economic Behavior, 53(2):170–207

Katok E., Roth A.E. (2004) Auctions of Homogeneous Goods with Increasing Returns: Experimental Comparison of Alternative Dutch Auctions. Management Science, 50(8):1044–1063

Krishna V., Rosenthal R.W. (1996) Simultaneous auctions with synergies. Games and Economic Behaviorm, 17:1–31

Rosenthal R.W., Wang R. (1996) Simultaneous Auctions with Synergies and Common Values. Games and Economic Behavior, 17:32–55

Chapter 9
Social Learning and Pricing Obfuscation

Maciej Latek and Bogumil Kaminski

Abstract We examine markets in which companies are allowed to obfuscate prices and customers are forced to rely on their direct experience and signals they receive from social networks to make purchasing decisions. We compare interventions by public regulators that impose constraints on the amount of price obfuscation with those that augment customers' cognitive capacities in order to determine which class of policies enhances social welfare the most in such a setting. We implement the strategic behavior of companies by a recursive simulation of n-th order rationality and extend the Experience Weighted Attractions framework to incorporate information from social networks for adaptive customers. Therefore, we search for market designs that are robust with respect to bounded rationality of companies and customers.

9.1 Introduction

Persistence of price dispersion for homogeneous products is one of the empirical conundrums of contemporary industrial organization. Despite being thick with dozens of companies selling similar products, some markets do not converge to one price. For example, Thompson and Thompson (2006) presents evidence for unexplained variation in prices and super marginal profits for web-hosting companies. Garrod (2007) obtains similar patterns for travel agencies. Price obfuscation by companies offers one explanation for observed price dispersion in such markets. For instance,

---

M. Latek
Department of Computational Social Science, George Mason University, U.S.A, e-mail: `mlatek@gmu.edu`

B. Kaminski
Decision Analysis and Support Division, Warsaw School of Economics, Poland, e-mail: `bkamins@sgh.waw.pl`

Baye *et al.* (2002), Ellison and Ellison (2004), and Clay *et al.* (2001) use data from websites devoted to comparing prices of consumer electronics to argue that retailers actively engage in price obfuscation practices that frustrate consumer search. Such practices include the companies' use of fictitious price comparisons or false sale signs to deter consumer search deceptively and profitably. Consumers' inability to reason about multi-dimensional goods and services exhaustively or to predict their future usage provides another venue for price obfuscation[1]. Obfuscation influences consumer surplus negatively (Gabaix and Laibson, 2003), therefore regulatory intervention gains salience. Supply-side regulatory intervention would most likely fail in markets like online retail websites. However, it can alter the structure of other markets like health insurance markets to ameliorate the impact of price obfuscation on consumers (Randall *et al.*, 2008).

Existing models of price obfuscation analyze equilibrium strategies of companies operating under monopoly (Rubinstein, 1993), Bertrand competition (Gabaix and Laibson, 2003), Stackelberg oligopoly (Spector, 2000) or monopolistic competition (Gabaix and Laibson, 2005; Wilson, 2004; Ellison and Wolitzky, 2008). These models also differ in how they describe consumer behavior, employing simple sampling scheme (Spiegler, 2006), perceptron-like architectures (Rubinstein, 1993), variations of Bayesian updating (Wilson, 2004) or costly search processes (Ellison and Wolitzky, 2008; Gabaix and Laibson, 2005). Our approach differs from the current models of obfuscation on three model requirements. First, we postulate that price obfuscation should be studied not as a static optimization problem, but as a concurrent and dynamic arms race among companies and customers. Second, a useful price obfuscation model should explicitly include the customers' limited cognitive capabilities and companies' limited computational capacity (Rust, 1997). Lastly, strong evidence suggests that complexity causes customers to use social networks to help with purchasing decisions (Frank and Lamiraud, 2006); the model needs to account for this fact. Implementation of these three postulates should lead to the identification of a market design that (*a*) is robust with respect to behavioral and social assumptions and (*b*) maximizes social welfare over trajectories rather than just at equilibrium[2]. Under these assumptions, we wish to answer the following questions:

1. What market designs and regulatory instruments can be used to induce companies engaged in price obfuscation to increase social welfare?
2. How does the social efficiency of such interventions depend on the specification of the bounded rationality of market participants?

Our model allows regulators to weight the social effectiveness of supply-side interventions that impose strategy constraints on competitors versus that of demand-side

---

[1] Telecommunication markets provide an apt example for a situation where consumers find it difficult to predict their future usage of airtime and other dimensions of service such as voice, data, sms and mms (Hatton, 2005).

[2] Axtell (2000) argues for trajectories instead of equilibria and highlights the danger of focusing on unstable equilibria, those not attained by boundedly rational agents or those obtained asymptotically but not realized over long periods.

interventions that increase the responsiveness of customers[3]. We focus on domains such as health insurance markets, telecommunications or Internet services providers markets where customers make a few decisions in their lifetime but can observe the outcomes of decisions made by their peers. We discuss the architecture of a prototype model in Section 9.2 and present sample dynamics and results in Section 9.3.

9.2 Model Architecture

9.2.1 Obfuscation Game and Dimensions of Intervention

The market consists of K expected-profit maximizing companies offering perfect substitutes and N consumers. Companies play a simultaneous-move, complete information game. A strategy for company i is a discrete distribution p_t^i over feasible price-levels $\{0\ldots L-1\}^4$. If customer k chooses to use company j as the service provider, k's payoff is equal to $L-x$, where x is a random draw from the distribution p_t^j. Company j receives revenue of x and we set all marginal costs to 0. Each company is n-th order rational. The full description of this approach to modeling strategic interactions is given in Latek et al. (2009) and summarized in Section 9.2.2. Each customer chooses a service provider using Experience Weighted Attraction learning (Ho et al., 2004). In Section 9.2.3 we generalize EWA learning to account for presence of the social network.

For certain experiments, customers are given two additional choices other than choice of service providers. They can (1) abstain from participating in the market and receive a reservation payoff of R or (2) defer the choice of the provider or `optout` to a special agent called `oracle` whose advice guarantees the highest expected payoff: `oracle` is a function that returns the index of the best choice $\texttt{oracle}(i) = \mathrm{argmax}_{(k\in 1\ldots K)\cup \texttt{optout}} \left(L - \mathrm{E}_{p_t^k} x \right) \cup R$. Even though `oracle` reduces uncertainty for customers, customer treat `oracle` the same as they would any other choice and need to learn its performance[5]. Mechanism of `oracle` is introduced as a proxy for demand-side regulatory intervention. The supply-side regulatory instruments constrain policies p_t^i by imposing the reward penalty of `varianceModifier` $\times \mathrm{var}\left(p_t^i\right)$ on each transaction of company i [6]. All penalties are considered transfers and do not influence social welfare.

---

[3] In the U.S., health insurance plans are subject to both obfuscation due to multi-dimensional services with usage uncertainty and to regulatory oversight at a significant annual cost of 2×10^{11} USD (Johnston, 2007). The same market also features instruments that increase the customers' cognitive capability. For example, Microsoft or Google health portfolios or the website http://ratemyplan.com/ deliver personalized evaluation of the contingencies customers may face.

[4] Technically, p_t^i is intended to approximate a continuous distribution with finite support. Increasing L increases the precision of the approximation. We denote period number by subscript and company number by superscript.

[5] A good study of online comparison websites and factors that make customers trust them is Mayer et al. (2005).

[6] $\mathrm{var}\left(p_t^i\right)$ is variance of policy p_t^i. Condition `varianceModifer` $= 0$ corresponds to the unperturbed competition. This approximates the real life scenario in which probability of being caught

Measures of market performance include prices, number of customers that entered the market and social welfare. Social welfare metric is decomposed into companies profit, the sum of customer rewards and variance penalties. Market prices are viewed both ex-ante by aggregating obfuscation distributions before consumer choice has been made and as ex-post as averages of final draws from respective $p_t^\bullet$ done by customers on their own or acting on the advice of `oracle`.

9.2.2 Recursive Companies

We implement our model as a multi-agent simulation using the MASON simulation framework (Luke et al., 2005). The state of the simulation at time t, denoted as C_t, is defined as all relevant information, including the state of adaptive customers and social connections among them. The set of obfuscation policies for all companies at time t is denoted as a $\boldsymbol{p}_t$, a K-dimensional vector of policies.

The simulation is as a map Ψ that for a given C_t and a fixed set of policies $\boldsymbol{p}_t$ returns both the next state C_{t+1} and the vector of rewards $\boldsymbol{r}_t = (r_t^1, \ldots, r_t^K)$ for each company:

$$(\boldsymbol{r}_t, C_{t+1}) = \Psi(\boldsymbol{p}_t, C_t). \tag{9.1}$$

We shall give companies access to Ψ and to use it as a forecasting tool. Superimposing Ψ produces forecasts about future rewards $\boldsymbol{r}_t, \ldots, \boldsymbol{r}_{t+h}$ and future states of the simulation $C_{t+1}, \ldots, C_{t+h}$ for any horizon h and scenario of policy trajectories $\boldsymbol{P}_{t,h} = (\boldsymbol{p}_t, \ldots, \boldsymbol{p}_{t+h})$.

Company i maximizes the expected discounted stream of rewards for a certain planning horizon h by controlling policies $(p_t^i, \ldots, p_{t+h}^i)$:

$$\max_{(p_t^i, \ldots, p_{t+h}^i)} \sum_{j=0}^{h} \gamma^j E\left(r_{t+j}^i\right), \tag{9.2}$$

where γ is the discount rate[7].

Companies are n-th order rational (Stahl and Haruvy, 2003). Denote by

$$\Xi^i(d,h) = (\Xi_0^i(d,h), \ldots, \Xi_h^i(d,h)), \tag{9.3}$$

the optimal policy trajectory $(p_t^i, \ldots, p_{t+h}^i)$ of the i-th company with planning horizon h assuming that it's order of rationality is equal to d. A 0-order rational company replicates its last policy for h periods forward:

$$\Xi^i(0,h) = \underbrace{\left(p_{t-1}^i, \ldots, p_{t-1}^i\right)}_{h+1}. \tag{9.4}$$

---

and being penalized for breaking consumer protection laws is an increasing function of magnitude of violation (Kato).

[7] Customers are activated at random and an element of randomness is incorporated in the definition of $p_t^\bullet$. Therefore, $(\boldsymbol{r}_t, C_{t+1})$ are random variables and companies need to average over multiple trajectories of Ψ, using the same initial conditions, to obtain reward expectations.

The solutions to Ξ for companies having rationality order $d > 0$ are defined recursively. In each period d-th order rational company i assumes that other companies ($k \neq i$) are playing $(d-1)$-th order rational strategies $\Xi^k(d-1,h)$. Therefore the i-th company optimizes:

$$\Xi^i(d,h) \equiv \underset{(p^i_t,\ldots,p^i_{t+h})}{\operatorname{argmax}} \sum_{j=0}^{h} \gamma^j E\left(r^i_{t+j}\right)$$

subject to:

$$\forall j \in \{0,\ldots,h\}: (r_{t+j}, C_{t+j+1}) = \Psi(\boldsymbol{p}_{t+j}, C_{t+j})$$
$$\boldsymbol{p}_{t+j} = p^i_{t+j} \cup \{\Xi^k_j(d-1,h)\}_{k \neq i}$$

Solving $\Xi(\bullet,\bullet)$ generates an extended best-response dynamics. For $d=1$, the best response is calculated while $d=2$ yields the best response to a company's expectations of the other companies' best responses. Parameter h controls how myopic the companies are. Finally, we introduce the cost of strategy adjustment of $\alpha \left\| p^i_t - p^i_{t+1} \right\|$ deduced from company revenues[8].

9.2.3 Adaptive Customers

In each period, each customer selects one of the companies as the service provider, chooses to stay out of the market or defers to `oracle`, should the last two choices be available. If customer i chooses option j at time t, we denote such a condition as $s_i(t) = j$. The reward the customer receives, $r_i(j)$, is calculated as follows:

$$r_i(j) = \begin{cases} L-x, \ x \sim p^i(t) & \text{if } j \in 1\ldots K \\ R & \text{if } j = \texttt{optout} \\ r_i(\texttt{oracle}(t)) & \text{if } j = \texttt{oracle}. \end{cases}$$

This formulation assumes that all rewards obtained when acting on `oracle`'s advice are attributed to `oracle` directly, rather than to the actual final choices. Additionally, customers have access to information on choices and rewards of other customers who belong to their social neighborhood $n(i)$.

The core of decision making and adaptation scheme of customers is the EWA model (Ho et al., 2004, Camerer and Ho, 1999), modified to account for social networks. The baseline EWA model relies on two variables. The first variable $N(t)$ is interpreted as the number of æobservation-equivalentsÆ of past experiences. The second variable A^j_i is consumer iÆs attraction of company j after period t. Variables $N(t)$ and $A^j_i(t)$ begin with prior values, set here as $N(0) = 1$ and $\forall_j A^j_i(0) = 1$. Updating is governed by two rules. First, $N(t) = \rho N(t-1) + 1$, $t \geq 1$. The parameter ρ is a depreciation rate that measures the impact of previous experiences, compared to

---

[8] Parameter α is proxy for the cost of communicating a new policy to consumers and the ensuing operational adjustments. Large α allows customer learning to catch up with strategy changes more easily.

one new period. Second, i's own experiences and social network signals informing i about forgone payoffs are integrated into attractions table:

$$A_i^j(t) = \begin{cases} \dfrac{\phi N(t-1)A_i^j(t-1) + (1-\delta)r_i(t)}{N(t)} & \text{if } s_i(t) = j \\ \dfrac{\phi N(t-1)A_i^j(t-1) + \delta r_k(t)}{N(t)} & \text{if } \exists k \in n(i) : s_k(t) = j \\ \dfrac{\phi N(t-1)A_i^j(t-1) + \delta R}{N(t)} & \text{else.} \end{cases} \quad (9.5)$$

The factor ϕ is a discount factor or decay rate that depreciates previous attraction. Factor δ is used to weight direct experience versus information about foregone payoffs obtained through social interactions. If customer i observes more than one peer using the same provider, a sample is drawn at random. In the second equation, we extend EWA by using the social network as a source of information about the foregone payoffs. Should the customer neither experience the choice himself nor receive information about it from his social network, the reservation payoff R is used to update respective attraction. We call our modification Social Experience Weighted Attractions (SEWA).

Attractions determine probabilities of choosing option j by customer i $\Pr_i^j(t)$ using the logit transformation:

$$\Pr_i^j(t) = \frac{e^{\lambda A_i^j(t)}}{\sum_{k=1}^{K} e^{\lambda A_i^k(t)}}. \quad (9.6)$$

Such a formulation satisfies all of the four requirements for a learning rule to stack up against humans in a minimal competency test given by Arifovic and Ledyard (2004)[9]. Summarizing, each of the customers is characterized by 4 parameters: $\{\phi, \delta, \rho, \lambda\}$ and his social neighborhood $n(i)$. We used an Erdős-Rényi random graph with average number of neighbors 3 as a model of social network (Newman et al., 1999).

9.3 Experiments

This section starts with the description of a sample baseline market dynamics. Later, we investigate 6 different market designs varianceModifier $\in \{0,1,2\} \times$ oracle $\in \{on, off\}$, defaults for other parameters are bolded in Table 9.1.

---

[9] Those are (1) the use of hypothetical to create history, (2) the ability to focus only on what is important, (3) the ability to forget history when it is no longer important, and (4) the ability to try new things.

9 Social Learning and Pricing Obfuscation

Table 9.1 Simulation parameters used during experiments from Section 9.3. Website https://www.assembla.com/wiki/show/recursiveengines contains simulation itself as well as data for full parameter sweeps. Bolded values are used as defaults.

Group	Parameter	Range	Meaning
Firms	d	{1,**2**,3}	Depth of recursion
	h	{1,**3**,5}	Planning horizon
	L	{3,**5**,7}	Number of strategy dimensions
	α	{0,**50**,100}	Cost of strategy change
Customers	λ	[0...**4**...5]	Attraction sensitivity
	ϕ	[0...**0.9**...1]	Discount factor or attraction decay rate
	δ	[0...**0.3**...1]	Weight of direct versus social information
	ρ	[0...**0.9**...1]	Depreciation rate / inertia
	R	{0,**2**,4}	Reservation payoff for staying out of the market
Markets	N	{20,**50**,1000}	Number of adaptive customers
	K	{**1**,2,3,4,5}	Number of recursive companies
	oracle	**on**,off	Can customers refer to oracle for advice
	optout	**on**,off	Can customers opt-out of the market
	varianceModifier	{**0**,1,2}	Variance penalty imposed on transactions
	averageDegree	{**0**,3,6}	Average degree of the social network

9.3.1 Baseline Behaviors

This section outlines the default behavior of the model, with the exception of $L = 3$ and $R = 1$. First, Figures 9.1(a) and Figures 9.1(b) give the sample dynamics of attractions $A_i^j(t)$ for a single customer i and the population average $\bar{A}^j(t)$. At the individual level, we observe rapid changes correlated with the inflow of new information and exponential decay to baseline values in the absence thereof. The integration of information from the customer's social network accounts for multiple concurrent spikes. The evolution of the average population attractions has these spikes smoothed out, with the oracle's attraction being a little bit larger than companies' later in the run. This is caused by oracle amplifying differences in relative attractiveness and always selecting even marginally cheaper offers.

Figures 9.1(c) and 9.1(d) present the evolution of pricing policies as well as associated ex-ante averages for each company. Attractions for companies follow paths of average prices with a lag of 5 to 10 periods. Figures 9.1(e) and 9.1(f) present how attractions were translated into actual choices before and after oracle's intervention. After ex-ante prices converged among companies, oracle's influence resulted in a price war, where each company enjoyed a group of steady followers but contends for a large flock of switchers acting on the oracle's advice.

As shown in Figure 9.1(d), there was always at least one company offering expected ex-ante price of less than R. Thus, oracle would never recommend exiting the market. Nevertheless, even if a customer has subscribed to the optimal company, we sample his experience. Therefore, a few bad experiences of his own or his social network can cause him to consider exiting the market, see Figures 9.1(e) and 9.1(f).

9.3.2 Efficiency of Market Intervention

The long-term statistics used in discussing the effects of intervention are gathered on three Figures. Figure 9.2 presents average market policies $\bar{p}$. Social welfare, alongside the ex-post prices, based on customer choices, are presented on Figure 9.3. Finally, Figure 9.4 shows distributions of market prices and number of entrants induced by behavioral uncertainty of the customers. Figure 9.2 averages the behavioral profiles out whereas other figures represent it by either plotting individual data points (Figure 9.4) or providing error bars for outcomes (Figure 9.3).

Observe that price obfuscation allows companies to avoid competition. Consider the first column of Figure 9.2, where oracle = off and varianceModifier = 0. When oracle is not enabled, increasing the number of competitors has little effect on strategies of companies, even in presence of opt-out option. When varianceModifier is increased, the companies respond by a decrease in the variance of policies with no change in average ex-ante or ex-post prices. The associated decrease in social welfare follows, Figure 9.3, as more undesirable events (draws of extremely high prices) are even more frequent and customers start exiting the market.

With oracle enabled, the problem of the monopolist does not change significantly. On the other hand, for duopolies and triopolies, enabling oracle spurs competition and leads to decrease in all prices, without collapsing companies' profits. Companies maintain their profit levels because the overall size of the market increases significantly when oracle is present. This positive effect is destroyed by increase in varianceModifier that causes companies to compensate for penalties paid.

Lastly, another positive effect of oracle is seen on Figure 9.4. Oracle causes a decrease in the behavioral uncertainty of social outcomes, measured as the spread between the worst and the best observed outcomes. Therefore, the design of markets with oracle is robust. Moreover, for duopolies and triopolies, the influence of oracle goes beyond presenting customers with one additional no-optout option[10].

---

[10] Suppose there are K companies in the market and share x of customers decided to stay in the market when oracle=off. Assume that oracle never recommends the optout option. If customers can defer choices to oracle, we would expect a fraction $\frac{(K+1)x}{K+x}$ of customers to remain in the market. Increase in the number of entrants predicted using this simple model is presented on Figure 9.4.

9 Social Learning and Pricing Obfuscation

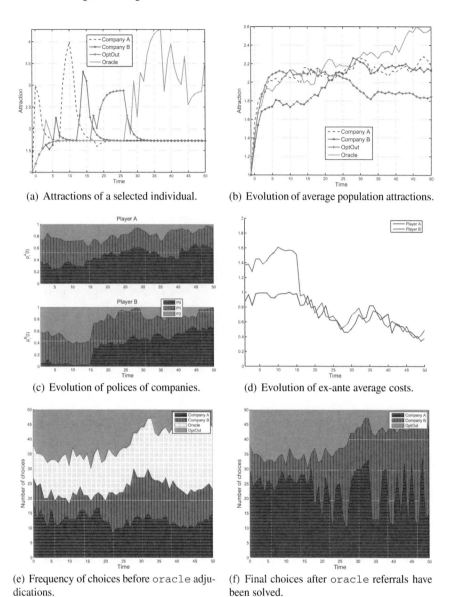

(a) Attractions of a selected individual.

(b) Evolution of average population attractions.

(c) Evolution of polices of companies.

(d) Evolution of ex-ante average costs.

(e) Frequency of choices before `oracle` adjudications.

(f) Final choices after `oracle` referrals have been solved.

Fig. 9.1 Dashboard for a sample run with social EWA customers and two companies with $L = 3$ and $R = 1$. Rest of default parameters from Table 9.1 apply. Parameter L has been reduced to enable plotting strategies in two-dimensional space.

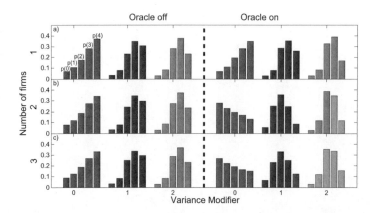

Fig. 9.2 Average long-run obfuscation strategies used on markets differing in number of competitors (rows), presence of `oracle` (major columns) and variance penalty (colored minor columns). Each group of bars corresponds to shape of policy $\bar{p}$, such that individual bars correspond to components $\bar{p}(0), \ldots, \bar{p}(L-1)$ for $L = 5$. As policies are probability distributions, for each group, sum of heights of bars is equal to 1.

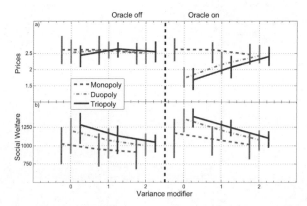

Fig. 9.3 Ex-post market prices (top row) and combined measure of social welfare (bottom row) as a function of number of competitors (colors), presence of `oracle` (major columns) and variance penalty (minor columns). The influence of behavioral uncertainty is coded using error bars corresponding to 5th and 95th percentile of respective distributions of outcomes.

9.4 Conclusions

We have analyzed an environment in which companies are allowed to obfuscate their pricing and adaptive consumers use different sources of information to decide which service provider to buy from. Under the no intervention scenario, pricing obfuscation increases the market power of companies, producing higher markups in

9 Social Learning and Pricing Obfuscation

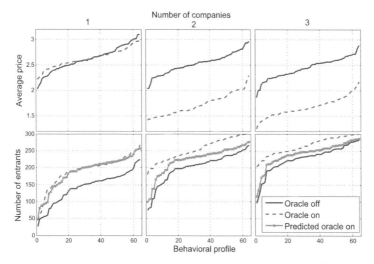

Fig. 9.4 Distributions of measures of market performance as a function of behavioral specification (variables parameterizing SEWA algorithm, $\lambda, \phi, \delta, \rho$, see Table 9.1). All values are long-run and come from markets differing in number of competitors (columns) and presence of `oracle` (lines). As proved earlier, the `varianceModifier` is inefficient instrument of intervention, thus we set it to 0. For each outcome and market combination, behavioral profiles have been sorted in an increasing order.

comparison to the pure Bertrand competition and preventing competition as number of companies increases.

The most positive outcome of intervention is achieved when customers are provided with additional information sources, but no constraints on transaction or policies of competitors are enforced. Imposing strategy constraints is counterproductive and might lead to the collapse of the market. These results are robust with respect to the number of competitors, behavioral specification and learning capabilities of customers.

Website `https://www.assembla.com/wiki/show/recursiveengines` contains codes necessary to run our simulation, supplementary materials and additional links.

References

J. Arifovic and J. Ledyard. Scaling up learning models in public good games. *Journal of Public Economic Theory*, 2004.

R. Axtell. Why agents? on the varied motivations for agent computing in the social sciences. Technical Report 17, Center on Social Dynamics, The Brookings Institution, 2000.

M. Baye, J. Morgan, and P. Scholten. Persistent price dispersion in online markets. 2002.

C. Camerer and T. H. Ho. Experience-weighted attraction learning in normal form games. *Econometrica*, 67:827–874, 1999.

K. Clay, R. Krishnan, and M. Smith. *The Great Experiment: Pricing on the Internet.* 2001.

G. Ellison and S. F. Ellison. Search, obfuscation and price elasticities on the internet. 2004.

G. Ellison and A. Wolitzky. A search cost model of obfuscation. 2008.

R. G. Frank and K. Lamiraud. Choice, price competition and complexity in markets for health insurance. 2006.

X. Gabaix and D. Laibson. Pricing and product design with boundedly rational consumers. pages 1–23, 2003.

X. Gabaix and D. Laibson. Shrouded attributes, consumer myopia and information suppression in competitive markets. 2005.

L. Garrod. Price transparency and consumer naivety in a competitive market. 2007.

L. Hatton. A case study in complex systems evolution: consumer price obfuscation and mobile/cell phone tariff pricing. pages 1–13, 2005.

T. H. Ho, C. F. Camerer, and J.-K. Chong. The economics of learning models: A self-tuning theory of learning in games. 2004.

C. Johnston. *Medicare Part D: an Institutional Analysis.* PhD thesis, George Mason University, 2007.

M. Kato. Transitoriness of market power and antitrust activity.

M. Latek, R. Axtell, and B. Kaminski. Bounded rationality via recursion (forthcoming). In *Proceedings of the Eighth International Conference on Autonomous Agents and Multiagent Systems*, 2009.

S. Luke, C. Cioffi-Revilla, L. Panait, K. Sullivan, and G. C. Balan. Mason: A multi-agent simulation environment. *Simulation*, 81(7):517–527, 2005.

R. N. Mayer, J. Huh, and B. J. Cude. Cues of credibility and price performance of life insurance comparison web sites. *Journal of Consumer Affairs*, 39:71–94, 2005.

M. Newman, D. Watts, and S. Strogatz. Random graph models of social networks. In *Proc. Natl. Acad. Sci.*, 1999.

C. Randall, J. Rebitzer, L. Taylor, and M. Votruba. Unhealthy insurance markets: Seach frictions and quality of health insurance. *NBER Working Paper Series*, (October), 2008.

A. Rubinstein. On price recognition and computational complexity in a monopolistic model. *Journal of Political Economy*, 101:473–485, 1993.

J. Rust. Dealing with the complexity of economic calculations. 1997.

D. Spector. The noisy duopolist. 2000.

R. Spiegler. Competition over agents with boundedly rational expectations. *Theoretical Economics*, 1:207–231, 2006.

D. O. Stahl and E. Haruvy. Level-n bounded rationality on a level playing field of sequential games. 2003.

M. Thompson and S. Thompson. Pricing in a market without apparent horizontal differentiation: Evidence from web hosting services. *Economics of Innovation and New Technology*, 15(7):649–663, 2006.

C. M. Wilson. Price deception, market power and consumer policy. 2004.

Part IV
Finance

Chapter 10
Mutual Funds Flows and the "Sheriff of Nottingham" Effect

Lucia Milone and Paolo Pellizzari

Abstract Investors in mutual funds appear to reward disproportionately the best performing funds with large inflows while, at the same time, avoid to withdraw similar amounts from the poorly managed funds. We show that this peculiar flat-convex shape of the flow-performance curve for mutual funds can be generally explained by a model where profit chasing customers punish the bad funds by switching a fraction of their wealth to the best ones ("Sheriff of Nottingham" effect). In the absence of external flows, the model provably produces a constant curve when the standard deviation of excess returns is much larger than the level of the returns. This for the most part explains the apparent insensitivity of flows to below-average returns. The introduction of exogenous injections of money invested in the top funds complete the model and provides a realistic increase in the flows of the funds yielding above-average returns. We finally show by simulation that our results are robust to variations in the values of the parameters of the model.

10.1 Introduction

Flows into and out of mutual funds have an interesting dynamics and exhibit some puzzling features. We focus in this paper on the shape of the flow-performance curve that shows an asymmetric reaction of households to past returns. Customers appear to chase (excess) profits, "flocking to funds with the highest recent returns, though failing to flee from poor performers" (Sirri and Tufano, 1998). This results in flat-convex (*J*-shaped) curve suggesting that customers are pretty insensitive to low and

---

L. Milone
Dept. of Applied Mathematics, University Ca' Foscari of Venice, Italy, e-mail: `lucia.milone@unive.it`

P. Pellizzari
Dept. of Applied Mathematics and SSE, University Ca' Foscari of Venice, Italy, e-mail: `paolop@unive.it`

average performances and appears to care about extremely positive returns only. In other words, the (positive) inflow into the best performing funds has a much bigger magnitude than the (negative) outflow from the poorly managed funds. More subtly, in the intermediate range of returns a rather good (but not exceptional) fund is likely to experience the same flow pattern of a rather bad (but not awful) fund, even though the difference in the (properly adjusted) performance is quite substantial.

The empirical evidence robustly supporting this finding is abundant and some recent papers offer possible explanations that go beyond the high search costs and lack of sophistication on the part of clients that were initially proposed. Berk and Tonks (2007) observe that there is a mechanical reason partly explaining the puzzle: only people who have invested in the worst funds can withdraw money from them while all investors have the option to invest in the best funds, producing a higher positive growth rate. In second place, they observe that the apparent smaller sensitivity to bad performance is due the heterogenous willingness to realize losses capital: only a part of the investors in the fund escape away after one poor yearly return but others are less responsive to past returns and funds with two consecutive negative returns have small outflows. The work in Lynch and Musto (2003) supports the view that some apparent indifference to bad returns is linked to the ambiguous inference that can be drawn from a negative outcome: from the one hand, it can be interpreted as a signal of poor managerial skills and disappointing future performances. Hence, investors can switch their capital away. On the other hand, poor performance is also leading to a change in the strategy of the manager that (exactly because of the past failures) wants to modify his trades and/or risk exposure. In this respect, inferior returns are not indicative of future prospects and clients may hold their shares in the funds.

Del Guercio and Tkac (2008) consider the 5-star Morningstar rating as a performance measure and show that most of the features of the flow dynamics are not strictly dependent on return-based rankings: a 5-star rating induces a disproportionate abnormal inflows, while other changes are less relevant (but still economically significant at times).

In this work, we describe a model of internal and exogenous flows among mutual funds that is driven by the simple principle "take from the poor (performer) to give to rich (one)". This deliberate negation of the famous Robin Hood's catchphrase suggested to name this behaviour the "Sheriff of Nottingham" effect. All the explanations provided so far in the literature indeed specialize in some clever way a general kind of behaviour where customers move part of their wealth away from the worst performers to invest in the best funds. The specific details or the motivation for this partial shift may change and there have been various suggestions in the aforementioned literature but we offer some theoretical insight and extensive simulation to argue that any "Sheriff of Nottingham"-like behaviour can produce a remarkably flat flow-performance curve.

Our work does not fully model all the actors in the fund industry, namely customers and funds. In fact, we leave aside the customers to model a given number N of funds that experience flows due to the action of investors. If a specific fund ranks in the worst x funds, based on some performance measure in a reference period, then a fraction α of its net asset value (NAV) is withdrawn and moved (randomly) to one of the best x performing funds. The asymmetric reaction to bad performances can be easily justified from a psychological point as the disutility of a loss is larger than the utility of a similar gain (Kahneman and Tversky, 1979). Moreover, the idea that there is a large blurred intermediate area where all performances look the same is somewhat intrinsic in the structure of the basic information that is presented to funds' customers. The ratings provided by Morningstar and other vendors, for example, assign stars on the basis of a subdivision of funds into "quintiles" of performances, somewhat suggesting that there are worse and better funds but also giving a rather coarse and indistinct picture.

The change in the wealth of the funds can be interpreted as the result of many individual agents switching to other and possibly more skilled managers. We do not keep track of the single investors but only study the funds and how their growth rates are changed by this behaviour of the agents. In the presence of internal flows only (i.e., if there are not external flows pouring into the mutual funds), the flow-performance curve turns out to be very flat for a wide set of parameters, provided that the standard deviation of the returns is relatively large (as it is the case in reality).

In order to capture the excessive growth rate of the best performing funds, we additionally assume that customers with fresh wealth invest among the best mutual funds. In detail, we assume that only the best x funds receive net inflows, amounting to a fraction β of their NAV. Our general model is able to robustly generate a flat flow curve for average and below-average funds and much larger growth rates for the top performing products in the industry. Putting things together, we reproduce the empirical observations with a general process, few principles and repeated interactions in terms of flow exchange and injections among the funds (leaving behind the curtains the individual investors that ultimately drive the whole dynamics).

The paper goes on as follows. Section 2 presents our ideas in a simplified probabilistic and tractable framework. We formally prove that flat curves can be obtained in the limit when the standard deviation of returns is large. Section 3 describes our model, gives the details of the switching mechanism and presents results using simulations. We conclude in Section 4.

10.2 A Simple Example and One Analytical Result

This section presents a simple example of rank-based flows among funds. Assume that households can invest in four mutual funds yielding excess returns (or alphas) distributed as normal independent normal random variables $X_{1t}, X_{2t}, X_{3t}, X_{4t}$ in year t. Letting $X_{jt} \sim N(\mu_j, \sigma), \mu_1 \leq \mu_2 \leq \mu_3 \leq \mu_4$, we can interpret the mean of the excess return as the skill of the manager, so that the fourth manager is on average the best one. The clients, however, do not observe the μ_js but only the yearly realizations of the four funds. For concreteness, the following figures are representatives of the actual universe of mutual funds split in quartiles (see Kosowski et al., 2006):

$\mu_1 = 4.25\%, \mu_2 = 5.40\%, \mu_3 = 6.48\%, \mu_4 = 8.40\%$, with a common standard deviation $\sigma = 14.81\%$.

How would you allocate wealth in a similar situation? Waiting for a few decades to estimate the means with high precision does not seem realistic and one reasonable response would be a "Sheriff of Nottingham" behaviour that periodically takes from the poor fund to transfer to the rich one[1]. This section shows how the flows between funds are affected by this commonsensical switching strategy.

Clients of the funds myopically try to optimize their excess return ranking the funds every year on the base of the realized $X_{1t}, X_{2t}, X_{3t}, X_{4t}$ and moving some wealth from the worst to the best performer. The precise details are described in the following section but the important thing to realize is that the probability of an in(out)-flow for a specific fund is depending on the probability to be ranked first or last in a year. Let $abcd$ be a permutation (ranking) of the set $\{1,2,3,4\}$. We are interested by the probability P_{abcd}, namely

$$P_{abcd} = Pr(X_a \leq X_b \leq X_c \leq X_d), \tag{10.1}$$

where we omit t for notational simplicity. Defining $Y_{ij} = X_i - X_j, i \neq j \in \{1,2,3,4\}$, the above probability can be rewritten as $P_{abcd} = Pr(Y_{ab} \leq 0, Y_{bc} \leq 0, Y_{cd} \leq 0)$. Each Y is the difference of independent normal variates and we have $E[Y_{ij}] = \mu_i - \mu_j, Var[Y_{ij}] = 2\sigma^2$. The density of the 3-dimensional random variable $Y = (Y_{ab}, Y_{bc}, Y_{cd})'$ is normal with covariance matrix Σ that can be easily derived. For example,

$$\begin{aligned} Cov(Y_{ab}, Y_{bc}) &= E[Y_{ab}Y_{bc}] - E[Y_{ab}]E[Y_{bc}] \\ &= E[(X_a - X_b)(X_b - X_c)] - (\mu_a - \mu_b)(\mu_b - \mu_c) \\ &= (\mu_a\mu_b - \mu_a\mu_c - (\sigma^2 + \mu_b^2) + \mu_b\mu_c) - (\mu_a\mu_b - \mu_a\mu_c - \mu_b^2 + \mu_b\mu_c) \\ &= -\sigma^2, \\ Cov(Y_{ab}, Y_{cd}) &= E[Y_{ab}Y_{cd}] - E[Y_{ab}]E[Y_{cd}] \\ &= E[(X_a - X_b)(X_c - X_d)] - (\mu_a - \mu_b)(\mu_c - \mu_d) \\ &= 0. \end{aligned}$$

Equipped with

$$\mu = (\mu_a - \mu_b, \mu_b - \mu_c, \mu_c - \mu_d)' \text{ and } \Sigma = \begin{pmatrix} 2\sigma^2 & -\sigma^2 & 0 \\ -\sigma^2 & 2\sigma^2 & -\sigma^2 \\ 0 & -\sigma^2 & 2\sigma^2 \end{pmatrix}, \tag{10.2}$$

the probability P_{abcd} can be computed as

$$P_{abcd} = \Phi_{\mu,\Sigma}(0,0,0). \tag{10.3}$$

---

[1] For the sake of precision, clients divert money each year from the worst to the best performing fund.

Table 10.1 Probabilities to experience an inflow, u, and outflow, d, for each of the four funds. Data are based on the excess returns provided in Kosowski et al. (2006).

	X_1	X_2	X_3	X_4
u	0.208	0.232	0.256	0.305
d	0.295	0.265	0.240	0.200

In turn, the probabilities u_j and d_j to be ranked best or worst and, as a result, to experience an inflow or outflow, can be computed for each fund ($j = 1,\ldots,4$) using (10.3) and summing over the appropriate subset of permutations. Table 10.1 shows for each fund the chances to have positive (u) and negative (d) flows, using the aforementioned values. The probabilities in Table 10.1 show that the chance for the less skilled manager X_1 to get a positive inflow are exceeding 20%. Moreover, intermediate funds X_2 and X_3 have virtually the same probabilities to be ranked at opposite extremes. This means that real mutual funds in the second and third quartiles of performance are likely to be very similar in terms of flows, despite considerable difference in returns. In other words, myopically switching funds from the worst to the best performer is consistent with the flat performance-flow curve that is empirically documented for mutual funds.

This result holds under general conditions about the size of μ and σ.

Theorem 10.1. *The probability P_{abcd} is constant (independent of the permutation) if*

$$\frac{\mu}{\sigma} \to 0. \qquad (10.4)$$

Proof. We can write P_{abcd} using (10.3) as

$$P_{abcd} = Constant \times \int_{-\infty}^{0}\int_{-\infty}^{0}\int_{-\infty}^{0} \exp\left(-\frac{1}{2}(\mathbf{x}-\boldsymbol{\mu})'\Sigma^{-1}(\mathbf{x}-\boldsymbol{\mu})\right) d\mathbf{x}, \qquad (10.5)$$

where $\mathbf{x} = (x_1, x_2, x_3)$ and $\boldsymbol{\mu} = (\mu_a - \mu_b, \mu_b - \mu_c, \mu_c - \mu_d)'$. Changing variables by the position $\mathbf{y} = (\mathbf{x} - \boldsymbol{\mu})/\sigma$ we have

$$P_{abcd} = Constant \times \int_{-\infty}^{-\frac{\mu_a-\mu_b}{\sigma}}\int_{-\infty}^{-\frac{\mu_b-\mu_c}{\sigma}}\int_{-\infty}^{-\frac{\mu_c-\mu_d}{\sigma}} \exp\left(-\frac{1}{2}\mathbf{y}'\begin{pmatrix} 2 & -1 & 0 \\ -1 & 2 & -1 \\ 0 & -1 & 2 \end{pmatrix}^{-1}\mathbf{y}\right) d\mathbf{y}. \qquad (10.6)$$

Taking the limit for $\mu/\sigma \to 0$ and observing that the integrand does not depend on the permutation trough $\mu_a,\ldots,\mu_d$ proves the result. □

Theorem 1 shows that in the limit case in which the standard deviation of the excess returns is very large relatively to the mean excess returns, then every rank is equally likely. Hence, the inflows and outflows are equally probable resulting in a (totally) flat performance curve. The result is insightful as the standard deviation measures the confusion arising in the process to pick the best manager: if σ is (infinitely) large, customers are unable to reward consistently the best manager and the flows are flat. The proof can be easily generalized to many funds along the same lines.

However, Theorem 1 crucially depends on extreme assumptions and does not provide ways to compute the switching probabilities for any actual and bounded set of values for μ and σ. Moreover, were customers switching every T years or according to a performance measure computed on a time window of length T, the mean-standard deviation ratio relative to T years would become $\mu T/\sigma\sqrt{T}$ which, for large T, could be bounded away from 0. The theorem offers in this case little guide, if any.

To overcome these limitations, we now describe a richer computational model of flows into and out of mutual funds.

10.3 A Computational Model

In this section we describe a micro-simulation model to explore some departures from the over-simplified setup that can be treated analytically. In this respect, this section is an effort to explain the empirical regularity of the flow-performance curve using an agent-based model, in the spirit of Lettau (1997). As we made clear previously, we model N mutual funds that have identic and independent yearly excess return described by a normal distribution $N(\mu_i, \sigma_i), i = 1,\ldots,N$. In the absence of any flow, the net asset value w_{it} of fund i at time t changes due to the return R_{it}:

$$w_{it} = w_{i,t-1}(1+R_{it}), \qquad (10.7)$$

where R_{it} is a random draw from $N(\mu_i, \sigma_i)$.

Every year all the funds are ranked according to the mean past excess return over T years. We assume that (due to the action of customers that are not modelled), each of the worst x funds loses a fraction α of its net asset value that is randomly transferred to one of the best x performing funds. The "Sheriff of Nottingham" behaviour ensures that all the x-worst funds lose some money but the x-best funds do not receive equal inflows and (unrealistic) symmetries are avoided due to the random picking of the recipient. Observe that different choices for x and α give rise to different situations. Setting, say, $x = N/4$ is resemblant of the setup described in Section 2, while $x = N/5$ is somewhat mimicking the 5-star Morningstar rating. Another important parameter in the model is α, the percentage of wealth that is removed from the bad funds to flow to the best ones. In general, we assume that α is much smaller than 100%, meaning that poor performing funds face some outflows but not massive withdrawals. Among the reasons there are, as seen in the Introduction, heterogenous willingness of investors to remove capital from the manager and the problematic inference about future returns that can be drawn. We think that another obvious reason is a simple diversification effect. Customers may indeed draw away only a part of the wealth invested low-return funds in order to stay invested in different mutual funds to avoid to keep all the eggs in the same basket.

So far the model cares only about "internal" flows, that depends on x, α and on the distributions $N(\mu_i, \sigma_i)$. However, the growth rates of the value under management are obviously contingent on the flow of exogenous wealth that is injected in the funds. The magnitude of this external flow clearly impact the growth rates and data show that a great part of the increment in the funds' NAV is due to the entry of fresh capital. Hence we introduce external flows in the model and assume that (all of) the best x funds acquire new customers so that their NAV is increased by a factor $1 + \beta$. The fact that new customers select one of the best funds for their new investment is rather natural and the previously mentioned papers offer some guidance in the choice of the size of β, which is realistically in the range 20%–40%, see also Ding et al. (2008). Of course, letting $\beta = 0$ is *de facto* allowing for internal flows only and it is an important special case for our model. We compare this benchmark with the case $\beta > 0$ to better enhance the effects of external flow on the flow-performance curve.

10.3.1 Results

All our results are based on averages computed using 200 simulations for different values of the parameters. We do not adventure ourselves in the estimation of the parameters, but to keep some resemblance to real situations and to the literature, we consider $N = 500$ funds over a period of 20 years. Representative values for excess returns (that are periodically used by customers to rank the funds) are listed, say, in Kosowski et al. (2006). The $\mu_i(\sigma_i)$ are obtained grouping funds in deciles based on the yearly performance (in percent): $\mu_1 = 3.36\,(15.28)$, $\mu_2 = 4.80\,(14.46)$, $\mu_3 = 5.04\,(14.27)$, $\mu_4 = 5.40\,(13.86)$, $\mu_5 = 5.52\,(13.75)$, $\mu_6 = 6.36\,(13.89)$, $\mu_7 = 6.48\,(14.13)$, $\mu_8 = 6.96\,(14.58)$, $\mu_9 = 7.92\,(15.55)$ and $\mu_{10} = 9.36\,(18.36)$. Observe that the observed σ's are approximately constant and that excess returns are often an order of magnitude smaller than the standard deviation. The assumptions of Theorem 1 are very roughly met but there is clearly scope for simulations to explore the effects of departures from that setting.

The simulation of N funds when only deciles-based statistics are known requires some caution. We could replicate $N/10$ times the values listed above for μ_i and σ_i but this produces a very granular set of funds. Moreover, every simulation would have the very same set of values for the parameters while deciles do not determine a single composition of the set. Hence, we resort to a resampling algorithm described in Thompson (2000). The method, called SIMDAT, allows for the creation of pseudo-samples of arbitrary size given a matrix of reference observations $\mathbf{X}$ (in this case $X_i = (\mu_i, \sigma_i), i = 1, \ldots, 10$). The pseudo-samples are generated by first picking at random one of the X_i and then blending its components using linear combinations with its k-nearest neighbors. The shape of the resulting distribution can be tuned modifying k and, as extreme cases, we can sample from the singular distribution that gives equal non-null mass to the points X_i when $k = 1$ or from a unique multivariate density $N(E[\mathbf{X}], Cov(\mathbf{X}))$ when k approaches infinity. We take a

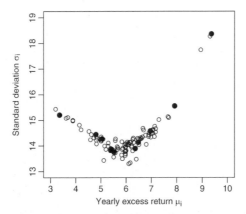

Fig. 10.1 Simulated excess returns and standard deviations for 100 funds (circles). The points are a pseudo-sample of the 10 deciles statistics quoted in the text (solid circles) and are obtained using SIMDAT with $k = 5$.

reasonable compromise in the generation of the pseudo-samples and set $k = 5$ that produces a cloud of point visually approximating fairly well the deciles statistics plotted on a $\mu\sigma$-plane, as shown in Figure 10.1. Additional details on the SIM-DAT algorithm can be found in Thompson's book and the code can be freely downloaded at http://lib.stat.cmu.edu/S/gendat. We tried other values of k to check that our results do not change in any significant way.

The yearly growth rate of a fund i at time t is defined as:

$$gr_{it} = \frac{w_{it} - w_{i,t-1}(1 + R_{it})}{w_{i,t-1}}. \tag{10.8}$$

Each year, funds are ranked based on their mean excess return over the previous T years and flows are generated as described before (because of internal movements driven by α and exogenous streams related to β). It is difficult to estimate the length T for the revision window used by investors. Most probably there is notable heterogeneity among different kinds of mutual funds' customers but there is evidence that long horizons are sometimes used. Financial media, for example, often report also 3- and 5-year returns for funds' investments. The average holding period of funds' shares may be related to the revision frequency, even though they may not be necessarily equal. Informal evidence is supportive of average holding periods of several years and Sirri and Tufano (1998) reports time-spans as long as 7 years. We investigate values for T in the set $\{1, 3, 5\}$.

We select $\alpha = 10\%, 15\%, 20\%$ so that only a portion of the invested monies are switched away in a single year after a poor outcome. The previous discussion also motivates our choice to pick x in $\{25, 75, 125\}$. As $N = 500$ this means that being ranked in the worse 5% to 25% of funds causes some outflow by the invested agents.

We present our results having in mind a somewhat representative benchmark configuration where $(\alpha^*, x^*, T^*, \beta^*) = (15\%, 75, 3, 30\%)$. We then move one parameter

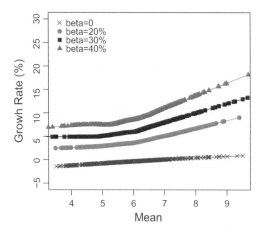

Fig. 10.2 Flow-performance curves for $\beta \in \{0, 20\%, 30\%, 40\%\}$. The graphs are obtained averaging the results of 200 simulations.

at a time, keeping the others fixed to investigate the individual effects and the sensitivity of our findings.

Figure 10.2 depicts the arithmetic average growth rate of the funds as a function of the mean excess return. Different values for β are considered and we clearly see the flat and convex shape of the flow-performance curve. There are two interesting features in the graph. The left part of the curves is nearly constant, demonstrating that the flow pattern of a bad fund is pretty similar to the one of the median performer. The right part of the curve is, instead, seen to be rising steeply. In stark contrast with the low μ zone, this means that the best funds enjoy much higher relative inflows than the relative outflows of the worst ones. The picture shows that this effect is depending on the size of β, that has also the unsurprising effect to raise the level of the whole curve brought by increased external flows infused in the economy.

It is also worthwhile noticing that the position $\beta = 0$ produces a remarkably flat curve. This situation devoid of any external flow is very close to the assumptions of Theorem 1 and indeed the theoretical result, predicting a constant curve, is a decent portrait the simulations. A similar, almost constant outcome is found for other values of the parameters, provided that β is held at 0.

The right panel of Figure 10.3 shows the flow-performance curves for $\alpha = 10\%, 15\%, 20\%$. The sensitivity with respect to α is relatively low and the same realistic shape is robustly generated. The level of the curves increases with α and this holds even in the right part of the μ-axis. Two effects are competing here: a bigger α leads to bigger outflows from the worst funds and this reduce the average growth rate. At the same time, however, a fund with low μ occasionally ranks high and receives a relatively large and even outlying inflow. This lucky event has non-negligible probability in view of the insights given by Theorem 1 and more than compensate the more commonly observed negative growth rates when taking averages.

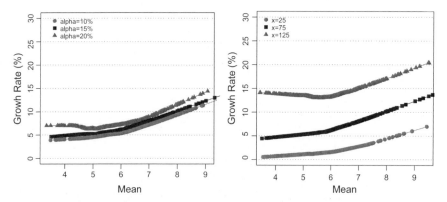

Fig. 10.3 Flow-performance curves for $\alpha \in \{10\%, 15\%, 20\%\}$, on the left, and $x \in \{25, 75, 125\}$, on the right. The graphs are obtained averaging the results of 200 simulations.

The left panel of Figure 10.3 shows the results of our simulations when $x = 25, 75, 125$. The value of x measure the extent of the region where below-average funds are considered "bad" and consequently experience outflows that are gained by symmetrically positioned good funds. The flow-performance curves relative to $x = 25, 75$ are both convex and show the usual shape with a flatter region followed by a increasing section on the right. Setting $x = 25$, i.e. allowing only 5% of the funds to be faced with withdrawals, produces a mild curvature and probably $x = 75$ is a better choice that enhances rather appropriately the rise in the growth rate of the best performers. Increasing x has some interesting effects. On the one hand the set of funds that suffers outflows or enjoys inflows is much larger. Due to the sizeable standard deviations of the returns used to rank the funds, this results in (relatively) many cases where bad to average funds rank in the top part of the standing. On the other hand, the U-shaped graph shows that the previously described effect for α enters the stage here as well. Even if inferior funds lose wealth more often than not, nonetheless they are some occasions when they get inflows that are huge in relative terms. As there is no evidence of a U-shaped curve in the empirical literature, the examination of the whole picture lead to the belief that investors are probably escaping from a fund when the performance is extremely negative (worse 5 or 15% of the industry), implicitly tolerating without any action a rank close to the 3-rd quartile.

The effect of varying T in the set $\{1, 3, 5\}$ is depicted in Figure 10.4. Only the left part of the flow-performance curve is visibly affected. Low values for T produce volatile periodic rankings and, being the T-period average excess return smaller than the corresponding dispersion, the dynamics predicted by Theorem 1 is at work (flat curve), with the usual distortion on the right due to the external inflows. The economic intuition is clear: investors found their decision on short term performance and, hence, easily mistake the good fund with the bad. If, conversely, a longer period

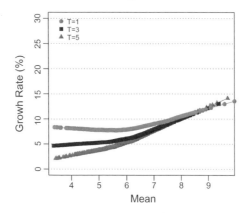

Fig. 10.4 Flow-performance curves for different values of $T = 1, 3, 5$ years. The graphs are obtained averaging the results of 200 simulations.

is used for the evaluation, the ranking is more consistent because more observations are used. Moreover, for many funds μT is of the same order of magnitude of $\sigma\sqrt{T}$ when $T = 5$ and indeed the flow-performance curve almost linearly penalizes the poor-performers in favour of the funds with higher values of μ. Again this fits quite well with the basic intuition that careful investors, taking some years to assess the ability of their managers, can better pick and reward funds with average superior returns. The finding that slower and more cautious agents are less prone to generate puzzling outcomes is not surprising and was reported in famous agent-based papers like in Lettau (1997), where longer T cut down the size of the risk exposure taken by the agents, or in Arthur *et al.* (1997) where infrequent activation of the learning device suffices to obtain prices not far from the rational-expectations equilibrium.

10.4 Conclusion

We have shown that a "Sheriff of Nottingham" behaviour of profit-chasing clients of mutual funds can robustly produce a fairly flat performance-flow curve, in the absence of external flows. The main ingredients of the model are moderate levels of x and α, the number of funds that are rated as bad/good and the fraction of invested wealth that is moved away, respectively. Our model can robustly generate flow-performance curve that are qualitatively close to the empirically observed ones, if some exogenous flow is taken into account. Various papers in the literature offer interesting (and distinct) explanations for the flat-convex shape of the flow-performance curve and all the proposed mechanisms are in a sense versions of this model. We have proved a proposition that shows that a constant curve is indeed produced (for any x and α) when the ratio between average returns and standard deviation goes to zero. This analytical result stresses that investors are incapable to reward skilled managers in a confused world where average excess returns are contaminated by high randomness due to the sizeable standard deviation of the same returns.

We show that a sufficient condition to bend up the right part of the curve is to assume that fresh funds are invested in the best x-funds that have their net asset value increased by a factor $1 + \beta$. The parameter β, combined with x, controls the amount of exogenous flows and affects the level and curvature of the curve.

By simulations and comparative static exercises, we demonstrate that our results are robust and hold for large intervals of the parameters. Most notably, large values for x are disruptive in that they cause unrealistic U-shaped curves. Finally, we show that the length T of the time-span used by agents to evaluate the average returns of the funds has some impact. Allowing for longer T gives raise to an almost linear curve, while shorter horizons are more likely to produce realistic flow-performance curvature. This behaviour is an indirect test of Theorem 1 as an increase in T makes the required assumptions more and more inaccurate.

References

Arthur, W., Holland, J., LeBaron, B., and Taylor, P. (1997). Asset pricing under endogenous expectations in an artificial stock market. In Arthur, W., Lane, D., and Durlauf, S., editors, *The economy as an evolving complex system II*. Addison-Wesley.

Berk, J. B. and Tonks, I. (2007). Return persistence and fund flows in the worst performing mutual funds. NBER Working Papers 13042, National Bureau of Economic Research, Inc.

Ding, B., Getmansky, M., Liang, B., and Wermers, R. R. (2008). Investor Flows and Share Restrictions in the Hedge Fund Industry. *SSRN eLibrary*.

Del Guercio, D. and Tkac, P. (2008). Star power: The effect of monrningstar ratings on mutual fund flow. *Journal of Financial and Quantitative Analysis*, 43(04):907–936.

Kahneman, D. and Tversky, A. (1979). Prospect theory: An analysis of decision under risk. *Econometrica*, 47(2):263–91.

Kosowski, R., Timmermann, A., Wermers, R., and White, H. (2006). Can mutual fund "stars" really pick stocks? new evidence from a bootstrap analysis. *Journal of Finance*, 61(6):2551–2595.

Lettau, M. (1997). Explaining the facts with adaptive agents: the case of mutual fund flows. *Journal of Economic Dynamics and Control*, 21:1117–1147.

Lynch, A. and Musto, D. (2003). How investors interpret past fund returns. *Journal of Finance*, 58(5):2033–2058.

Sirri, E. and Tufano, P. (1998). Costly search and mutual fund flows. *Journal of Finance*, 53(5):1589–1622.

Thompson, J. (2000). *Simulation: a Modeler's Approach*. Wiley.

Chapter 11
Foundations for a Framework for Multiagent-Based Simulation of Macrohistorical Episodes in Financial Markets

Bàrbara Llacay and Gilbert Peffer

Abstract Questions about methodology and model design are subject to constant debate in the emerging field of agent-based modelling and simulation. This article intends to make progress on some of the more foundational aspects affecting method and design. Our primary focus is on a much neglected area of agent-based modelling, namely that of large-scale, spatio-temporal phenomena in financial markets. We argue that multiagent-based models are ideally suited to tackle this class of problems, but that as of yet simulation research has not delivered the methods and tools necessary for this task. The lack of a methodological framework tailored to this complex research object, due in part to a persistent coloration of research questions and interests in positivist shades, is an evident obstacle to progress. We hold that simulation research in finance should set its own methodological agenda, and propose that the mechanism-centric philosophy of critical realism is moved to the centre stage. Our framework encourages researchers to be mindful of existing knowledge and insight in finance without being kept hostage to it and to embrace the historic turn and look out for synergies in qualitative research.

11.1 Introduction

The turmoil that has ravaged financial markets and institutions over the last two years, and which has now spilled over with a vengeance into the national economies of industrial and developing countries has laid bare perhaps more than anything else the shortcomings of standard economic models and their relative ineffectiveness in the context of financial stability. When Lehman Brothers, an investment bank, collapsed in September 2008 for instance, regulators were as much left in the dark as investors all over the world about the true exposures of this systemically important

B. Llacay · G. Peffer
Dept. for Economic, Financial, and Actuarial Mathematics, University of Barcelona, Av. Diagonal 690, 08034 Barcelona, Spain, e-mail: bllacay@ub.edu, g.peffer@ub.edu

institution, and hence about the impact on the financial system of the widely expected counterparty defaults and write-offs.

Mechanisms of bank runs, market failure, and payment system disruptions have been extensively described in the microeconomic literature since the 1980s (Allen and Gale, 2007). While early models focussed mainly on bank panics, subsequently competitive markets were included into the analysis to explain how interlinkages between financial institutions and markets can amplify and propagate small liquidity shocks. Contagion, whereby shocks spread through the system via interlocking deposits and asset holdings has been the target of various theoretical and empirical studies (e.g. Upper and Worms, 2004). While these important developments have highlighted a number of salient features of instability, and have alerted policy makers to the dangers of inefficient intermediation and liquidity shortages in financial markets, they do not offer the comprehensive framework needed for effective crisis modelling. Macroeconomic models, especially those currently in use in Central Banks around the world, also suffer from a number of flaws that makes them unsuitable for the purpose of financial stability modelling (ECB, 2008).

In this article, we ask whether multi-agent based simulation (MABS) can play a constructive and perhaps novel role in modelling large-scale, complex phenomena in financial markets, and sketch the outline of a comprehensive though still preliminary and evolving methodological framework that can move MABS closer to realising its full potential in this critical field of application.

11.2 What is Wrong with MABS?

Agent-based models are routinely advocated from social simulation and agent-based computational economics quarters as a new and promising instrument in financial research (LeBaron, 2001), with a clear potential to remedy many of the perceived shortcomings of mainstream economics, or more specifically, neoclassical finance (Tay, 2006). The vast empirical literature on financial markets and institutions, and the extensive theoretical explorations into their functioning certainly provides a tremendous wealth of insights and knowledge on which to build extensive agent models of the financial system and the economy.

Despite the bullish assurances by simulation practitioners however, and notwithstanding the evident benefits held out by MABS, attempts to harness its full potential have fallen well short of expectations – and quite evidently so in light of the marked advances that finance as a multifaceted academic discipline and a field of practice has made elsewhere[1]. We believe that the reasons for this failure can be

---

[1] The simulation literature gives at times the erroneous impression that most of financial research is either deductive-nomological (e.g. neoclassical finance) or experimental and psychological (in particular behavioural finance), with little in-between. However, there are quite a few lines research that are prominent scientific disciplines in their own right, quite independent of neoclassical and behavioural finance: naturalistic decision making and expertise research in finance, neuroeconomics and neurofinance, social studies of finance, cultural economics, and so forth.

found in: (1) a general disregard for empirical evidence (Moss, 2008) beyond market data or stylised facts, and, perhaps more importantly, a latent dislike to take on board the central questions and insights that have emerged over time, particularly in mainstream financial research and practice over time; (2) a lurking commitment to elements of positivist doctrine when, at the same time, this has been central to the simulationist criticisms raised at orthodox finance; and (3) a not uncommonly held belief that MABS is an alternative to finance theory when in fact multiagent systems (MAS) are atheoretical as far as finance is concerned. Some of these issues have been tentatively raised in a few occasions in the simulation literature (e.g. LeBaron, 2006).

It is of course perfectly legitimate to build agent models of largely academic interest that explain for instance financial market puzzles or stylised facts. Nor is there much to argue about the penchant to create models with minimal-size parameter sets, although the criterion of parsimony is pretty hard to translate into an operational and cost-effective modelling strategy. What we intend to say however is that these taken-for-granted 'default options' of MABS philosophy, once they become an unquestioned part and parcel of our modelling practice, pose a formidable obstacle in harnessing the full power of the agent-based social simulation paradigm, at least as far as complex financial modelling is concerned. Let us now have a look in turn at the three limiting factors – empirical groundedness, conceptual and descriptive validity, theory pluralism – hinted to above, and their implications for a yet to materialise MABS framework.

11.2.1 Barriers to MABS for Macrohistorial Research in Finance

Empirical research in mainstream finance is dominated, on one side by econometric analyses that build on the idea of event regularities of the type 'whenever X then Y', and on the other side by formal models that aim to replicate so-called stylised facts discerned from financial market data. Agent-based modelling strategies commonly employed in studying financial market phenomena quite often draw or learn on these teachings. Moreover, research questions in MABS often seem to align with the more traditional cognitive interests of financial scholarship, and simulation research rarely if at all tackles problems that have a clear relevance in financial practice. But what is the alternative to a practice informed by the positivist tradition of building small, incremental models or searching for constant event conjunctions in large data sets?

This question cannot be answered meaningfully without reference to model *use*. The key motivation behind our proposal is to develop historical explanations, exploring and testing alternative hypotheses about generating mechanisms, intervening factors, decision points, event processes and so on, that link hypothesised causes to observed outcomes. Our focus here is on financial crises, that is, complex socio-economic processes that typically involve a medley of interdependent markets, institutions, and infrastructures, and commonly show a dynamics that depends in complicated ways on the strategic interaction of social, political, and economic actors, on contractual exposures, and on the 'physical' linkages in the underlying payment and settlement systems. The characteristics of our research object and the questions we are focussing on strongly suggest a role for qualitative research instruments, and in particular for the cross and within-case methods found in comparative history, international relations, and other fields of the social and political sciences. We propose that through the appreciation of the comparative strengths of qualitative research – and particularly of within-case study methods – that the potential of MABS for macrohistorical financial episodes can be more evidently discerned.

Why is it that the social simulation literature as it pertains to financial modelling has shown scant interest, if any, for the vast array of methods and insights from qualitative historical and social research, despite the fact that there is an extremely diverse and, compared to the rather formal research pieces typically found in financial economics, fairly accessible literature on this research tradition? We believe that part of the reason for this state of affairs are the epistemological and methodological aims, assumptions, and preferences that spill over from mainstream econometrics and economics into the realm of MABS in an uncritical and largely taken-for-granted fashion. It is largely this, perhaps inadvertent, influence from positivist thinking, we argue, which ultimately limits progress by holding back the development of a more suitable method adapted to the nature of MAS. In a relatively recent article on validation for instance, Windrum *et al.* (2007) discuss a number of core issues that all agent models presumably have to come to terms with. What strikes us as particularly worrying is not only that a vocabulary geared to cognitive interests that largely reside in the confines of statistical research is uncritically recruited for sweeping methodological judgements on the merits of quite different research traditions. What is more troubling though is that all these issues have been widely discussed in the relevant literature, where the discrediting arguments from statistic quarters have been quite successfully rebutted (see e.g. George and Bennett, 2005, on the misapplication of the "degrees of freedom problem").

While epistemological and methodological predilections in mainstream economics are an important hurdle for MABS to overcome, proponents on the social simulation side of the fence are doing little to remove the obstacles. Rather, as a reaction to the predominance of orthodox economic thought, and especially neoclassical finance, they to present MABS as an alternative to finance theory. Whatever the merits and limitations of formal modelling in finance, we reject this stance for three reasons. First, MABS is a modelling framework while, say, neoclassical finance is a theory – MASs are atheoretical as far as finance is concerned. Second, an attitude that is hostile towards traditional research streams runs the danger of putting off researchers from widely reading the financial literature and (mindfully and knowledgeably) tapping into it when designing agent models. Fact is that apart from the purely mathematically oriented literature in finance, a large number of highly rated publications inside and outside of the mainstream that contain a wealth of knowledge, commentaries, and interpretations on financial markets and behaviour that can hardly be ignored in any serious attempt to building models of ecological validity and relevance. Third, and more importantly for the discussions that follow, both the formal and the experimental financial literature contain detailed and often insightful discussions on mechanisms that drive institutional, market, and individual behaviour. In fact, the idea that hidden, and possibly latent and contingent mechanisms work jointly to generate observed real-world processes and events lies at the core of critical realism, a scientific paradigm that has received much attention over recent years, and which, or so we suggest, might form the basis for a more methodological approach to MABS. Thus, in the context of our framework, the likely role to be played by the kind of stylised models discussed in mainstream economics is to provide a pool of mechanisms (e.g. social imitation, information diffusion, or price discovery) into which we can tap when the available evidence is incomplete or equivocal.

To sum up, epistemological and methodological questions are of great import in MABS, not only because any methodological proposal that focuses on improving agent modelling practice needs to address these questions at some point, but also because progress in MABS practice is hampered by largely imported concerns about statistical and formal deductive methods from econometrics and financial economics. Although there are as of yet no operational proposals for a method specifically tailored to MABS, judging from the literature it is unlikely that the simulation community would be content with a world where MABS were little more than a methodological extension grafted onto the mainstream project.

Based on these discussions, the key issues we believe that need tackling are how to bring richer sets of empirical evidence to bear on model specification and evaluation, what exactly to replace the formal deductive mode of reasoning and the regular conjunctions framework from econometrics with, and in what ways and by what methodological means theoretical insights from other fields of the social sciences, including financial economics can play a role in the MABS process. Before turning to the discussion of our proposal, we think it is important to reemphasise that multi-agent systems, to which MABS is intimately linked, are both atheoretical and amethodological as far as the human sciences are concerned. To improve the quality of MABS in view of intended use and to avoid the problem of arbitrary model design, social simulation research in finance will, to a fuller or lesser extent, have to become more sensitive to theoretical concepts and insights from scientific disciplines that are pertinent to the object of research, while at the same time remain open to and adopt wherever possible, proven research methods and techniques from social research that are best suited to the pursued aim.

For sure, the social simulation literature has extensively discussed issues related to methodology and put forward a number of proposals to improve the process of agent model design and implementation (e.g. Richiardi *et al.*, 2006, Gilbert, 2007). Most of these recommendations are however notoriously vague on how to put them into practice or, in some cases, are just not practicable for our purpose. Still, some elements of our approach are not new and have been advocated at various occasions by simulation researchers. In fact, our proposal for domain analysis and model specification, design, and implementation resonates to some extent with the methodological deliberations of Boero and Squazzoni (2005), although the authors neither show how to translate their recommendations into a procedure for model building (which in all fairness wasn't the aim of their article) nor do they discuss case-based models on terms proper to case study research. The authors furthermore tell us at several occasions that agent models are well suited to describe and explain "empirical reality in a mechanism-based style of analysis" (Boero and Squazzoni, 2005:1.15), without however providing any details of how this might be done. If one carefully considers the implications of the mechanism-centric, critical realist mode of inference in a complex world, that is, in a world where mechanisms can join together in contingent and possibly counteracting ways to bring about an observed process, event, or structural change, then it becomes rapidly clear that there is no quick fix to drastically simplify the retroductive move from empirical observations to possibly equifinal or multifinal sets of interacting and perhaps contingent mechanisms as their likely cause. We discuss further below how historical research grapples with this problem and, as a result, suggest that our MABS framework should make use of process tracing, an important qualitative research tool that examines complex causal mechanisms to uncover the ways in which they link putative causes to observed events within a particular historical case or across a small number of cases.

The foregoing discussion forms a tentative basis and the starting point for a more comprehensive MABS framework, which we will outline in the discussions that follow. At the core of the framework lies a commitment to critical realism, and in particular to the notion of a stratified reality where structures, mechanisms, and tendencies that are not accessible through our sense experiences and impressions produce, govern, affect, and constrain the observable events and states of affairs (Lawson, 1997). While on a conceptual level our descriptive and explanatory style is intimately linked to the project of critical realism, we have to look further afield for inspiration as to the possible logic, role, and function of structures and mechanisms in the actual context of macrohistorical analysis (e.g. McAdam *et al.*, 2001). A key characteristic of our approach, and here we lean quite strongly on historical and case research practice, is that no type of empirical evidence is by necessity excluded from the analysis. On the contrary, especially at the initial stages, and before we can start specifying a model, it is crucial that the researcher gains a thorough understanding of the crisis episode by examining a whole raft of evidence available from news papers, journals, regulatory reports, archive material, hearing transcripts, and so forth. A further important element of the approach are typological and general theories and models from the social sciences and from finance that provide us with conceptual scaffolding when and where needed in the model building process. Finally, in terms of implementation, we opted for a formal modelling language – AML – rather than a particular agent software or environment since this offers a more rigorous specification for MABS models and greater flexibility at the time of implementation. In the following section, we discuss the different elements of our approach in more detail, explain how they are related to each other, and formulate the steps to build a MABS implementation in AML based on rich evidence available about the episode and the concepts borrowed from selected theories.

11.3 Proposal for a MABS Framework

In what follows it is important to keep in mind that we pursue a particular research purpose, namely to shed light on historical crisis episodes by identifying the possibly contingent mechanisms that operated jointly over a period of time to generate the observed real world processes thought responsible for the salient conditions, key events, and state of affairs. Some of the key characteristics of our research object – complex and enduring interleaved behavioural, social, and economic processes on one side and singular episodes with mostly superficial commonalities when compared with other crisis events on the other – pose severe limitations to the applicability of formal modeling techniques and of statistical methods, and hence to the transferability of epistemological concerns and methodological strategies to our field of study. This is not to say that there is no place in our approach for formal descriptions of isolated mechanisms or for econometric analysis of simulation results – in fact there is – but that our research strategy should not be kept hostage by methodological injunctions and concerns from mainstream economics and econometrics. To paraphrase George and Bennett (2005), we believe that statistical analysis, MABS, and formal models should be regarded as complementary, rather than competitive. Clearly then, there is not much to be gained in pursuing a one-size-fits-all strategy for MABS model building. As we have said before, the fact that MABS is not only an atheoretical but also an amethodological modeling framework means that it cannot possibly be an alternative *method* to econometrics or formal modeling. As a consequence, simulation researchers need to look elsewhere in order to specify the methodological make-up of MABS. We have chosen case study methods in social research as our source of inspiration since research aims, objects, and questions studied there show some evident alignments with those we are confronted with here (see e.g. Stern and Sundelius, 2002).

In the recent past there has been a noticeable increase in interest from researchers across social science disciplines, including economics, in historical explanation. Even the social simulation literature has become witness to the wide ranging imprint the 'historic turn', calling for researchers to pay more attention to qualitative methods in simulation research (e.g. Squazzoni and Boero, 2007). In fact, one reason why case study methods have become an appealing research tool for social scientists is that they are well-suited to the task of minutely exploring the complex causality that typically underlies context-dependent event processes (Gupta and Wang, 2004:218), and that they are seen as complementary to rather than competing with statistical and formal methods.

What is case study research? George and Bennett (2005) define a case in very general terms to be "an instance of a class of events", where the 'class of events' represents a particular type of phenomenon, such as the dry-up of market liquidity during financial turmoil. A case study is then "a well-defined aspect of a historical episode" and the "decision about which class of events to study and which theories to use determines what data [...] are relevant to her or his study of it" (George and Bennett, 2005:18). Case studies have a number of distinct advantages compared to large-N statistical methods and formal deductive models, which are particularly pertinent in the context of our research aims and questions. Where statistical studies typically (have to) amalgamate data of unalike cases or characteristics into unified, high-level concepts, and where formal models need to reduce the parameter space for the sake of tractability, and thus may have to exclude germane causal features from the analysis, case methods allow researchers to drill down the conceptual structures and make context part and parcel of hypothesis development and contingent generalisations about causal mechanisms. While both statistical and formal deductive methods by themselves offer little in terms of identifying new variables or generating new hypotheses, the rich evidence that comes to the fore during field and archival research in the social sciences are highly conducive to scientific creativity by stimulating researchers to generate new explanatory hypotheses or altering existing ones at each stage of the analysis. To sum up, case study research permits us quite naturally to increase the conceptual depth of analysis while at the same time opening up the possibility of generating new concepts and hypotheses drawing on a wealth of evidence from field, experimental, and archival sources and studies. Two additional advantages brought to us by case study research are closely aligned with and have in part also motivated our interest for the mechanism-centric explanatory style of critical realism. The detailed analysis of a single or a small number of cases allows us for instance to zoom in where we suspect conditions that might activate hypothesised mechanisms or where counteracting forces might conceal these intervening mechanisms. Exploring causal mechanisms and the conditions under which they operate can help us for instance explain historical episodes or test alternative hypotheses about specific occurrences. Moreover, while complexity is a real problem especially in the context of the formal, deductive mode of explanation, case studies are particularly well-suited to investigate complex causal inter-actions including multiply dependent feedback loops, path dependence, and causal relations of equifinality and multifinality.

11.3.1 A Bird's Eye View of the Framework

We shall start by providing a summary overview of the methodological framework and its constituent elements before describing the different modelling steps in more detail and showing how they relate to each other. The modelling process revolves around a rich set of descriptions for a given situation or episode, of which we would like to model a salient aspect in order to, say, test conflicting explanatory accounts or develop a hypothesis about likely causes. The empirical evidence we thus accumulate during the MABS process represents what experiences and impressions we have of the world, though we should bear in mind that theoretical interests and interpretive work may be hidden in and thus have shaped some such descriptions. At the end of the modelling process, we should hope to obtain a formal model implementation – in our case in AML – that satisfies the evaluation criteria we have established at the outset, possibly in agreement with stakeholders and aligned with their needs. Evaluation, though an important aspect of any MABS framework, is

11 Foundations for AB Simulation of Macrohistorical Financial Episodes 137

beyond the scope of this article. Now, whatever form the MABS process in the end takes, it needs to be geared towards generating an AML representation, a crucially important hurdle in view of the fact that much of the evidence we are typically confronted with has more often than not a processual character, and also that there is no natural way of representing in a MAS a truly mechanism-centric view of the world as propounded by critical realism.

Let us go back now to where we started off, that is to the set of descriptions of a historical episode. Evidence from observations, measurements, or oral accounts, though by all means necessary for our aims, is generally insufficient to create a functioning model, especially one that needs to be formulated as a MAS. In our case, AML takes the role of a formal specification of the MAS, and hence whatever concepts and modelling mechanisms it offers, we have to be sensitive to the fact that, at a minimum, (a subset of) these concepts and mechanisms need to acquire a clear meaning in our conceptualisation of the world, above and beyond what we can extract from the data and other such 'pure' kinds of evidence. The buck doesn't stop here however. While AML obliges us to look out for, identify, and eventually implement its own types of entities, relations, or behaviours, we need to complement this barren world view with concepts, categorisations, mechanisms, and (typically mid-range) theories developed in the many disciplines of the human sciences[2]. Again, these will have to be mapped eventually onto the agent model (in AML), which for some theories or concepts is less troublesome than for others. For instance, although we might find useful hints in the microstructure literature about different pricing mechanisms, those that are formulated as optimisation or control problems cannot be implemented in a (necessarily) straightforward manner in a multi-agent world.

We have now established three key building blocks of our framework: empirical evidence, theoretical descriptions, and an implementation language. The fourth, and final element of the framework covers several functions and, in essence, is motivated by Tony Lawson's reading of critical realism (Lawson, 1997), a philosophy of science that emerged in reaction to the perceived shortcomings of positivism and brought to prominence by the influential writings of Bhaskar (1978). Key precepts from critical realism that underlie our understanding of how the world works and which accordingly make up the foundation of our methodological framework are 'mechanisms', 'structures', 'processes', 'powers', and 'retroduction'. In the following, we define each of these concepts in turn, drawing directly on Lawson's text (Lawson, 1997), and briefly outline the operational role they take on as part of the modelling process.

Science, according to the critical realist view expounded by Lawson "aims at identifying and illuminating the structures and mechanisms, powers and tendencies, that govern or facilitate the course of events. The scientific objective is to identify relatively enduring structures and to understand their characteristic ways of acting"

---

[2] If for instance we decide that one aspect of our model involves herding, the best bet to uncover the actual mechanism by which social actors imitate is through fieldwork, which might be guided by theories of imitation from social psychology. In many cases, fieldwork is too costly so the alternative here is to use secondary sources and empirically supported theoretical accounts.

(Lawson, 1997:23). The implication for agent models is that, and here we paraphrase Lawson, they have to support, or better 'accommodate', an account of those structures, mechanisms, powers, and tendencies that, singularly or in combination, have the capacity to contribute to the production or facilitation of some already identified phenomenon of interest. *Structures* are central to this account and are understood as some generally enduring, power wielding, intrinsic feature of systems or complex situations. A structure possesses causal powers, that is, "potentials, capacities, or abilities to act in certain ways and/or to facilitate various activities and developments." It follows then that complex systems and situations "have powers *in virtue of* their structure" (Lawson, 1997:21). Within this conception then, a mechanism is seen as "a way of acting or working of a structured thing" (Lawson, 1997:21).

The relevance of the critical realist's concepts of structure and mechanism for our framework is that they represent, at the most fundamental level, all that can be provided for *explicitly* by a MABS implementation. The set of (AML) modelling entities – agents, relations, behaviour, resources, and so on – can be understood, always from this perspective, that is, as either structural or mechanistic 'things' *capable* of generating or facilitating a simulacrum of the phenomenon, in the artificial world, by way of executing, or simulating, the agent model. However, and herein lies one of the difficulties of modelling around this particular theory of science, structures and mechanisms are but part of what conditions or determines a MABS implementation. Structures and mechanisms can join up in quite distinct ways, usually not under the exclusive control of the researcher, exhibiting in some occasions "causal powers which, when triggered or released, act as generative mechanisms" that may actually *not* determine, or not have the strong potential to determine, the phenomenon of interest or part thereof. It is these causal powers that emanate from structures and mechanisms, which in a dynamic balance of forces, constrain and enable the succession of events and the processes that characterise "the genesis, reproduction, and decline of some structure, mechanism, or thing" (Lawson, 1997: 34). And it is these powers, potentially active in a simulation, that our MABS model has to *implicitly* implement, in addition to the *explicit* representation of structures and mechanisms. Needless to say that a thorough understanding of the historical episode, and the conditions and drivers underlying the experienced events is essential for a successful move from the empirical evidence to an implementation which is perceptive and faithful to the causal powers exhibited by the structures and mechanisms that are characteristic and representative of the target system. While the essential style of reasoning in critical realism proceeds from "the knowledge of some surface phenomenon [...] to a knowledge of mechanisms at a deeper level or strata of reality, which contributed to the generation of the original phenomenon of interest" (Lawson, 1997:26), we have to make sure that once we have made this move, our implementation not only incorporates the knowledge about mechanisms and structures, but is also sensitive to the possibly latent and contingent powers intrinsic in the implementation[3].

---

[3] Surely now, if we think about the issue of validation in the context of this critical realist's perspective on modeling, it ought to be clear that positivists injunctions such as those exposed in Windrum *et al.* (2007) are neither necessary, in that exact form, nor sufficient to guarantee a valid model.

11.3.2 The Modelling Process

Before discussing the different modelling stages, we will first offer a succinct overview of the MABS process. For the purpose of illustrating the different components of the framework, we distinguish between several conceptual levels that characterise the development process, though in practice, modelling will actually proceed in an iterative fashion. Three of these levels, use and benefits, simulation, and evaluation are outside the scope of this article. Here, we focus on the levels of description, analysis, and implementation.

At the level of description, multiple sets of descriptions and narratives obtained from archival documents, interviews, reports, news commentaries and so on provide the evidential basis for the MABS model. This knowledge base typically grows and evolves during the iterative modelling process, to accommodate the need for additional information or to contrast competing hypotheses, explanatory variables, or AML representations. In addition to empirical evidence in its original or raw form, we generate knowledge maps in different formats, including tables, graphs, and diagrams to summarise, partition, and visualise the information embedded in the empirical accounts. Qualitative methods, in particular those from case study research, guide us in this task. The (continual) outcome of these activities will subsequently be examined at the level of analysis.

At the level of analysis there are four interleaving modes of organising and studying the empirical evidence: case analysis, structural analysis, theory-driven analysis, and MAS-centric analysis. Case analysis basically draws on traditional methods of case research to analyse the evidence from our case knowledge base. This ought to provide, as a minimum, a thorough understanding of those aspects of the episode that are relevant for the modelling exercise. Narratives of historical episodes, which in traditional financial modelling are commonly ignored, are of particular interest here since they provide us with a processual perspective, which, as we have seen, is central to our word view.

Structural analysis is motivated by our reading of critical realism and draws on the elements we have previously discussed. Again, we make use here of case methods, in particular of process tracing on the one hand and on the mode of analysis expounded in McAdam *et al.* (2001), on the other. Process tracing "attempts to identify the intervening causal process – the causal chain and causal mechanism – between an independent variable (or variables) and the outcome of the dependent variable" (George and Bennett, 2005:206). Process tracing, which supports explanation via causal mechanisms, shows distinct strengths as a tool for theory development and evaluation, complementing statistical analysis which operates on a different level of causal inference. In a similar vein, though focused on typological theory development, McAdam and colleagues propose a mechanism-centred analytical framework to explain a wide range of historically, geographically, and

---

Positivists are interested in constant event conjunctions without reference to deeper strata of reality. In that world view, there is no need to be attentive to, say, the latent and contingent powers of structures or mechanisms. Validation in the critical realist's world however has to incorporate the aspect of causal power, and ensure that an model actually exhibits these powers in whatever form.

culturally divergent episodes of political strife. Specifically, the authors' intention is to overcome the impossible search for generalisable accounts of war, revolution, or social movements by identifying combinations of recurring mechanisms and processes that play a crucial role in seemingly disparate occurrences of contention in world history. The particular value of the authors' book for us lies in the concrete idea it provides of the empirical work – be it directly or through secondary sources – involved in identifying recurring mechanisms across a wide variety of historical episodes.

Structural analysis proceeds in a two-way fashion, from empirical evidence to the process level, and back, from putative structures and mechanisms inferred via retroduction to the causal powers that, when active, constrain, enable, and generate the observed event sequences and change processes. Again, tables, graphs, and diagrams help shape, document, track, and visualise the analytical procedures. Structural analysis is intimately linked to the different framework components at the level of description, analysis, and implementation. It incorporates the data from the empirical knowledge base, borrowing the working concepts, categories, structure, and mechanism precepts from typological (mid-range) theories and the formal AML specification. In turn, this stage of analysis may raise new questions and generate new hypotheses, for which additional empirical evidence might be sought, different theories might become relevant, and the AML model specification might need to be altered. The crucial and perhaps the most problematic aspect here is to make sure that the causal powers inherent in the model structures and mechanisms are seen to facilitate and constrain the identified processes in a properly balanced fashion, that is, the powers neither determine the processes nor make them an unlikely outcome, always judged of course by the available evidence.

It would be extremely difficult, if not impossible, to design a complex model of a crisis episode without any reference to existing theoretical work or models. Nor would it be desirable or particularly constructive to take decisions about the overall model content and composition light-heartedly and in an arbitrary fashion. There are of course situations where little empirical evidence is available, let alone theoretical propositions, but as far as finance is concerned there is a good chance that most aspects of interest have been well-researched and that some foundational knowledge, even in limited form, is available. Theory-driven analysis serves several functions in our framework. First, the theoretical literature can provide us with competing models or explanations for a particular section of the available evidence, support theory development by eliciting new research questions and proposals, or help us reject untenable theory propositions. Second, narratives and descriptions of the episode will almost necessarily leave some gaps unfilled or parts of the episode vaguely defined. Theory may give us some indications of how we might reasonably and meaningfully extend the incomplete or add the missing parts. Also, available empirical research that either confirms, criticises, or rejects a theory – in general or for a particular area of application – will allow us to decide whether such a theory is suitable for our case. Third, categories and concepts used or developed in particular models, theories, and research paradigms particularly from the human sciences are potential candidates for our model ontology, that is, for the elements and relationships that need to be represented meaningfully in our MABS model. Fourth, the theoretically-oriented literature plays an active role at every stage of the structural analysis for all the reasons just mentioned.

The implementation is a key milestone in the MABS process, and the formal modelling language we a reusing sets a number of strict conditions and requirements on the kind of entities and mechanisms that it allows us to represent. The MAS-centric analysis has some parallel aims to the theory-driven analysis in that it encourages the use of AML concepts at an early modelling stage. Specifically, evidence from the knowledge base and selected theories (identified at the theory-driven analysis stage) are filtered by the AML specification to generate a preliminary idea of the kind of entities, features, and relationships that might find their way into the model. Moreover, and this is one side of the challenging task of incorporating the mechanisms and structures that wield the causal powers, the AML specification prescribes, recommends, and constrains, in a general way, key entities in the structural analysis in a way that these structures and mechanisms can be become operational at the level of implementation. It is to implementation where we turn next. Despite the fact that the physical and software implementation of an agent model is of key importance and an exigent task, we have opted for a formal implementation language for reasons of rigour and generality at the implementation level. In specific, we have chosen AML (Cervenka and Trencansky, 2007), an extension to the widely used UML2.0, since it incorporates all necessary MAS concepts and components, the language specification is very well documented, and the rigour and extensibility of UML2.0 translates directly into AML, leaving the door open for a more domain-specific specialisation (e.g. AML adapted to modelling financial markets). AML provides the tools to model social, interactional, behavioural, and mental (e.g. cognitive or emotional) aspects of the agent system. Social aspects that can be modelled include a system's organisational structure, social relationships, agent roles, and social interaction. Moreover AML can represent interactions between multiple entities, decoupled messaging, speech act extensions, perceiving acts, service provision, and mechanisms that allow for dynamic change, triggered by interaction, of structural features such as organisation or roles.

The previous stages of analysis will have produced a range of concepts, entities, mechanisms and so on that have to be represented at the implementation level. Since AML played a role in shaping the outcome of previous analysis stages, there is a good chance that much of what came out of these analyses can be implemented in a relatively straightforward manner. However, and here we refer back to our previous discussions, one aspect of implementation in the mechanism-centric world is delicate. The structures and, to some extent, the mechanisms are unlikely to pose a major challenge since AML provides the necessary tools to deal with these (although emergence is an issue here that we haven't addressed). However, the resulting processes generated and constrained by these structures and mechanisms will depend on how the latter are linked up or how they interact, some of which is beyond *direct* control of the modeller. We can have neither determinism, nor impossibility; the causal powers that emanate from the make-up of the model need to be able to facilitate or capacitate the observed processes consistent with the empirical and theoretical evidence. *Ex ante*, we might employ one of the several available process tracing methods to identify the mechanisms and complex interaction effects, or the conditions under which structures exert causal influence or mechanisms are active or triggered, or to map out the causal paths and determine the causal import of intervening variables, all of which will give us a better idea of the ways that structures and mechanisms incorporated into our model shape or affect event processes or structural change. *Ex post* we can simulate the model over a range of configurations to investigate how likely or enduring the resulting processes are compared to the evidence given to us.

11.4 Conclusions

Although agent-based simulation is widely hailed as a promising tool for social scientists, economists, and financial market researchers, it also poses some important methodological challenges. We have argued that agent-based models of macrofinancial episodes ought to be grounded in the alternative epistemology of critical realism and that they should take on board the methods and recommendations from qualitative research, in particular from case study research. Moreover, we have sketched the outline of a comprehensive framework to design and implement multi-agent models of financial markets.

The MABS framework proposed here[4] focuses on an area that has to date not attracted much attention from the agent simulation community, namely large-scale spatio-temporal processes in finance[5]. More specifically, such a framework is intended to help us shed light on complex issues such as the emergence of financial innovations in credit derivatives markets and the mounting interest in moving towards 'originate to distribute' type business models, or the role these events have played in the 2007 collapse of credit markets and institutional arrangements.

While epistemological and methodological considerations carried over from the more traditional financial disciplines have hindered progress on building complex MABS models that have practical relevance, such models are in fact necessary and called for in many areas of policy making, including financial stability. There have recently been concerted efforts to design model toolkits that thoroughly explore the systemic vulnerabilities which affect the stability and orderly functioning of financial markets, institutions, and infrastructures. The Bank of England for instance has a very high-priority commitment to develop a modelling framework that enables decision makers to deliver a much improved assessment of the vulnerability of firms, markets, and infrastructure to extreme shocks, gain a much deeper appreciation of the often contingent and latent contagion channels, and spot and tackle weaknesses and faults in the financial system early on (Jenkinson, 2007).

---

[4] More information, examples, and resources can be found on http://www.financialecology.info/remabs

[5] See however http://www.eurace.group.shef.ac.uk/ for an infrastructure for large-scale agent modelling of the European economy

Thus the challenge is on. Whether there will come a time when MABS meets that challenge and becomes a serious contender in the world of financial modelling depends of course on many considerations, some of which are more difficult to handle or control than others. We have argued that simulation research in finance should set its own methodological agenda, be mindful of prior research in the field without being kept hostage to it, embrace the historic turn and look out for synergies in qualitative research, and then 'get on with it'.

References

Allen A, Gale D (2007) Understanding financial crises. Oxford University Press, Oxford

Bhaskar R (1978) A realist theory of science. Harvester Press, Hassocks

Boero R, Squazzoni F (2005) Does empirical embeddedness matter? Methodological issues on agent-based models for analytical social science. JASSS 8, No. 4. Available online at http://jasss.soc.surrey.ac.uk/8/4/6.html

Cervenka R, Trencansky I (2007) The agent modeling language - AML. A Comprehensive Approach to Modeling Multi-Agent Systems. Birkhäuser, Basel

ECB (2008) Simulating Financial Instability. Proceedings of the Conference on stress-testing and financial crisis simulation exercises, Frankfurt am Main, 12-13 July 2008.

George A, Bennett A (2005) Case studies and theory developments in the social sciences. The MIT Press, Cambridge

Gilbert N (2007) Agent-based models. Sage Publications, London

Gupta V, Wang J (2004) From corporate crisis to turnaround in East Asia: a study of China Huajing Electronics Group Corporation. Asia Pac J of Manage, 21:213–233

Jenkinson N (2007) Developing a framework for stress testing of financial stability risks. Comments to the ECB High Level Conference on "Simulating Financial Instability" on 12-13 July 2007

Lawson T (1997) Economics and reality. Routledge, London

LeBaron B (2001) A builder's guide to agent-based financial markets. Quant financ 1:254–261

LeBaron B (2006) Agent-based computational finance. In: Judd K and Tesfatsion L (eds) The Handbook of Computational Economics, Volume 2, Elsevier, Amsterdam

McAdam D, Tarrow S, Tilly C (2001) Dynamics of contention. Cambridge University Press, Cambridge

Moss S (2008) Alternative approaches to the empirical validation of agent-based models. JASSS 11, No. 1. Available online at http://jasss.soc.surrey.ac.uk/11/1/5.html

Richiardi M, Leombruni R, Saam N, Sonnessa M (2006) A common protocol for agent-based social simulation. JASSS 9, No. 1. Available online at http://jasss.soc.surrey.ac.uk/9/1/15.html

Stern E, Sundelius B (2002) Crisis management Europe: an integrated regional research and training program. Int Stud Perspect 3:71–88.

Squazzoni F, Boero R (2007) The relevance of empirical foundations of agent-based simulations in the social sciences. Presented at the EMAEE 2007 Conference on "Globalisation, Services and Innovation: The Changing Dynamics of the Knowledge Economy", Manchester, 17-19 May.

Tay N (2006) Agent-based models of financial markets. In: Few C and Lee A (eds) Encyclopedia in finance, Springer, New York.

Upper C, Worms A (2004) Estimating bilateral exposures in the German interbank market: Is there a danger of contagion? Eur Econ Rev 48:827–849

Windrum P, Fagiolo G, Moneta A (2007) Empirical validation of agent-based models: alternatives and prospects. JASSS 10, No. 2. Available online at http://jasss.soc.surrey.ac.uk/10/2/8.html

Chapter 12
Explaining Equity Excess Return by Means of an Agent-Based Financial Market

Andrea Teglio, Marco Raberto and Silvano Cincotti

Abstract The observed values of equity premium, i.e., the excess return required by investors to hold equities instead of risk-free securities, are usually far larger than values foreseen by consumption capital asset pricing models with realistic aversion to risk. In order to tackle the problem form a different point of view, we present a model of an artificial economy, where different heterogeneous agents are interacting in the financial market. Households, firms, and a commercial bank make endogenous financial decisions which involve portfolio investments for households, capital structure and dividends policy for firms, and lending and borrowing rates for the commercial bank. In particular, households are characterized by behavioral rules derived from prospect theory. Labor income for households and earnings for firms are exogenous determined, according to independent stochastic processes. From simulation experiments it emerges that the model offers new interesting insights on the issue, confirming some hypothesis about the influence of households psychological features on the equity premium dynamics. In particular, the model shows that the length of time over which agents aggregate and evaluate returns, called evaluation period, has a significant role in explaining equity excess returns.

A. Teglio
DIBE-CINEF, University of Genova, Via Opera Pia 11a, 16145, Italy, e-mail: teglio@i2.unige.it

M. Raberto
School of Science and Engineering, Reykjavik University, Kringlan 1, 103 Reykjavik, Iceland, e-mail: raberto@ru.is

S. Cincotti
DIBE-CINEF, University of Genova, Via Opera Pia 11a, 16145, Italy, e-mail: cincotti@i2.unige.it

12.1 Introduction

The combination of high equity premium, low risk free rate, and smooth consumption, which has been observed in real data, is difficult to explain with plausible levels of risk aversion within the rational-expectations consumption-based asset pricing models, as first pointed out by the seminal paper of Mehra and Prescott (1985); see also Mehra and Prescott (2008) for a comprehensive survey.

This work aims to study the equity premium puzzle by means of an artificial financial economy where households behavior under uncertainty is modeled according to findings and assumptions of prospect theory (Kahneman and Tversky, 1979; Tversky and Kahneman, 1992). In particular, households financial preferences encompass important behavioral assumptions, namely, loss aversion (losses cause a disutility which is higher than the utility due to an equal gain) and mental accounting of portfolio gains and losses. A model by Barberis *et al.* (2001) showed interesting results in encompassing two prospect theory insights, i.e., loss aversion and reference points, within the standard agents' utility framework based on the intertemporal maximization of consumption. In this respect, the difference is that our approach is agent-based instead of being based on the analytically-tractable general equilibrium modeling paradigm and that we separate portfolio allocation decisions by households from their consumption decisions, which are modeled according to an empirically grounded rule-of-thumb (Deaton, 1992). Consumption decisions affect only the size of portfolio investment through the budget constraints, but not the weights of assets in the portfolio, see our former contribution (Cincotti *et al.*, 2007) to appreciate how the dynamics of consumption may affect asset prices in an agent-based model.

Households portfolio allocation is then modeled according to a preference structure based on a key prospect theory insight, i.e., the myopic loss aversion, which depends on the limited foresight capabilities characterizing humans when forming beliefs about financial returns. Benartzi and Thaler (1995) showed that loss aversion combined with mental accounting, i.e., frequent evaluation of portfolio, is able to explain the equity premium puzzle. That combination has been dubbed myopic loss aversion. It is worth noting that myopic loss aversion, due to its algorithmic nature, can be hardly addressed within a general equilibrium analytical model; the agent-based approach seems then to be the suitable framework to model this behavioral feature; see e.g. Tesfatsion and Judd (2006) for a recent survey on this approach.

Besides households, the model is populated by firms, a commercial bank, a central bank and a government, which interact with households through a multi-asset financial market. As portfolio allocation for households, also decisions by firms about dividends payment are endogenously determined and constrained by two exogenous stochastic processes, namely labor wages for households and returns on investments for firms. The Government and the Central Bank make fiscal and monetary policy decisions by setting tax and interest rates, respectively. A particular attention is devoted to the balance sheets, considering the dynamics of the financial flows among agents. Firms and bank's equity are divided into shares among households and traded in the financial market. Firms also recur to debt financing, asking for bank loans. The bank collects households deposit and accesses to the standing facilities of the central bank, that sets the interest rate. The government collect taxes and pays bonds coupons to bondholders.

The paper is divided into sections as follows. In Section 2, we present the agent-based model, Section 3 reports computational experiments, while the last Section presents our conclusions.

12.2 The Model

The distinctive feature of the model is that agents' financial decisions are endogenously determined by behavioral rules. Conversely, due to the absence of a labor market, the wage level is exogenously determined by means of a stochastic process.

Two nested time units characterize the time structure of the model, namely, the day, indexed by t, and the month, indexed by τ. Firms, the commercial bank, the Government and the central bank make decisions on a monthly basis, while the financial market operates daily as well as households' financial investment decisions. Each month is divided into a given number of days.

12.2.1 Firms

Each firm, indexed by j, is described by a balance sheet, characterized by a fixed endowment of physical capital A^j on the asset side, and both equity E_τ^j and debt D_τ^j as liabilities. Given the dynamics of debt, the book value of equity at any time τ is given by:

$$E_\tau^j = A^j - D_\tau^j, \tag{12.1}$$

where the endowment of physical capital is supposed to be measured in term of the same monetary numeraire of both equity and debt liabilities. Claims on firm equity capital and future profits stream are dividend into $\mathcal{N}^j$ shares, and traded by households in the stock market. The initial price of each firm share p_0^j is set to $E_0^j/\mathcal{N}^j$. The debt is a loan provided by the commercial bank.

Each firm is also characterized by a time-varying return on physical capital (ROA) ξ_τ^j, modeled according to an exogenous autoregressive stochastic process, i.e.,

$$\xi_\tau^j = \alpha \xi_{\tau-1}^j + \sigma \varepsilon_\tau^j, \tag{12.2}$$

where ε_τ^j is a Gaussian white noise, i.e., $\varepsilon_\tau \sim N(0,1)$, and α and σ are parameters uniform across firms, characterized by the usual constraints, i.e., $0 < \alpha < 1$ and $\sigma > 0$. Noises are uncorrelated across firms. The quantity $\xi_\tau^j A^j$ sets the earnings obtained by the firm, before interests and taxes. Net earnings π_τ^j are then given by:

$$\pi_\tau^j = \xi_\tau^j A^j - r_{\tau-1}^L D_{\tau-1}^j - T_\tau^j, \tag{12.3}$$

where T_τ^j are taxes paid to the Government on gross earnings, after deducting interest payment, and r^L is the commercial bank lending rate. A constant fraction θ^j of net earnings, if positive, is paid to shareholders by means of dividends, while the remaining part is retained to reduce debt. Per share dividends d_τ^j are then given by $\theta^j \max(\pi_\tau^j, 0)/\mathcal{N}^j$ and the dynamics of firm debt is determined as follows,

$$D_\tau^j = D_{\tau-1}^j - \pi_\tau^j + \mathcal{N}^j d_\tau^j. \qquad (12.4)$$

The book value of equity at month τ is then computed according to Eq. 12.1. $\mathcal{E}_\tau^|$ denotes the market value of equity at month τ and is given by $\mathcal{E}_\tau^| = \mathcal{N}^j p_\tau^j$, where p_τ^j is the stock price observed during the last day of month $\tau - 1$. In principle, the values of $\mathcal{E}_\tau^|$ and E_τ^j can be very different; however, fundamentalist trading behavior is based on the difference between stock market capitalization and the book value of equity, see paragraph 12.2.2, thus determining a not diverging behavior in the long run.

12.2.2 Households

Households are simultaneously taking the roles of workers, consumers and market traders. They receive an exogenously given labor income, if employed, and an unemployment subsidy from the government, if unemployed. Savings-consumption decision has been modeled within the framework of the buffer-stock theory of consumption (Carroll, 2001; Deaton, 1992). The main attractive feature of this approach is that consumption behavior can be articulated in very simple and intuitive terms. Consumers have a target level of cash on hand to income ratio $\bar{x}^i$, i.e., a target buffer stock of liquid assets with respect to permanent income, that they use to smooth consumption in the face of an uncertain income stream. If their buffer stock falls below target, their consumption level C_τ^i will be lower than their expected income and liquid assets will rise, while if they have assets in excess of their target they will spend freely and assets will fall.

Households can either invest their savings in the asset market, by trading stocks or bonds, or can put them in a saving account that pays a fixed, risk-free interest rate. They form beliefs about assets future returns considering a common forward horizon of three months. The implied idea is that households are able to foresee assets trends only for short periods of time, also if they plan to hold their assets for a longer period. Besides, each household i is characterized by an evaluation period ε_i which is a multiple of the forward horizon and is used to compute preferences and evaluate investments, see Benartzi and Thaler (1995) for a discussion about the importance of the evaluation period. Beliefs are formed according to three stylized behavior, i.e., random, chartist and fundamental. In particular, expected asset returns for each asset j, issued by the j-th firm, are given by a linear combination of three terms: a scalar random component $\rho_{j,i}^r$, a set of past returns $\rho_{j,i}^c$ computed in a backward time

12 Explaining Equity Excess Return by Means of an Agent-Based Financial Market

window, and a fundamentalist scalar term $\rho^f_{j,i}$. In order to compute the fundamental return, each household estimates a fundamental price

$$p_{j,i} = (E^j_\tau + \widehat{\pi}^j)/\mathcal{N}^j, \qquad (12.5)$$

taking into account the equity capital of firm j and the expected retained earnings $\widehat{\pi}^j$ in the forward horizon. Given the fundamental price and considering the last market price, the household derives the expected fundamental return $\rho^f_{j,i}$. Composing the three terms and adding expected cash flow yields $y^e_{j,i}$ (i.e., dividends for stocks and coupons for bonds), households determines a set of total expected returns $\rho_{j,i}$ as

$$\rho_{j,i} = \alpha^r_i \rho^r_{j,i} + \alpha^c_i \rho^c_{j,i} + \alpha^f_i \rho^f_{j,i} + y^e_{j,i}, \qquad (12.6)$$

where α^r_i, α^c_i and α^f_i are household's weights that sum to one. Then households build a normalized histogram $H[\rho_{j,i}]$ where the set of total expected returns is grouped in M_i bins. It is worth noting that a large number of bins M_i means that the household is more careful when examining the asset's past performance, taking into account more elements (it uses a higher resolution to build the histogram).

The histogram $H[\rho_{j,i}]$ can be seen as a prospect

$$\mathscr{P} = [\rho^H_{j,i}, p^H_{j,i}] \qquad (12.7)$$

where $\rho^H_{j,i}$ are the bins center values of the expected total returns histogram and $p^H_{j,i}$ are the associated probabilities, i.e., the level of the normalized histogram. If the evaluation period of the household is longer than the forward horizon used in the beliefs formation, it means that the prospect should be iterated accordingly. To this aim, we modelled how the structure of a prospect varies when the evaluation period changes. Following the concepts of myopic loss aversion, we introduce a new prospect $\mathscr{P}^n$ that represents the mental accounting (Benartzi and Thaler, 1995) of the agent when considering the risky investment, that means an n times iteration of prospect $\mathscr{P}$. Accordingly, the number of elements of the iterated prospect $\mathscr{P}^n$ will pass from M_i to $\mathscr{M}_i$. Thus, each household will face a new prospect

$$\mathscr{P}^n = [\rho^{H_n}_{j,i}, p^{H_n}_{j,i}] \qquad (12.8)$$

depending on its evaluation period.

In order to clarify this aspect we show one iteration of a belief structure where the household expects, for a given asset, a negative return of 1% with 50% probabilities and a positive return of 2% with 50% probabilities.

- Initial Prospect: $[(-0.01, 0.5), (0.02, 0.5)]$.
- Utility: $U = 0$ ($\lambda = 2$).
- Iterated Prospect: $[(-0.02, 0.25), (0.01, 0.5), (0.04, 0.25)]$.
- Utility: $U = 0.005$ ($\lambda = 2$).

It can be noted how, in the example, a single iteration can determine a raise in the utility of the asset, and therefore in the relative demand for it.

Prospect theory utility is defined over gains and losses, i.e., returns ρ^{H_n}, rather than levels of wealth. The value function for the ith household has the following form:

$$v_i(\rho_{j,i}^{H_n}) = \begin{cases} (\rho_{j,i}^{H_n})^\alpha & \text{if } \rho_{j,i}^{H_n} \geq 0, \\ -\lambda_i(-\rho_{j,i}^{H_n})^\beta & \text{if } \rho_{j,i}^{H_n} < 0, \end{cases} \quad (12.9)$$

where λ_i is the coefficient of loss aversion of household i.

Given the histogram of composed expected returns, the ith household may calculate the utility of asset j as,

$$U_{j,i} = \sum_{\mathcal{M}_i} p_{j,i}^{H_n} v(\rho_{j,i}^{H_n}), \quad (12.10)$$

where $p_{j,i}^{H_n}$ are the probabilities associated to $\rho_{j,i}^{H_n}$. These utilities are finally normalized and mapped into assets weights by means of a linear transformation. Once the assets weights are available, the household can build its desired portfolio and emit orders consequently. Orders are therefore submitted to a clearing house that determines assets new prices.

12.2.3 The Banking Sector

The commercial bank collects households deposits B_τ, provides loans L_τ to firms, and holds a buffer account C_τ at the central bank, which can be positive or negative. The commercial bank sets the lending rate r^L to firms according to a mark-up rule on the central bank policy rate r, i.e., $r_\tau^L = \mu_L r_\tau$, where $\mu_L > 1$ is the mark-up. The rate on households deposits r^B is determined by $r_\tau^B = \mu_B r_\tau$ where μ_B is lesser than one. Net earnings are given by

$$\pi_\tau^b = r_{\tau-1}C_{\tau-1} + r_{\tau-1}^L L_{\tau-1} - r_{\tau-1}^B B_{\tau-1} - T_\tau^j, \quad (12.11)$$

where T_τ^j are taxes as a fraction of gross earnings paid to the Government. The capital structure of the bank is composed by both equity capital E^b and debt financing, i.e., the Central Bank account and households deposits. The bank equity is divided into shares among households and traded in the financial market. Given the amount of L and B set by firms and households, respectively, and the dynamics of equity $E_\tau^b = E_{\tau-1}^b + \hat{\pi}_\tau^b$, where $\hat{\pi}^b$ are the retained earnings, the bank adjusts C according to the budget constraint $C_\tau = E_\tau^b + B_\tau - L_\tau$.

The central bank implements monetary policy decisions by means of a policy rate r_τ which is used both as a borrowing or lending rate for the commercial bank account.

12.2.4 The Government

The Government runs a financial budget. Income is given by a mixture of different taxation policies, that include taxes on households wages, on corporate earnings, and on capital income. Expenditures depend on unemployment benefits, that are expressed as a percentage of the current wage level, and on the interest rates on government debt. Taxation is adjusted adaptively in order to finance expenditures, running a zero budget target. The government may issue both short-term or long-term bonds in order to finance the budget deficit. Bonds have a face value which is paid at the maturity date, and pay fixed coupons to bondholders anchored to the central bank policy rate.

12.3 Simulation Results

The model described in section 12.2 has been simulated on a cluster of 24 parallel processors and the current section shows some of the computational results. In particular, we focused our investigation on the effects of households psychological traits (i.e., loss aversion and evaluation period) on the financial market. Loss aversion represents the idea that the damage caused by a loss overcomes the utility produced by an equally large gain. The evaluation period is the length of time over which an agent aggregates and evaluates returns, that in the case of the model coincides with the period an agent intends to hold an asset. We propose a set of experiments where we verify the effects of variations in households loss aversion and evaluation period on the financial market and, in particular, on the equity premium.

In order to interpret these results, the reader should reckon with two essential aspects of the model. The first aspect is that households have three different available solution for their financial investments: a risk free bank account, government bonds with a low risk profile, and firms stocks which are characterized by a higher risk. It is reasonable to expect that changes in households loss aversion or evaluation period should modify the distribution of agents wealth among these different assets. The second aspect to keep in mind is that the total number of assets in the model is constant over time, because the government does not issue new bonds during the simulation. Considered that the entirety of the assets is distributed among households, it is worth noting that, in average, the percentage of a specific asset in households portfolio turns out to be fixed, and in particular, this implies that, in average, the ratio between stocks and bonds in households portfolio is constant.

We present the results of computational experiments performed with a model populated by 2000 households, 3 firms, a commercial bank, a central bank and a government. Firms are endowed with a constant physical capital and make no new investments. They adopt different dividends pay-out strategies and use retained earnings to increase their equity base. Traders are divided among fundamentalists (10%), chartists (10%) and random traders (80%). The commercial bank dividend policy consists in paying 100% of its net earnings. The government applies a fixed

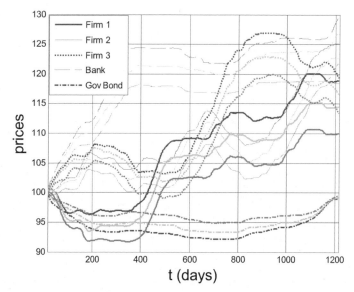

Fig. 12.1 Assets price level for different values of loss aversion: $\lambda = 1.5$ (black line), $\lambda = 2$ (light gray line), $\lambda = 2.5$ (dark gray line)

tax rate both on capital income of households and on corporate earnings of the firms and the bank. In the financial market 3 stocks and one government bond are traded. There is no issuing of new government bonds, and their maturity date is set at the end of the simulation.

Figure 12.1 shows assets prices trajectories for a sample simulation where the central bank interest rate is $r = 0.05$ and households evaluation period corresponds to 2 times the forward looking window, i.e., $\varepsilon = 6$ months. The three gray levels identify three different values for loss aversion: $\lambda = 1.5$ (black), $\lambda = 2$ (light), $\lambda = 2.5$ (dark).

Let us make some general observations on the plot. The government bond price is far less volatile than stocks prices; this is mainly due to the the bond face value, which strongly anchors the expectations of price dynamics, and to the bond cash flow, that corresponds to a constant coupon. The different price trajectories among firms depend on their different dividends pay-out strategies. If a firm pays high dividends, at the beginning of the simulation the price of its asset grows faster, but later this effect tends to be compensated by the higher equity base of firms that have a lower dividends pay-out policy, and whose price will raise pushed by fundamentalists traders. Finally, it is worth noting that the price processes exhibit jumps, crashes and periods of low volatility, realistic features which clearly depend on the interplay of random, chartist and fundamental strategies.

Figure 12.1 shows that in the presence of higher values of loss aversion stocks price levels decrease, while in contrast the price of the government bond grows. This effect is given by the higher volatility of stocks, because households overestimate

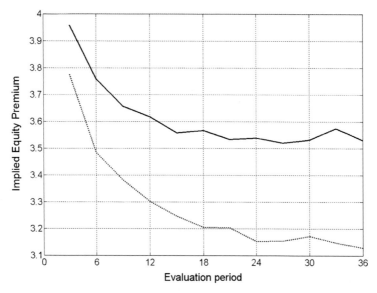

Fig. 12.2 The implied equity premium for different values of the evaluation period. Stocks/bonds ratio is 50% (dotted line) or 66% (continuous line)

the risk of loosing money, when their loss aversion is stronger, and therefore prefer to buy government bonds.

What we would like to show, with the help of Figures 12.2 and 12.3, is that the magnitude of the equity premium strongly depends on the evaluation period. Of course other variables, like the interest rate, or the loss aversion, contribute to set the equity premium, but this could have been easily foreseen. On the other hand, the dependence on the evaluation period is more subtle and interesting because, given certain standard values of the interest rate and of the loss aversion, the model permits to infer how frequently households are supposed to evaluate their investments in order to explain an observed empirical value of the equity premium. Using a similar approach Benartzi and Tahler find that, in order to justify the historical value of the equity premium, households should have an evaluation period of one year (Benartzi and Thaler, 1995).

Figure 12.2 shows a dotted line, referred to a stock/bonds ratio of 50% and a continuous one referred to a ratio of 66%. What emerges looking at the downward slope of these curves is the following concept: if we suppose that households have a shorter evaluation period, we should expect a higher equity premium in order to justify a given stocks/bonds ratio. This supports the thesis of myopic loss aversion as a determinant of a very high level of equity premium, because if a short evaluation is supposed, a high equity premium should be expected.

The continuous line (66% ratio) exhibits the same trend of the dotted (50% ratio) but for higher values of the equity premium. Obviously, if we suppose households holding more stocks, we should also expect the presence of higher stock returns attracting them.

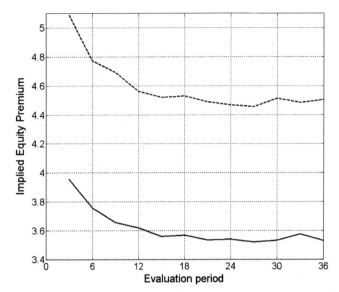

Fig. 12.3 The implied equity premium for different values of the evaluation period. Central bank interest rate is set at 3% (dashed line) or at 4% (continuous line).

Figure 12.2 compares the continuous line of figure 12.2, with a dashed one (66% stocks/bonds ratio) corresponding to a central bank interest rate that decreases from 4% to 3%. The increase of the equity premium is evident and it appears to compensate the decrease in interest rates, but it also should be remarked that this increase is slightly less that the reduction of the central bank policy rate (corresponding to 1%). This is probably due to second order effects that still has to be investigated. Actually, the impact of the interest rate on the equity premium is probably a thorny policy issue that we will take in more exhaustive consideration in future works.

Figure 12.4 has been obtained by averaging, for each evaluation period, the value of the equity premium using 10 different seeds for the underlying stochastic processes (ROA and wages). Again, it clearly shows that, if we suppose that households have a shorter evaluation period, we should expect a higher equity premium in order to justify a given stocks/bonds ratio in their portfolio.

12.4 Conclusions

The explanation of equity excess returns with respect to relatively risk free treasury bills has been quite a thorny issue for the economists since the problem has been raised from Mehra and Prescott. Among several possible solution that have been proposed in the last decades, Benartzi and Tahler suggested that the nature of the mental accounting that characterizes traders could explain this apparent contradiction derived from the rational expectations asset pricing approach. In particular,

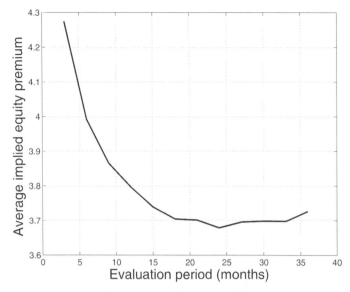

Fig. 12.4 The average implied equity premium for different values of the evaluation period.

according to Benartzi and Tahler, the length of time over which an agent aggregates and evaluates returns, called evaluation period, plays a crucial role in the matter.

The work presented in this paper is based on a agent-based model of a financial economy where the behavioral decisions of agents are endogenously taken. The model incorporates the main actors of the financial scenario, including households, firms, banks and government, and is particularly complete in terms their economic interaction.

A particular attention has been dedicated to the beliefs formation mechanism of households trading in the asset market, and on their preferences structure that is designed in order to take into account some of the main features of prospect theory.

The computational experiments presented in the paper show that households distinctive parameters (like loss aversion and evaluation period) clearly influence asset prices. In particular, the equity premium turns out to be appreciably dependent on households evaluation periods. In this respect, we show that households with a short evaluation period are not inclined to buy risky assets (firms stocks in our case) and tend to look for government bonds, or to keep their money in the bank account. This determines a strong presence of relatively non-risky assets in their portfolio, despite the higher returns of stocks. Our results are coherent with the analysis of Benartzi and Tahler and support their explication of myopic loss aversion as a determinant of the equity premium puzzle.

In the end, we would like to underline how our model is an open and complex framework where we plan to perform further scientific experiments in order to get a better comprehension of the economic key aspects underlying the dynamics of a financial economy.

Acknowledgements This work has been partially supported by the University of Genoa and by the European Union under IST-FET STREP Project EURACE.

References

N. Barberis, M. Huang, and T. Santos. Prospect theory and asset prices. *Quarterly Journal of Economics*, 116(1):1–53, February 2001.

S. Benartzi and R. H. Thaler. Myopic loss aversion and the equity premium puzzle. *The Quarterly Journal of Economics*, 110(1):73–92, 1995.

C. D. Carroll. A theory of the consumption function, with and without liquidity constraints. *Journal of Economic Perspectives*, 15(3):23–45, 2001.

S. Cincotti, M. Raberto, and A. Teglio. Towards an agent-based approach to financial economics: integrating houseolds' consumption and investment decision making. In *Proceedings of 2007 European Conference on Complex System*, 2007.

A. Deaton. Household saving in ldcs: credit markets, insurance and welfare. *The Scandinavian Journal of Economics*, 94(2):253–273, 1992.

D. Kahneman and A. Tversky. Prospect theory: an analysis of decision under risk. *Econometrica*, 47(2):263–292, March 1979.

R. Mehra and E. Prescott. The equity premium puzzle. *Journal of Monetary Economics*, XV:145–161, 1985.

R. Mehra and E. C. Prescott. The equity premium. ABCs. In R. Mehra, editor, *Hanbook of the Equity Risk Premium*, pages 1–36. Elsevier, 2008.

L. Tesfatsion and K. Judd. *Agent-Based Computational Economics*, volume 2 of *Handbook of Computational Economics*. North Holland, 2006.

A. Tversky and D. Kahneman. Advances in prospect theory: cumulative representation of uncertainty. *Journal of Risk and Uncertainty*, 5(4):297–323, October 1992.

Part V
Financial Markets

Chapter 13
Bubble and Crash in the Artificial Financial Market

Yuji Karino and Toshiji Kawagoe

Abstract In this paper, we investigate bubble and crash in the artificial financial market. Based on Ball and Holt (1998)'s experiment in the laboratory with real human beings, we create a simple artificial financial market using an agent-based simulation. In this simulation, we model each agent with different characteristics with respect to expectation formation and time discounting. We found that the case of prospect theory plus exponential time discounting is most resemble with the price dynamics found in Ball and Holt's experiment and real world price bubble and crash. We also examine whether Ball and Holt's and our experiment are really judged as a bubble and crush with some indexes so far proposed. Then, Ball and Holt' experimental result is judged not as a price bubble but as a divergent oscillation, while our result is judged as a bubble.

13.1 Introduction

In this paper, we investigate bubble and crash in the artificial financial market. Many attempts have been made to explain why and how bubble and crash occur in the financial market (see, for example, Friedman and Abraham, 2007). Due to the lack of relevant information about insider information of the business companies and psychological process of market participants, the problem is still unsolved. Thanks to the emergence of the artificial financial market approach, we can go one step further to investigate this very important topic in financial economics[1]

Y. Karino · T. Kawagoe
Future University - Hakodate, 116-2 Kameda Nakano cho, Hakodate, Hokkaido, 041-8655 Japan,
e-mail: g2108012@fun.ac.jp, kawagoe@fun.ac.jp

[1] Izumi and Ueda (2000) states that the research in an artificial financial market can be divided as follows.

1. Analyzing and replicating emergence phenomenon in real financial market (See Arthur *et al.*, 1997).
2. Verifying economic theory (See Chen *et al.*, 1999).
3. Using as an experimental tool for educational purpose (See U-Mart Project).

Our study is clearly classified with the type 1 study in these categories.

Based on Ball and Holt (1998)'s experiment in the laboratory with real human beings, we create a simple artificial financial market using an agent-based simulation. In this simulation, we model each agent with different characteristics with respect to expectation formation and time discounting. For expectation formation aspect, we compare traditional expected utility theory (see, for example, Schoemaker, 1982) with prospect theory (Kahneman and Tversky, 1979), which is currently a basis of behavioral finance theory. For time discounting aspect, we compare traditional exponential discounting formula with hyperbolic discounting formula (see Loewenstein and Prelec, 1991, and Frederick et al., 2002). Hyperbolic discounting formula is regarded more realistic than exponential one by researchers of behavioral finance.

So we have totally four different combinations of trading agent's characteristics. Then we test all these types of agents in an artificial financial market à la Ball and Holt (1998)'s experiment. Our results show that the combination of prospect theory and exponential discounting formula is the best fit to replicate a bubble and crash phenomenon in real financial market as well as in Ball and Holt's experiment.

Recently researchers studying behavioral finance advocate both prospect theory and hyperbolic discounting because each of them is regarded as a better model for replicating real human behaviors. But our simulation shows that only prospect theory is enough for replicating a bubble and crash in the financial market.

We also examine whether Ball and Holt (1998)'s experimental results are really judged as a bubble with some indexes so far proposed (See Takayasu and Takayasu, 1999, and Li et al., 2002). Then, Ball and Holt' experimental result is judged not as a bubble but as an divergent oscillation, while our result is judged as a bubble and crash.

The organization of the paper is as follows. Section 13.2 describes our settings of an artificial financial market. It also gives an overview of agents model and trading system. Section 13.3 presents our simulation results, and in Section 13.4 we conclude.

13.2 An Artificial Financial Market

13.2.1 Market Settings

In this section, we will explain the structure of an artificial financial market utilized in our agent-based simulation. The design of our artificial financial market is based on Ball and Holt (1998)'s experiment[2].

The market setting is as follows. Each trader begins the trade with three stocks, which can be bought or sold during 10 trading periods. They have $20 to finance trading. Traders can earn money from stocks in three ways. First, each stock held by an agent at the end of a trading period will pay a $1 dividend. Second, they can earn profits from buying and selling stocks. Third, any stock that still exists at the end of 10th trading period will pay $6. However, not every stock will survive until

---

[2] Their experiment is also a simplified version of Smith et al. (1988).

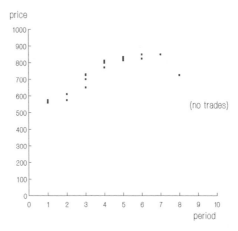

Fig. 13.1 Time series data of prices in Ball and Holt (1998)'s experiment

the last period. After the $1 dividend is paid at the end of each trading period, there is a 1/6 chance that any individual stock will be destroyed.

We can calculate the fundamental value of each stock as follows. The stock value at the start of period 10 is $6. Working backward to the beginning of period 9, the expected value in period 9 is calculated in this way:

$$V(9) = 1.00 + [5/6] * 6.00 = 6.00. \tag{13.1}$$

From this, we have a general recursive formula:

$$V(t) = 1.00 + [5/6] * E[V(t+1)], \tag{13.2}$$

where $E[*]$ means taking expectation. Solving this formula with initial value $V(10) = 6$, it become clear that the value should be $6 in all the periods. So in this simulation, the fundamental value of the stock is always $6.

For Ball and Holt (1998)'s experimental result, the trajectories of transactions prices is depicted in Fig. 13.1. In Fig. 13.1, prices are measured along the vertical axis in cent, and the 10 trading periods are shown on the horizontal axis. Compared these transaction prices with the fundamental value, we can see intuitively that a typical price bubble pattern appears. We will examine later in this paper whether their results are really judged as a price bubble.

As their experiment is a laboratory experiment with real human, it is not so clear what causes the bubble. To clarify the causes of price bubble in the experiment, we have to know the information about expectation formation and time discounting of each agent, but such an information is hardly available in the laboratory experiment. So, we decided to investigate what causes bubble in the financial market by using various types of artificial agents with respect to expectation formation and time discounting. So then, we will explain what types of agent we utilized in this simulation in the next subsection.

Table 13.1 The formulae for expectation formation and time discounting

Expected utility theory (EUT)	$w(q) = q$
Prospect theory (PT)	$w(q) = \frac{\delta q^\gamma}{\delta q^\gamma + (1-q)^\gamma}$
Exponential discounting (ED)	$V(x,t) = \frac{V(x,T)}{(1+r)^{(T-t)}}$
Hyperbolic discounting (HD)	$V(x,t) = \frac{V(x,T)}{1+(T-t)}$

q: objective probability, $w(q)$: probability weight function r: interest rate
$V(x,t)$: value function of the item x at time t, $\delta (0 < \delta \leq 2)$: attractiveness
$\gamma (0 < \gamma \leq 1)$: a curve rate, T: The terminal period, t: Current period

13.2.2 Trading Agents

In this section, we will explain the design of trading agents. First, we will show what kind of expectation formation and time discounting we utilized in our simulation. Next, the algorithm for buying and selling decision-making will be explained.

13.2.2.1 Expectation formation and time discounting

In our simulation, we compare two kinds of expectation formation. The one is the expected utility theory (EUT) and its probability weight function is linear (see Von Neumann and Morgenstern, 1944). The other is the prospect theory (PT) and its probability weight function is nonlinear (Kahneman and Tversky, 1979). Prospect theory was proposed initially as a refined model to overcome some paradoxical phenomena against EUT in decision-making under risk. For prospect theory, many variant specifications are proposed. Among these, we employ a flexible and tractable Gonzalez and George (1999)'s type as a bench mark.

As for time discounting, we compare exponential discounting (ED)[3] with hyperbolic discounting (HD)[4]. Though exponential discounting is the standard model in financial economics, many psychological experiments revealed that human beings in real world show some time inconsistent behaviors in the decision-making involving intertemporal choices. Then, hyperbolic discounting was proposed as a refinement for the exponential discounting formula.

Specifications of these models are also shown in Table 13.1. So we have totally four different types of trading agents; i.e., agent who follows (1) EUT and ED, (2) EUT and HD, (3) PT and ED, and (4) PT and HD. Among these, standard financial economic model is based on (1) EUT and ED, and behavioral finance model is based on (4) PT and HD. Then we test all these agents in an artificial financial market à la Ball and Holt (1998)'s experimental settings described in Section 13.2.1.

---

[3] See Samuelson (1937).
[4] See Thaler (1981).

13 Bubble and Crash in the Artificial Financial Market

Table 13.2 The algorithm for buying and selling decision-making

State of the market		type of order
Neither bid nor ask exists	$p(t) > E(t)$	sell in limit order
	$p(t) \leq E(t)$	buy in limit order
Only ask price exists	$Ask \leq E(t)$	buy in order without limit
	$p(t) < E(t) < Ask$	buy in limit order
	$E(t) < Ask \leq p(t)$	sell in limit order
Only bid price exists	$Bid \geq E(t)$	sell in order without limit
	$p(t) > E(t) > Bid$	sell in limit order
	$E(t) > Bid \geq p(t)$	buy in limit order
Both bid and ask prices exist	$Ask \leq E(t)$	buy in order without limit
	$p(t) < E(t) < Ask$	buy in limit order
	$Bid \geq E(t)$	sell in order without limit
	$p(t) > E(t) > Bid$	sell in limit order

Note : If an agent doesn't have any stock, it cannot make a selling order. Similarly, if an agent doesn't have enough money to buy, it cannot make a buying order.

Bid : the best bid price in the market
Ask : the best ask price in the market
p(t) : current market price
E(t) : expected discounted value of the stock

In each session of our simulation, we create totally 100 agents, and the parameter values of expectation formation and time discounting are given at random. We call each 10 trading period a session, then replicate such a session 30 times, and finally evaluate these results in taking the average over the 30 sessions.

13.2.2.2 The Algorithm for Buying and Selling Decision-Making

Agents make buying and selling orders according to its expected discounted payoff (Audet *et al.*, 2002). Agents can buy and sell only one stock for one period. Each agent makes an order sequentially according to a prespecified order. The order is determined at random in the beginning of each trading period. The algorithm of buying and selling decision-making is shown in Table 13.2. Initial value of market price is set to 600 cents. An agent who makes an order first has to make a limit order. The following agents compare the market price $p(t)$ with the expected discounted value of the stock, $E(t)$. If the expected value is larger than the market price, the agent decides to sell with a randomly chosen price between $E(t)$ and $p(t)$, and otherwise the agent decides to buy with a randomly chosen price between $E(t)$ and $p(t)$. Here $E(t)$ is defined as follows.

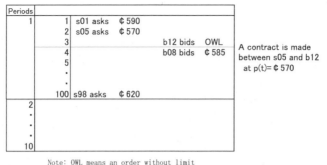

Fig. 13.2 Transaction example

$$E(t) = w\left(\left(\frac{5}{6}\right)^{10-t}\right)V(600,t) + \sum_{\tau=1}^{t} w\left(\left(\frac{5}{6}\right)^{\tau}\right)V(100,\tau). \quad (13.3)$$

The first term is expectation with respect to the probability weighted function w of the discounted value of the final period payment, 600 cents, at time t, and the second term is expectation with respect to the probability weighted function w of the discounted value of the sum of dividends, 100 cents, at time t. Next, if $E(t)$ is lower than the current best bid (the highest buying price in the market), the agent sells in order without limit when the best bit exists. Similarly, if $E(t)$ is higher than the best ask (the lowest selling price in the market), the agent buys in order without limit when the best ask exists. Otherwise the agent makes a limit order.

13.2.3 Transaction System

Contracts among agents are determined by an double auction (Friedman and Rust, 1993). As we have described above, each agent can make a limit order or an order without limit. If the contract is made with the limit order, transaction price is determined at the limit price. If the contract is made with the order without limit, transaction price is determined at the highest price in the market if the ask price is limit order or the lowest price if the bid price is limit order. For making a contract, the order without limit is given more priority than limit order.

Fig. 13.2 shows an example of this transaction process. Firstly, agent $s01$ whose expected discounted payoff $E(t) = 590$ makes a selling order in limit price chosen at random between 590 and 600 cents because its $E(t)$ is lower than the initial market price (600 cents). Here we assume that the limit order is determined at 590 cents. Then, agent $s05$ with $E(t) = 560$ makes a selling order in limit price chosen between 560 and 590 cents because its $E(t)$ is lower than the market price (600 cents) and lower than best ask (590 cents). Here the limit price is determined at 570 cents.

13 Bubble and Crash in the Artificial Financial Market

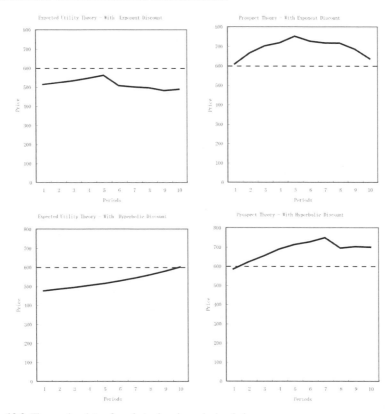

Fig. 13.3 Time series data of market prices in each simulation.

Then, agent $b12$ with $E(t) = 610$ makes a buying order without limit because its $E(t)$ is higher than best ask price (570 cents). As the selling order in limit price 570 cents is the lowest ask in this case, a contract is made at this price. Then, the market price is updated to $p(t) = 570$ cents.

13.3 Results

13.3.1 Simulation Results

Fig. 13.3 shows the time series data of average of stock prices in each simulation. As for the expectation formation, the figures in the left hand side are the cases of expected utility theory, and the ones in the right hand side are the cases of prospect theory. As for the time discounting, the top two figures are exponential discounting cases, and the bottom two are hyperbolic discounting cases. In each graph, vertical axis is price in cent, and horizontal axis is trading period.

First, note that there is none of expected utility theory cases that prices go beyond the fundamental value, $6 (600 cents). That is, no bubble is observed when agent follows expected utility theory as expectation formation. On the other hand, in prospect theory cases, prices go beyond the fundamental values in both cases, i.e. we safely say that price bubbles occur in these cases. So, we can conclude that which agent following prospect theory is a necessary condition for price bubble to occur in the financial market of Ball and Holt (1998)'s type.

Next, we can see that different time discounting formula makes price dynamics quite different in both expected utility and prospect theory cases. In general, we can say that (1) exponential time discounting gives single-peaked mountain-shaped price dynamics, (2) upward price dynamics occurs in hyperbolic discounting cases. Of these, the case of prospect theory plus exponential time discounting is most resemble with the price dynamics found in Ball and Holt (1998)'s experiment as well as in real world price bubble and crash.

13.3.2 Definition of Price Bubble

To the best of our knowledge, there is only a few index so far proposed to measure whether price bubble occurs. REE (Rational Expectation Equilibrium price) spread at time period t, Δ_t, is frequently used as an index that measures the degree of divergence from fundamental value. The definition of REE spread is as follows.

$$\Delta_t = \frac{1}{t} \sum_{\tau=1}^{t} (p(\tau) - V),$$

where $p(\tau)$ is market price at period τ and V is fundamental value.

Fig. 13.4 shows REE spread for each time period. The figures in the left hand side are the cases of expected utility theory, and the ones in the right hand side are the cases of prospect theory. On the other hand, the top two figures are exponential discounting cases, and the bottom two are hyperbolic discounting cases. In expected utility cases, REE indx are always negative, while the index are almost always positive in prospect theory cases. Among expected utility cases, when agents follows hyperbolic time discounting, REE index shows upper trend slightly, while when agents follows exponential time discounting, no such upper trend is observed. In both prospect theory cases, upper trend of REE index are clearly observed.

Next index is proposed by researchers in econophysics (Takayasu and Takayasu, 1999, and Li et al., 2002). Based on price adjustment dynamics in the market, their index measures the degree of stability of the market price. The adjustment dynamics of the market is characterized by the following three dynamical equations.

First, it is assumed that change of the market price is proportional to the difference between the current market price, $p(t)$, and the market equilibrium price $V(t)$

13 Bubble and Crash in the Artificial Financial Market

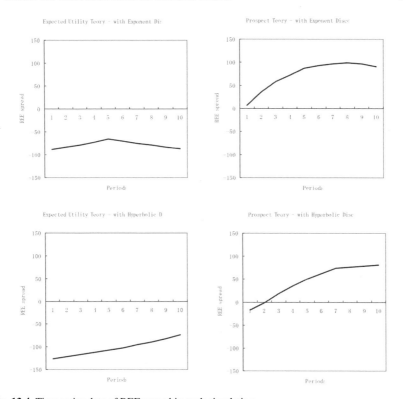

Fig. 13.4 Time series data of REE spread in each simulation.

(in our case, fundamental value). So, we have the following equation.

$$p(t+\Delta t) - p(t) = -A(t)(p(t) - V(t)) + f(t), \qquad (13.4)$$

where $A(t)$ is the inverse of the elasticity of the market price, which means a strength of the tendency toward equilibrium price, and $f(t)$ is a random shock. Then, dynamics of market equilibrium price $V(t)$ is assumed as follows.

$$V(t+\Delta t) = V(t) + f^*(t) + B(t)\{p(t) - p(t-\Delta t)\}, \qquad (13.5)$$

where $B(t)$ is a measure of sensibility of the trading agents for the change of the market price, and $f^*(t)$ is a random shock.

For obtaining a stationary state, we assume that $f(t) = f^*(t) = 0$ and that coefficients A and B are constant, then following equation is derived from equations (13.3) and (13.4).

$$\delta p(t+\Delta t) + (A-1)\delta p(t) - AB\delta p(t-\Delta t) = 0, \qquad (13.6)$$

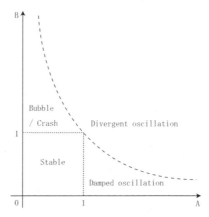

Fig. 13.5 Classification of price dynamics.

where $\delta p(t)$ is $p(t) - V(t)$. State of this dynamics can be classified into the following four types. See also Fig. 13.5.

1. Stable: In this area, as coefficients A and B are small, market price $p(t)$ converges to equilibrium price $V(t)$.
2. Bubble / crash : In this area, as coefficient A is small but B is large, equilibrium price $V(t)$ changes with great degree than market price $p(t)$, while as A is small, magnitude relation between $p(t)$ and $V(t)$ is preserved. As a result, market price increases or decreases exponentially in short period.
3. Damped oscillation : In this area, as coefficient A is large but B is small, $p(t)$ asymptotically converges to $V(t)$ with oscillation. So, dynamics of the market price shows damped oscillation.
4. Divergent oscillation: In this area, as both coefficients A and B are large, both $p(t)$ and $V(t)$ are unstable and diverge with large oscillation.

Table 13.3 shows the average values of coefficients A and B for our simulation and Ball and Holt (1998)'s experiment. In both expected utility theory cases, price dynamics is classified as Stable. On the other hand, in both prospect theory cases, these cases are classified as Bubble / crash. However, contrary to our intuition, Ball and Holt's experiment results is classified not as Bubble but as Divergent oscillation.

Table 13.3 Estimated values of coefficients of A and B in the price dynamics.

Coefficients	Ball and Holt	EUT and ED	EUT and HD	PT and ED	PT and HD
A	1.196	0.2842	0.2669	0.4133	0.2657
B	2.1817	0.792	0.3001	1.837	1.4199
State	Divergent oscillation	Stable	Stable	Bubble / Crash	Bubble / Crash

13 Bubble and Crash in the Artificial Financial Market

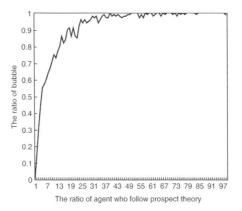

Fig. 13.6 The frequency of the occurrence of bubble conditional on the ratio of the agents who follow prospect theory

13.3.3 Sensibility Analysis

We also investigate the situation where agents who follow prospect theory enter into the population that consists of the agents who follow expected utility theory. Then we change the ratio of the prospect theoretic agents in the population to see how many such agents are necessary for the emergence of bubble and crash. In Fig 13.6, the frequency of the occurrence of bubble is depicted. The vertical axis is frequency of the occurrence of bubble and the horizontal axis is the ratio of the agents who follow prospect theory in the population. This graph shows that it is enough to occur price bubble in the market that the ratio pass over only 30 percent.

13.4 Conclusion

In this paper, we tried to replicate bubble and crash in the real world by utilizing agent-based simulation. We examined various combination of expectation formation and time discounting of trading agents, and found that the market with agents who follow prospect theory and exponential discounting tended to cause a bubble and crush. We also investigate whether Ball and Holt (1998)'s experimental result is really judged as a bubble with some indexes. Our result indicated that their experimental result cannot be classified as a bubble. In fact, according to the index we used, Ball and Holt' experimental result was an divergent oscillation rather than a bubble and crush. We also examine how much prospect theoretic agents is necessary for emergence of bubble and crush in the financial market, we found that only 30% of those agents is necessary.

References

Arthur, W.B., J. H. Holland, B. LeBaron, R.G. Palmer, and P. Tayler (1997) "Asset Pricing Under Endogenous Expectations in an Artificial Stock Market," In The Economy as an Evolving Complex System, 2, pp. 15-44.
Audet, M., T. Gravelle, and J. Yang (2002) "Alternative Trading Systems: Does One Shoe Fit All," Bank of Canada Working Paper.
Ball, S. and C. Holt. (1998) "Classroom Games: Speculation and Bubbles in Asset Markets," Journal of Economic Perspectives, 12, pp. 207–18.
Chen, S.C, C.-H. Yeh, and C.-C. Liao (1999) "Testing the rational expectations hypothesis with the agent-based model of stock markets," In Proceedings of ICAI99, pp. 381–387.
Friedman, D. and R. Abraham (2007) "Bubbles and Crashes: Escape Dynamics in Financial Markets," SCCIE WORKING PAPER, 7.
Friedman, D. and J. Rust (1993) The Double Auction Market: Institutions, Theories, and Evidence. Addison-Wesley.
Frederick, S., G. Lowenstein, and T. O'Donoghue (2002) "Time discounting and time preference: A critical review," Journal of Economic Literature, 40, pp. 351–401.
Gonzalez, R. and W. George (1999) "On the Shape of the Probability Weighting Function," Cognitive Psychology, 38, pp. 129–166.
Izumi, K. and K. Ueda (2000) "Introduction to Artificial Financial Market," Magazine of Academic Society in Population Intelligence, 15, pp. 941–950.
Kahneman, D. and A. Tversky (1979) "Prospect Theory: An analysis of Decision under Risk," Econometrica, 47, pp. 263–291.
Laibson, D (1997) "Golden Eggs and Hyperbolic Discounting," The Quarterly Journal of Economics, 112, pp. 443–77.
Li, M.G, A. Oba, and H. Takayasu (2002) "Parameter Estimation of a Generaized Langevin Equation of Market Price," In Empirical Science of Financial Fluctuations - The Advent of Econophysics, Springer Verlag.
Loewenstein, G. and D. Prelec (1991) Choices Over Time, Russell Sage Foundation.
Samuelson, P (1937) "A note on measurement of utility," Review of Economic Studies, 4, pp. 61–155.
Schoemaker P. J. H (1982) "The Expected Utility Model: Its Variants, Purposes, Evidence and Limitations," Journal of Economic Literature, 20, pp. 529–563.
Smith, V, L., L. Suchanek, and W. Arlington (1988) "Bubbles, Crashes and Endogenous Expectations in Experimental Spot Asset Markets," Econometrica, 56, pp. 1119–1151.
Takayasu, H. and M. Takayasu (1999) "Critical fluctiatopms of demand and supply," Physica, 269, pp. 24–29.
Thaler, R, H (1981) "Some Empirical Evidence on Dynamic Inconsistency," Economic Letters, 8, pp. 201–207.
U-Mart Project Web Site, http://www.u-mart.org/.
Von Neumann, J. and O. Morgenstern (1944) Theory of Games and Economic Behavior, Princeton University Press.

Chapter 14
Computation of the Ex-Post Optimal Strategy for the Trading of a Single Financial Asset

Olivier Brandouy, Philippe Mathieu and Iryna Veryzhenko

Abstract In this paper we explain how to compute the maximum amount of money one investor can earn in trading a single financial asset under a set of trading constraints. The obtained algorithm allows to identify the ex-post optimal strategy $S*$ over a set of (known) prices, which is unconventional in Finance. We deliberately adopt such a simplification to show that *even* if one posits a complete knowledge of the "future", the determination of $S*$ is far from triviality, especially in a framework with transaction costs. We review some solutions that are exponential and propose a new polynomial algorithm. Among others, our results shed light on a not so documented aspect of financial markets complexity, propose an absolute boundary for the profits one can realize in a specific time window and against which any investment strategy can be gauged.

14.1 Introduction

Obtaining good (even acceptable) performances with active management strategies in finance is a fairly hard challenge. Theoretically speaking, tenants of the efficient market hypothesis claim, with strong arguments, that a rational investor should stick to a simple *"Buy and Hold"* strategy for a correctly diversified portfolio (see for example Sharpe, 1991, or Malkiel, 2004). Said differently, an active management,

---

O. Brandouy
LEM, UMR CNRS-USTL 8179,Université de Lille 1, France, e-mail: `olivier.brandouy@univ-lille1.fr`

P. Mathieu
LIFL, UMR CNRS-USTL 8022,Université de Lille 1, France, e-mail: `philippe.mathieu@lifl.fr`

I. Veryzhenko
LEM & LIFL,,Université de Lille 1, France, e-mail: `iryna.veryzhenko@univ-lille1.fr`

linked to hypothetical managerial skills for *market timing* or *stock picking* would mostly generate transaction costs without real benefit. Nevertheless, this debate is far from being closed (see for example Brock *et al.*, 1992, Shen, 2003) as well as the whole discussion on the profitability of active *versus* passive portfolio management styles.[1] In this paper, we do not discuss the opportunity of such active strategies based on *market timing* nor we describe an operational process allowing fund managers to find out how to identify states in the market where "buying" or "selling" is particularly appropriate. We also depart from the "portfolio-choice" framework in focusing on the trading of a single financial asset (for example, a market index tracker). Thus, we neither propose a method that ranks various active strategies in terms of risk-return performance (although our framework might be extended to this bi-criteria approach).

First of all, one well established reason for doubting that active strategies can earn excess risk-adjusted returns is linked to the high level of randomness of financial markets. In other terms, these markets are hardly predictable. On the other hand, we stress in this paper that the realization of these excess returns is complex task due to an additional computational issue. Our contribution is focused on this additional complexity that renders smart trading particularly tough. We especially show that *even if* future prices were perfectly predictable, determining how to behave optimally with respect to this knowledge can be extremely complicated, and, in many cases, intractable. Therefore, the bottom-line of this research is to identify an optimal strategy $S*$ providing the maximum profit one can obtain in trading a single financial commodity, under a predefined set of constraints and with a complete knowledge of its price motion.

This question will be called the $S*-determination$ problem. We show that this latter problem is far from being trivial, even if this target immediately evokes many popular models that most frequently prove to be completely inefficient. Among others, we provide a new algorithm that decreases the complexity class of this problem and propose a new method delivering *an absolute performance indicator* geared towards the evaluation of a wide range of trading strategies. This algorithm establishes, for any series of prices, a boundary (in terms of maximum profit) that has not been characterized before to our knowledge.

One potential application for this algorithm could be to estimate the *ex-post* performance of investment strategies or fund management principles that are formulated *ex-ante* the realization of prices over which these are deployed. It also provides an alternative to the relative rankings of investment strategies delivered by traditional methods.

This paper is organized as follow. We first formalize the framework we start from and define explicitly the $S*-determination$ problem. In a second section we present the mathematical frameworks related to these questions as well as a new algorithm geared at identifying the $S*$ strategy. In a last section we illustrate this

---

[1] See for example Jensen, 1968 for an argumentation about why actively managed funds should be avoided and, among others, Elton *et al.*, 1996 or Carhart, 1997 for empirical arguments or other developments.

latter algorithm and provide some practical implementations to gauge the absolute performance of a few trading strategies.

14.2 Elements of the Game and Formalizations

Consider the idealised situation in which one investor has the complete knowledge of a finite series of financial prices $\overrightarrow{p} = \{p_t | t \in [0,n]\}$, for example daily closing prices for one given stock, index or fund. This investor is also supposed to have the opportunity to rebalance his holdings at each date t without affecting these prices.[2] These holdings at date t are a combination of cash C_t and a number of assets A_t : $H_0 = A_0 + C_0$.

Let us now define the rules of a game for this investor, or said differently, a series of rules constraining her behaviour:

- At time $t = 0$, the initial holdings of any agent is only composed of cash (C_0); they do not hold any asset ($A_0 = 0$).[3]
- Having the knowledge of the entire (future) price series, the idealised investor must decide for each date $t \in (1,n)$ one specific action that can alter her holdings: "buy", "sell" and "stay unchanged", resp. coded B, S and U. In other terms, the investor has to compose a "sentence" of size n using characters in B, S, U. The interpretation of each of these actions is as follows:

  Buy: One can write B *if and only if* $H_{t-1} = C_{t-1}$. If B is written at date t, all the investor's cash is converted into assets (delivering a new quantity for $A_t \neq 0$). Assuming transaction costs at a $c\%$ rate,

  $$A_t = \frac{H_{t-1}}{p_t \times (1+c)}. \tag{14.1}$$

  Additionally, the first character in any sentence must be a B.

  Sell : if and only if $A_{t-1} \neq 0$, the investor can write S and convert her position into cash. Considering an identical rate of transaction costs c,

  $$C_t = A_{t-1} \times (p_t \times (1-c)). \tag{14.2}$$

  Stay unchanged: Whatever the nature of H_{t-1} (cash or assets), she can also decide to write U and let her position unchanged at date t : $H_t = H_{t-1}$.

- This "sentence" is one investment strategy S_i over $\overrightarrow{p}$ chosen in a set of strategies $\{S\}$.

Each instance S_i can be gauged in terms of relative performance with regards to another strategy $S_{j, j \neq i}$ (and reciprocally). What we propose here is to determine

---

[2] In other terms, we posit a price-taker framework.
[3] At date $t = 1$ –beginning of the game we posit C_1 to be equal to the first price of the considered time series.

an absolute performance indicator for each of these instances with respect to the best possible strategy in $\{S\}$ defined in terms of maximum profit $H_{t+n} - H_t$. As we will show later, this best strategy, denoted $S*$, is relatively easy to identify when transaction costs are not implemented. On the contrary, when transaction costs alter profits, this identification is far more complex.

A trivial method to solve this identification problem when transaction costs are implemented is to generate all possible sentences and to compute the net earning one can obtain with these to identify $S*$. This set is of finite size 2^n, thus exponential. As we will show now, there are at least two ways to improve efficiently the computation of the optimal strategy $S*$, whatever the level of transaction costs is. One is based on a simplex method; the other is based on the search of an optimal path in an oriented bipartite network.

In this section, we show that the identification of $S*$ can be described as a linear programming problem with a classical Simplex solution. Unfortunately, this approach is relatively inefficient since the Simplex algorithm is non-polynomial in the worst case (*i.e.*, one can lack the necessary computing resources to obtain a result as soon as the size of $\vec{p}$ becomes important.)

14.2.1 Initial Simplification

Before formal results are presented, we introduce two theorems that are necessary to simplify the problem we face and to find an efficient solution.

First simplification: *filtering the price sequence.*

Let's consider the price vector $\vec{p}$ consisting of three consecutive prices p_t, p_{t+1}, p_{t+2} and the function

$$R(x,y) = y(1-c) - x(1+c). \tag{14.3}$$

In equation 14.3, the $R(x,y)$ function computes net earnings of successive "buy" and "sell" actions with $c\%$ transaction costs. In this equation, x denotes the price at which one buys and y the price at which one sells. By definition, y appears later in the time sequence than x. We show that $S*$ in $\vec{p}$, as defined page 173, can be identified in a subset of $\vec{p}$ denoted $\vec{fp}$[4] consisting of the extreme points in the price sequence (peaks and troughs) ignoring any intermediary points (here, p_{t+1}).

In the first step of the demonstration, we assume $p_{t+2} \geq p_{t+1} \geq p_t$. Therefore $R(p_t, p_{t+2}) > R(p_t, p_{t+1})$ and $R(p_t, p_{t+2}) > R(p_{t+1}, p_{t+2})$. In this latter case, p_{t+2} is a "peak" while p_t is a trough.

Theorem 14.1. *Ignoring intermediary points:*
To identify $S*$, p_{t+1} can be ignored.

Proof. Proof by contradiction:
If it were not the case, since it is not allowed to buy and sell at the same date:

---
[4] *i.e.* $\vec{fp}$ for "filtered $\vec{p}$"

$$R(p_{t+1}, p_{t+2}) > R(p_t, p_{t+2}). \tag{14.4}$$

Therefore: $p_{t+2}(1-c) - p_{t+1}(1+c) > p_{t+2}(1-c) - p_t(1+c)$, which can be simplified: $p_{t+1} < p_t$.
By definition $p_{t+1} > p_t$ which is contradictory with the preceding result.
Q.E.A ✻

Notice that the same demonstration can be made by analogy in the case where $p_{t+2} \leq p_{t+1} \leq p_t$.
As a consequence, if p_{t+1} is an "intermediary" point as exposed previously, it can be ignored to identify S∗. In other terms, if one considers a complete price sequence $\overrightarrow{p}$, only peaks and troughs should be selected to identify S∗. This sub-series made of peaks and troughs will be denoted $\overrightarrow{fp}$.

Lemma 14.1. *No inclusion of losses : to identify S∗, one can ignore all situations in which $R(x,y) < 0$*

Literally, no trade with negative net earnings can be included in the best strategy.

Determining two vectors of prices for *potential* "buy" and "sell" actions.

From theorem 14.1 we know that it is necessary and sufficient to focus on extremum points in the price sequence. We now show that $\overrightarrow{fp}$ can itself be sliced in two separate sub-vectors of "peaks" and "troughs". These sub-vectors define two independent sets of potential "buy" and "sell" positions in $\overrightarrow{p}$ (resp. denoted $\overrightarrow{fp_B}$ and $\overrightarrow{fp_S}$).
To introduce the next theorem, let's consider four consecutive prices p_t, p_{t+1}, p_{t+2}, p_{t+3} such as $p_{t+1} > p_t$, $p_{t+3} > p_{t+2}$ and $p_{t+2} < p_{t+1}$.[5]

Theorem 14.2. *To identify S∗, none of the $\overrightarrow{fp_B}$ can receive a S and none of the $\overrightarrow{fp_S}$ can receive a B.*

Proof. (i) Since $p_{t+1} > p_t$, it is obvious that $R(p_t, p_{t+3}) > R(p_{t+1}, p_{t+3})$. Then $(p_t \leftarrow B) \succ (p_{t+1} \leftarrow B)$
(ii) Similarly, since $p_{t+2} < p_{t+1}$ it is obvious that $R(p_{t+2}, p_{t+3}) > R(p_{t+1}, p_{t+3})$. Then $(p_{t+2} \leftarrow B) \succ (p_{t+1} \leftarrow B)$
From lemma 1 we know that the situation in which $p_{t+3} < p_t$ must be ignored; Therefore, from (i), (ii) and lemma 1 :
– whether $(p_t \leftarrow B)$ and $(p_{t+1} \leftarrow U)$ from (ii); thus $(p_{t+2} \leftarrow \{U\}$ and $(p_{t+3} \leftarrow \{U \text{ or } S\})$
– or $(p_t \leftarrow U)$ and $(p_{t+1} \leftarrow U)$; thus $(p_{t+2} \leftarrow \{U \text{ or } B\})$ and $(p_{t+3} \leftarrow \{U \text{ or } S\})$
$(p_t, p_{t+2}) \leftarrow \{U \text{ or } B\})$; $\overrightarrow{fp_B} = \{p_t, p_{t+2}\}$
$(p_{t+1}, p_{t+3}) \leftarrow \{U \text{ or } S\})$; $\overrightarrow{fp_S} = \{p_{t+1}, p_{t+3}\}$
Q.E.D ∎

---
[5] In this latter case, we do not consider the situation in which $p_{t+2} > p_{t+1}$ since it is equivalent to the initial simplification case exposed previously.

This theorem does not state where to buy or to sell in the subsets $\overrightarrow{fp_B}$ and $\overrightarrow{fp_S}$ in order to identify $S*$. It uniquely states that it is not worth buying in any element of $\overrightarrow{fp_B}$ and selling in any element of $\overrightarrow{fp_S}$.

14.2.2 A Linear Programming Method For the Identification of S*

A first way to solve the $S*$ determination problem is to use a linear programming method. The basic idea here is to maximize an objective function subject to a set of constraints formalizing the rules in which this problem is embedded. We now expose how this program should be written.

Let denote $a(i,j)$ the potential benefit one can obtain if $p_i \in \overrightarrow{fp_B}$ and $p_j \in \overrightarrow{fp_B}$. Notice $a(i,j)$ is computed using equation 14.3. Let $x(i,j)$ be a dummy variable coding 0 or 1 that will be used to ignore (resp. to identify) transitions between any two prices p_i and p_j. If $p_i \leftarrow$ (S or U) or $p_j \leftarrow$ U then $x(i,j) = 0$, else $x(i,j) = 1$. Using these notations, the identification of $S*$ can be done solving the following linear problem:

$$\max \sum_{(i,j) \in \overrightarrow{fp_B} \cup \overrightarrow{fp_S}} a(i,j) x(i,j), \tag{14.5}$$

$$\sum_{(i,j) \in S*} x(i,j) \leq n, \tag{14.6}$$

$$\sum_j x(j,i) + x(i,j) \leq 1, \ \forall i \in \overrightarrow{fp_B}, \tag{14.7}$$

$$x(i,j) + \sum_{k=1}^{j} +x(i+1,k) \leq 1, \ \forall i \in \overrightarrow{fp_B}, j \in \overrightarrow{fp_S}, \tag{14.8}$$

$$x(i,j) + \sum_{k=j+1}^{n} x(i+1,k) \leq 2, \ \forall i \in \overrightarrow{fp_B}, j \in \overrightarrow{fp_S}, \tag{14.9}$$

$$0 \leq x(i,j) \leq 1, \ \forall i \in \overrightarrow{fp_B}, j \in \overrightarrow{fp_S}. \tag{14.10}$$

Literally, the objective function (14.5) states one seeks to maximize the total benefits in trading (that is, to identify $S*$). Constraint (14.6) implies that $S*$ cannot be composed of more than n prices while constraint (14.7) imposes the uniqueness of the solution. Constraints (14.8)-(14.9) do not allow backwards in the price series with respect to their sequential ordering. Constraint (14.10) requires that $x(i,j) = 1$ if a trade occurs between position i and j in $\overrightarrow{f_p}$, otherwise, $x(i,j) = 0$. This latter constraint means that the problem can be solved by simplex method.

However, it is virtually impossible to explicitly enumerate all these constraints as soon as $\overrightarrow{f_p}$ is of moderate size. It is also recognized that the simplex algorithm is exponential even if it can be solved for certain cases in polynomial time. We now propose to develop an alternative approach for this problem allowing an efficient

14.2.3 Embedding the Identification of S∗ in a Graph Structure

Let each price in $\vec{fp}$ be depicted as a vertex in a network. $Card(\vec{fp}=k)$. Each vertex is indexed with an integer with respect to its place in the price series. We show now how to construct a bipartite, oriented and weighted network $\mathcal{N}(E,\vec{fp_B},\vec{fp_S})$ connecting points in $\vec{fp_B}$ and $\vec{fp_S}$.

Definition 14.1. Let $\aleph_X$ the subset of vertices succeeding vertex X. The network $\mathcal{N}$ is defined by the successors of each vertex.

Graph construction:

The initial situation from which we start is : $\forall X \in \vec{fp}, \aleph_X = \emptyset$. From this situation, two different kind of edges can be build :

Trading edge $(TE_{i,j})$: for any two vertices $i \in \vec{fp_B}$ and $j \in \vec{fp_S}$, vertex $j \in \aleph_i$ if and only if :

1. $j > i$ (which ensure temporal consistency)
2. c being the rate of transaction costs,

$$R_{i,j} = p_j(1-c) - p_i(1+c) \geq 0. \qquad (14.11)$$

Forward edge $(FE_{m,n})$: for any two vertices $m \in \vec{fp_S}$ and $n \in \vec{fp_B}$, $n \in \aleph_m$ if and only if :

1. $n > m$ (which ensure temporal consistency)
2. $\aleph_n \neq \emptyset$

Notice we impose a "time consistency rule"[6] to avoid backward connections in this bipartite oriented graph. This means that a starting vertex p_{t+k} cannot be connected to a ending vertex p_{t+l} with $k \geq l$.

The rule presented in equation 14.11 obviously determines a profit as in equation 14.3. For any two vertices, these profits can be analyzed as weights for the corresponding edges of $\mathcal{N}$.[7]

Consequently, we receive a balanced, bipartite, weighted and directed network. We propose to interpret weights computed with 14.11 as distances between two vertices in the following proposition:

---

[6] Similar to equations 14.8 end 14.9
[7] Provided these profits are positive.

Proposition 14.1. *S∗ in this framework is a* longest path problem.

We now introduce a third theorem that is necessary to understand that $S*$ is equivalent to a longest path.

Theorem 14.3. *For $c > 0$ and any four consecutive prices p_t, p_{t+1}, p_{t+2}, p_{t+3} in a filtered price series such as $\overrightarrow{fp}$ (see section 14.2.1) with $R(t,t+1) > 0$, $R(t,t+3) > 0$, $R(t+2,t+3) > 0$:*
$R(t,t+1) + R(t+2,t+3) > R(t,t+3)$

Proof.
$-p_t(1+c) + p_{t+1}(1-c) - p_{t+2}(1+c) + p_{t+3}(1-c) > -p_t(1+c) + p_{t+3}(1-c)$
$p_{t+1}(1-c) > p_{t+2}(1+c)$
$p_{t+1}/p_{t+2} > (1+c)/(1-c)$
$c > 0 \Rightarrow (1+c)/(1-c) > 1 \Rightarrow p_{t+1}/p_{t+2} > 1$ by definition.
Q.E.D ■

In the construction of $\mathcal{N}$, one can notice that the number of edges depends upon the level of transaction costs c:

- The greater c the fewer the number of edges in $\mathcal{N}$ and the easier the solution of the problem as well.
- When $c \rightsquigarrow 0$, the graph tends to be more and more connected. For a specific threshold θ, $\mathcal{N}$ is fully connected (with respect to the time consistency rule). θ can be computed linearly; for any two consecutive prices in $\rightarrow fp$, $p_t \in \overrightarrow{fp_B}$ and $p_{t+1} \in \overrightarrow{fp_S}$:

$$\theta = min(p_{t+1} - p_t)/(p_{t+1} + p_t). \tag{14.12}$$

When $c < \theta$, $\mathcal{N}$ in fully connected. In this situation, we can derive from theorem 14.3 the following corollary:

Corollary 14.1. *No backtracking:* $\forall c < \theta, S* = \sum_{i=1}^{k-1} TE_{i,j=(i+1)}$.

In other terms, when $c < \theta$, it is proved that $S*$ is the path connecting all the edges as they appear in sequential order (see figure 14.1(a)). $S*$ connects all vertices. When $c > \theta$, this result cannot be established. For example, in figure 14.1(b), we posit c such as $R(t+2,t+3) < 0$; one cannot follow a path in the price series connecting all vertices: many potentially interesting paths can be discovered (see

(a) Complete Bipartite Network : no backtracking

(b) Uncomplete Bipartite Network : backtracking

Fig. 14.1 Illustration of the "No Backtracking Theorem"

figure 14.1(b)) [8] and therefore must be compared to determine $S*$. One way to tackle this *backtracking* problem could be to compute all possible paths, which would deliver again an exponential algorithm.

We now show how we decrease the complexity class of this problem using a new algorithm to determine $S*$ in this graph formalism.

14.2.4 The $S*-determination$ Algorithm

In this section we develop a new algorithm adapted to the determination of $S*$ in the graph framework. This algorithm derives from a technique exposed by Floyd (1969). Floyd originally developped this algorithm for finding a shortest path between every pair of vertices in a graph. This algorithm is transformed and adapted to fit our constraints.

We first introduce some notations and present the Floyd shortest-path algorithm; then we expose the $S*-determination$ algorithm itself.

Identifying the shortest path in $\mathcal{N}$ with the Floyd algorithm

Let $d^k{}_{ij}$ denote the length of a shortest path from vertex i to vertex j, where only the first k vertices are allowed to be intermediate vertices. If no such path exists, then let $d^k{}_{ij} = \infty$. Using this definition of $d^k{}_{ij}$, it follows that $d^0{}_{ij}$ denotes the length of a shortest path from i to j that uses no intermediate vertices.

Let $d^0{}_{ii} = 0$ for all vertices i. Furthermore, $d^n{}_{ij}$ represents the length of a shortest path from i to j.

Let D^k denote the $n \times n$ matrix whose i, j^{th} element is $d^k{}_{ij}$. If we know the length of each edge in the graph, then we can determine matrix D^0. Ultimately, we wish to determine D^n, the matrix of shortest path lengths. The Floyd shortest-path algorithm starts with D^0 and computes D^1 from D^0. Then, the algorithm calculates D^2 from D^1. This process is iterated until D^n is computed from D^{n-1}. Notice that only the elements of matrix $D^k - 1$ are needed to compute the elements of D^k. Moreover, these computations can be performed without reference to the underlying graph (see Minieka, 1978).

Therefore, the Floyd shortest-path algorithm can be expressed in pseudo-code as in Figure 14.2.

Notice it is established that the total amount of computation required by the Floyd algorithm is proportional to $2n^3$, which means that the Floyd algorithm requires $O(n^3)$ running time.

---

[8] Two of these paths are presented, one with plain lines, the other with hash lines. As soon as a TE between consecutive vertices is missing this kind of situation may appear.

```
for k=1 to n
    for i=1 to n
        for j=1 to n
            path[i][j]=min ( path[i][j], path[i][k]+path[k][j]
```

Fig. 14.2 Floyd Algorithm

Operating the $S*-$determination algorithm

If the Floyd algorithm is performed with a maximisation procedure instead of a minimisation operation, this latter algorithm will produce the *maximum longest path* which corresponds, in our formalism, to $S*$.

The pseudo-code of the $S*-$*determination* algorithm is presented in Figure 14.3.

```
for k=1 to n
    for j=k to n
        path[0][j]=max ( path[0][j], path[0][k]+path[k][j])
```

Fig. 14.3 $S*-$*determination* algorithm

We now present in details how the $S*-$*determination* algorithm can be used for finding the longest path between the initial edge in $\overrightarrow{fp_B}$ to any other edge in $\mathcal{N}$. One has to follow three steps:

1. Setting-up D^0
   a. Number the vertices of $\mathcal{N}$ $1,...,n$.
   b. Determine the matrix D^0 whose i,jth element equals the length of the longest arc from vertex 1 to vertex j if any.
   c. If no such arc exists, let $d_i^0 j = -\infty$.
   d. Let $d_i^0 i = 0$ for each i.

2. Recursive computations of D^k
   a. For $k = 1,...,n$ successively determine the elements of D^k form elements of D^{k-1} using the following recursive formula:
   $$d_i^k j = \max\{d_{ik}^{k-1} + d_{kj}^{k-1}, d_{ij}^{k-1}\}. \tag{14.13}$$
   b. As each element is determined, record the path that is represents.

3. Upon termination, the i,jth element of matrix D^n represents the length of a longest path from vertex i to vertex j.

The optimality of this algorithm follows inductively from the fact that the length of a longest path from i to j allowing only the first k vertices to be intermediate vertices must be the bigger of (i) the length of a longest path from i to j allowing only the first $k-1$ vertices to be intermediate vertices and (ii) the length of a longest path from i to j that allows only the first k vertices as intermediate vertices and uses the kth vertex once as an intermediate vertex.

The complexity of the $S*-determination$ algorithm has now to be established. One must remember the Simplex solution is exponential and so is the simple enumeration of all possible paths in the network. In our case, the longest path from vertex 1 to every other vertex is searched. During the first iteration one must go over $n-1$ vertices. Hence, $n-1$ additions and $n-1$ minimisations have to be processed. Thereby, the first iteration consists of $2(n-1)$ operations. Similarly, it is possible to show that the second iteration consists of $2(n-2)$ operations and so on.

$$\sum_{i=1}^{i=n} 2(n-i) = n(n-1). \tag{14.14}$$

Thereby, the $S*-determination$ algorithm requires $O(n^2)$ running time and therefore $\in PSPACE$. Notice this new algorithm clearly outperforms the other existing techniques presented previously and decreases the complexity class of our problem.

Notice we should also build other longest-path algorithms able to take into account the constraints we face on solutions such as the one proposed by Dantzig, 1966 or Shier, 1973. The first solution is similar to Floyd, 1969 although the order in which the calculations are performed is different. The second algorithm, known as the *double-sweep algorithm*, finds the k shortest path lengths between a specified vertex and all other vertices in the graph and can also be tuned to our problem.

14.3 Numerical Illustrations and Conclusive Remarks

In this paper, we show that the best investment $S*$ can be defined using a linear programming framework and solved with a Simplex approach. Nevertheless, if this method is theoretically correct, it suffers from severe limitations in terms of computability (the underlying algorithm being non-polynomial in the worst case). We therefore propose to embed this question in a graph theory framework and show that the determination of the best investment behavior is equivalent to the identification of an optimal path in an oriented, weighted, bipartite network.

We now propose one application of the $S*-determination$ algorithm using the daily Dow-Jones index from 2/12/1980 to 20/02/2009 (*i.e.* 7156 observations). No one can seriously defend the idea that one particular economic agent could be able to predict with some accuracy the next 7156 closing prices of the Dow-Jones Index by Dec., 2nd, 1980. However, notice that *even if* it were possible (which is most improbable), taking advantage of this knowledge under the constraints enumerated in

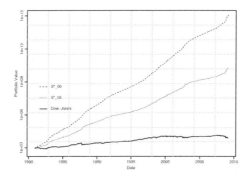

Fig. 14.4 $S*$ with resp. $c = 0\%$ and $c = 0.5\%$ and Dow-Jones Index (y axis in log scale)

section 14.2 would also be extremely difficult, if simply possible, without using the $S*-determination$ algorithm. With this algorithm, we determine the best behavior with transaction costs c respectively at 0% and 5%. The maximum wealth one should obtain in these two cases is bigger than 1.10E+15 in the first case and bigger than 1.83E+10 in the second case. These figures seem extraordinarily important: one must keep in mind they are simply impossible to obtain because of the global unpredictability of the market motions at date $t+n$ with regards to the available information at date t. In figure 14.4 we present the evolution of an investor's wealth adopting $S*$ in both contexts of transaction costs and absence of transaction costs.

Nevertheless, on shorter horizons, some agents claim they can produce such predictions or at least detect specific dates where it is worth entering the market or shorting their positions. For example, technical traders claim they can observe signals or patterns in past prices associated with potential market reversals.

Among others, one popular model for technical traders consists in comparing two moving averages based on past prices.[9] One is computed over a long range period L, the other on a short time window s. If MM_s crosses MM_L from the top to the bottom, some technical traders would predict a further decrease in stock prices and try to sell immediately their holdings. On the contrary, if these moving average cross from the bottom to the top, the signal would be seen as "buy" signal.

In Figures 14.5 we generated such signals using the same Dow-Jones data; we also computed the corresponding investment positions one idealized technical trader would have obtained in managing her investment positions with respect to the obtained signals.[10] Notice that the "moving average" strategies provide a perfect instanciation of the "rules of the game" presented in section 14.2 since it delivers alternatively "buy" or "sell" signals. Concerning the *signals* sub-figures, we only present a limited time window for graphical clarity reasons. The *investment positions*

---

[9] The moving average with i lags MM_i is equal to $(1/i)\sum_i (p_{(t-i+1)})$.

[10] To make this computations, we endowed this idealized trader with an amount of cash equal to the Dow-Jones index value at date 1 (974.40).

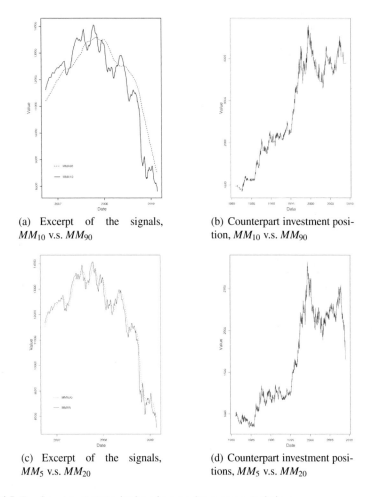

(a) Excerpt of the signals, MM_{10} v.s. MM_{90}

(b) Counterpart investment position, MM_{10} v.s. MM_{90}

(c) Excerpt of the signals, MM_5 v.s. MM_{20}

(d) Counterpart investment positions, MM_5 v.s. MM_{20}

Fig. 14.5 Two investment strategies based on moving averages techniques

subfigures report the evolution of an investor's wealth using these signals in context of 0% transaction costs.

In Figure 14.5(a), MM_s is based on 10 days while MM_L is based on 90 days. With these values we can generate 135 signals in the complete time window. In Figure 14.5(c), these moving averages are respectively based on 5 and 20 trading days which delivers 469 signals.

One can easily rank these strategies in term of overall profitability : MM_{10} v.s. MM_{90} seems to perform better than MM_5 v.s. MM_{20} in this price sample since the first one bears an overall profitability of +299% (terminal value of investments = 3886.36) against +70% for the second (terminal value : 1657.18). In any case, one can also measure how far these two strategies are from the optimum $S*$. Here, notice none of these strategies is interesting in any manner in *absolute terms* while the first one appears to outperform the second one in *relative terms*.

Said differently, whatever the relative performance of any trading strategy, $S*$ can be used to gauge its absolute performance.[11]

Notice again that resolving the $S*-determination$ problem does not give insights on the kind of signals one should feed automatic trading systems with, nor indicate a plausible behavior for any real-world investor. It simply establishes a boundary that was, to our opinion, largely unknown, and proposes a reference in terms of maximum-profit trajectory against which any population of investment trajectories can be gauged.

References

Brock, W., J. Lakonishok, and B. LeBaron (1992): "Simple Technical Trading Rules and the Stochastic Properties of Stock Returns," *Journal of Finance*, 47(5), 1731–1764.

Carhart, M. M. (1997): "On Persistence in Mutual Fund Performance," *Journal of Finance*, 52(1), 57–82.

Dantzig, G. (1966): "All Shortest Routes in a Graph," in *Theory of Graphs, International Symposium, Rome*, pp. 91–92. Gordon and Breach, New York.

Elton, E. J., M. J. Gruber, and C. R. Blake (1996): "The Persistence of Risk-Adjusted Mutual Fund Performance," *Journal of Business*, 69(2), 133–57.

Floyd, R. (1969): "Algorithm 97, Shortest Path Algorithms," *Operations Research*, 17, 395–412.

Jensen, M. C. (1968): "The performance of mutual funds in the period," *Journal of Finance*, 23, 389–416.

Malkiel, B. (2004): "Can Predictable Patterns in Market Returns be Exploited Using Real Money?," *Journal of Portflio Management*, 30, 131–141.

Minieka, E. (1978): *Algorithms for Networks and Graphs*. Marcel Dekker.

Sharpe, W. F. (1991): "The Arithmetic of Active Management," *The Financial Analysts' Journal*, 47(1), 7–9.

Shen, P. (2003): "Market timing strategies that worked – based on the E/P ratio of the S&P 500 and interest rates.," *Journal of Portfolio Management*, 29, 57–68.

Shier, D. (1973): "Iterative Methods for Determining the k Shortest Paths in a Network," *Networks*, 6, 205–230.

---

[11] In our example, both MM_{10} v.s. MM_{90} and MM_5 v.s. MM_{20} were poor performing strategies. A simple Buy and Hold behavior "buying" the market at date 1 and selling it at date 7156 would have performed far better than these two moving average techniques. Nevertheless, one can suppose some automatic trading strategies could outperform this B&H strategy, for example in a context of high frequency data.

Chapter 15
A Generative Approach on the Relationship between Trading Volume, Prices, Returns and Volatility of Financial Assets

José Antonio Pascual and Javier Pajares

Abstract The relationship among trading volume, prices, returns, etc., of financial assets is complex, but its proper understanding may be of great influence on the development of financial theories. Throughout the last half century, many researchers have faced the issue, but a general consensus has not been reached. In this paper, we propose to use agent based simulation, a methodology that allows us to recreate different scenarios to reproduce the observed behavior in financial markets.

15.1 Introduction

Following previous studies focused on the analysis of some of the representative statistical patterns of real financial markets, such as: the behavior Integrated order one (I(1)) of the price series, excess kurtosis in returns and volatility clustering (see Pascual and Pajares, 2007; Pascual *et al.*, 2006), in this work we study the presence of another regularities in the behavior of financial markets, as is the correlation between the trading volume, prices, returns and volatility.

During the last decades, many financial economists have analyzed these kind of relations, usually by means of empirical data, but a general consensus about their existence and causes has not been reached. In this paper, we explore how a generative approach contribute to explain these phenomena, by means of the simulation based on agents of a financial market. Karpoff (1987) shown the importance of the understanding of the relationship between stock price and volume. He gives us four reasons:

J.A. Pascual
Grupo InSiSoc, Departamento de Organización de Empresas y C.I.M., Universidad de Valladolid.
Paseo del Cauce 59, C.P. 47011, Valladolid, Spain, e-mail: pascual@eis.uva.es

J. Pajares
Grupo InSiSoc, Departamento de Organización de Empresas y C.I.M., Universidad de Valladolid.
Paseo del Cauce 59, C.P. 47011, Valladolid, Spain, e-mail: pajares@eis.uva.es

- The empirical relationship between returns and volume helps us to discriminate between different theories on how information is disseminated in financial markets.
- The implementation of the tests and the validity of the inferences depend on the joint distribution of returns and volume, for event studies that use combinations of returns and volume data to infer the information content of the event.
- The relationship among return and volume is critical in the evaluation of the distribution of returns themselves.
- The technical analysis is based on the statistical structure of volume and returns, so that a better understanding of these structure will provide better results to us.

Once revealed the importance of the understanding of the relation between stock prices and volume, we proceed to comment the structure of this article. The paper has been structured according to this scheme. At first, after a brief review of some of the preliminary work on the subject, and once covered the findings made by them, we see that the absence of a common agreement on certain results, stimulates the search of new routes of study that contribute new results, which leads us to propose a simulation based on agents. Then describe the methodology used in this analysis, along with some of the technical study, which will move to the next section that sets out the results.

15.2 Historical Precedents and Motivation

Since the pioneering work by Osborne (1959), in which changes in the prices of financial assets were modeled according to a lognormal distribution with dependent variance on the volume traded, there have been many studies on the empirical relation among the prices of financial assets, and the volume traded for them (See Granger and Morgenstern, 1963; Rogalski, 1978; Smirlock and Starks, 1985, 1988; Hiemstra and Jones, 1995, for more details).

Epps (1975, 1977) and Karpoff (1987) reflects the previous analysis and conclusions of the principal authors on this topic. Most authors support the existence of a contemporary positive correlation among trading volume of the assets and the absolute value of changes in their prices. Karpoff (1987) showed that the ratio of volume against price changes (from indices) in absolute value was higher for up-ticks transactions than for downticks, but other authors found the opposite.

Copeland (1976) and Lakonishok and Levi (1982), among others, look for the existence of a contemporary relation among price increases and volume traded, through different causal contrasts. Some authors hold that increases in the traded volume, for motives of speculation, cause greater volatility in prices. Therefore, it is possible to establish a cause effect relation, among volume and returns. Others, nevertheless, establish the opposite relation.

The association between volatility and volume was analyzed by Karpoff (1987) and Brock and LeBaron (1996) among others. Recently, stochastic time series models of conditional heteroscedasticity have been applied to analyze this relation

(Lamoureux and Lastrapes, 1990). They conclude that there is evidence of strong relation between volume and volatility.

Since the publication of the work by Karpoff (1987), the existing relation between volume and volatility remains a topic of ongoing controversy. There are basically two theories that explain the empirical evidence on the existence of positive correlation between volume and volatility in prices.

The first one (Clark, 1973) is based on Mixture of Distribution Hypothesis. According to this theory, volume and volatility depend together on a variable, which can be interpreted as the amount of information flowing into the market, so that both variables change contemporary opposite to this variable. The other one is based on the Sequential Information Models by Copeland (1976), who suppose the existence of a series of intermediate balances throughout the day and the balance observed at the end of the day is the result of the evolution of the first ones.

This article discusses an aspect still not analyzed in previous financial literature, at least up to where our knowledge comes: The influence of the composition of the market, that is, the agents' proportion behaving with different trading rules.

Therefore, with the study of the behavior of the markets we understand that they can raise two complementary approaches. The first one, is eminently descriptively in that it is attended principally to the study of the characteristics, proper of the financial series, correlations between variables, relations of lead and lag, etc. The other one, is an experimental or generative approach, in that the understanding of the behavior is looked to level added of the market departing from the individual behavior of the agents who integrate it.

15.3 Methodology

In Pascual and Pajares (2007), and Pascual *et al.* (2006), we saw the market model, and that there was a relationship between the market composition and the major statistical patterns of behavior observed in real markets. Now, we analyze the influence of the market composition in the relations between the price series, volume and volatility.

In particular we analyze what happens in the market (price-volume, return-volume, volume-volatility, relations) as the proportion of technical agents (TF) increases with respect to a market populated entirety by fundamental agents (BF), and then analyze that it happens when the psychological (KT) ones burst on the market together with the fundamental ones.

15.3.1 The ISS-ASM Model

The model has been inspired in the one by LeBaron *et al.* (1999), a reference to study artificial financial markets. It's in the line of other models (see Samanidou *et al.*, 2007, for a review of the literature).

The ISS-ASM is the InSiSoc Arificial Stock Market, a agent based model that have been programmed in Java, inside the InSiSoc Group in the University of Valladolid.

As in the SF-ASM, a single risky stock is traded and it is also possible to borrow/lend money at the risk free interest rate. The amount of dividends paid by the risky stock follows an order one auto-regressive model. Prices emerge endogenously as a consequence of bids and offers. We have extended the SF-ASM in order include more investors behaviour patterns:

- Fundamental investors. (BFagents) They process all the market's relevant information and form expectations about the value of future price + dividend. Then, they buy/sell shares depending on these expectations, their confidence about the forecast, and depending on their risk aversion as well. Following LeBaron *et al.* (1999), the demand of shares for agent i at time t can be computed as:

$$x_{i,t} = \frac{E_{i,t}[p_{t+1} + d_{t+1}] - p_t * (1 + r_f)}{\lambda * \sigma^2_{i,t,p+d}}, \qquad (15.1)$$

  where item p_t and d_t are prices and dividends in period t, E means expectations, λ is a measure of the risk aversion, and σ^2 is the forecast variance.
  According to the eq. (1), agents build their demands comparing their expectations about the future value of $p_{t+1} + d_{t+1}$ with the money they will get investing p_t monetary units at the risk free interest rate. Agents, then correct this amount, taking into account the variance of their forecasts and their risk aversion. For this reason, the higher the value of λ, the lower the demand is; in this way, agents behaving with less aversion to risk will try to form portfolios with a higher proportion of risky assets than no risky assets.

- Psychological investors. (KTagents) Their behaviour is similar to the one exhibited by the fundamental investors but their risk aversion changes over time depending on their previous wealth, as suggested in some experiments by Kahneman and Tversky (1979). In particular, can take a couple of values: agents move to the higher one when the 10 periods average wealth of an agent is lower than his/her present wealth; the lower one is used otherwise.
  This means that if an agent has lost money with respect to previous periods, he/she will become more averse to risk and the value of λ will be increased.

- Technical traders. (TFagents) They take their decisions using technical rules. In particular they compute moving averages with different periods and the use the crosses between them as trading signals. technical trades compute a low order (MA(l)) and a high order moving average (MA(h)) of prices; they buy shares when the MA(l) crosses from down to up to the MA(h) and sell stocks if MA(l) crosses the other one from top to down.

15.3.2 Dataset.

The dataset (10000 data) analyzed is composed of the series of market prices and trading volume gained through the simulation of different market compositions with the ISS-ASM model. The showed results are the average values after different simulations with different random seeds.

15.3.3 Cross-Correlations and Causal Relation

First we analyze the relation among price and volume, changes in prices (by means of returns) and the volume and finally between volume and volatility, simply by calculating cross-correlation coefficients (Corr)

With these data we will develop graphs of Corr $[P_t, V_{t-j}]$, Corr $[R_t, V_{t-j}]$, Corr $[SR_t, V_{t-j}]$. Where $[P_t, V_t, R_t, SR_t]$, are respectively the price, volume traded, return, and square return in the t instant, which will be used as a measure of volatility. The cross-correlations are use to analyze the contemporary correlation the price and different delays and advances of the volume, as well as of returns and volatility, also for different advances and delays of the volume (indicated these delays/advances for the value of j).

But besides this contemporary relation between $[P_t, V_t, R_t, SR_t]$, later we will extend the analysis examining the causal relation. To verify the causality is important because it may help us better understand the market microstructure. I'll use the Granger causality test (Granger and Morgenstern, 1963).

Then we want to examine the dynamic relationship or causal relation. The correlation between variables might suggest the presence of causality. Therefore we investigate this hypothesis using the Granger Causality Test. Based on the premise that the future can not cause the present or the past.

The causality tests allow us to know which variable causes the other. The tests are normally conducted by testing whether there is a relation between the lagged values of the two series. Consequently, to test whether volume leads return or return leads volume, we employ Granger causality tests, as has been done in previous research on developed markets (e.g., Smirlock and Starks, 1985, 1988; Assogbavi *et al.*, 1992).

15.4 Conclusions - Results

In this section we represent and analyze, the influence of the market compositions in the relations price-volume, return-volume, and volatility-volume by mean of the cross-correlations between $[P_t, V_t, R_t, SR_t]$, and Granger Causality test.

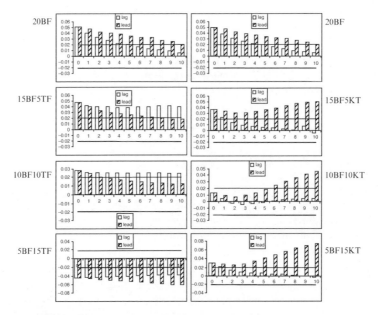

Fig. 15.1 Cross-Correlation Price-Volume for different market compositions. BF and TF (left side) and BF and KT (right side) $[P_t, V_{t-j}]$ lags, $[P_t, V_{t+j}]$ leads

15.4.1 Price-Volume Relationship

From Fig. 15.1 we can deduce that for all combinations of fundamental and technical agents analyzed, there is a small but significant contemporary correlation between price and trading volume. The correlation is even weaker, but significant, for the correlations among prices and volume lags and leads.

Focusing on market's compositions:

- A market populated only with fundamental agents shows a rapid exponential decay by the time in cross-correlations for lags and leads.
- As the number of technical increases the significant correlations for the delays becomes almost constant.
- The positive correlation becomes negative when the technical agents are in greater proportion on the market.

On the other hand, when we analyzed the presence of psychological agents, we observed that the decay of the significant delays is much faster, ceasing to be significant before, as it increases the agents' proportion of this type. With the advances the opposite happens, instead of being more rapid the decay, we appreciate that as the proportion of technical increases, there is an exponential increase in the level of significance, though in the first advances they are insignificant.

15 A Generative Approach on the Relationship between V-P-R-SR of Financial Assets

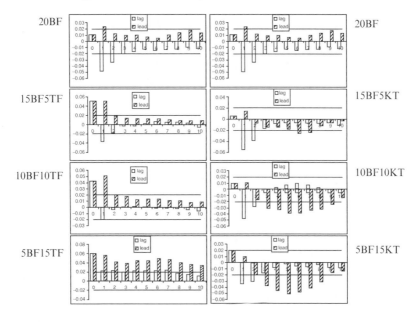

Fig. 15.2 Cross-Correlation Return-Volume for different market compositions. BF and TF (left side) and BF and KT (right side) $[R_t, V_{t-j}]$ lags, $[R_t, V_{t+j}]$ leads

15.4.2 Return-Volume Relationship

From Fig. 15.2 we can see that for 20 fundamental agents there is no positive significant correlation between returns and trading volume. But there is a small significant correlation between returns and one lead (positive) and three delays (negative) of the volume.

When the technical agents come into the market, there is contemporary significant positive correlation between returns and volume. The relation among returns and lags and leads in volume continues though weak, except for the case of 15 technicals, in which the advances are, even up to the order 10, highly significant.

When the psychological sharing the market with the fundamentals, we see that the correlation structure between return and volume for different delays is not affected by the presence of these KTagents. However, leads move from positive correlations but not significantly, to negative not significant when there are few psychological, but becoming more significant as their proportion is increasing.

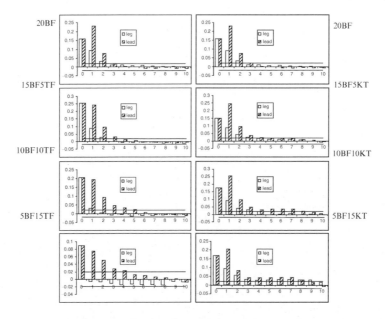

Fig. 15.3 Cross-Correlation Volatility-Volume for different market compositions. BF and TF (left side) and BF and KT (right side) $[SR_t, V_{t-j}]$ lags, $[SR_t, V_{t+j}]$ leads

15.4.3 Volatility-Volume Relationship

Fig. 15.3 shows that there is a positive relationship between contemporary trading volume and volatility for different combinations of fundamental and technical agents.

Moreover, there is a significant positive relationship between the delayed volume and volatility when all the agents are fundamental or are dominant, the significance decreases as the ratio of technical agents increases, and even disappear when these dominate the market. Among anticipated volume and volatility, there is a significant positive correlation practically independent of the tested combination.

It also shows a clear asymmetry in the levels of significance, around zero, of the cross-correlations

The positive relation among contemporary trading volume and volatility is also appreciated for different combinations of fundamental and psychological agents. Furthermore, the positive significant relationship between retarded volume and volatility and between anticipated volume and volatility exists independently of the analyzed combination, and the number of significant leads and lags grows with the psychological agents' proportion.

It also notes that there is asymmetry in the cross-correlation around zero, as in the previous case. This agrees with the results of Brock and LeBaron (1996).

15.4.4 Causal Relationship

The contemporary relationship between P and V, R and V, and in particular between SR and V, leads us to think about whether trading activity may be identified as a potential source of the observed serial dependence (persistence) in volatility.

Till now we have focused on the contemporary relationship between $[P_t, V_t, R_t, SR_t]$. Now we will examine the dynamic relationship or causal relation. The procedure used in this study verifies if volume precedes price, returns, or volatility, or vice versa.

The correlation between variables can be a first indication of the presence of causality. Therefore we investigate this hypothesis using the Granger Causality Test. Based on the premise that the future cannot cause the present or the past.

Table 15.1, Table 15.2 and Table 15.3 present the results of the tests of causal relation based on the model explained before, together with F-statisticians and the corresponding levels of significance for each market's composition. The last column in these tables indicate if there is, or not, causal relation, (Yes represents that the causal relation is significant at 5 %).

Table 15.1 shows that firstly, trading volume Granger cause prices and vice versa, when the market is formed (trained) only by fundamental agents or for fundamental and technical. Whereas when on the market there coexist agents of psychological type with the fundamental ones the volume Granger cause price. But price not Granger cause volume when the psychological ones dominate the market or are in equal proportion that the fundamental ones.

Table 15.2 indicates us that trading volume Granger cause price's variation in all the analyzed combinations. This implies that, besides the contemporary relation between volume and returns, volume may provide some predictive power on future returns in presence of present and past returns. This agrees with some theoretical

Table 15.1 Ganger causality tests on price-volume relation

Markets Composition	Null Hypothesis:	F-Statistic	Probability	Causal Relationship
20BF	V does not Granger Cause P	17.67	0.00	Yes
	P does not Granger Cause V	6.42	0.00	Yes
15BF5TF	V does not Granger Cause P	26.58	0.00	Yes
	P does not Granger Cause V	10.64	0.00	Yes
10BF10TF	V does not Granger Cause P	16.62	0.00	Yes
	P does not Granger Cause V	13.18	0.00	Yes
5BF15TF	V does not Granger Cause P	6.96	0.00	Yes
	P does not Granger Cause V	17.03	0.00	Yes
15BF5KT	V does not Granger Cause P	23.00	0.00	Yes
	P does not Granger Cause V	3.90	0.01	Yes
10BF10KT	V does not Granger Cause P	23.75	0.00	Yes
	P does not Granger Cause V	1.13	0.46	No
5BF15KT	V does not Granger Cause P	19.02	0.00	Yes
	P does not Granger Cause V	1.92	0.13	No

Table 15.2 Ganger causality tests on return-volume relation

Markets Composition	Null Hypothesis:	F-Statistic	Probability	Causal Relationship
20BF	V does not Granger Cause R	17.32	0.00	Yes
	R does not Granger Cause V	2.24	0.09	No
15BF5TF	V does not Granger Cause R	22.81	0.00	Yes
	R does not Granger Cause V	7.27	0.00	Yes
10BF10TF	V does not Granger Cause R	15.54	0.00	Yes
	R does not Granger Cause V	13.27	0.00	Yes
5BF15TF	V does not Granger Cause R	3.84	0.01	Yes
	R does not Granger Cause V	8.80	0.00	Yes
15BF5KT	V does not Granger Cause R	21.13	0.00	Yes
	R does not Granger Cause V	2.54	0.06	No
10BF10KT	V does not Granger Cause R	20.07	0.00	Yes
	R does not Granger Cause V	4,83	0.00	Yes
5BF15KT	V does not Granger Cause R	4,95	0.00	Yes
	R does not Granger Cause V	15.22	0.00	Yes

Table 15.3 Ganger causality tests on volatility-volume relation

Markets Composition	Null Hypothesis:	F-Statistic	Probability	Causal Relationship
20BF	V does not Granger Cause SR	21.01	0.00	Yes
	SR does not Granger Cause V	160.13	0.00	Yes
15BF5TF	V does not Granger Cause SR	15.19	0.00	Yes
	SR does not Granger Cause V	124.97	0.00	Yes
10BF10TF	V does not Granger Cause SR	8.30	0.00	Yes
	SR does not Granger Cause V	94.38	0.00	Yes
5BF15TF	V does not Granger Cause SR	21.10	0.00	Yes
	SR does not Granger Cause V	23.32	0.00	Yes
15BF5KT	V does not Granger Cause SR	11.86	0.00	Yes
	SR does not Granger Cause V	236.23	0.00	Yes
10BF10KT	V does not Granger Cause SR	8.17	0.00	Yes
	SR does not Granger Cause V	227.17	0.00	Yes
5BF15KT	V does not Granger Cause SR	3.70	0.02	Yes
	SR does not Granger Cause V	135.32	0.00	Yes

models who argue that the information contained in volume concerns the future returns.

When the market is fully formed by fundamental agents, and when they dominate it together with a small proportion of psychological, the inverse relationship is not verified, i.e. the returns not Granger cause volume. In other cases returns Granger cause volume.

Table 15.3 indicates us that between volume and volatility (measure as the square of returns), there is a feedback. That is, trading volume helps to predict volatility and vice versa. Because volume Granger cause volatility and vice versa.

15.5 Summary

The price-volume relation in financial stock markets has received considerable attention over the past decades. Although numerous studies have attempted to establish the empirical and theoretical structure of this relation, a consensus is yet to be reached.

Given the divergent conclusions of this research, further insights should be obtained through investigations on alternative sets of financial data, and we think that the data from artificial stock markets could help us to understand this relationships.

In particular from the data of the ISS-ASM, we conclude that:

- For all the agents' combinations there is a small but significant contemporary correlation between price and trading volume, contemporary significant positive correlation between returns and volume and there are asymmetry around zero in cross-correlation of returns and trading volume.
- Volume Granger cause price and vice versa, when the market is populated only by fundamental agents or for fundamental and technical.
- When in the market coexist psychological with fundamental agents, volume Granger cause price, but price not Granger cause volume if the psychological ones dominate or are in equal proportion that the fundamental ones.
- Volume Granger cause returns in all the analyzed combinations, so volume may provide some predictive power on future returns in presence of present and past returns.
- Returns Granger cause volume in all analyzed combinations except that the market is fully formed by fundamental agents, or when the fundamental agents dominate the market together with a small proportion of psychological.
- For all the scenarios volume Granger cause volatility and vice versa. Volume may provide some predictive power on future volatility and vice versa.

Acknowledgements The authors have benefited from the financial support of the Spanish Ministry of Education and Science (project TIN2008-06464-C03-02) and of the Junta de Castilla y León (projects VA006B09 and VA006A09). We are also very grateful to Adolfo López-Paredes and Cesáreo Hernández for many important ideas and their contributions to this work.

References

Assogbavi, T., Khoury, N., and Yourougou, P. (1992) La Causalité du Lien Volume-Prix de l'indice Toronto 35 Et Son Marché Ó Terme, Co-autored by Khoury and Yourou-gou, FINECO, vol 2, 55–65.

Brock, W. A., and LeBaron B. D. (1996). A dynamic structural model for stock return volatility and trading volume. The Review of Economics and Statistics 78:94–110.

Clark, P. K. (1973). A subordinated stochastic process model with finite variance for speculative prices. Econometrica 41:135–155.

Copeland, T. E. (1976). A model of asset trading under the assumption of sequential information arrival. Journal of Finance 31:1149–1168.

Epps, T. W. (1975). Security price changes and transaction volumes: Theory and evidence. American Economic Review, 65:586–597,

Epps, T. W. (1977). Security price changes and transaction volumes: Some additional evidence. Journal of Financial and Quantitative Analysis, 12:141–146.

Granger, C.W.J. and Morgenstern, 0., (1963). Spectral analysis of New York stock market prices. Kyklos 16 (1): 1–27.

Hiemstra, C. and Jones, J.D., (1995). Testing for linear and nonlinear Granger causality in the stock price-volume relationship. Journal of Finance 49, 1639–1664.

Kahneman D., and Tversky A (1979) Prospect theory: An analysis of decisions under risk. Econometrica, 47, 313–327.

Karpoff, J. (1987). The relation between price changes and trading volume: A survey. Journal of Financial and Quantitative Analysis 22:109–126.

Lakonishok, J. and Levi, M. (1982). Weekend effects on stock returns: A note. Journal of Finance, 37:883–889.

Lamoureux, C. G. and Lastrapes, W. D. (1990). Heteroskedasticity in stock return data: Volume versus GARCH effects. The Journal of Finance 45(1):221–229.

LeBaron B., Arthur W.B. and Palmer R. (1999) Time series properties of an artificial stock market. Journal of Economic Dynamics and Control,vol 23, 1487–1516.

Osborne, M. (1959). Brownian motion in the stock market, Operations Research 7, 145–173.

Pascual J. A. and Pajares, J. (2007). The role of risk aversion and technical trading in the behavior of financial markets. In Social Simulation: Technologies, Advances and New Discoveries. 169–179. Edited By: B. Edmonds, K. G. Troitzsch, C. Hernández.

Pascual J. A., Pajares, J. and López A. (2006). Explaining the statistical features of Spanish stock market from the bottom-up. Lecture Notes in Economics and Mathematical Systems. Vol. 594. 282–294

Rogalski, R.J., (1978). The dependence of prices and volume. Review of Economics and Statistics 60 (2), 268–274.

Samanidou E, Zschischang E, Stauffer D, et al. (2007) Agent-based models of financial markets REP PROG PHYS, 70, 3, 409–450.

Smirlock, M. and Starks, L.T., (1985). A further examination of stock price changes and transactions volume. Journal of Financial Research 8 (3), 217–225.

Smirlock, M. and Starks, L.T., (1988). An empirical analysis of the stock price-volume relationship. Journal of Banking Finance 12 (1), 31–41.

Part VI
Information and Learning

Chapter 16
Comparing Laboratory Experiments and Agent-Based Simulations: The Value of Information and Market Efficiency in a Market with Asymmetric Information

Florian Hauser, Jürgen Huber and Michael Kirchler

Abstract In this paper agent-based simulations are employed to deepen our understanding of results from experimental asset markets with asymmetric fundamental information. Beside the experimental treatment, we implement two simulation settings: a base-case simulation with all agents using their fundamental information and an equilibrium solution in which agents can choose from a set of three different strategies. We find that the behavior of the human subjects closely matches a strategy based on using the fundamental information provided, even when other strategies would have resulted in higher earnings. As a consequence, efficiency in the human markets is lower than in most of the simulated markets.

16.1 Introduction

The value of information in the context of asset markets is – and has always been – one of the most heavily debated issues in finance. To overcome the limitations analytical models pose when dealing with this topic, experimental as well as agent-based approaches have become popular methods among researchers. In this paper we set up a model of an asset market with an asymmetric information structure. We conduct laboratory experiments with human subjects as well as agent-based simulations to deliver results on the value of information in this model. Using both methods allows us to allay the weaknesses of both approaches: for the agent-based simulations, one has to make strict assumptions about the behavior of the traders that may not correspond with reality. In contrast, experiments with human subjects can be considered as a kind of black box, as the behavior of the human subjects cannot be controlled and sometimes not even explained (Gode and Sunder, 1993).

Florian Hauser · Jürgen Huber · Michael Kirchler
Department of Department of Banking and Finance, Innsbruck University School of Management, Universitaetsstrasse 15, A-6020 e-mail: [Florian.Hauser,Juergen.Huber,Michael.Kirchler]@uibk.ac.at

Thus we pick up an idea of Duffy (2006) by using the agent-based simulations to better interpret results from the experiment. In the optimal case this allows to draw conclusions about how human traders in the experiments interact and how their asymmetric information is aggregated.

We conduct eight experimental asset markets with asymmetric information and set up two agent-based simulations with the same market model as in the experiments. In the first simulation setting all agents trade according to their fundamental information and in the second simulation agents select their optimal strategy from a set of three. We find that insiders outperform all other traders clearly in the experiment and in the agent-based simulations. In the experiment and in the simulation with all traders applying a fundamental strategy, the average informed traders end up worst and are outperformed by the uninformed random traders who reach the market return. When agents can choose their optimal strategy in the second simulation setting, market efficiency increases clearly and hence insiders outperformance is lowered. Some of the average informed now switch to a non-fundamental strategy and end up with approximately the market return. Consequently, the uninformed random traders are exploited and reach the lowest returns.

The paper is organized as follows: In Sec. 16.2 the market model is introduced. In Sec. 16.3 we describe the experimental implementation as well as the agent-based simulations. Section 16.4 presents the results and Sec. 16.5 concludes.

16.2 Market Model

We use a model of an asset market based on prior studies by Huber (2007) and Kirchler (2009). Thus, 10 traders i trade securities of a (virtual) risky company in a continuous double-auction market. Traders are able to submit limit orders to an open order book, as well as market orders which are executed instantaneously. Submission of orders is only restricted by holdings of stocks and cash. All traders start with equal initial endowments, holding 40 securities as well as 1600 units of virtual currency (Taler). The market runs for 24 periods k, each lasting 100 seconds.[1]

It is assumed that for each period k, the best available estimator for the fundamental value (FV) of the security is given by the following stochastic value process:

$$FV_k = FV_{k-1} \cdot (1 + \varepsilon_k); \ \varepsilon \sim N(\mu = 0.005, \sigma = 0.072). \tag{16.1}$$

To provide traders with heterogenous information on the value of the security, we introduce five information levels $I_{j \in [0;4]}$, each given to two traders. Based on the idea of Hellwig (1982), we assume that traders with higher information levels get information on the fundamental value of the security earlier than those associated to lower information levels. Hence, the best available estimator for the fundamental value of the security by a trader with information level I_j is calculated in period k as

$$CV_{j,k} = FV_{k+j-4}. \tag{16.2}$$

---

[1] Holdings of securities and virtual currency are carried over from one period to the next.

According to this, only the insiders with information level I_4 know the fundamental value in each period. Traders with information level I_3 will only receive information about the fundamental value of the previous period, and accordingly the information provided to traders with information level I_2 and I_1 has a lag of 2 and 3 periods, respectively. Traders in the category I_0 do not receive any information on the fundamental value at all. Furthermore, securities are liquidated at the end of the experiment at the fundamental value FV_{24}.

16.3 Experimental Implementation and Simulation

Experiments and simulations are conducted with eight different realizations of the value process (referred to as m in the following) described in (16.1). Four of them are generated randomly, the other four are mirrored at the conditional expected value (EV) as shown in Fig. 16.1.

We conducted eight experimental sessions (with ten traders each), one with each realization of the value process. At the beginning of a session, experimental subjects were briefed with written instructions, and they practiced with the trading interface during 4 trial periods which did not affect their final payment. Subjects were informed about the information structure and they knew their own information level. For our experiments we recruited business students who already had experience from previous economic experiments. However, no subject participated more than once in any session reported here. All sessions were conducted at the University of Innsbruck, the average payment for the subjects was 19 EUR, with the individual payment realization depending on their trading performance with an exchange rate of EUR/Taler of 1/175. The trading interface was programmed and conducted with z-Tree 3.0.6 (Fischbacher, 2007).

In the experiments as well as in the simulations, the two uninformed traders in I_0 were implemented as computerized random traders. They will serve as a benchmark

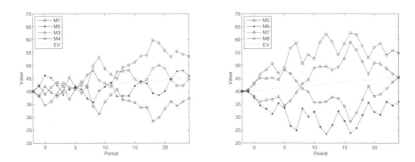

Fig. 16.1 Fundamental value, FV, as a function of period for the eight markets.

and their trading performance will allow us to compare experiments and simulations more carefully as will be shown in Sec. 16.4. Both random traders were bound to submit limit orders (bid or ask with equal probability) with a reservation price R_t, being calculated by the last market price P_t and a random variable:

$$R_t = P_t \pm \varepsilon_t; \; \varepsilon \sim N(\mu = 0, \sigma = 1). \tag{16.3}$$

The first random trader was programmed as a rather active trader, submitting orders for on average 50 shares per period with an average waiting time between orders of 6 seconds. The second random trader was less active, submitting orders for on average 20 shares in each period with a waiting time of 15 seconds.

After the experiments were completed agent-based simulations were conducted according to the same rules as applied in the experiment with only one difference: To limit the degrees of freedom of our agents, the number of securities traded in one order was fixed to three shares. To minimize random effects in the simulation, all results are based on 100 replications of each realization of the value process, so we conducted 800 runs in total. Beside of the random traders in I_0, which were programmed as described above, we considered two further trading strategies for the remaining eight agents in each market.

A *fundamental agent* will form his reservation price with respect to the conditional value associated with his information level. He is willing to buy the security for a price $R_t \leq CV_{j,k} - 0.1$ and he wants to sell a stock for $R_t \geq CV_{j,k} + 0.1$. When a fundamental agent wakes up, he will first check the order book for any existing limit orders fulfilling his restrictions. In this case, he will accept the according limit order, otherwise he will place a limit order (with equal probability for bid and ask) according to his reservation price.

A *marginal trader* has the incentive to keep his holdings close to his initial endowment and to submit the best bid or ask to the order book. He will not accept any existing limit orders. When he comes to trade, he will decide to place a bid if his holdings in stocks are smaller than 40, and he will submit an ask if he holds more than 40 shares. When he holds exactly 40 shares, he will place a bid or ask with equal probability. His reservation price is $R_t = P_{best\_bid} + 0.1$ for a bid and $R_t = P_{best\_ask} - 0.1$ for an ask, with P_{best_bid} (P_{best_ask}) being the best bid (ask) in the order book at the time he places his order. The fundamental and the marginal trading strategy are associated with an average wake-up time (i.e. waiting time between orders) of 18 seconds with a standard normally distributed error term.

To identify an equilibrium, meaning a situation where all traders adopt their optimal strategy and no single trader has the incentive to switch to another trading strategy, we apply a simple algorithm: We start with all informed traders $I_{[1;4]}$ adopting a fundamental strategy. This will be referred to as the "base-case simulation" or "T2" in the following. Next, we randomly choose one of the informed traders and calculate his abnormal return for all three possible trading strategies, assuming that all other traders stick with their original strategy. Now the chosen trader adopts the strategy delivering him the highest return and another trader is chosen for optimization. This loop is repeated until we arrive at a stable situation where no trader has an incentive to change his strategy. When running this optimization for 100 times, we arrive at an equilibrium after approximately 30 runs which is characterized by an unique strategy mix: in equilibrium, we always find three traders, one in each information level $I_{[1;3]}$, to adopt a marginal trader strategy, while all other informed traders stick with a fundamental strategy. This equilibrium situation will be referred to as "T3" in the following.

16.4 Results

In this section, we present results on payoff distributions and on market efficiency to investigate differences between the experimental approach and the agent-based simulations.

16.4.1 Distribution of Returns

Based on the final wealth of trader i (FW_i defined as the number of securities held multiplied with FV_{24} plus cash), we calculate his abnormal return as

$$AR_i = \ln(FW_i) - \ln(\overline{FW}). \tag{16.4}$$

Here $\overline{FW}$ defines the average final wealth across all traders in the market. The benchmarking on the market average is crucial to eliminate the idiosyncratic influence of different markets due to different fundamental value paths.

Figure 16.2 presents results on abnormal returns (left panels) and trading volumes (right panels) for the experiment (T1, black bars), the base-case simulation (T2, grey bars in both top panels) and the equilibrium case simulation (T3, grey bars in both bottom panels). Note that traders 1 and 2 are endowed with information level I_0, traders 3 and 4 with I_1,..., and traders 9 and 10 with I_4. We find very similar patterns regarding abnormal returns and trading volumes for both the experiment and the base-case simulation. Insiders clearly outperform the market and all other traders, while average informed traders I_1 and I_2 end up performing worst. Randomized traders I_0 come close to the market return in T1 and T2, a result which is in line with prior research (see Huber, 2007).

This J-shaped relationship between information level and return probably merits some explanation: a market is a place of strategic interaction where game-theoretic thinking is required. Receiving outdated information, as I_1, I_2, and to a certain degree I_3 do, can thus systematically reduce a trader's net return, as this information is already (at least partly) incorporated in prices by the actions of the insiders (I_4). Only the uninformed I_0 are "immune" to these systematic mistakes as their actions do not rely on any fundamental information – they trade randomly and thus receive a return close to zero in the base-case simulation and the human experiments.

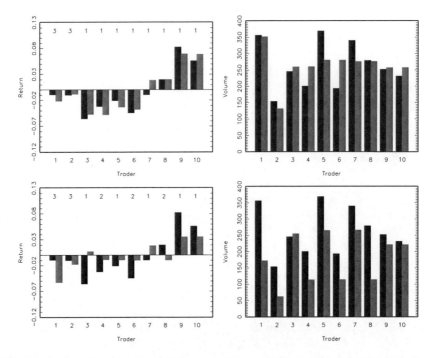

Fig. 16.2 Abnormal returns to the market average (left panels) and trading volumes (right panels) for the experiment T1 (black bars), the base-case simulation T2 (grey bars in both top panels) and the equilibrium case simulation T3 (grey bars in both bottom panels). The numbers in the top of both abnormal return plots indicate the trading strategies with "1" standing for fundamentalists, "2" indicating a marginal trader strategy and "3" representing the random strategy.

In the bottom panels T1 and T3 are compared. Here we see striking differences in returns and volume: in the simulation randomized agents I_0 perform worst, while the remaining fundamentalists for I_1 and I_2 improve and earn approximately the market return (the numbers in the top of both abnormal return plots indicate the trading strategies T_a as defined in Sec. 16.2, with "1" standing for fundamentalists, "2" indicating a marginal trader strategy and "3" representing the random strategy). The markedly lower return for the randomized agents I_0 in the equilibrium simulation T3 stems from the activities of marginal traders: both trader groups do not look at fundamental information, but while random agents I_0 place random orders, marginal traders add/deduct a small increment to current bids/asks. Thus many profitable orders that were executed for the random traders in the base-case simulation are no longer accepted in the equilibrium simulation as marginal traders lower bid-ask spreads here. Random traders I_0 thus mostly conduct trades that they lose money on and thus end up with strongly negative net returns. It is also worth noting that the traders with the older fundamental information of I_1 earn higher returns than those with the fundamental information of I_2. Even fundamental traders with I_3 only marginally outperform traders with I_1.

The three marginal traders only trade approximately half as much as fundamentalists in I_1 to I_3, but earnings of the two strategies are comparable and close to the market average. Insiders still outperform the market, though with lower excess returns than in the experiment and in the base-case simulation T2.

In terms of trading volume the base-case simulation appears to be well calibrated. Results for all traders are in most respect comparable to the experiment, and especially for the computerized random traders we can observe almost identical results here. Turning to the equilibrium simulation, it shows that trading volume of the random agents is less than half as high as in the experiment. Due to the marginal traders that successfully lower the bid-ask-spread, the limit orders submitted by the random agents have a much lower chance of being executed. Note again that even though the random agents trade much less than the fundamental agents in T3, returns of the former decrease considerably compared to T2.

Our first conclusion from these results is that in the experiments subjects for the most part relied on the fundamental information provided to them. The equilibrium simulation attests that for the low- and medium informed traders, a very simple alternative strategy which uses only the information provided by the order book instead of the private signal can earn them a considerably higher return. Obviously, most human subjects in the experiments did not consider that their private signal may be misleading, even though they should have realized during 24 periods that their trading strategy causes them systematic losses.

To see whether abnormal returns are different from zero within one market and to detect whether the differences between the information levels are significant we set up the following OLS-regression model:

$$AR_{i,m} = \beta_0 I_0 + \beta_1 I_1 + \beta_2 I_2 + \beta_3 I_3 + \beta_4 I_4 + \varepsilon_{i,m}. \tag{16.5}$$

Here, i stands for an individual trader in market m and I_0 to I_4 are binary dummy variables for the various information levels.[2] As we do not implement an intercept α, each coefficient is tested for the null hypothesis of being different from zero. Thus, by looking at the coefficient values we can easily check whether the different information levels outperform the market. Furthermore, by using Wald-coefficient tests, we test for pairwise differences in abnormal returns between the information levels.

To test on the differences between the experiment and the base-case simulation we modify Eq. (16.5) in a way that the coefficients I_0 to I_4 test for the differences within each information level. Therefore, we introduce the difference in abnormal returns for each information level j in each market m between the experiment and the base-case simulation as dependent variable ($AR_{j,m}^{T1} - AR_{j,m}^{T2}$):

$$AR_{j,m}^{T1} - AR_{j,m}^{T2} = \beta_0 I_0 + \beta_1 I_1 + \beta_2 I_2 + \beta_3 I_3 + \beta_4 I_4 + \varepsilon_{j,m}. \tag{16.6}$$

Table 16.1 presents the results. In the experiment and the base-case simulation insiders significantly outperform the market by 6.9 and 6.8 percentage points,

---

[2] With ten traders in each session, we arrive at 80 observations per treatment.

Table 16.1 OLS-Regression measuring the impact of the different information levels on abnormal returns AR for the experiment, the base-case simulation, and the equilibrium. In columns seven and eight we test on the differences in abnormal returns between the experiment and the base-case simulation within each information level.

	Experiment		Base-Case Sim		Sim. Equil.		T1–T2	
	Coef.	P-val.	Coef.	P-val.	Coef.	P-val.	Coef.	P-val.
I_0	−0.010	0.514	−0.017	0.060	−0.038	0.000	0.007	0.659
I_1	−0.044	0.004	−0.047	0.000	0.011	0.337	0.003	0.830
I_2	−0.033	0.031	−0.037	0.000	−0.011	0.330	0.004	0.785
I_3	0.005	0.742	0.022	0.015	0.019	0.094	−0.017	0.291
I_4	0.069	0.000	0.068	0.000	0.036	0.000	0.001	0.957
MM	–	–	–	–	−0.010	0.148	–	–
R^2	0.322		0.609		0.396		0.040	
n	80		80		80		40	

respectively, while traders with I_1 end up worst with a significant underperformance of 4.4 and 4.7 percentage points, respectively. In both treatments the computerized random traders I_0 earn the market return as their slight underperformance is not different from zero.[3]

When turning to the results of the simulation with the equilibrium strategy mix (T3), we find clear differences. As we now find three traders to adopt a marginal strategy, we modify our regression model in Eq. (16.5) by adding a binary marginal trader dummy (MM) as sixth independent variable. From the columns five and six we see that the random traders I_0 now significantly underperform the market and end up worst of all traders. The major losers in the base-case simulation and in the experiment, I_1 and I_2, now earn approximately the market return which goes at the expense of the insiders whose abnormal return is lowered by 3.2 percentage points with respect to the base-case simulation. Furthermore, all three marginal traders as a group (MM) end up with the market return. Interestingly, as the number of fundamentalists decreases due to the switching of low and average informed traders to a marginal trader strategy, the remaining low and average informed fundamentalists improve their performance.

In columns 7 and 8 one can further see that the experiment (T1) and the base-case simulation (T2) provide almost identical results, as abnormal returns in both treatments are indistinguishable from each other within each information level.

We run the same regression model with trading volume as independent variable to check whether our agents in the base-case simulation are well calibrated compared to the traders in the experiment. For each information level the differences in trading volumes are insignificant as can be seen in Table 16.2. This gives further evidence

---

[3] We find no significant difference between the active and the passive random trader in both the experiment and the base-case simulation (Panel regression according to (16.5) with additional dummies for both agents).

Table 16.2 OLS-Regression measuring the difference in trading volume for the experiment and the base-case simulation.

	T1–T2 Coef.	P-val.
I0	12.867	0.726
I1	−36.996	0.314
I2	0.826	0.982
I3	33.164	0.367
I4	−15.873	0.665
R^2	0.028	
n	80	

to our argumentation that results from the base-case simulation are in most respect in line with results from the experiment.

16.4.2 Market Efficiency

To analyze informational efficiency of our markets, we calculate the mean average absolute error of all tick prices in one market m as

$$MAE_m = \sum_{z=0}^{Z} \frac{|P_{z,k,m} - FV_{k,m}|}{Z}, \qquad (16.7)$$

with Z being the total number of tick prices observed in this market and $FV_{k,m}$ denoting the fundamental value of the security in period k, as provided to the insiders.

Figure 16.3 reports the mean average absolute errors (MAE) of tick prices in our markets. Comparing the results for both simulations (dark grey bars denote MAE's of the base-case simulation T2 where all informed agents process information, the light grey bars refer to the equilibrium simulation T3) we can observe mispricing to be much less pronounced in the equilibrium simulation. This can be attributed to the average informed agents that ignore their information and adopt a marginal strategy in T3. Their price impact decreases as their strategy only allows them to lower bid-ask-spreads, hence the fundamental information of the best informed agents has a much better chance to disseminate into market prices. This result is in line with prior research by Schredelseker (2001) and Hauser (2008), showing that informational efficiency will increase when average- and low-informed traders ignore their fundamental information and free-ride on the information provided by market prices.

Turning to the results of the experimental sessions (black bars), we can observe that prices in all experimental markets track fundamental values worse than in the equilibrium simulation T3. This corroborates that the inferior information of the medium- and low-informed traders distorted market prices in the experiment. Note

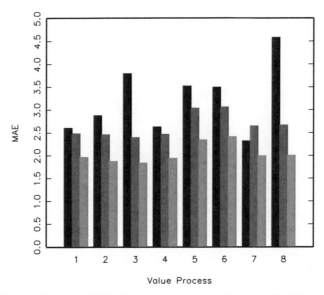

Fig. 16.3 Mean absolute error (*MAE*) for all eight experimental sessions T1 (black bars), and the simulation T2 (dark grey) and T3 (light grey).

that this also gives the insiders in the market a better chance for generating abnormal returns, as their private signal reflects the best available information and thus indicates them any distortion of market prices. Referring again to Fig. 16.2, the relatively high efficiency of market prices in T3 leads to considerably lower returns for insiders as they have a much lower chance for exploiting systematic errors of the other traders.

Before we observed, that when looking at the return distribution T1 (humans) was closer to T2 (base-case) than to T3 (equilibrium). This also holds when looking at market efficiency: Again the experimental results are better explained with the base-case simulation T2. Although inefficiency is higher for the experimental sessions in seven out of eight cases, the *MAE*'s are at least comparable between T1 and T2. When we test on significant differences between the treatments we find no difference in *MAE* and hence in market efficiency between the experiment T1 and the base-case simulation T2 (*Mann-Whitney U-Test, n=16, p=0.161*).[4] Instead, the equilibrium simulation T3 shows significantly higher levels of market efficiency compared to T1 and T2 (T1 vs. T3: *Mann-Whitney U-Test, n=16, p=0.001* and T2 vs T3: (*Mann-Whitney U-Test, n=16, p=0.000*)). This leaves us again with the impression that the average informed human traders did mostly rely on their private signals. By trading on this biased information, humans make joint mistakes which in turn leads to a relatively high mispricing in the experiment.

---

[4] As we have only one observation for each market we choose a non-parametric test at this stage.

16.5 Conclusion

In this paper we presented asset markets with asymmetric information which were run separately with both the experimental and simulation method. For the agent-based simulations we considered two different treatments: in the base-case simulation all informed traders relied on their private fundamental information while in the equilibrium simulation each trader choose his optimal strategy form a set of three alternatives.

Considering the value of asymmetric fundamental information, we observed that in the experiment and in the base-case simulation the average informed traders performed worst and the computerized random traders earned the market return. The insiders outperformed all other traders in all three treatments, but they earned less in the equilibrium simulation – with prices tracking fundamental values closer there is less money to be earned by the best informed. In the equilibrium simulation, we found the computerized random traders to end up with the lowest returns of all traders. This can again be attributed to the relatively high market efficiency in this treatment: now half of the (formerly losing) average informed no longer traded on information, but instead adopted a marginal trader strategy. This exposed especially random traders, as their (random) orders might have matched the marginal traders' orders. Hence, the latter earned some money and created losses for the former.

When looking at the informational efficiency of our markets, we found that prices in the equilibrium simulation track the fundamental values of the asset considerably better than in the other two treatments. As some of the average informed traders no longer trade on their biased signals, insider information has a much higher influence on market prices in the equilibrium simulation.

Considering the striking similarities of the results from the base-case simulation and the experiment, we conclude that the subjects in the experiments mostly relied on their fundamental information and the average-informed were not able to develop alternative trading strategies that would have allowed them to enhance their trading performance.

Acknowledgements The authors would like to acknowledge the Tyrolean Science Foundation and the Austrian National Bank (OeNB grant 12789) for financial support. Further thanks appertain to two anonymous referees for their extensive and very helpful comments on this paper.

References

John Duffy. Agent-based models and human subject experiments. In Tesfatsion and Judge, editors, *Handbook of Computational Economics 2*, pages 949–1011. Elsevier, 2006.

Urs Fischbacher. z-tree: Zurich toolbox for ready-made economic experiments. *Experimental Economics*, 10(2):171–178, 2007.

Dhananjay K. Gode and Shyam Sunder. Allocative efficiency of markets with zero intelligence traders: Market as a partial substitute for individual rationality. *Journal of Political Economy*, 101:119–137, 1993.

Florian Hauser. Trader's incentives to process information and market efficiency. In Michael Hanke and Jürgen Huber, editors, *Information, Interaction and (In)Efficiency in Financial Markets*, pages 11–24. Linde, 2008.

Martin Hellwig. Rational expectation equilibrium with conditioning on past prices, a mean-variance example. *Journal of Economic Theory*, 26:279–312, 1982.

Jürgen Huber. ôjö-shaped returns to timing advantage in access to information û experimental evidence and a tentative explanation. *Journal of Economic Dynamics and Control*, 31:2536–2572, 2007.

Michael Kirchler. Underreaction to fundamental information and asymmetry in mispricing between bullish and bearish markets. an experimental study. *Journal of Economic Dynamics and Control*, 33:491–506, 2009.

Klaus Schredelseker. Is the usefulness approach useful? some reflections on the utility of public information. In Stuart McLeay and Angelo Riccaboni, editors, *Contemporary Issues in Accounting Regulation*, pages 135–153. Kluwer Academic Publishers, 2001.

Chapter 17
Asset Return Dynamics under Alternative Learning Schemes

Elena Catanese, Andrea Consiglio, Valerio Lacagnina and Annalisa Russino

Abstract In this paper we design an artificial financial market where endogenous volatility is created assigning to the agents diverse prior beliefs about the joint distribution of returns, and, over time, making agents rationally update their beliefs using common public information. We analyze the asset price dynamics generated under two learning environments: one where agents assume that the joint distribution of returns is *IID*, and another where agents believe in the existence of regimes in the joint distribution of asset returns. We show that the regime switching learning structure can generate all the most common stylized facts of financial markets: fat tails and long-range dependence in volatility coexisting with relatively efficient markets.

17.1 Introduction

In this paper we design an artificial financial market to investigate what are the implications for market dynamics of alternative belief structures. In particular, we model an electronic financial market in which N risky securities can be exchanged. M risk-averse agents trade to reach their desired asset allocations. We assume that agents have incomplete information and, starting from heterogeneous beliefs, must learn about unobservable features of the economy from observable public data. In this framework, agents asset allocation choices, and thus market prices, will depend on the evolution of the uncertainty.

The goal of the paper is to study how the asset price dynamics is affected by the dynamics of beliefs under alternative learning schemes. We compare two learning environments: a first one where agents assume that the underlying joint distribution

---

E. Catanese · A. Consiglio · V. Lacagnina · A. Russino
Dip. di Scienze Statistiche e Matematiche "Silvio Vianelli", University of Palermo, Italy. Corresponding author: Annalisa Russino, e-mail: russino@unipa.it

of returns is *IID*; and a second one where agents assume a regime switching model for the joint distribution of returns (*HMM*).

The paper is related to the recent literature trying to highlight the economic mechanisms generating typical asset-pricing anomalies such as the heavy tails of the unconditional distribution of returns, the excess volatility with respect to the exogenous variability of fundamentals, volatility clustering and long-memory[1].

The theoretical work trying to explain financial market anomalies can be divided into two different strands. On one hand we have papers relaxing the assumption of individual rationality either through the belief-formation process or through the decision-making process. Alternatively, a growing number of papers has been focusing on exploring the consequences of relaxing the assumption of correct beliefs while maintaining the assumption of individual rationality[2]. Allowing agents to hold diverse prior beliefs, that are rationally updated over time using common public information, generates endogenous uncertainty which depends on the distribution of agents' beliefs, on the frequency of change in agents' beliefs, and on the correlation among beliefs. In this paper, we follow the last approach designing a market where agents' heterogeneity is introduced through diverse prior beliefs. All agents are rational: they update their beliefs over time using public information and are expected utility maximizers.

The main ingredients of our agent-based model can be summarized as follows. First, we design a market where heterogeneous investors interact in a multi-risky asset market. We overcome the traditional distinction between rational and irrational traders (*fundamentalists* and *chartists*) used in heterogeneous agent models[3], designing a market where all agents are *ex-ante* rational but imperfectly informed. Second, we concentrate our attention on the endogenous component of volatility and therefore we do not explicitly model a fundamental price process. Third, in our model the same information is available to all agents: they differ in terms of prior beliefs that are rationally adjusted over time using the realized historic returns. Thus, we do not introduce asymmetric information and any direct "social-interaction" mechanism among agents. Finally, we explicit the microstructure of the market designing a continuous double-auction trading mechanism.

The paper is structured as follows. Section 17.2 describes the market model and the statistical measures implemented to monitor the dynamics of population heterogeneity. Section 17.3 presents the calibration used for our simulations, and discusses the overall results obtained.

---

[1] See Pagan (1996); Cont (2001, 2005).

[2] See Bossaerts (1999); Brennan and Xia (2001); Kurtz and Motolese (2001); Lewellen and Shanken (2002); Timmermann (1993).

[3] See Hommes (2005), for a recent survey on heterogeneous agent models.

17.2 The Model

17.2.1 The Market Setting

We consider an economy with M agents and N risky assets. For each asset we design a continuous double-auction automated system based on an order-book divided in a buy and sell side. Agents enter the market sequentially. At each time step k within a trading day t we make the probability of entering the market for the i-th agent, $P_i(E)$, depend on the total imbalance between the target and the current portfolio, i.e. $P_i(E) = f(\Delta_i)$ where,

$$\Delta_i = \sum_{j=1}^{N} \left| h_{ij}^*(\tau) - \frac{x_{ij}^t(k) P_j^t(k)}{W_i^t(k)} \right|, \qquad (17.1)$$

where $h_{ij}^*(\tau)$ is the agent's optimal target allocation for asset j, $x_{ij}^t(k)$ represents the agent's current holding in asset j, $P_j^t(k)$ is the current price for asset j, and $W_i^t(k)$ is the agent's total wealth given current prices and agent's holdings. Thus, the activation function $P_i(E)$ reflects the urgency of trading for the candidate agent.

Agents' behavior is specified in terms of order flow strategy (number of units to buy or to sell) and order–type submission strategy (market or limit order).

Agents trade to rebalance their portfolio according to their optimal target allocations. At time step k during trading day t, the number of units of the j-th asset that the i-th agent is willing to trade is given by,

$$q_{ij}^t(k) = \left\lfloor \frac{h_{ij}^*(\tau) W_i^t(k) - x_{ij}^t(k) P_j^t(k)}{P_j^t(k)} \right\rfloor, \qquad (17.2)$$

where $\lfloor \cdot \rfloor$ denotes the integer part, The target allocations $h_{ij}^*(\tau)$, are the optimal solutions of the agent's portfolio choice problem with τ investment horizon. If $q_{ij}^t(k) > 0$, the trader issues a buy order; if $q_{ij}^t(k) < 0$, the trader issues a sell order. Agents are cash constrained. In particular, borrowing and short-selling are not allowed.

Agents can trade immediately at current quotes placing market orders. Alternatively, they can submit limit orders that will be stored in the exchange book until the end of the trading day and, if a matching order arrives, will be executed using first price priority and then time precedence. We simplify the agents' choice set fixing the order type submission strategy: all agents submit a market order for the quantity available at the best quote and, if the quantity they want to trade is higher, they place, for the residual quantity, a limit order at a price such that their order will be first in the queue of orders written in the book[4].

---

[4] See Consiglio et al. (2005) for a detailed description of the trading mechanism we implement.

17.2.2 The Portfolio Model

Agents are homogeneous in their trading strategy: they all trade to rebalance their portfolio according to their optimal target allocations. We assume that investors choose their portfolio maximizing their expected power utility defined over terminal wealth, $W_{t+\tau}$,

$$u(W_{t+\tau}) = \frac{W_{t+\tau}^{1-\gamma}}{1-\gamma}, \tag{17.3}$$

where τ is the investment horizon, γ is coefficient of relative risk aversion, and t is the updating time. Whenever agents review their beliefs, they solve their asset allocation problem. Assuming continuous compounding, the wealth equation turns out to be,

$$W_{t+\tau} = W_t \left(\omega_t' \exp(\mathbf{R}_{t+\tau}) \right), \tag{17.4}$$

where $\mathbf{R}_{t+\tau} = \sum_{i=1}^{\tau} \mathbf{r}_{t+i}$ is the vector of continuously compounded risky returns over the τ-period investment horizon.

We use Monte Carlo methods for the expected utility computation, and follow Barberis (2000) to approximate the integral in the expected utility functional as follows,

$$\max_{\omega_t} S^{-1} \sum_{s=1}^{S} \frac{(\omega_t' \exp(\sum_{i=1}^{\tau} \mathbf{r}_{t+i,s}))^{1-\gamma}}{1-\gamma}, \tag{17.5}$$

where S is the number of simulated paths of returns generated according to the agents' beliefs. It is worth to notice that in the regime switching setting, forward scenarios are generated using draws from a model that, starting from a state ψ drawn according to the agent filtered probability distribution Π_t, allows regimes to shift randomly as governed by the transition matrix $\hat{\mathbf{P}}$. Thus, in this setting scenarios follow a temporal structure in which any return of the sequence depends on past returns, while in the *IID* learning setting, each return is drawn according to a joint time-invariant distribution.

17.2.3 The Learning Process

17.2.3.1 The IID Setting

We allow agents to hold arbitrary arbitrary marginal prior densities for asset returns. We model the prior marginal return distribution of each asset as a Dirichlet with parameters $(\alpha_1, \ldots, \alpha_C)$ where C is number of classes of the support of the return distribution. Thus, we assign to the agents populating our economy arbitrary prior densities given by,

$$f_j^i(\theta) = \frac{\Gamma(\alpha_{ij1} + \ldots + \alpha_{ijC})}{\Gamma(\alpha_{ij1}) \ldots \Gamma(\alpha_{ijC})} \theta_1^{\alpha_{ij1}-1} \ldots \theta_C^{\alpha_{ijC}-1}, \tag{17.6}$$

where $\theta_1, \ldots, \theta_C \geq 0$; $\sum_{c=1}^{C} \theta_c = 1$, $i = 1, \ldots, M$, and $j = 1, \ldots, N$. Agents will use the history of observed market returns to update their beliefs in a Bayesian fashion.

Letting v_{jc} be the number of returns observed, for the j-th asset, in class c during the time period between two successive updating days, the posterior distribution of the i-th agent for the returns of asset j will be Dirichlet with parameters $((\alpha_{ij1} + v_{ij1}), \ldots, (\alpha_{ijC} + v_{ijC}))$. We concentrate our attention on analyzing the impact of a learning process about the marginal distributions of returns assuming that agents have a constant common view of the asset association structure. We use a Gaussian copula to model the dependence structure between the risky asset. Given their own marginal univariate return distributions and the assigned copula, agents correctly extract from the multivariate distribution of returns a number S of scenarios.

17.2.3.2 The HMM Setting

Agents assume a state-contingent multivariate gaussian return distribution with known parameters, but they do not observe the state variable. Agents share a common view about the parameters of the state-contingent multivariate gaussian return distribution, but they have diverse prior beliefs about the state probability distribution and the transition probability matrix governing regime switches. That is, we introduce heterogeneity allowing agents to have different initial probability distributions over states, Π_0, and different irreducibles transition matrices, $\mathbf{P}_0$. Regime switches among the Ψ states are driven by a first-order Markov chain. At each point in time, agents must form an opinion about the probability that the economy is in any particular state, and about the transition probabilities, using the information filtration generated by the observed multivariate time series of returns.

The updating process follows two steps[5]. First, given a realized sequence of the return vector, $\mathbf{R}_\tau = \{\mathbf{r}_1, \mathbf{r}_2 \ldots \mathbf{r}_\tau\}$, agents update the transition matrix $\mathbf{P}$ by the forward-backward Baum-Welch algorithm. The algorithm allows parameter estimation of the $\hat{\mathbf{P}}$ of an *HMM* given only emissions as training data. That is, given an observation sequence $\mathbf{R}_\tau$ of return vectors, and a prior transition matrix $\mathbf{P}$, and letting $N_\psi(\mathbf{r}_t)$ be the state-contingent multivariate density of observation $\mathbf{r}_t$, the updated transition probabilities are given by,

$$\hat{p}_{dl} = \left(\sum_{t=1}^{\tau} \alpha_{t-1}(d)\beta_{t-1}(d) \right)^{-1} \sum_{t=1}^{\tau} \alpha_{t-1}(d) p_{dl} N_l(\mathbf{r}_t) \beta_t(l), \qquad (17.7)$$

where $d, l \in \Psi$, and $\alpha_t(l)$ and $\beta_t(l)$ are recursively computed as forward and backward likelihood functions,

$$\alpha_t(l) = L(\mathbf{r}_1, \ldots \mathbf{r}_t, \psi_t = l) = \sum_{\psi=1}^{\Psi} \alpha_{t-1}(\psi) p_{\psi l} N_l(\mathbf{r}_t), \quad t = 1, \ldots, \tau,$$

$$\beta_t(l) = L(\mathbf{r}_{t+1}, \ldots, \mathbf{r}_\tau \mid \psi_t = l) = \sum_{\psi=1}^{\Psi} \beta_{t+1}(\psi) p_{l\psi} N_\psi(\mathbf{r}_{t+1}), \quad t = \tau-1, \ldots, 1,$$

with boundary conditions $\alpha_0(l) = \pi_t(l)$ and $\beta_\tau(l) = 1$.

---
[5] See Bhar and Hamori (2004).

Second, using the updated transition matrix, agents optimally revise their beliefs about the underlying state by computing filtered probability distributions,

$$\hat{\pi}_{t+i}(\psi) = \frac{(\hat{P}'\pi_{t+i-1}(\psi))N_\psi(\mathbf{r}_{t+1})}{\sum_{\psi=1}^{\Psi}\left(\hat{P}'\pi_{t+i-1}(\psi)\right)N_\psi(\mathbf{r}_{t+1})}, \quad i=1,\dots,\tau. \quad (17.8)$$

17.2.4 Statistical Measures of Population Heterogeneity

To analyze the impact on market dynamics of the evolution of population heterogeneity under the two learning structures, we use two measures of population heterogeneity: a measure of dissimilarity among agents' beliefs and a measure of distance among agents' optimal asset allocations.

Following the information theory point of view, we measure how likely on average it would be that an agent with different beliefs generates another agent's scenarios and viceversa. A natural generalization of a probabilistic distance measure for monitoring the dissimilarity between pairs of *HMMs*, a measure that is consistent with the re-estimation technique, is the symmetrized *KullBack-Leibler (KL)* divergence evaluated on the sequences of returns generated by the Markov sources (i.e. the agents' beliefs). If each agent represents a *Hidden Markov Model* with his own transition matrix, and state probability vector, $\lambda_i = \{\mathbf{\Pi}_t^i, \hat{\mathbf{P}}^i\}$, then the symmetrized *KL* divergence between the belief structures of two different agents is defined as follows,

$$D_{kl}(i,m) = \frac{1}{2\tau}\left(\int\left(\ln\mathbb{P}_{O^i}^i - \ln\mathbb{P}_{O^i}^m\right)d\mathbb{P}_{O^i}^i + + \int\left(\ln\mathbb{P}_{O^m}^m - \ln\mathbb{P}_{O^m}^i\right)d\mathbb{P}_{O^m}^m\right), \quad (17.9)$$

where O^i, and O^m are sets of observation sequences generated under the belief structure of agent i and m respectively, while $\mathbb{P}_{O^i}^i = L(O^i|\lambda_i)$ is the likelihood associated with the sequence of observations O^i and the parameters of the i-th agent. We evaluate the above integral on the simulated scenarios. Using Monte Carlo approximation we get,

$$E\left[\ln\frac{\mathbb{P}_{O^i}^i}{\mathbb{P}_{O^i}^m}\right]_{\mathbb{P}_{O^i}^i} = \frac{1}{S}\sum_{s=1}^{S}\ln\left(\frac{\mathbb{P}^i(\mathbf{R}_{\tau,s}^i)}{\mathbb{P}^m(\mathbf{R}_{\tau,s}^i)}\right), \quad (17.10)$$

where $\mathbf{R}_{\tau,s}^i$ are the scenario returns simulated by agent i

In the *IID* setting the joint distribution has a finite support since for each asset the *Dirichlet* distributions have non-zero values for a class only if returns have been observed for that class. Since the *K-L* divergence is not defined whenever the distributions have not the same support, and, furthermore, is sensitive to histogram binning (i.e. the classes), in the *IID* setting we implement an empirically derived modification of the *K-L* divergence, the *Jeffrey* divergence, that is numerically stable, symmetric and robust with respect to noise and the size of histogram bins. This measure, matching only pairs of bins that have the same index, is defined as,

$$D_J(i,m) = \sum_b\left(f_b^i\ln\frac{f_b^i}{f^*} + f_b^m\ln\frac{f_b^m}{f^*}\right), \quad (17.11)$$

where b are the bins, $f^* = (f_b^i + f_b^m)/2$, and f^i, f^m are the joint density distributions of agent i and m respectively.

In the case of Normal copula, with correlation matrix ρ, the joint density function $f(r_1,\ldots,r_N)$ turns out to be:

$$f(r_1,\ldots,r_N) = \frac{1}{|\rho|^{\frac{1}{2}}} \exp\left(-\frac{1}{2}r^\mathsf{T}(\rho^{-1} - \mathbb{I})r\right) \prod_{j=1}^{N} f_j(r_j). \tag{17.12}$$

In our specific case, after some calculus, the Jeffrey divergence turns out to be,

$$D_J(i,m) = a + \sum_{j=1,c=1}^{N,C} \left(f_{j,c}^i \ln f_{j,c}^i + f_{j,c}^m \ln f_{j,c}^m\right) + \\ - 2E\left[\ln\left(\prod_{j=1}^{N} f_j^i(r_j) + \prod_{j=1}^{N} f_j^m(r_j)\right)\right]_{f^*}, \tag{17.13}$$

where $a = 2\ln 2$, C are the classes, $f_{j,c}^i$ are defined as in equation 17.6, and the expected value is evaluated by Monte Carlo approximation using the scenario returns simulated by both agents i and m.

Differences in beliefs will have an impact on returns dynamics indirectly through agents' optimal allocation choices. Thus, in addition, we analyze the evolution of population heterogeneity in terms of optimal asset allocations. We look at the temporal behavior of the population average optimal asset allocations $\bar{h}_{jt} = 1/M \sum_{i=1}^{M} h_{ijt}^*$, and of the dispersion, $\sigma_{jt}(h_{ijt}^*)$, around these mean values. Moreover, we build a compact measure of the population heterogeneity in terms of optimal portfolio choices, summing, at each point in time, the *Euclidean distance (ED)* between each pair of optimal allocation vectors. Letting $a = M(M-1)/2$ be the number of EDs for a population of M agents, we get,

$$ED(h^*) = \sum_{1}^{a} \left(\sum_{j=1, i<m}^{N} (h_{j,i}^* - h_{j,m}^*)^2\right)^{1/2}. \tag{17.14}$$

17.3 Calibration and Results

17.3.1 Simulation Parameters

We run our simulations with a population of $M = 6000$ potentially active traders, $T = 4000$ trading days, and $N = 3$ risky assets. Each trading day is divided in $K = 360$ time steps. Every agent gets an initial endowment in each of the N stocks of our economy of 50 shares, and a cash endowment of $C_i = €\,1000$. Initial prices are set equal to €\,100. Agents are divided in $G = 12$ equally sized groups. All the agents in a group share the same view about the joint distribution of returns. In both settings agents share, the same investment horizon of $\tau = 240$ days, the same parameter of relative risk aversion γ. The updating process is asynchronous and it is triggered by the agents' difficulty to reach optimal portfolios. Every twenty days, at the beginning of the trading day, one group is extracted for updating. The probability of extraction is proportional to $\Delta_g(t)$, a function that combines the group portfolio unbalance with the number of attempts to trade, since the last updating time, of the agents in the g-th group,

$$\Delta_g(t) = \sum_{i \in g} \Delta_i \sum_{i \in g, j=\tau_g^*}^{t} I(i,j), \qquad (17.15)$$

where $g = 1, \ldots, 12$, τ_g^* is the last updating time of group g, $I(i,j) = 1$ whenever agent i entered the market at time j, 0 otherwise. The mechanism implemented is such that each group is extracted for updating on average once a year.

To calibrate the parameters of the model, we follow Guidolin and Timmermann (2007), which have estimated a multivariate gaussian regime switching model using US monthly time series data. Specifically, we borrow the number of states, $\Psi = 4$, and the state-contingent structure of the multivariate gaussian return distribution. Under the specified parameter calibration, the three assets can be interpreted as representing a specific asset class (large stocks, small stocks, and long-term bonds), while the states represent a particular state of the economy: *crash* (negative returns, highly volatile); *slow-growth* (small positive returns, low volatility); *bull* (sustained growth on average, low volatility) *recovery* (highest drifts, highly volatile).

To make the two learning settings comparable, we set the correlation matrix in the *IID* setting equal to the one obtained estimating the parameters of a single state model. Moreover, we set the parameters of the marginal return distributions to ensure that the initial population heterogeneity, measured empirically in terms of distance among scenarios, is of the same magnitude in the two settings.

All the simulations are initialized using a common historical path of returns, and assigning, before the first updating date[6], random target allocation vectors sampled from a Dirichlet(1,...,1;1).

We analyze how the dynamics of the distribution of beliefs over time affects market volatility, and how results change varying $\gamma \in \{2.5, 4, 5.5, 7.5, 10\}$.

17.3.2 Comparison between the Learning Models

In general, both settings generate fat-tails, serial dependence in volatility, and return series generally uncorrelated. But the two settings have very different characteristics when γ varies.

In Figure 17.1 we show the temporal evolution of population heterogeneity, both in terms of optimal allocations and in terms of beliefs, under the two settings.

---

[6] At day 220 all agent groups completed the first round of the asynchronous updating process.

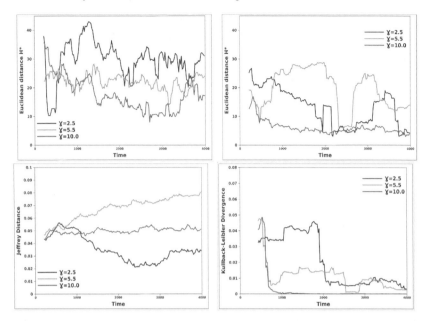

Fig. 17.1 Temporal evolution of the measures of population heterogeneity under the two learning structures for different levels of γ. In the upper panels, from left to right, we display the *Euclidean* distance among optimal allocations for the **IID** and the **HMM** setting. In the bottom panels we show the distance in beliefs: from left to right, the *Jeffrey* divergence for the **IID**, and the *K-L* divergence for the **HMM** setting.

In the *IID* setting the parameter of risk aversion does not seem to affect the evolution of population heterogeneity. For all γ, the *Euclidean* distance among optimal allocations strongly fluctuates over time around initial levels. Correspondingly, the *Jeffrey* dissimilarity measure, regardless the level of risk aversion, shows a tendency to diverge.

Additionally, as shown in Table 17.1, the asymptotic population allocation vectors stabilize to similar values regardless of the risk aversion (both $\bar{h}_j$, and $\sigma_j(h^*_{ij})$ stay constant when γ changes). In the long run, independently of γ, the population average allocation vectors are mainly concentrated on long-term bonds and small stocks: large stocks tend to disappear from the market[7].

On the contrary, in the *HMM*, as γ increases, the population becomes more homogeneous both in terms of beliefs (scenarios) and in terms of allocation vectors[8]. Consistently, as shown in Table 17.1, the asymptotic standard deviations of optimal

---

[7] This tendency is particularly strong when $\gamma = 2.5$. In this case the large stock survives in the market only for about 250 days. The scarcity of time series data is the reason why we do not compute α, and n^{acf} for this asset.

[8] When $\gamma = 5.5$ the *Euclidean* distance among allocation vectors appears to fluctuate strongly over time in spite of the declining trend of the *KL* divergence. That happens because the agent population converges to believe that the economy will keep on switching between state 1 and 4, that are the states with the greatest difference in allocation vectors.

Table 17.1 Asymptotic population choices and global summary of the distribution properties of the daily absolute returns for the different simulations and different assets. $\bar{h}_j$ and $\sigma_j(h_{ij}^*)$ stands for the asymptotic mean and standard deviation of the population optimal allocations. α stands for the angular coefficient of the 5% tail of the normalized distribution of $|r_t|$, and n^{acf} represents the number of lags where the autocorrelation of $|r_t|$ is significantly greater than 0.

	γ	large-cap h^*		$|r_t|$		small-cap h^*		$|r_t|$		long-term bond h^*		$|r_t|$	
		$\bar{h}_j$	$\sigma_j(h_{ij}^*)$	α	n^{acf}	$\bar{h}_j$	$\sigma_j(h_{ij}^*)$	α	n^{acf}	$\bar{h}_j$	$\sigma_j(h_{ij}^*)$	α	n^{acf}
HMM	2.5	.79	.120	-3.15	300	.18	.042	-3.20	250	.03	.088	-2.32	250
	4.0	.81	.130	-2.93	350	.12	.023	-3.09	350	.07	.115	-2.72	300
	5.5	.76	.167	-3.36	350	.11	.019	-3.32	300	.13	.158	-3.02	250
	7.5	.72	.092	-3.56	600	.10	.016	-3.21	500	.17	.091	-3.38	450
	10.0	.62	.045	-4.60	450	.11	.012	-4.15	450	.27	.043	-4.57	450
IID	2.5	.01	.032	n.c.	n.c.	.35	.189	-4.03	40	.65	.180	-3.94	40
	4.0	.03	.097	-4.5	5	.43	.128	-3.40	10	.54	.095	-4.09	10
	5.5	.01	.029	-3.80	20	.41	.094	-4.48	5	.58	.083	-4.70	5
	7.5	.06	.097	-4.00	20	.42	.131	-3.87	20	.53	.105	-5.25	5
	10.0	.02	.049	-3.50	20	.40	.158	-3.73	20	.58	.128	-3.80	5

portfolio allocations decreases as gamma increases. Moreover, the overall mean allocation to stocks declines with γ, while the population average asymptotic allocation to long-term bonds increases (the $\bar{h}$ of long-term bonds goes from 3% when $\gamma = 2.5$ to 27% when $\gamma = 10$). Additionally, the population heterogeneity tends to decrease over time.

The two learning settings have also different characteristics in terms of endogenous volatility. In Figure 17.2 we plot, for the three assets, the time series of absolute returns generated under the two learning frameworks. Clearly, returns are much more volatile in the *IID* setting, and maintain a high level of volatility over time. Conversely, in the *HMM* setting the volatility of returns decreases over time.

Moreover, only the regime switching setting is able to produce long-memory in volatility. The long-memory behavior of the volatility series appears to be stronger at high levels of γ. A deeper analysis of the average perceived states of the economy shows that for high levels of γ states tend to be much more persistent. This, combined with the fact that the *K-L* distance lowers as γ increases, suggests that autocorrelation of volatility should decay much slower as gamma increases. Indeed, as shown in Table 17.1, we do observe that the autocorrelation of $|r_t|$ is significantly greater than 0 up to a lag that increases from an average value of 267 days ($\gamma = 2.5$), to an average value of 450 days ($\gamma = 10$). On the contrary, in the *IID* setting the autocorrelation function of absolute returns decays rapidly to zero resembling a short-memory process.

To better understand the behavior of the two models in terms of volatility, we plot in Figure 17.3 the time series of prices and population optimal allocations for the long-term bond when $\gamma = 4$ under the two learning schemes. Typically, in the *IID* setting the $\bar{h}_{jt}$ fluctuates over time more strongly than in the *HMM* setting. It seems that while in the *IID* setting volatility is substantially driven by movements of the

17 Asset Return Dynamics under Alternative Learning Schemes

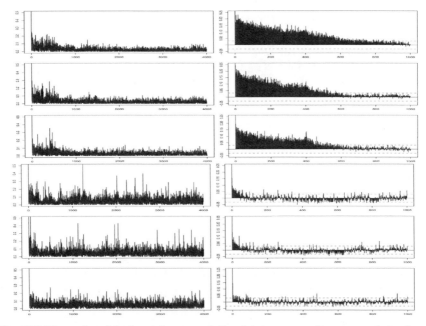

Fig. 17.2 Time series of absolute daily returns (left) and their corresponding autocorrelation function (right) for the different learning settings with $\gamma = 7.5$. In the upper three panels we display the **HMM** model, in the bottom three panels the **IID** setting. The three upper (bottom) panels show the *large-cap*, *small-cap*, and *long-term bond* respectively.

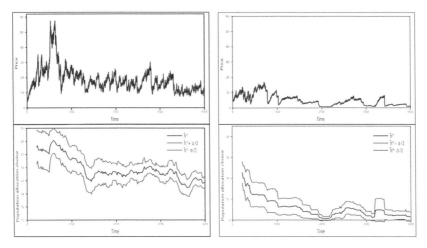

Fig. 17.3 Global overview of prices and population allocation choices of the *long-term bond* for the different learning settings with $\gamma = 4.0$. In the upper panels we display prices, while in the bottom panels we plot $\bar{h}_{jt}$ and $\sigma_{jt}(h^*_{ijt})$. From left to right, we show the **IID** setting and the **HMM** setting respectively.

population average allocation, in the *HMM* setting the pattern of volatility seems to be more related to the pattern of $\sigma_{jt}(h^*_{ijt})$.

In conclusion our simulations show that introducing learning is sufficient to reproduce stylized facts such as fat tails of the return distribution and serial dependence in volatility. We show that there is no need to reject the notion of *ex-ante* rationality as agent-based models normally do. In particular, we show that the regime switching learning structure can generate all the most common stylized facts of financial markets: fat tails and long-range dependence in volatility coexisting with relatively efficient markets.

References

N. Barberis. Investing for the Long Run when Returns are Predictable. *Journal of Finance*, 55:225–264, 2000.

R. Bhar and S. Hamori. *Hidden Markov Models. Application to Financial Economics*. Kluwer Academic, 2004.

P. Bossaerts. Learning–Induced Securities Price Volatility. Working Paper, California Institute of Technology, 1999.

M. Brennan and Y. Xia. Stock Price Volatility and Equity Premium. *Journal of Monetary Economics*, 47:249–283, 2001.

A. Consiglio, V. Lacagnina, and A. Russino. A simulation analysis of the microstructure of an order driven financial market with multiple securities and portfolio choices. *Quantitative Finance*, 5(1):71–87, 2005.

R. Cont. Empirical Properties of Asset Returns: Stylized Facts and Statistical Issues. *Quantitative Finance*, 1:1–14, 2001.

R. Cont. Volatility Clustering in Financial Markets: Empirical Facts and Agent-Based Models. In A. Kirman and G. Teyssiere, editors, *Long Memory in Economics*. Springer, 2005.

M. Guidolin and A. Timmermann. Asset Allocation under Multivariate Regime Switching. *Journal of Economic Dynamics and Control*, 31:3503–3544, 2007.

C. H. Hommes. Heterogeneous Agent Models in Economics and Finance. In K. L. Judd and L. Tesfatsion, editors, *Handbook of Computational Economics*, volume 2. Elsevier Science, 2005.

M. Kurtz and M. Motolese. Endogenous Uncertainty and Market Volatility. *Economic Theory*, 17:497–544, 2001.

J. Lewellen and J. Shanken. Learning, Asset-Pricing Tests, and Market Efficiency. *The Journal of Finance*, LVII:1113–1145, 2002.

A. Pagan. The Econometrics of Financial Markets. *Journal of Empirical Finance*, 3:15–102, 1996.

A. Timmermann. How Learning in Financial Markets Generates Excess Volatilty and Predictability in Stock Prices. *Quarterly Journal of Economics*, pages 1135–1145, 1993.

Chapter 18
An Attempt to Integrate Path-Dependency in a Learning Model

Narine Udumyan, Juliette Rouchier and Dominique Ami

Abstract The absence of information on the state of the resource is considered as one of the main reasons of resource collapses. In the current study, we propose a solution to this problem stemming from the resource users. They can perceive the resource dynamics by the impact it has on their profits. At a given time step, the state of the resource depends on its previous states and hence on the agents' past decisions. In this perspective, different perceptions are characterized by different weights that the resource users assign to the current and past actions in the profit formation. In order to capture these individual differences, we consider Schaefer-Gordon dynamic model. On its basis, we develop a learning model, adapted from Roth-Erev model. The simulation results show that the resource can be exploited in a sustainable manner if the past action is taken into account.

18.1 Introduction

Fisheries are part of common-pool resources (CPR), and display in consequence some of their dynamical and social characteristics. In particular, the depletion of these fisheries can be witnessed everywhere in the world (FAO, 2000) and a political and organizational answer to this depletion is still to be found, in a theoretical way as well as in many different fields.

One of the most important causes of natural resource loss and ecosystem degradation (FAO, 1998) is linked to the difficulties related to the estimation of the real degradation of the resource. It is not uncommon to wrongfully predict the absence

---

N. Udumyan · J. Rouchier
GREQAM, 2, rue de la Charité 13002 Marseille, France, e-mail: `narine.udumyan@univmed.fr`, `juliette.rouchier@univmed.fr`

D. Ami
IDEP DESMID, 2, rue de la Charité 13002 Marseille, France, e-mail: `dominique.ami@univmed.fr`

of overexploitation (Berkes *et al.*, 2001). These errors are dearly paid when the resource estimations represent a sort of reference for the public manager to define the most appropriated management tool. The perception of the state of the resource can be made by two ways: either direct observation or through an analysis of the captures. In fisheries, a direct stock observation is very costly and not necessarily accurate: most of the time the depletion of the resource becomes visible when it gets harder to get fishes. This indirect method of evaluation is accessible to managers, but also to actors on the field, and it could be interesting to see if those actors could use this information to choose the right quantity of fishes to capture.

In this study we would like to know if agents, even if completely unaware of the others, like a tale describing idealistic individualistic behaviours, could get to choose actions that do not destroy the resource they are using. And this unconscious communication could be done in a state of misinformation about the state of the resource and its dynamics.

To study the impact of our hypothesis, we use a dynamic framework that models the level of a CPR in time, transformed by its users' actions and its own internal evolution. The bioeconomic dynamics that is implemented is Schaefer-Gordon model (Gordon, 1954, Schaefer, 1954), very commonly used, which integrates reproduction of fishes and captures by fishers.

We add a social model which has an agent-based structure. Agent-based models (ABM) are regarded as appropriate to explore situations where agents have incomplete knowledge and to identify possible dynamics of complex systems (Janssen and Ostrom, 2006). According to our agent-based model, each agent makes only one individual decision: to decide the effort to exert on the resource. We suppose that the resource dynamics can be perceived via the impact it has on the agents' profits obtained in each time step. In our context, past actions of resource users have an impact on the state of the resource through its temporal dynamics (the current state of the resource depends on its past state and therefore the action that was performed previously). We then chose to consider that agents could learn by associating the profit they make not only to their current action, but also to the previous one. An agent assigns certain weights to the past and current actions, that represent an estimation of their respective role in the profit formation for the current time step. This element is original. It is a variation on the classical Roth-Erev in a context where agents know nothing about the structure of the game they are playing but try to extract the highest profit.

We show that taking into account the past actions for understanding the current profit allows to establish more sustainable situations[1] in the resource exploitation.

The paper is organized in the following manner. In the section 18.2 we explain the motivations of this study. In the section 18.3, main assumptions and a description of the model are given. In sections 18.4 and 18.5, the model is calibrated and main simulation results are presented. In the rest of this paper, we discuss obtained results and explore the perspectives of this study.

---

[1] "Sustainable" is seen here as the possibility to keep a stock of resource and of having positive profit in the long run.

18.2 Study of CPR Based on Information Issue

18.2.1 Lack of Information and Over-Exploitation

There exist empiric researches that study the impact of the uncertainty about the resource on the exploitation of the resource. For instance, Budescu *et al.* (1990) designed experiments where the size of the resource is uncertain to participants who have to decide on their level of exploitation. Their resource follows a uniformly distributed random variable, about which participants only know the lower and upper bounds of the distribution. They are free to request what they want from a common resource pool. In their experiment, as the width of the interval between these bounds increases so does the quantity of the requests, resulting in overharvesting. This finding was replicated several times under different assumptions: asymmetric, symmetric profits, different definition of uncertainty, simultaneous and sequential requests (Foddy, 1999). The uncertainty about resource dynamics was studied by Hine and Gifford (1996). They show that if the replenishment rate of the resource is unknown, overharvesting is also observed.

Cardenas *et al.* (2008) provide another empirical evidence of difficulties encountered by the real actors to make relevant decisions in response to temporal and spatial features of the resource dynamics. They design experiments in which the interactions produce a path-dependency and discuss the difficulties related to this feature of the game. In these experiments, participants know the impact of the effort on the state of the resource. Several access rules are considered, defining several treatment of the experiment. One of them is individual property rule. Overexploitation of the resource occurs in most settings, but also, surprisingly, when land is accessed with the property rule. Cardenas et al. refer to this situation as "fishery trap": once the participants overexploit the resource, even if they realize it, the individual attempts to decrease effort are not sufficient to replenish it.

The goal of the current study is to find out if some simple learning rule could enable agents to avoid this "fishery trap". For this, we rely on a dynamic framework that can reflect the temporal dependence of the state of the resource on the agents' current and past actions. The intuition behind the learning model is to give the agents the opportunity to perceive their past action as having an impact on their current profit.

18.2.2 Dealing with Scarce Information in ABM

The complexity of human choice is widely acknowledged, and is often referred to as bounded rationality. It has been documented in recent years thanks to extensive experimental research. These findings motivate scholars to use new tools to represent bounded rationality in models, and for this ABM are used in a quite general way.

With ABM, the researcher explicitly describes the decision process of simulated actors at the micro level.

In ABM applied to CPR issues, since in real life information about the evolution of the complex resource is not available, learning in the models is based on past actions and their results. A very widely used model that uses past information is reinforcement learning (Duffy, 2006). It is based on a basic psychological observation: actions that lead to rewards are chosen with a higher frequency in the future, while actions that cause punishment become less frequent. One of the first models for reinforcement learning is Roth-Erev model (explained in section 18.3.2). Erev and Roth (Erev and Roth, 1998, Roth and Erev, 1995) propose a model that is based on probabilistic choices: agents are faced with a given set of actions, each of which producing a particular reward at each time-step. The information about these rewards enables them to associate an action to a " propensity " ; all propensities are translated into probabilities to choose an action when the agent needs to act. Erev and Roth have shown that their model explains well the data collected from economic experiments on some social dilemma games. It embodies the most salient regularities observed in the decision-making behavior of human subjects across a wide variety of multi-agent experimental games.

There exist some variations of the standard Roth-Erev model such as the model of Nicolaisen *et al.* (2001) that modify the Roth-Erev rule to address the problems of parameter degeneracy and no probability updating in response to zero profits (the latter occurs in a double-auction context). Another variation, Bereby-Meyer and Erev model (1998) integrates the fact that the position of the reference point delineating the loss and gain domains could be a function of expectations, goals, and experience. Finally, a well-known model links reinforcement and belief learning, under a generalized Experience-Weighted Attraction (EWA) learning model (Camerer and Ho, 1999). Janssen and Ahn (2006) even consider the variation of the latter by including social preferences and signaling component in order to show that individuals have other-regarding preferences of inequality aversion and conditionally cooperative preferences. In these two last versions, the structure of the game needs to be known to agents, since they have to be able to compare their actual utility to what it would have been if they had chosen another action.

After discovering through some preliminary study that the standard Roth-Erev model leads to overharvesting of the resource in the ecological setting we chose, as a variation of this model we decided to incorporate the past actions of agents into their decision process.

18.3 The Model

18.3.1 Main Assumptions and General Framework

Environment. We place our agents in a bioeconomic environment represented by a standard dynamic model of resource exploitation. The biological environment consists of a unique area (one cell) and unique resource. We adopt the Schaeffer-Gordon model's assumptions concerning the harvests and profit function.

Time. Time is discrete. One period represents one day and values are set according to field values.

Resource access. We suppose that the population of Fishers is fixed (we refer to artificial agents as Fisher and real agents as fisher). This hypothesis is based on the fact that the artisanal fishery is exerted by small communities in which there is almost no entry (McGoodwin, 2003).

Cost and price. In the context of small fisheries, the quantity that is caught has very small impact on the price, considered as exogenous. In our main model, we fix this price for the whole simulation. We also fix the cost, homogenous in the population.

Agents. The Fishers do not have any information about the state or the dynamics of the resource and have no idea that other Agents are using the resource either. An Agent performs one choice per time-step: the effort that it puts on the resource. This effort is chosen among a set of possible values. Agents have the same set of values and the same learning model.

Learning. Agents use Erev and Roth model and our variation: they store all past information as an aggregate form (a propensities associated to each possible action) and translate the propensities in probabilities to choose an action at each step. This process includes a forgetting parameter (here φ), an experimentation parameter (ε) and a distinction parameter β to discriminate actions when translating the propensities. Here, for each profit, two actions can be seen as a causal factor: the one they performed at the current time-step and the one of the previous time-step, both are weighted with a parameter θ that integrates this fact in the learning model. We want to test the influence of θ.

Observation. We are interested in "sustainability" of our artificial system and our definition of sustainability is based on the economic criteria: no Fisher can ever have negative profit along a simulation.

18.3.2 Resource Dynamics and Probabilistic Choice of Effort

We consider N agents and assume that the resource dynamics follows Schaefer-Gordon model (Gordon, 1954, Schaefer, 1954):

$$X_{t+1} = X_t + F(X_t) - \sum H_t^i, \qquad (18.1)$$

where X_t denotes the biomass of the fish population at time t, $F(X)$ is a given function representing the natural growth rate of the fish population, E_t is the effort exerted by the agent at time t and where H_t^i is a function of harvests of the agent i at time t. Standard assumptions are made on the latter functions (for more details see Clark, 2005). $F(X)$ follows a logistic law:

$$F(X_t) = rX_t(1 - X_t/K), \qquad (18.2)$$

with r intrinsic growth rate, K environmental carrying capacity (saturation level). Harvests H are proportional to the resource's biomass and the fishing effort E:

$$H_t^i = kE_t^i X_t, \qquad (18.3)$$

where k is a catchability coefficient.

The economic component of the model is described by the profit provided by the fishery resource at each given level of effort E:

$$\Pi_t^i = pH_t^i - cE_t^i, \qquad (18.4)$$

where Π_t^i is the profit of the agent i at time t, p price per unit of resource, H_t^i harvests at time t, c cost per unit of effort, and E_t is the effort employed by the agent i at time t. As said before, the price p and the cost c are fixed and unique.

Suppose that each agent has M actions that represent feasible harvesting efforts (here $M = 41$). The agents base their decision about the effort on aggregated information about past exploitation of the resource called propensities $q_{ij}(t)$. They change over time and define the propensity to play the action j in period t for the agent i. Initial (period 1) propensities are equal $q_{ij}(1) = q_{im}(1)$ for all available actions j, m and all agents i, and $\sum_j q_{ij}(1) = S_i(1)$, where $S_i(1)$ is an initial strength parameter, equal to a constant that is the same for all players, $S_i(1) = S(1)$. Lower is the value of initial strengths, faster is the learning.

The probability $p_{ij}(t)$ that agent i plays action j in period t is made according to the exponential choice rule:

$$p_{ij}(t) = \exp(\beta q_{ij}(t)) / \sum_m \exp(\beta q_{im}(t)), \qquad (18.5)$$

where β is a distinction parameter that measures the sensitivity of probabilities to reinforcements. The parameter β reinforces the differences between the propensities $q_{ij}(t)$. The higher the value of the parameter β, more distinct are the values of $q_{ij}(t)$ and it is more probable that the system converge to a steady state.

Suppose that, in period t, agent i plays action k and receives a profit of x. Let $R(x_t) = x_t - x_t^{\min}$, where $x_t^{\min}$ is the smallest profit in the set of all profits obtained during t periods[2]. In the standard Roth-Erev model, $R(x_t)$ is entirely associated to the action k. We transform the Roth-Erev model so that it is possible for the agent to

---

[2] This definition of the payoff function $R(x_t)$ corresponds to the one described in a particular case of the Bereby-Meyer and Erev model (for more details, see Bereby-Meyer and Erev, 1998).

associate profit at t to its action in $(t-1)$³ and for this we introduce an additional parameter $\theta \in [0,1]$ that gives weight to past and current action. When $\theta = 0$ only the past action is associated to the profit; when $\theta = 1$ only the present action is; When $0 < \theta < 1$ the profit is partly associated to both actions.

Thus, agent i updates his propensity to play action j according to the rule:

$$q_{ij}(t+1) = \begin{cases} (1-\varphi)q_{ij}(t) + \theta(1-\varepsilon)R(\Pi_t) + \\ \quad + (1-\text{sgn}(\theta))\varepsilon R(\Pi_t)/(N-1), & \text{if } j = C, \\ (1-\varphi)q_{ij}(t) + (1-\theta)(1-\varepsilon)R(\Pi_t) + \\ \quad + (\text{sgn}(\theta-1)+1)\varepsilon R(\Pi_t)/(N-1), & \text{if } j = P, \\ (1-\varphi)q_{ij}(t) + \varepsilon R(\Pi_t)(N-1), & \text{if } j = NC, \end{cases} \quad (18.6)$$

where C is the action chosen in period t (current action), P is the action chosen in period $t-1$ (past action) and NC are the actions that were not chosen in periods t and $t-1$. φ is classically interpreted as a forgetting parameter that gradually reduces the role of past experience, ε an experimentation parameter that allows for some experimentation, and we define θ as the weight associated to the current action.

If $\theta = 1$, we have the standard Roth-Erev model. If $\theta = 0$ the profit obtained at t is entirely associated to the action performed at $t-1$. Finally, if $0 < \theta < 1$, the agents take into account both current and past actions with weights $1-\theta$ and θ respectively that determine the importance of each of the two actions in the formation of the current profit.

18.4 Simulations

Our model is calibrated on few studies that exist on artisanal fisheries in the French Mediterranean and in France in general. The parameters of the bioeconomic model were adjusted according to the real data provided by Jouvenel and Faure (2005) for the Prado bay, Marseilles, and more general data describing the French Mediterranean fishery (Berthou et al., 2001).

We fix two learning parameters $\varphi = 0.1$ and $\varepsilon = 0.1$ of the standard Roth-Erev model. These values are consistent with the ranges reported in Erev and Roth (1998), $0 < \varphi < 0.20$ and $0.02 < \varepsilon < 0.30$, that show the best fit to their experimental data covering twelve distinct types of human-subject games. The value of the parameter β is chosen so that the learning would converge. Note that for each number of agents and values of φ and ε, we fix β.

Two parameters are varying in our system, θ our crucial parameter, and the number of agents, which stays small. Values of θ are $0, 0.1, 0.25, 0.5, 0.75$ and 1. Values of N are $2, 8$ and 16. We observe more precisely two values of θ which are 0 and 1. We run 100 simulations for each set of parameters and 10000 periods. In order

---

[3] Here, we do not integrate more than one step in the past.

to analyze the impact of different learning models, we give here the following indicators, although we observed many more: percentage of economically sustainable scenarios; resource biomass in the final period; average global profit at last timestep. All these indicators except for the first one are given as average and standard deviation to judge their variations from simulation to simulation.

18.5 Results

In this section we will describe results, and those will be explained in the following section.

Among the values of θ we chose, the value of θ that corresponds to the classical Erev-Roth model ($\theta = 1$) is not performing as well as the others. In this case, the only situation where agents reduce their effort is when they get negative profit (and hence the simulation is not sustainable). With other high values of θ, $\theta = 0.5$ and $\theta = 0.75$ we get non sustainable outcomes (which also imply very low fish stock). When the resource can no longer provide positive profits, the agents do not immediately reduce their efforts, and it takes a long period of time to settle on efforts which are low enough to give sustainable situations. Most of the time, the learning phase is too long to have Fishers be able to stay in the fishery.

In simulations where past has more importance (for $0 \leq \theta \leq 0.25$), we mostly get sustainable simulations. These learning models imply faster learning, and Fisher do not need to approach negative profit to choose sustainable efforts.

In summary: the lower the value of θ, the more Fishers keep the resource available over a long period without negative profit, or said differently: the number of sustainable scenarios reduces as the value of θ increases (see for more details in Table 18.1). We will explain in the next section the reason why this fact emerges.

After observing the main differences among scenarios with two agents, we increase the number of Agents. In all settings, the total value of effort that is made by the Fishers remains the same and Fishers have the same number of possible efforts, with a smaller difference between each possible effort. This is the reason why we have to increase the value of β (discrimination parameter) to stabilize learning.

Considering that the Fishers learn with information based on their individual actions, it is to be expected that the presence of many others will reduce the impact of each Agent and hence disturb the learning system we have established. Increasing the number of agents indeed complicates the coordination of agents. The variability and of the system increases with the number of agents and its dynamics becomes more stochastic.

We report in Table 18.1 simulation results for 2, 8 and 16 Fishers. We have three main results: 1/ the higher the number of Fishers, the more severe the exploitation of the resource 2/ if $\theta = 0$, the higher the number of Fishers, the higher the profit 3/ when θ increases, the system gets less sustainable.

18 An Attempt to Integrate Path-Dependency in a Learning Model   231

Table 18.1 Statistics of 100 simulations for $N = 2$, 8 and 16, $\beta = 15$, 60 and 120 respectively, $\varphi = 0.1$, $\varepsilon = 0.1$. The values are the average of 100 simulations. In the brackets we present the standard deviation of each indicator

	2 Agents		
Value of θ	Econ. sust. scenarios (%)	Biomass end	Global Profit
0	83	254 (115)	0,8473 (0,2786)
0.1	72	217 (98)	0,8532 (0,3014)
0.25	40	210 (93)	0,8535 (0,3086)
	8 Agents		
Value of θ	Econ. sust. scenarios (%)	Biomass end	Global Profit
0	100	204 (85)	0,8776 (0,3114)
0.1	84	156 (62)	0,7404 (0,3192)
0.25	38	131 (53)	0,612 (0,3322)
	16 Agents		
Value of θ	Econ. sust. scenarios (%)	Biomass end	Global Profit
0	100	184 (55)	0,8979 (0,2423)
0.1	85	133 (46)	0,639 (0,2708)
0.25	37	92 (31)	0,3586 (0,2485)

18.6 Discussions

In this discussion we want to explain two facts that we observed in our model: the scenarios are more sustainable when θ is lower; the resource is less depleted when the number of agents is lower (although total maximum effort stays the same).

The fact that more scenarios are sustainable when the profit is associated to the past can be explained in a mechanical way but is also interesting in terms of global interpretation about coordination among individuals with private information. In the situation when the resource can lead to positive profit when it is harvested (like at the beginning of the simulation), and considering the values of price and cost, it is always the case that Fisher gets higher profit when its effort is higher. For example, if Agents use the basic Erev-Roth rule ($\theta = 1$) the only observation they can get is 'higher efforts yield higher profits'. The high efforts are hence chosen more frequently from the beginning of simulations which leads to the depletion of the resource and negative profits. This stays true, if the learning links profit to current action in an important way (here more than 0.5 for $\theta \geq 0.5$): Agents discover and learn that it is always better to choose a higher effort.

It could logically seem a bit strange that the "best" learning (according to our indicators) does not take into account present action. Clearly we disturb the straightforward causal link between effort and profit when we introduce the past action in the learning. In that case, it can seem like the Agents learn on the basis of "wrong" information. When an agent associate the profit to the past, it can associate a given profit to completely different preceding efforts, for example a very high one and a very low one, which would be impossible in the classical learning. This means that the possibility of associating high profit to low effort is possible. Considering our resource dynamics, it is even clear that it is not only possible, but also more frequent that profit get higher after the Agent chose a small effort (the resource is less depleted and any effort gives a higher profit than if the resource had been overused). The possibility of an association that could seem to be a wrong inference reveals itself to be an inference that is coherent with the dynamics of the resource. This is why our learning is working so well in our setting. This result is very interesting since it reminds a little bit of the fundamental result of Gode and Sunder (1993) whose Zero-Intelligent agents (with no learning at all) perform well just because the structure of interactions they evolve in forces them to behave well. Here, our Agents do not know why it is a good idea to believe that the current action has no impact on the profit (and it is wrong) but the structure of the resource is such that this misbelief is useful to them in the long term. It is to be noted that the role of misbelief in artificial (and real) societies has been shown by Doran some years ago (Doran, 1998).

Considering the dynamics of our model, we could interpret the difference in performance between these different learning models by saying that the case when $\theta \geq 0.5$ Fishers are directly sensitive to economic results, whereas when they have $\theta \leq 0.25$ they are indirectly sensitive to biological dynamics.

Increasing the number of agents affects the observed regularities induced by different perceptions of resource dynamics because it slows down the adaptation of the agents to the resource dynamics complicated by increased number of other agents' impacts to take into consideration. Therefore for large numbers of agents coordination is necessary between the agents in order to attain a sustainable exploitation of the resource. We need to increase the value of the discrimination parameter, since the difference between possible actions gets too small for agents to see difference in implied profits.

18.7 Conclusion

Our most important finding is that taking into account the previous action as having a role in the profit formation has an impact on global dynamics of fishing. This can be explained by the non-linear dependence between this action and the current state of the resource via growth function in contrast to the current action having linear impact to the state of the resource as well as on the current profits. Indeed, according to Cardenas *et al.* (2008), the difficulties of overcoming the fishery trap are related to the non linear relation between perceived profits and employed efforts via the resource dynamics. This finding explains why using the information on the past action enables the agents to exploit the resource in a sustainable manner.

Our study deals with a bio-economic system where the lack of information is central. Here, there is no intervention of exogenous manager, and resource users are the only ones who can make decisions about the resource. Even more, they act without communicating, so perceiving the resource as if they were the only ones. If they take into account the relationship between their past actions and current profits, overexploitation of the resource can be avoided. This can be interpreted as the possibility for users to perform well, although they are not constrained and they do not know the exact stock or dynamics of the resource (in our model they do not even "know" that there is a dynamics but they just perceive it indirectly). Being purely mechanical, this result can be potentially extended to real-life users of a common-pool resource.

Of course, users will never learn with Erev-Roth model. However, our simulations mainly underline the importance of taking into account the temporal features of the resource dynamics. This significant element can be integrated in awareness campaign targeting education of local communities in environmental issues. The relationship between their current and past behavior and their current benefits becoming more transparent with the help of awareness campaigns, it is possible to increase the conservational motivation of resource users. This could therefore become a powerful motivating tool leading to a more responsible resource use.

References

Bereby-Meyer, Y., I. Erev, 1998. On Learning To Become a Successful Loser: A Comparison of Alternative Abstractions of Learning Processes in the Loss Domain. Journal of Mathematical Psychology 42, 266–286.

Berthou, P., F. Daurès, O. Guyader, E. Leblond, C. Merrien, M. Jezequel, 2001. Synthèse des Pêcheries 2001, Flotte Méditerranée : PACA et Languedoc-Roussillon. Direction des Ressources Vivantes - Système d'Informations Halieutiques, Ifremer.

Berkes, F., R. Mahon, P. McConney, R. Pollnac et R. Pomeroy, 2001. Managing small-scale fisheries alternative directions and methods.

Budescu, D. V., A. Rapoport, A., R. Suleiman, 1990. Resource dilemmas with environmental uncertainty and asymmetric players. European Journal of Social Psychology, 20, 475–487.

Camerer, C. F., and T. H. Ho, 1999. Experience-weighted attraction learning in normal form games. Econometrica 67(4): 827–874.

Cardenas J.-C., M. Janssen, F. Bousquet, 2008. Dynamics of Rules and Resources: Three New Field Experiments on Water, Forests and Fisheries. Chapter submitted for a Handbook on experimental Economics and the Environment edited by John List and Michael Price (Edward Elgar Publishing).

Clark, C.W., 1990, 2005. Mathematical Bioeconomics, The optimal management of renewable ressources, John Wiley.

Doran J., 1998, Simulating Collective Misbelief, Journal of Artificial Societies and Social Simulation, 1 (1).

Duffy, J., 2006. Agent-Based Models and Human Subject Experiments, Handbook of Computational Economics, in: Leigh Tesfatsion & Kenneth L. Judd (ed.), Handbook of Computational Economics, edition 1, volume 2, chapter 19, pages 949–1011 Elsevier.

Erev, I., A. E. Roth, 1998. Predicting How People Play Games with Unique, Mixed-Strategy Equilibria, American Economic Review 88: 848–881.

Foddy, M., 1999. Resolving Social Dilemmas: Dynamic, Structural, and Intergroup Aspects, Psychology Press; 1 edition, 388 p.

Food and Agriculture Organization of the United Nations (FAO), ed. Scialabba, Nadia, 1998. Integrated coastal area management and agriculture, forestry and fisheries. FAO Guidelines, Rome. 256 p.

Food and Agriculture Organization of the United Nations (FAO), 2000. La situation mondiale des pêches et de l'aquaculture.

McGoodwin, J.R., 2003, Comprendre la culture des communautés de pêcheurs: élément fondamental pour la gestion des pêches et la sécurité alimentaire. FAO Document technique sur les pêches. No. 401. Rome, FAO. 2003. 335 p.

Gode D.K., S. Sunder, 1993, Allocative efficiency of markets with zero intelligence traders: markets as a partial substitute for individual rationality, Journal of Political Economy, 101, pp 119–137.

Gordon, H.S., 1954. The economic theory of a common property resource, Journal of Political Economy 62: 124–142.

Hine, D. V., and R. Gifford, 1996. Individual restraint and group efficiency in commons dilemmas: The effects of uncertainty and risk-seeking. Journal of Applied Social Psychology, 26, 993–1009.

Janssen, M.A., and T.K. Ahn, 2006. Learning, signaling, and social preferences in public-good games, Ecology and Society 11(2): 21.

Janssen, M.A., E. Ostrom, 2006. Chapter 30. Governing Social-Ecological Systems, Handbook of Computational Economics, Volume 2, 1465–1509.

Jouvenel, J.-Y., Faure, V., 2005. Etat zéro de la " pêche artisanale aux petits métiers " dans la baie du Prado (rade sud de Marseille) - Rapport final. Contrat P2A Développement - Ville de Marseille, Direction de la Qualité de Vie Partagée, Division Mer et Littoral, octobre 2005 : 92pp.

Nicolaisen, J., V. Petrov, L. Tesfatsion, 2001. Market Power and Efficiency in a Computational Electricity Market with Discriminatory Double-Auction Pricing, IEEE Transactions on Evolutionary Computation 5(5), 504–523.

Roth, A.E., Erev, I., 1995. Learning in Extensive Form Games: Experimental Data and Simple Dynamic Models in the Intermediate Run, Games and Economic Behavior 6: 164–212.

Schaefer, M.B., 1954. Some aspects of the dynamics of populations important to the management of commercial marine fisheries, Inter-American Tropical Tuna Commission, Bulletin, 1, p. 25–26.

Part VII
Methodological Issues

Chapter 19
A Model-to-Model Analysis of the Repeated Prisoners' Dilemma: Genetic Algorithms *vs.* Evolutionary Dynamics

Xavier Vilà

Abstract We study the properties of the well known Replicator Dynamics when applied to a finitely repeated version of the Prisoners' Dilemma game. We characterize the behavior of such dynamics under strongly simplifying assumptions (i.e. only 3 strategies are available) and show that the basin of attraction of defection shrinks as the number of repetitions increases. After discussing the difficulties involved in trying to relax the "strongly simplifying assumptions" above, we approach the same model by means of simulations based on genetic algorithms. The resulting simulations describe a behavior of the system very close to the one predicted by the replicator dynamics without imposing any of the assumptions of the analytical model. Our main conclusion is that analytical and computational models are good complements for research in social sciences. Indeed, while on the one hand computational models are extremely useful to extend the scope of the analysis to complex scenarios hard to analyze mathematically, on the other hand formal models can be extremely useful to verify and to explain the outcomes of computational models.

19.1 Introduction

In the growing field of Agent-Based computer simulations applied to social sciences, model replication is considered a key issue. Indeed, asserting whether the observed results of a particular simulation of a model are correct or generalizable is a difficult task when no formal (i.e. mathematical) proof is provided. Only replication, comparison, alignment, and other related techniques can shed some light on the validity of simulations. This work contains one such comparison. We put side-by-side two different analysis (mathematical and computational) of the same model: the evolution of strategies in the repeated prisoners' dilemma.

First, we consider the case in which the evolutionary system can be described by a deterministic dynamic system that uses expected values. Using strong simplifying

---

X. Vilà
Universitat Autònoma de Barcelona, Spain, e-mail: Xavier.Vila@uab.cat

assumptions we are able to solve this case and to produce a complete description of how the process behaves. We also discuss the problems involved when we try to relax some of the assumptions made.

The second approach is a computational simulation in which finite automata are used to represent the strategies played and a decentralized adaptive process based on the models of genetic algorithms to simulate the stochastic evolutionary process. With this technique we can relax some of the strong assumptions used in the first approach and still obtain the same basic results.

We like to think that the limitations of the first approach (analytical) provide a good motivation for the second approach (Agent-Based simulations). Indeed, although both approaches address the same problem, we show that the use of Agent-Based computational techniques allows us to relax hypothesis and overcome the limitations of the analytical approach. On the other hand, it is shown that the analytical model is extremely useful in order to explain the behavior and the causality of the results of the computational model.

The choice of the repeated prisoners' dilemma to conduct the experiment described above is not arbitrary. It is a well know and largely studied game, and many things about it have been learned thanks to the tools of formal game theory. But when the game is studied from an evolutionary perspective, the results are not always clear. The works by Boyd and Lorberbaum (1987) and Binmore and Samuelson (1992), for instance, show that evolutionary stable solutions may fail to exists in many versions of the game. Experiments and simulations, on the other hand, like the ones conducted by Axelrod (1984), Axelrod and Hamilton (1981), Nowak and Sigmund (1992), or Miller (1996), seem to suggest that Tit-for-tat (and other similar strategies) prevail in most of the situations. Thus, the interest of our research is putting these two approaches, analytical and computational, side-by-side to achieve a better understanding of the evolutionary behavior of players in the repeated prisoners' dilemma

19.2 The Analytical Model

The basic stage game (Prisoners' Dilemma) that players will play repeatedly is given by

	C	D
C	3,3	0,5
D	5,0	1,1

We now consider the repeated version of the game played a finite number of rounds R. In order to keep things simple, we only consider three possible strategies (as in Nowak *et al.*, 2004):

- D: Always defect
- C: Always cooperate
- T: Tit-for-Tat

as they are the three strategies that have deserved a higher attention in almost all the literature dealing with the Repeated Prisoner's Dilemma from an evolutionary point of view. The fact that we only consider 3 possible strategies clearly imposes a strong restriction to the analysis, as we will discuss later. Given the above, the repeated game can be represented as follows

	C	D	T
C	$3R, 3R$	$0, 5R$	$3R, 3R$
D	$5R, 0$	R, R	$5+(R-1), (R-1)$
T	$3R, 3R$	$(R-1), 5+(R-1)$	$3R, 3R$

Thus, for instance, when a D-type strategy meets a T-type strategy, the former gets 5 in the first round and then 1 in each subsequent round ($5+(R-1)$ in total), while the later gets 0 first and then 1 in each subsequent round ($R-1$ in total).

19.2.1 The Replicator Dynamics Analysis

Let $p_t(C)$ be the probability that, at time t, a player in this population is an "always cooperate" type, and the same for $p_t(D)$ and $p_t(T)$. We thus have that $p_t(C) + p_t(D) + p_t(T) = 1 \ \forall t$.

The replicator dynamics states that the rate of change of such probabilities is a function of the relative performance of each strategy with respect to the average performance of the population. In this sense, given $p_t(C), p_t(D), p_t(T)$, the expected payoff for each strategy is:

$$E_t \pi(C) = 3Rp_t(C) + 0p_t(D) + 3Rp_t(T) = 3R(P_t(C) + p_t(T)),$$
$$E_t \pi(D) = 5Rp_t(C) + Rp_t(D) + (5+(R-1))p_t(T),$$
$$E_t \pi(T) = 3Rp_t(C) + (R-1)p_t(D) + 3Rp_t(T)$$
$$= 3R(P_t(C) + p_t(T)) + (R-1)p_t(D),$$

and the average payoff will be:

$$E_t \bar{\pi} = E_t \pi(C) p_t(C) + E_t \pi(D) p_t(D) + E_t \pi(T) p_t(T). \tag{19.1}$$

Notice that since $p_t(C) + p_t(D) + p_t(T) = 1 \ \forall t$ only two dimensions matter. Hence, the replicator dynamics in this case is given by:

$$\frac{\partial p_t(C)}{\partial t} = p_t(C)(E_t \pi(C) - E_t \bar{\pi}),$$
$$\frac{\partial p_t(D)}{\partial t} = p_t(D)(E_t \pi(D) - E_t \bar{\pi}),$$

and the corresponding vector field showing the trajectories of the system is given in Figure 19.1 (the direction of the flows is form right to left).

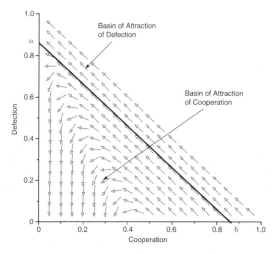

Fig. 19.1 Vector Field

The horizontal and vertical axis in Figure 19.1 correspond to $p_t(C)$ and $p_t(D)$ respectively. Thus, the three vertexes of the triangle $((1,0), (0,1), \text{and}\, (0.0))$, correspond to the states $p_t(C) = 1, p_t(D) = 1, \text{and}\, p_t(T) = 1$ respectively. The trajectories that represent the evolution of the system are divided in two areas or basins of attraction, one for Defection and another for Cooperation. Stationary points of the system are marked red: $(0,1)$ corresponding to everybody playing *always defect* $p_t(D) = 1$, $(0,(2R-4)/(2R-3))$, and all the points in the line that goes from $(0,0)$ to $(1,0)$ that corresponds to points with no *defectants*, that is, $p_t(D) = 0$ and $p_t(C) + p_t(T) = 1$. Only the point $(0,1)$ corresponding to $p_t(D) = 1$ is asymptotically stable in the sense that if the system is slightly perturbed away from $(0,1)$, any trajectory will bring it back to the same point. The singular point $(0,(2R-4)/(2R-3))$ can only be reached if the system starts somewhere in the line that goes from $(0,(2R-4)/(2R-3))$ to $((R-2)/(R-1),0)$, which occurs with zero probability.

An important result is that the relative size of these basins of attraction depends on the number of repetition R. That is, if the system starts at random, the probability of reaching the point $(0,1)$ (everybody defecting) or the line $(0,0) \rightarrow (1,0)$ (everybody cooperating) depends on R. Thus, we can compute what is the *expected per-round payoff* a priori depending on R.

$$E\bar{\pi} = \left(\frac{2R-4}{2R-3}\right)\left(\frac{R-2}{R-1}\right) \cdot 3 + \left(1 - \left(\frac{2R-4}{2R-3}\right)\left(\frac{R-2}{R-1}\right)\right) \cdot 1. \quad (19.2)$$

Figure 19.2 shows the behavior of the *expected per-round payoff* as a function of R. We observe that it grows rapidly as the number of repetitions (R) increases. In fact, $E\bar{\pi} \rightarrow 3$ as $R \rightarrow \infty$.

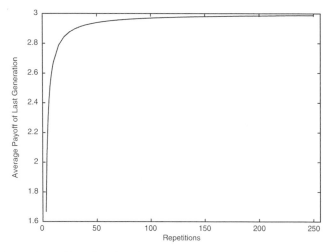

Fig. 19.2 Expected payoff as a function of R

19.3 The Computational Model

Given the analysis above, the dynamics seem to suggest that there is room for cooperation. At least for a broad range of initial conditions, the trajectories lead to some point in the horizontal axis corresponding to a population consisting of *only* C and T strategies.

Nevertheless, such analysis is extremely partial since we are only considering 3 strategies at a time, namely C, D, and T. One can easily see that extending this approach to a more general case (with more strategies considered) is a difficult task.

To overcome this limitation, we develop a computer simulation in which the strategies are represented by finite automata of size four (encoded as binary strings of 0's and 1's) and a Genetic Algorithm routine is used to simulate the evolutionary process as in Miller (1996). The algorithm was run for 5000 generations starting from an initial random population of 100 strategies using the standard single-cut crossover operator and with a probability of per-bit mutation of 0.005. In most of the cases, the results of such simulations produce the outcome in Figure 19.3, in which the evolution of the (per round) average payoff is displayed.

Because the final average payoff is 3 we can conclude that all players follow a cooperative strategy.

In other cases, though, cooperation is not the final result as the evolution of the average payoff results as in Figure 19.4, which corresponds to the case of all the players defecting.

In both cases, though, the resemblance between the vector field in Figure 19.1 and the evolution of payoffs in Figures 19.3 and 19.4 is very appealing. When the final result is *cooperation* (as in Figure 19.3), both in the replicator dynamic analysis and in the simulations, the evolutionary process seems to favor the growth of Defectant strategies at first, and then these disappear and Cooperative strategies start to replicate to end up with the payoff corresponding to the cooperative behavior. On

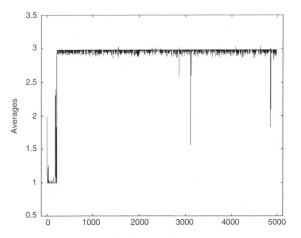

Fig. 19.3 Evolution of the average per-round payoff when Cooperation is the result

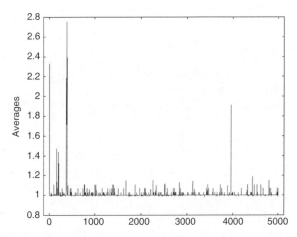

Fig. 19.4 Evolution of the average per-round payoff when Defection is the result

the contrary, when the final result is *defection*, the evolution goes "monotonically" towards that point.

How often each of these two results occurs? Given that in the analytical model we have found out that the answer to this question depends upon the number of repetitions R, we check whether R also has an effect in the computational model. In this sense, Figure 19.5 complements Figure 19.2 by showing how the final observed average payoff of the simulations[1] (the payoff of generation 5000) depends on R. For robustness, we do such exercise with two different crossover rules and with no crossover

---

[1] For each value of R we run 100 simulations and compute the average payoff of the last generation (5000)

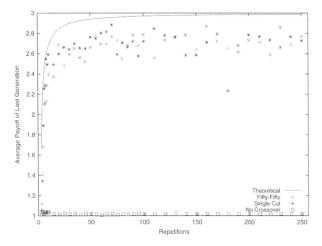

Fig. 19.5 Expected and observed payoffs as a function of R

Figure 19.5 shows how the behavior of the simulations also resembles what we obtained theoretically in the previous section. That is, as the number of repetitions R grows, the higher is the probability of reaching cooperation as the final result and hence, the higher is the average payoff (both theoretical and empirically).

In this sense, it seems that the use of Genetic Algorithms to simulate the evolutionary process closely matches the behavior predicted by the replicator dynamics while avoiding the strong limitation of considering only 3 possible strategies.

19.4 Conclusions

We have studied the evolution of strategies in the well known Repeated Prisoner's Dilemma using two different approaches: one analytical based on the replicator dynamics and one computational based on genetic algorithms. We show that the results obtained from the two approaches coincide almost completely in the sense that,

1. The two approaches produce the same two possible outcomes: evolution towards defection or evolution towards cooperation.
2. In the two approaches, the path towards the equilibrium are similar: monotonic when going towards defection, non-monotonic when going towards cooperation
3. In the two approaches, the proportion of times each of the two possible results occurs is also similar and depends on the number of repetitions of the game.

The scope of these conclusions, though, might be somehow limited. The reason is that, while in the analytical model only three strategies are considered (Always cooperate, Always defect, and Tit-for-tat), the computational model deals with finite automata of size 4, which can represent a very large number of different strategies. Nevertheless, one generally observes that from a starting random population of strategies (represented by finite automata), the genetic algorithm rapidly reduces the number of "working" strategies and, at the end, only strategies similar to the three used in the analytical model appear. Also, in Vilà (2008) we discuss other genetic algorithm operators that can deal with this issue, and the results are not different from the ones presented here. Another limitation of the present analysis is that it focuses exclusively on the Repeated Prisoner's Dilemma. On the one hand this might be considered a good research strategy as such game has been extensively analyzed and it is very easy to put in contrast the results obtained here with other results in the literature. On the other hand the same technique should be tested with other games to verify the conclusions drawn in this paper, which is the topic of future research. Nevertheless, in Vilà (2008) a similar approach (combining analytical and computational models) has been used to study a model of Bertrand competition with strategic sellers and buyers and the results there corroborate the main findings here: the outcomes from the replicator dynamics model and from the genetic algorithms model coincide to a high degree.

The results of this research seem to suggest that, in our opinion, analytical and computational models are good complements for research in social sciences. Indeed, while on the one hand computational models are extremely useful to extend the scope of the analysis to complex scenarios hard to analyze mathematically, on the other hand formal models can be extremely useful to verify and to explain the outcomes of computational models without the need of resorting to verbal and ad-hoc explanations.

Acknowledgements Financial support from grant ECO2008-04756 (Grupo Consolidado-C) from the Spanish Ministry of Science and Innovation, form grant SGR2005-0712 of the Generalitat de Catalunya, and the Barcelona GSE research network and CREA are gratefully acknowledged

References

Axelrod, R.: The Evolution of Cooperation. New York: Basic Books (1984)
Axelrod, R. and Hamilton, W.: The Evolution of Cooperation. Science **211** (1981) 1390–1396
Miller, J. H.: The coevolution of automata in the repeated PrisonerâÇÖs Dilemma. Journal of Economic Behavior and Organization **29** (1996) 87âÇô112
Binmore, K. and Samuelson, L: Evolutionary Stability in Repeated Games Played by Finite Automata. Journal of Economic Theory **57** (1992) 278–305
Boyd, R. and Lorberbaum J.: No Pure Strategy is Evolutionarily Stable in the repeated Prisoner's Dilemma Game. Nature **327** (1987) 58–59
Nowak, M. A., Sasaki, A., Taylor, C., and Fudenberg, D.: Emergence of cooperation and evolutionary stability in finite populations. Nature **428** (2004) 646 âÇô 650
Nowak, M. and Sigmund, K: Tit for Tat in Heterogeneous Populations. Nature **355** (1992) 250–253
Vilà, X.: A Model-To-Model Analysis of Bertrand Competition. Journal of Artificial Societies and Social Simulation **11(2)** (2008), http://jasss.soc.surrey.ac.uk/11/2/11.html.

Chapter 20
Impact of Tag Recognition in Economic Decisions

David Poza, Félix Villafáñez and Javier Pajares

Abstract In this paper we replicate the model by Axtell *et al.* (2000), a game where two agents ask for proportions of the same pie. After simulating the same scenarios, we get the same results, both in the cases of one-agent and two-agent types (tag model). Once we know the model has been properly replicated, we go one step further, by analyzing the influence in the observed behavior of the 'rational' decision rule and of the matrix payoff. First, we change the agent's decision rule, so that agents could decide playing a heuristic which is not so 'rational' as the original rule. We also evaluate the dependence of the results on the selected payoff matrix. We conclude that both the decisions rules and the payoff matrix could affect how and when the equilibrium and the segregation emerge in the system. This is particularly interesting for the tag model, as it is related to the role of group recognition in economic decisions.

20.1 Introduction

Agent-based modelling has become an extremely useful methodology. Restrictions in time and availability (among others) make it difficult to involve humans in experiments.

If both social sciences and economics are experimental sciences, they need a laboratory (López-Paredes *et al.*, 2002). By means of bottom-up models, social scientists have been able to analyze emergent social phenomena beyond the traditional simulation and experimental techniques. From micro behaviours and interactions among agents, we have been able to build stylized models explaining some of the relevant macro-observed facts.

D. Poza · F. Villafáñez · J. Pajares
INSISOC, Valladolid University, Paseo del Cauce 59, 47011 Valladolid, Spain, e-mail: e-mail: djpoza@gmail.com, villafafelix@yahoo.es, pajares@eis.uva.es

The pioneering works by Schelling and Axelrod showed us how computational sciences might help social scientists to develop models based on real assumptions about the behaviour of economic agents. However, we had to wait for several decades to put those pioneering works to the test. Thus, the research by Schelling (1971) was intensively extended by Epstein and Axtell (1996), who built up a real Universe (Sugarscape) by means of simple rules. More recently, Galán and Izquierdo (2005) discussed the meta-norm models by Axelrod (1986).

The efforts to replicate previous published models have grown during the recent years. Replication contributes to improve the reliability of the results and understanding of the system, as Sansores and Pavón (2005) stated. However, model replicating is a very tough task, as it was showed by Axelrod (1997), and Edmonds and Hales (2003). More recently, Wilensky and Rand (2007) proposed some interesting recommendations for improving diffusion and rigour in multiagent simulations. Anyway, replication is always the first step to improve and extending previous models, so that new hypothesis and new agent behaviours could be tested.

In this paper, we replicate the model by Axtell et al. (2000) (hereafter AEY), where two agents demand a portion of the same pie, and the portion a particular agent gets depends on the portion demanded by the other agent. Our results are in agreement with their conclusions, both with non distinguishable and distinguishable agents (the tag model), as Dessalles et al. (2007) also confirmed in a previous replication of this work.

But we try to go one step further. First, we have considered possible artefacts (Galán et al., 2009) and we have tested the influence on the results of minor changes in the agents decision rule (as López-Paredes et al., 2004, suggested), so that their decision depends on the most likely option taken by their opponents in previous games; in particular, agents decide based on the opponents decision in a "statistical mode". It is consistent with experimental research done in neuroscience which demonstrates that humans don't use statistical properties in their internal decision processes.

And secondly, we have tested how dependent are the results of the reward values on the pay-off matrix, to see how it affects the aggregated observed behaviour.

The main result of our research is that these simple changes may affect dramatically how and when the equilibrium is reached. Ito et al. (2007) empirically demonstrated that tags play a main role in the agents "rational" decisions. Our results confirm their findings.

20.2 Cognitive Foundations

Social Neuroscience offers an opportunity to design more realistic agent based models. Lieberman (2007) stated that human beings have two systems that control the manner they behave in social situations. These systems are the X-system and the C-system. The X-system is responsible for social process that would be designated as automatic and the C-system is responsible for social process that would be designated as controlled. In AEY's model, the agents take decisions at random with certain probability. This behaviour is a reflection of the decisions that one takes when his X-system is activated. On the other hand, the situations in which the agents take decisions in a rational way can be considered as an action taken by the C-system.

Ito *et al.* (2007) state that human beings take different decisions depending on several cues (tags) such as the gender, race or age they distinguish in others (we create stereotypes to facilitate the decision process). Their work justify that these cues are the cause of prejudices and different behavioral paths in the relationship with others. In the AEY's model we study, the agents only distinguish a tag but there is not a differentiated rule of behaviour (there is not prejudice at all in the society). Agents use the same rule of decision, founded in past experience (in some way, looking to create a stereotype) but they save the record of the reward at each round (the opponent's choice) in a different memory set. The consequence is that segregation in the society emerges occasionally (even without prejudices). We find that this result is very interesting, and can explain the mechanism that drives the emergence of cluster in a wide range of economic problems: industrial districts, spatial monopolies, etc.

20.3 The Model

We begin by replicating the bargaining model by AEY in which two players demand some portion of a pie. They could demand three possible portions: low, medium and high. As long as the sum of the two demands is not more than 100 percent of the pie, each player gets what he demands; otherwise each one gets nothing.

The authors assume a population of n agents that are randomly paired to play. Each agent has a memory in which he records the decision taken by his opponents in previous games. The agent uses the information stored in his memory to demand the portion of the pie that maximizes his benefit (with probability $1-\varepsilon$) and randomly (with probability ε).

At first, the authors assume that the agents are indistinguishable from one another, except for their memories about previous games. They conclude that, whenever there are not observable differences among the agents (the agents have not a distinguishable tag), there is only one possible state of equilibrium in which all the agents demand half of the pie. Otherwise, all the agents are either aggressive or passive (some of them demand low and some of them demand high), and no equilibrium is reached.

Secondly, the authors let the agents be distinguishable from one another by introducing a tag: they create two types of agents, each of whom with a different tag. The agents are capable of identifying their opponents' tag and they keep the portion of the pie demanded by their opponents in their memories, both with the same and different tag. In this case, the authors prove that, just by adding different tags to the players, discriminatory states can emerge under certain conditions, in which agents with different tags follow different behaviours.

20.4 The Model with One Agent Type

20.4.1 Replication

First, we have replicated the AEY's model. We used the original payoff matrix (i.e. the combination of values for the different demands): 30 percent for low; 50 percent for medium and 70 percent for high. We also used the original decision rule.

Problem approach
n - number of agents ε - uncertainly parameter
m - memory length of each agent
S_i - space of agent's ($i = 1, \ldots, n$) possible strategies
$$\rightarrow j \in [L, M, H]/M = 50, H = 100 - L, L < H$$
(L - select Low, M - select Medium, H - select High)
$[v_1, v_2, \ldots, v_m]^i$ - memory array of agent i, which stores the strategies
$v_k \in [L, M, H]$ chosen by the opponents in the m previous rounds
$[A, B]$ - couple of agent randomly paired / $\frac{n}{2}$ randomly pairs by round
If agent A chooses $i \in S_A$, and agent B chooses $j \in S_B$, they will receive $[i, j]$ if $(i+j) \leq 100$, and $[0, 0]$ if $(i+j) > 100$ (see Table 20.1, Combination of payoffs)

Decision rule
n_j^A - number of positions with value $j \in [L, M, H]$ in the memory array of agent A
$[v_1, v_2, \ldots, v_m]^A$

$Pr(B_j^A) = \dfrac{n_j^A}{m}$ - Probability estimated by the agent A for the possibility that the opponent B selects the strategy j (equivalent to the relative frequency of occurrence of value j in the memory array of agent A)

The utility function for agent A when selects the strategy $i \in S_i = [L, M, H]$ is:
$U(A_i) = i \cdot \sum_{j \in S_B}[Pr(B_j^A) \cdot V(i, j)]$
/ $i \in S_A$; $V(i, j) = 1$ if $(i+j) \leq 100$; $V(i, j) = 0$ if $(i+j) > 100$

Then, each agent A selects with probability $(1 - \varepsilon)$ the strategy i that maximizes its utility function:
A select $i \in S_A = [L, M, H]$ / $EU(A_i) = \max U(A_i)$
And selects a random option $i \in S_A$ with probability ε.

Example
$n - 10; m - 5;$
$L = 30, M = 50, H = 70$
$\Rightarrow S_A = [L, M, H] = [30, 50, 70]$ - space of possible strategies for agent A
if $[j_1, j_2, \ldots, j_m]^A = [30, 30, 50, 70, 30]$ - current memory array of agent A

$n_{30}^A = 3, n_{50}^A = 1, n_{70}^A = 1 \Rightarrow Pr(B_{30}^A) = \dfrac{3}{5}, Pr(B_{50}^A) = \dfrac{1}{5}, Pr(B_{70}^A) = \dfrac{1}{5}$

$U(A_{30}) = 30 \cdot Pr(B_{30}^A) \cdot V(30, 30) + 30 \cdot Pr(B_{50}^A) \cdot V(30, 50) + 30 \cdot Pr(B_{70}^A) \cdot V(30, 70) =$

$$30 \cdot \frac{3}{5} \cdot 1 + 30 \cdot \frac{1}{5} \cdot 1 + 30 \cdot \frac{1}{5} \cdot 1 = 30$$

$$U(A_{50}) = 50 \cdot Pr(B^A_{30}) \cdot V(50,30) + 50 \cdot Pr(B^A_{50}) \cdot V(50,50) + 50 \cdot Pr(B^A_{70}) \cdot V(50,70) = 50 \cdot \frac{3}{5} \cdot 1 + 50 \cdot \frac{1}{5} \cdot 1 + 50 \cdot \frac{1}{5} \cdot 0 = 40$$

$$U(A_{70}) = 70 \cdot Pr(B^A_{30}) \cdot V(70,30) + 70 \cdot Pr(B^A_{50}) \cdot V(70,50) + 70 \cdot Pr(B^A_{70}) \cdot V(70,70) = 70 \cdot \frac{3}{5} \cdot 1 + 50 \cdot \frac{1}{5} \cdot 0 + 50 \cdot \frac{1}{5} \cdot 0 = 42$$

Agent A selects 70 with probability $(1 - \varepsilon)$, as it maximizes its utility function.
$EU(A_{70}) = \max U(A_i) = 42$
And selects a random option $i \in S_A = [30, 50, 70]$ with probability ε.

A simulation of this replication is shown in Figures 20.1 and 20.2. Both simulations were run with the same initial parameters (the same number of agents -n-, the same memory size -m-, and the same uncertainty parameter -ε-). Figure 20.1 shows an equitable equilibrium of the system after 100 iterations. Figure 20.2 shows a fractious state after 53 iterations.

After running a great number of simulations with the same parameters, we conclude that the probability of getting the fractious state (Figure 20.2) is very low in comparison with the probability of reaching an equitable equilibrium (Figure 20.1). The reason for this is that, in the long term, the benefit of choosing M becomes higher than choosing L or H, and thus, the agents tend to choose M, reinforcing the system tendency towards the equitable equilibrium. All the agents are initialized with random memories. Therefore, there is still a little chance that the initial values in the agents' memories lead to a fractious state like the one shown in Figure 20.2.

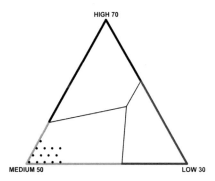

Fig. 20.1 Replication of AEY's model with a number of agents $n = 30$, memory size $m = 20$ and uncertainty parameter $\varepsilon = 0.2$. Equitable equilibrium

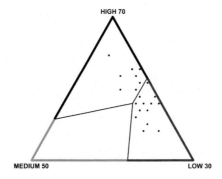

Fig. 20.2 Replication of AEY's model with a number of agents $n = 30$, memory size $m = 20$ and uncertainty parameter $\varepsilon = 0.2$. Fractious state

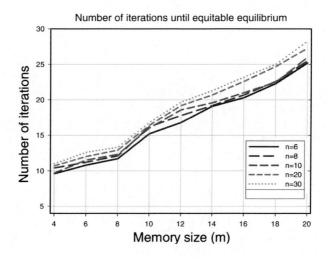

Fig. 20.3 Replication of AEY's model with uncertainty parameter $\varepsilon = 0$. Number of iterations to equitable equilibrium, as a function of the memory size; various n (number of agents)

Both models, AEY's and our replication, produce the same result in relation with the time it takes for the system to reach an equitable equilibrium starting from random initial conditions: it increases as the memory size grows. This is plotted in Figure 20.3.

20.4.2 Introduction of a New Decision Rule

After replicating the original scenario, we changed AEY's decision rule so that the agents demanded the pie portion maximizing their benefits against the most likely option taken by their opponents in previous games (mode of their memory). An agent will choose H if L is the most frequent decision taken by his opponents in the previous matches; If the most repeated value in his memory is M, the player will choose M. If previous matches show that H is the most frequent decision taken by his opponents, the agent will choose L.

New decision rule
Each agent A selects, with probability $(1-\varepsilon)$, its strategy i according to the statistical mode (Mo) of its memory array as follows:

$Mo[v_1, v_2, ..., v_m]^A = i \ / \ \max n_j^A = n_i^A \ \forall j \in S_A$
If $Mo[v_1, v_2, ..., v_m]^A = L \Rightarrow A$ select $i = H$
If $Mo[v_1, v_2, ..., v_m]^A = M \Rightarrow A$ select $i = M$
If $Mo[v_1, v_2, ..., v_m]^A = H \Rightarrow A$ select $i = L$
And selects a random option $i \in S_A$ with probability ε.

Example
$n = 10; m = 5;$
$L = 30, M = 50, H = 70$
$\Rightarrow S_A = [L, M, H] = [30, 50, 70]$ - space of possible strategies for agent A
if $[v_1, v_2, ..., v_m]^A = [30, 30, 50, 70, 30]$ - current memory array of agent A

$n_{30}^A = 3, n_{50}^A = 1, n_{70}^A = 1 \Rightarrow Mo[30, 30, 50, 70, 30] = 30 \Rightarrow$ Agent A selects 70 with probability $(1-\varepsilon)$, and selects a random option $i \in S_A = [30, 50, 70]$ with probability ε.

When the agents used this new decision rule, the chances of reaching the equitable equilibrium were considerably reduced (as López-Paredes *et al.*, 2004, concluded). In fact, the probability of reaching the equitable equilibrium was not higher than reaching a fractious state.

Furthermore, even when the equity equilibrium was reached, the time to get it was longer in comparison with the same conditions in the experiment with AEY's decision rule. Figure 20.4 and Figure 20.5 show this comparison. Notice that the decision borders change after introducing the new decision rule.

20.4.3 Introduction of a Variable Payoff Matrix

In AEY's model, the values of the possible demands are fixed: 30 percent of the pie for low; 50 percent of the pie for medium and 70 percent of the pie for high. We

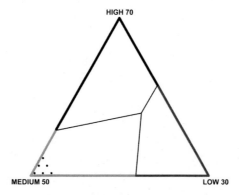

Fig. 20.4 Replication of AEY's model with a number of agents $n = 30$, memory size $m = 20$ and uncertainty parameter $\varepsilon = 0.1$. Original decision rule

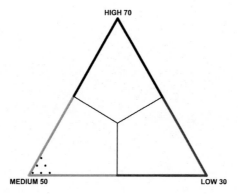

Fig. 20.5 Replication of AEY's model with a number of agents $n = 30$, memory size $m = 20$ and uncertainty parameter $\varepsilon = 0.1$. New decision rule

have studied different combinations for low and high rewards to analyze the effects on the behaviour of the system[1].

The combination of payoffs is shown in Table 20.1.

The simulation shows that the higher the value assigned to "low", the longer it takes for the system to reach the equitable equilibrium. The reward an agent receives when he demands low is always L, independently of what his opponent demands. When the value assigned to L is increased, the agents are not given an incentive to choose M or H, because the reward of choosing one of these options gets lower than choosing L. Whereas the expected benefit of choosing L is fixed (L), the expected benefit of choosing M or H depends on the opponent's decision, which is conditioned by the values stored in his memory. This is the reason why in the first stages of the simulation, the agents tend to move towards the bottom-right corner of the

---

[1] In any case, the sum of the values of L and H is equal to the 100 percent of the pie.

Table 20.1 Possible payoff matrices (demand combinations).

	H	M	L
H	0,0	0	**95,5**
M	0,0	50,50	50,5
L	**5,95**	5,50	5,5

	H	M	L
H	0,0	0	**80,20**
M	0,0	50,50	50,20
L	**20,80**	20,50	20,20

	H	M	L
H	0,0	0	**65,35**
M	0,0	50,50	**50,35**
L	35,65	**35,50**	35,35

	H	M	L
H	0,0	0	**90,10**
M	0,0	50,50	50,10
L	**10,90**	10,50	10,10

	H	M	L
H	0,0	0	**75,25**
M	0,0	50,50	50,25
L	**25,75**	25,50	25,25

	H	M	L
H	0,0	0	**60,40**
M	0,0	50,50	50,40
L	**40,60**	40,50	40,40

	H	M	L
H	0,0	0	**85,15**
M	0,0	50,50	50,15
L	**15,85**	15,50	15,15

	H	M	L
H	0,0	0	**70,30**
M	0,0	50,50	50,30
L	**30,70**	30,50	30,30

	H	M	L
H	0,0	0	**50,45**
M	0,0	50,50	50,45
L	**45,55**	45,50	45,45

simplex. Due to this behaviour, after a number of iterations, the appearance of L's in the agents' memories increases. Therefore, at some point, the expected benefit of choosing M becomes higher than the benefit of choosing L, and eventually all the agents choose M, reaching an equitable equilibrium. An analysis of this scenario is shown in Figure 20.6.

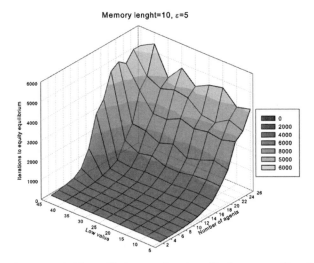

Fig. 20.6 Iterations to equitable equilibrium as a function of L (lowest payoff) and n (number of agents); uncertainty parameter $\varepsilon = 5$ and memory length m = 10.

20.5 The Model with Two Agent Types (the "Tag" Model)

In a second experiment, AEY attaches a tag to each agent, so that players are distinguishable from one another. There is only one tag in the model: the agent's colour. One half of the population will have a dark colour and the other half will have a light colour. The agents are capable of distinguishing the opponent's colour.

Although the decision rule does not change if the opponent has the same tag or not, the decision taken by the same-tag opponents are stored in a different memory set than the decisions taken by different-tag opponents.

AEY states that discrimination can emerge, both when the agents play with other agents of the same type (intra-type games) and when the agents play against players with different tag (inter-type). To analyze the results of the experiment, AEY uses two simplexes (Figure 20.7). The simplex on the left represents the memory of the agents when they play against players with the same tag (intratype matches). The simplex on the right shows the memory of the agents when they play against players with different tag (intertype matches).

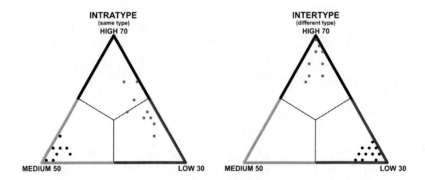

Fig. 20.7 Emergence of discrimination between players with different tags in our replication of AEY's model

After simulating this scenario, we concluded that segregation did not appear in the model. This is why we tried changing the decision rule so that the agents chose the best reply against the most frequent decision taken by their opponents in previous matches (mode of the memory vector), as described in section 20.4. Once the decision rule was changed, we could appreciate all the cases of segregation that emerged in AEY's model, in both intratype and intertype games.

In Figure 20.7, segregation has emerged in both, intratype and intertype games. In the case of intratype games (matches among players with the same tag), the dark agents have learned to compromise and finally reach an equitable equilibrium. However, the light agents tend to choose L or H and reach a fractious state. In relationship with intertype games (matches among players with different tag), the system has reached a fractious state: the dark agents become aggressive and tend to demand H and the light players become passive and tend to demand L.

20.6 Conclusions

In AEY's model, segregation processes emerge spontaneously. There is not a behaviour rule making agents behave in a different way when they play against agents with their same tag or with different tag. The only difference among the agents is the tag and the memories about the previous games. A priori one may think that the tags will not affect the agents decision as it is an exogenous property.

Initially, the two types of agents are initialized with the same criteria to get a random memory. After a series of iterations with other agents, they "learn" how to behave depending on whether the agent they meet is same-tag opponent or a different-tag opponent.

After replicating the model we conclude that our results are in accordance with the original AEY's work. In this paper, trying to go a step further, we have inquired about the effects of new decision rules and new payoff matrix. We conclude that simple changes within the original model can produce dramatic changes in the studied system.

In future lines of research, we will include new decision rules, such as using moving averages when taking a decision and endorsement techniques to assign more relevance to the decisions taken in the recent games than in the older ones. We are currently working in playing the game in a 2D grid and with different social networks topologies, to study if the segregation results will change if the agents are not randomly paired.

Acknowledgements The authors have been benefited from the financial support of the *Spanish Ministry of Education and Science* (TIN2008-06464-C03-02) and of the *Junta de Castilla y León* (projects GREX251:ABACO and VA006A09). We are also grateful to anonymous referees for their comments. Usual disclaimers apply.

References

Axelrod, R. M. (1986). An Evolutionary Approach to Norms. *American Political Science Review*, 80(4), pp. 1095–1111.

Axelrod, R. M. (1997). Advancing the Art of Simulation in the Social Sciences. Published in *Rosario Conte, Rainer Hegselmann and Pietro Terna (eds.), Simulating Social Phenomena*, pp.21–40. Berlin: Springer, 1997.

Axtell, R.; Epstein, J.M. and Young, P.(2000). The Emergence of Classes in a Multi-Agent Bargaining Model. *Brookings Institution - Working Papers No.9*.

February 2000. http://www.brookings.edu/~/media/Files/rc/reports/2000/02fixtopicname_axtell/classes.pdf

Dessalles, J.L., Müller, J.P. and Phan, D. (2007). Emergence in Multi-agent Systems. *Conceptual and Methodological Issues. Agent-Based Modelling and Simulation in the Social and Human Sciences.* 14, pp. 327–355. The Bardwell Press, Oxford.

Edmonds, B. and Hales, D. (2003). Replication, replication and replication: Some hard lessons from model alignment. *Journal of Artificial Societies and Social Simulation*, 6(4), 2003.

Epstein, J. and Axtell, R. (1996). Growing artificial societies: social science from the bottom up. *Washington, DC: Brookings and Cambridge, MA: MIT Press.*

Galán, J. M. and Izquierdo, L. R. (2005). Appearances Can Be Deceiving: Lessons Learned Re-Implementing Axelrod's 'Evolutionary Approach to Norms'. *Journal of Artificial Societies and Social Simulation* 8(3)2. http://jasss.soc.surrey.ac.uk/8/3/2.htm

Galán J.M., Izquierdo, L.R., Izquierdo, S., Santos J.S., del Olmo, R., López-Paredes, A. and Edmonds, B. (2009). Errors and Artefacts in Agent-Based Modelling. *Journal of Artificial Societies and Social Simulation vol. 12, no. 1 1.* January 2009. http://jasss.soc.surrey.ac.uk/12/1/1.html

Ito, T.A., Willadsen-Jensen, E.C., and Correll, J. (2007). Social neuroscience and social perception: New perspectives on categorization, prejudice, and stereotyping. In *E. Harmon-Jones & P. Winkielman (Eds.), Social Neuroscience: Integrating Biological and Psychological Explanations of Social Behavior*, pp. 401–421. New York: Guilford.

Lieberman, M.D. (2007). The X- and C-Systems. The neuronal basis of automatic and controlled social cognition. In *E. Harmon-Jones & P. Winkielman (Eds.), Social Neuroscience: Integrating Biological and Psychological Explanations of Social Behavior*, pp. 290–315. New York: Guilford.

López-Paredes A., Hernández C., Pajares J. (2002). Towards a New Experimental Socio-economics. Complex Behaviour in Bargaining. *Journal of Socioeconomics 31*, pp. 423–429, 2002.

López-Paredes A., Hernández C., Pajares J. (2004). Social intelligence or tag reasoning?. *2nd ESSA Conference.* www.uni-koblenz.de/~essa/ESSA2004/files/papers/Lopez_Hernandez_Pajares_ESSA04.pdf

Sansores, C. and Pavón, J. (2005). Agent-based simulation replication: A model driven architecture approach. In *Gelbukh A F, de Albornoz A, and Terashima-Marín H (Eds.) MICAI 2005: Advances in Artificial Intelligence, 4th Mexican International Conference on Artificial Intelligence, Monterrey, Mexico, November 14–18, 2005, Proceedings. Lecture Notes in Computer Science 3789*, pp. 244–253. Berlin Heidelberg: Springer.

Schelling, T. (1971). "Dynamic Models of Segregation." *Journal of Mathematical Sociology 1:* pp. 143–186. 1971.

Wilensky, U. and Rand, W. (2007). Making Models Match: Replicating an Agent-Based Model. *Journal of Artificial Societies and Social Simulation.* October 2007.

Chapter 21
Simulation of Effects of Culture on Trade Partner Selection

Gert Jan Hofstede, Catholijn M. Jonker and Tim Verwaart

Abstract The criteria that traders use to select their trade partners differ across cultures. The rational criterion of expected profit of the next contract to be negotiated dominates the decision in individualistic, egalitarian, uncertainty tolerant cultures. In other cultures, criteria like personal relations, group membership, status difference and trust may strongly influence trade partner selection. There also exist differences in the level of information about potential partners that traders require before entering into business contacts. This paper models the role of culture at the level of individual agents, based on Hofstede's five dimensions of culture. The model is applied in multi-agent simulations, that are designed as a research tool for supply chain research. The model is implemented as a random selection process, where potential partners have unequal probabilities of being selected. The factors influencing the probabilities are: expected profit and trust (learnt from previous contacts with potential partners or reputation), common group membership, societal status, and personal relations. Results are presented, that indicate that Hofstede's model can be used to simulate the effect of culture on the formation and maintenance of business relationships.

21.1 Introduction

Strategies for selecting trade partners are known to be heterogeneous among traders operating in the same environment. For instance, Kirman (2008) describes trade on the Marseille wholesale fish market: according to recorded transaction data of this

---

G.J. Hofstede
Wageningen University, Hollandseweg 1, 6706 KN Wageningen, The Netherlands, e-mail: gertjan.hofstede@wur.nl

C.M. Jonker
Delft University of Technology, Mekelweg 4, 2628 CD Delft, The Netherlands, e-mail: c.m.jonker@tudelft.nl

T. Verwaart
LEI Wageningen UR, Postbus 29703, 2502 LS Den Haag, The Netherlands, e-mail: tim.verwaart@wur.nl

C. Hernández et al. (eds.), *Artificial Economics*, Lecture Notes in Economics and Mathematical Systems,
DOI: 10.1007/978-3-642-02956-1_21, © Springer-Verlag Berlin Heidelberg 2009

market, some buyers are loyal to sellers, while others persistently display shopping behaviour, moving from seller to seller. Weisbuch *et al.* (2000) showed how this heterogeneous behaviour can be reproduced in a multi-agent simulation. The approach is based on reinforcement learning of expected profitability of trade relations, where the length of an agent's memory and its sensitivity to past experience are parameters that differentiate agent behaviour. An interesting observation in that research is, that both loyal buyers and shopping buyers survive in this market.

Literature on international business, e.g. Hofstede and Hofsteade (2005), Trompenaars and Hampden-Turner (1993), suggests that the distribution of the parameters introduced by Weisbuch *et al.* (2000) - i.e. the length of memory and loyalty to business relations versus the drive to explore new opportunities - will be different across different cultures. Furthermore, besides expected profit, phenomena like trust and personal relations are relevant and are known to have different influence on trade partner selection and network formation across cultures (Hofstede, 2007). In some societies, economic systems may be based on trust, in other societies on opportunism. Gorobets and Nooteboom (2006) showed by means of a multi-agent simulations that both types of systems might be viable in different societies. However, in intercultural trade these differences may hamper trade relations, because trust and opportunism may be appreciated differently. Also, loyalty may be appreciated differently across cultures.

The relation between culture and international trade has been studied at the macro level, e.g. (Gou, 2004; Kónya, 2006). The research reported in the present paper models the relation between culture and trade partner selection at the micro level. The purpose is the development of multi-agent simulations that can be used as an instrument in supply network research, in combination with human gaming simulations (Jonker *et al.*, 2006; Meijer *et al.*, 2006) The simulations and the human games are based on the paradigm of transaction cost economics (Williamson, 1985; 1998), with focus on asymmetric information, opportunism and trust. The main processes to be modeled in the agents are trade partner selection and bargaining in the pre-contract phase, and the decisions to either cooperate or defect and either trust or monitor and enforce in the post-contract phase of transactions. The present paper focuses on the process of trade partner selection.

The computational models of the effects of culture are based on the work of G. Hofstede (2001). Hofstede identified five dimensions of national cultures, that can be measured by a numerical index. The dimensions are: individualism versus collectivism, inequality of power, uncertainty avoidance, masculinity versus femininity, and long-term versus short-term orientation. G.J. Hofstede (2006; 2008a; 2008b; 2008c; 2009) describe production rule models of the influence of culture on trade processes for each of the individual dimensions. Section 21.2 of the present paper summarises the analyses reported in these models in as far as they are relevant for trade partner selection.

Although other dimensional models of culture could certainly be used for similar purposes, Hofstede's framework was chosen over possible other candidates (such as Hall, 1976; House *et al.*, 2004; Schwartz, 1994; Trompenaars and Hampden-Turner, 1993) for various reasons. First, Hofstede's work is parsimonious and accessible, with only five dimensions compared to GLOBE's 18, and with its 1-to-100 scales. Second, it has a wide scope, compared to Trompenaars and Hampden-Turner, whose dimensions are statistically intercorrelated and can be described as aspects of only individualism and power distance (Smith *et al.*, 1996) or Hall who focused on the dimension of individualism (low-context communication) versus collectivism (high-context communication). Those models miss out on issues related to gender roles, anxiety and Confucian values. Third, it has the greatest empirical base of these studies, with a well-matched sample of 117.000 respondents to the original study plus hundreds of replications during a quarter century that validate the model (Kirkman *et al.*, 2006; Schimmack *et al.*, 2005). Fourth, it is the most widely used. It has survived fashions and hasty storms of criticism (Smith, 2006; Sóndergaard, 1994). Fifth and most important, it shows continued predictive value for many societal phenomena (Hofstede, 2001; Smith, 2002). The most likely candidates for extension of the Hofstede model are the new dimensions found by Minkov using World Value Survey data (Minkov, 2007).

This paper aims to integrate the rules for the individual Hofstede dimensions into a model of the partner selection process, simultaneously taking all five dimensions into account. The basis of the model is the reinforcement learning model proposed by Weisbuch *et al.* (2000), enhanced with "non-rational" aspects that are relevant from the culture perspective. Section 21.3 describes the model.

The main goal of the authors' current research is to assess the feasibility of the Hofstede dimensions for agent-based simulation of the effects of culture on international trade, in particular in international supply chains of food products, where intensive trade among many small-scale firms occurs, and where usually product quality information is asymmetric. Section 21.4 presents results of simulations that indicate that believable simulation results can be obtained by applying the Hofstede model. Section 21.5 concludes the paper.

21.2 Hofstede's Dimensions and Trade Partner Selection

Behaving as a good, upstanding member of the group is at the core of the lives of all beings that live in social groups (Wilson, 2007). Human beings are intensely social and spend up to twenty years being taught how to act as virtuous members of society. But how to be virtuous? Different societies have found different answers to that question. In some, rationality is a prominent virtue; in others, common sense. In some, virtue consists primarily in honouring tradition; in others, it consists more of becoming prosperous. Although traders basically attempt to maximize profits, their cultural background sets limits to the means they use, to the partners they deal with, to the extent they get personally involved with partners, to loyalty, to the time spent on establishing relations, to bargaining tactics, to duration of bargaining etc. (Hofstede and Hofsteade, 2005; Trompenaars and Hampden-Turner, 1993).

In a series of papers, G.J. Hofstede et al. (2006; 2008a; 2008b; 2008c; 2009) proposed a process model of trading agents, inspired by the context of the trust and tracing game and transaction cost economics, and described the effects of culture on the processes for each of the individual five dimensions of culture as identified by G. Hofstede (2001). The relevant processes are:

- Trade goal selection: sell or buy, what product, quality level;
- Partner selection: search for a partner to deal with, agree to start negotiation;
- Negotiation: bargain about conditions and guarantees, resulting in a contract;
- Delivery: deliver according to the contract or use opportunities to defect;
- Monitoring and enforcing: spend resources on tracing or trust the partner;
- Belief update: while dealing, record experience to apply it in the future.

The present paper focuses on partner selection. The next paragraphs summarize the effects of culture on trade partner selection for each dimension.

Individualism versus collectivism. In individualistic societies people primarily feel to be an individual, responsible for his or her personal actions and well-being. Traders in individualistic societies traders actively build and maintain relations, and cut-off in case of insufficient utility. In collectivistic societies people have given group memberships and relations, that cannot be cut-off, and feel responsible for and loyal to their ingroup. Traders prefer ingroup partners, but outgroup partners can get ingroup status by mutual investment in the relation.

Power distance. This dimension differentiates between hierarchical societies where the less powerful accept that power is distributed unequally, and egalitarian ones where power relations are functional, as in principal-agent relations. In hierarchical societies, traders prefer business partners with equal status. They avoid the more powerful, but cannot refuse business proposed by a more powerful.

Uncertainty avoidance. In extremely uncertainty avoiding societies, people fear what they are unfamiliar with (xenophobia) and feel uncomfortable in uncertain situations. Uncertainty avoiding traders are distrusting and do not deal with strangers and people belonging to different social classes. Traders from uncertainty-tolerant societies may actively search for new partners without limits.

Masculinity versus femininity. In masculine societies people are oriented toward competition, performance, and material success. Traders actively search for new partners, or better: opponents, and experience trade as a game to be won. In feminine societies, people are oriented toward cooperation and take care for others. They prefer relations with a good atmosphere, prefer getting acquainted before doing business, forgive betrayal but avoid repetitive cheaters.

Long-term versus short-term orientation. In long-term oriented societies, thrift and perseverance are respected as virtues. Traders actively build and maintain network relations and see them as an asset for future prosperity. In short-term oriented societies consumption, social obligations, and face are important, for instance showing off by doing business with a high status partner.

21.3 Representation in Agents

Data for the trade partner selection process is modeled into the agents as follows:

- the agent's culture $<IDV^*, PDI^*, UAI^*, MAS^*, LTO^*>$: five variables that represent the Hofstede indices, scaled to the interval $[0, 1]$;

21 Simulation of Effects of Culture on Trade Partner Selection

Table 21.1 Partner model information taken into account for computing preference

Culture Type	Trust/ relation	Distrust	Ingroup	Outgroup	Status difference	Partner status
Individualist	+					
Collectivist			+			
Hierarchical					−	
Egalitarian						
Unc.avoiding		−		−	−	
Unc.tolerant						
Masculine						
Feminine	+					
LT-oriented	+					
ST-oriented						+

+ indicates that the partner trait increases preference in the particular type of culture;
− indicates that the trait has a negative influence on preference.

- parameters β and γ that represent an agent's loyalty (β) and learning characteristic (γ), according to the model of Weisbuch *et al.* (2000);
- a *partner model* (a set of variables) for each potential partner;
- *labels* that represent an agents group memberships and societal status.

An agent's labels are visible to other agents; the other information is private.
A *partner model* for partner j represents an agent's beliefs about j:

- the expected utility J'_j, learnt in previous business contacts, as a basis for preference in partner selection;
- experience-based trust t_j: a subjective probability that the partner will cooperate once a contract has been closed, also representing the experienced quality of the relation;
- group distance D_j, between partner and self, computed from *group labels*;
- belief about the partners societal status s_j, and the status difference $S_j = s_j - s_i$ with self, observed from *status labels*.

Note that the agents are not modeled to be aware of other agents' cultures.

The mechanism for partner selection is based on the reinforcement learning of expected utility proposed by Weisbuch *et al.* (2000). Agents select their partners at random, with probability:

$$P_j = \exp(\beta J_j) / \sum_{j'} \exp(\beta J_{j'}), \qquad (21.1)$$

where β is a parameter that represents an agent's loyalty to partners with high values of J_j; J_j represents the preference for a particular partner, based on experience of profitability of previous deals with that partner, and effected by the agent's culture. The effects of culture on partner preference are summarized in Table 21.1.

Table 21.1 presents 5 factors that increase the preference for another agent, depending on culture. In individualistic, feminine, or long-term oriented cultures the quality of the trusted relation with the partner is more important than in other cultures. In collectivistic cultures ingroup partners are more probable to be selected than outgroup partners. In short-term oriented cultures, there is a special preference for partners with a high societal status. The increasing effect of culture on preference for J_j is computed as follows:

$$e_j^+ = \max\{IDV^*t_j, (1-MAS^*)t_j, LTO^*t_j, (1-IDV^*)(1-D_j), (1-LTO^*)s_j\},$$

so influence of a single factor is modeled as the product of the normalized Hofstede index and the value of the relevant belief in the partner model, all represented on the interval [0, 1], and from these the maximal value is selected.

The decreasing effect is computed similarly:

$$e_j^- = \max\{UAI^*(1-t_j), UAI^*D_j, PDI^*|S_j|, UAI^*|S_j|\}. \tag{21.2}$$

The total effect of culture, $e_j = e_j^+ - e_j^-$, is used to compute the agent's preference for partner j, taking the history of previous dealing J'_j and culture into account:

$$J_j = (1+e_j)^\alpha J'_j, \tag{21.3}$$

where the parameter α determines the extent of the cultural impact on preference.

The resulting preference J_j is used in eq. 21.1 to compute the probability that j will be selected. Parameter β in eq. 21.1, representing loyalty, also depends on an agent's culture. We expect it to be increased to a maximal value in long-term oriented societies, and to be decreased to a minimal value in uncertainty-tolerant or masculine societies.

$$b = \max\{LTO^*\} - \max\{1-UAI^*, MAS^*\}, \tag{21.4}$$
$$B = \beta' + (\beta^{\max} - \beta')(|b|+b)/2 - (\beta' - \beta^{\min})(|b|-b)/2, \tag{21.5}$$

where β' represents a parameter that is assigned to the agent at initialization, with $0 < \beta^{\min} < \beta' < \beta^{\max}$.

The experience of dealing with agent j is processed after each negotiation:

$$J'_j(n) = (1-\gamma)J'_j(n-1) + \gamma u_j(n), \tag{21.6}$$

where $u_j(n)$ is the utility of the n-th negotiation result with j; $u_j(n) = 0$ if the negotiation was terminated without agreement. The value of γ is expected to depend on culture: an higher value in feminine, a lower value in uncertainty avoiding cultures:

$$c = 1 - MAS^* - UAI^*, \tag{21.7}$$
$$\gamma = \gamma' + (\gamma^{\max} - \gamma')(|c|+c)/2 - (\gamma' - \gamma^{\min})(|c|-c)/2. \tag{21.8}$$

Parameter γ' is assigned to the agent at initialization, with $0 < \gamma^{\min} < \gamma' < \gamma^{\max} < 1$.

After a agent has targeted a partner, applying eq. 21.1 it sends a proposal to negotiate about a deal. The receiver may either accept or ignore the proposal. The proposing agents waits for some time, and if it receives no reply, it updates J'_j with $u_j = 0$, see eq. 21.1, and than tries and targets a partner again.

If an agent has no negotiation going on, it checks for received proposals. It may have recent proposals from several agents simultaneously. From the simultaneous proposers, it selects the one with the maximum preference. There is one additional effect: agents from hierarchical societies that face a higher-ranked proposer are inclined to accept even if they do not prefer the partner, because it is not done to refuse in that case. The acceptability is calculated for all proposers:

$$a_j = J'_j / \max_{j'}(J'_{j'}) + (1 - J'_j)PDI^* \max(S_j, 0) . \quad (21.9)$$

Subsequently the agent selects, from the agents that proposed to negotiate, an agent k with maximal acceptability and decides whether to accept its proposal or to start looking for a partner by itself, with probabilities:

$$p(\text{start negotiation with } k) = a_k , \quad (21.10)$$

$$p(\text{start new partner selection}) = 1 - a_k . \quad (21.11)$$

21.4 Simulation Results

This section presents two series of simulation results. In the first series, the effects of the individual Hofstede dimensions are investigated by varying the index of one dimension, while keeping the other indices constant. These simulations are run in culturally homogeneous societies, i.e. all agents having equal cultural settings and, in some simulations, different group memberships or different societal status. The purpose of this first series of experiments is to verify the implementation of the model. In the second series, Hofstede's indices for some imaginary countries are used to simulate trade patterns emerging in multicultural settings. The results show that believably differentiated patterns can be generated. However, the model needs further tuning and validation with real-word data in order to generate realistic results for real countries.

Table 21.2 presents results of simulation runs in different cultural settings. The simulation model is based on Meijer *et al.* (2006). In the simulation, agents can select partners, negotiate, deliver, and process the experience gained in these activities, to update belief about expected utility J'_j and trust or quality of the relation-ship t_j. The agents are homogeneous: all agents have equal parameter settings. In all runs, eight supplier agents and eight customer agents were trading, all with parameters $\alpha = 1$, $\beta' = 1.5$, $\beta^{\min} = 0.3$, $\beta^{\max} = 3$, $\gamma = 0.3$, $\gamma^{\min} = 0.1$, $\gamma^{\max} = 0.5$. The normalized indices of culture were all set to 0.5, except one, which was set to either 0.1 or 0.9. The agents had no group distance or status difference.

As may be expected from eq. 21.4, Table 21.2 shows that long-term orientation, uncertainty avoidance and masculinity effect the emerging loyalty. As Table 21.3 shows, increasing the basic values of β' and $\beta^{\max}$ increases average loyalty, but the cultural effect remains. In particular, the increasing effect of LTO* is very strong with the high value of $\beta^{\max}$, because of the non-linearity of eq. 21.1. A similar effect occurs with low IDV* in this setting. Because of increased preference for ingroup

Table 21.2 Loyalty, expressed as percentage of trade contacts with the most frequently contacted partner in different (artificial) cultural settings $\alpha = 1$, $\beta' = 1.5$, $\beta^{min} = 0.3$, $\beta^{max} = 3$, $\gamma' = 0.3$, $\gamma^{min} = 0.1$, $\gamma^{max} = 0.5$; all agents have status 0.5 and common group labels

Value of index PDI*	UAI*	IDV*	MAS*	LTO*
0.9	28	21	28	26	45
0.1	31	32	30	35	24

PDI* = 0.9 : hierarchical; PDI* = 0.1 : egalitarian;
UAI* = 0.9 : uncertainty avoiding; UAI* = 0.1 : uncertainty tolerant;
IDV* = 0.9 : individualistic; IDV* = 0.1 : collectivistic;
MAS* = 0.9 : masculine; MAS* = 0.1 : feminine;
LTO* = 0.9 : long-term oriented; LTO* = 0.1 : short-term oriented.

Table 21.3 Loyalty, with increased $\beta' = 3$, $\beta^{max} = 10$ (other setting as in Table 21.2)

Value of index PDI*	UAI*	IDV*	MAS*	LTO*
0.9	28	21	33	34	71
0.1	40	36	51	44	29

partners, together with increased β and the non-linearity of eq. 21.1, the agents stick to partners they selected in the beginning of the simulation. Further experiments are run with $\beta' = 1.5$, $\beta^{min} = 0.3$, $\beta^{max} = 3$.

In similar experiments, it was found that reducing γ' to 0.1 reduced the learning of loyalty so that no differentiation was found; increasing it to 0.5 did not produce results significantly different from Table 21.2. In all further experiments $\gamma' = 0.3$.

Table 21.4 presents results with heterogeneous agents with respect to group distance, in homogeneous cultures. The results indicate that in uncertainty avoiding, collectivistic, and, surprisingly, long-term oriented societies ingroup partners are preferred; in uncertainty avoiding societies due to aversion against anything unfamiliar; in collectivistic societies due to ingroup preference. In the LTO society, loyalty makes agents stick to ingroup partners they selected in the beginning (when individual preferences are equal) because IND* = UAI* = 0.5.

Table 21.5 displays the effects of culture on trade situations with unequal societal status. Trade with partners from different classes is not done in hierarchical societies. In uncertainty avoiding societies, the aversion against what is different reduces cross-class shopping. In the simulations with masculine agents, the agents are less loyal, have no threshold toward contacting lower classed agents, and the powerful agents rapidly learn exploit their power, resulting in increased cross-class shopping.

The results presented so far concern artificial cultures. Table 21.6 presents results obtained with cultural settings that are similar to actual average Hofstede indices of national cultures. The results illustrate that differentiated behavior emerges with differentiated loyalty and different inclination to outgroup shopping. Results for China show a weak inclination to outgroup shopping. This may seam contradictory with China's position on the world market. In Chinese culture ingroup trading is preferred, but after getting acquainted and mutual investment in the personal relation,

Table 21.4 Outgroup shopping, expressed as percentage of trade contacts with outgroup partners; settings as in table 21.1, except group distance: both suppliers and customers are divided into equally sized groups 1 and 2 with group distance $D_j = 1$

Value of index PDI*	UAI*	IDV*	MAS*	LTO*
0.9	31	20	35	28	16
0.1	27	41	18	30	42

Table 21.5 Cross-class shopping, expressed as percentage of trade contacts with partners having a different status; settings as in table 21.1, except status: half of suppliers and half of customers have status 0.01, the others have status 0.99; group distance $D_j = 0$

Value of index PDI*	UAI*	IDV*	MAS*	LTO*
0.9	24	27	34	40	35
0.1	36	35	36	31	34

Table 21.6 Average loyalty and inclination to outgroup shopping in societies of agents with two groups, with group distance Dj = 1, no status difference, other parameters as in Table 1; the cultures are modeled with some similarity to actual national cultures

Culture similar to	PDI*	UAI*	IDV*	MAS*	LTO*	loyalty	outgroup shopping
China	0.7	0.3	0.1	0.7	0.9	68	8
India	0.7	0.5	0.5	0.5	0.7	38	22
Russia	0.9	0.9	0.3	0.3	0.3	36	15
Sweden	0.3	0.3	0.7	0.1	0.3	32	44
USA	0.5	0.5	0.9	0.7	0.3	23	42

an outgroup partner may become accepted as ingroup. Once the relational barriers are broken, uncertainty avoidance and masculinity come to effect.

The results for outgroup shopping of Sweden and USA are similar, in spite of the different cultures. In experiments eight customer agents with USA-like configuration and eight customer agents with Swedish-like configuration traded with eight Chinese-like supplier agents. Different patterns of customer loyalty emerged, as displayed in Tables 21.7 and 21.8. The tables display the number of successful transactions between each supplier and each buyer. In the simulation with USA-like agents, the number of empty cells is 24 on 203 transactions, and average customer loyalty equals 46 percent. In the simulation with Swedish-like agents, the number of empty cells is 31 on 293, and average customer loyalty equals 56 percent.

21.5 Conclusion

The contribution of this work is that it shows how a model of culture can be formulated to simulate culturally differentiated behavior of agents. The model of Hofstede

Table 21.7 Number of successful transaction between 8 USA-like customer agents and 8 Chinese-like supplier agents, in 500 time steps

Agent	S1	S2	S3	S4	S5	S6	S7	S8
C1	2	1	1	9	5		8	
C2	1	1	5		5	1	1	25
C3			15					1
C4		6			10	6	6	4
C5		3		5		7	3	2
C6	1	6		3	5		3	
C7	6	4	5	11	1			
C8	10	1		3			1	10

Table 21.8 Number of successful transaction between 8 Swedish-like customer agents and 8 Chinese-like supplier agents, in 500 time steps

Agent	S1	S2	S3	S4	S5	S6	S7	S8
C1		1	3		6	30		
C2		1	17	9			2	6
C3	4	20				1	2	
C4	2	11		4			22	
C5	2		18			13		
C6	30			2	1		8	
C7	1		11	3	15			10
C8	7				8		11	12

(2001) has been applied to partner selection in international trade in a context where personal relations between traders are important. The partner selection is based on the model of Weisbuch et al. (2000). Culture is modeled to effect preference for particular partners and parameters of the partner selection mechanism (the loyalty parameter and the learning parameter).

The model is implemented in agents. Multi-agent simulations have been run to verify the correct implementation of the model and to produce example results. Although further refinements are possible, the results show that believable behaviors emerge. The results qualitatively represent effects expected on the basis of Hofstede's theory. However, validation against empirical data in the situations that the model aims to describe, is required to calibrate parameters to actual trader's behavior and to scale Hofstede's indices to the simulation indices.

The situation that is modeled is a common market place. All agents can be aware of all other agents. The model does not include network extensions: the population of agents is fixed. The agents are free to select any partner, and the partner is free to enter into negotiations or to ignore proposals. The agents have labels that indicate their group memberships and societal status. Labels are visible to all agents and can be used for partner selection. The information about transactions is private. It is only available to the transaction partners. They can use it for future partner selection. An important characteristic of the present model is that agents do not have a theory of culture. They act according to their cultural programming, but they are not aware of cultural difference with partners.

The purpose of this model of partner selection is to simulate the behavior of players in trade games (Jonker *et al.*, 2006; Meijer *et al.*, 2006). In order to validate the model for this purpose, it has to be integrated with models of bargaining and contract fulfillment. The combined models can be tuned to results obtained in human gaming simulations, and their usefulness for supply chain research can be assessed. Those tasks remain for future research.

References

A. Gorobets A, B. Nooteboom. In C. Bruun, editor, Advances in Artificial Economics, Lecture Notes in Economics and Mathematical Systems 584: 121–132. Springer, Berlin, 2006.

R. Guo. How culture influences foreign trade: evidence from the U.S. and China. Journal of Socio-Economics 33: 785–812, 2004.

E.T. Hall. Beyond culture. Anchor, Garden City NY, 1976.

G. Hofstede. Culture's Consequences, 2nd Edition. Sage, Thousand Oaks CA, 2001.

G. Hofstede, G.J. Hofstede. Cultures and Organizations: Software of the Mind. Third Millennium Edition. McGraw-Hill, New York, 2005.

G.J. Hofstede. Trust and Transparency in Supply Netchains: a Contradiction? In W.Y.C. Wang et al., editor, Supply Chain Management: Issues in the New Era of Collaboration and Competition. Idea Group, Hershey PA: 2007.

G.J. Hofstede, C.M. Jonker, S. Meijer, T. Verwaart. Modelling Trade and Trust across Cultures. In K. Stølen, W.H. Winsborough, F. Martinelli, F. Massacci, editors, Trust Management: 4th International Conference, iTrust 2006, Proceedings, LNCS 3968: 120–134. Springer, Berlin, 2006.

G.J. Hofstede, C.M. Jonker, T. Verwaart. Modeling Culture in Trade: Uncertainty Avoid-ance. 2008 Agent-Directed Simulation Symposium (ADSS 2008), Spring Simulation Multiconference 2008: 143–150. SCS, San Diego, 2008a.

G.J. Hofstede, C.M. Jonker, T. Verwaart. Individualism and Collectivism in Trade Agents. In N.T. Nguyen, L. Borzemski, A. Grzech, M. Ali, editors, New Frontiers in Applied Artificial Intelligence, Proceedings of IEA/AIE 2008, LNAI 5027: 492–501. Springer, Berlin, 2008b.

G.J. Hofstede, C.M. Jonker, T. Verwaart. Long-term Orientation in Trade. In K. Schredelseker, F. Hauser, editors, Complexity and Artificial Markets, Lecture Notes in Economics and Mathematical Systems 614: 107–119. Springer, Berlin, 2008c.

G.J. Hofstede, C.M. Jonker, T. Verwaart. Modelling Power Distance in Trade. In N. David, J.S. Sichman, editors. Multi-Agent-based Simulation IX, MABS 2008, Revised Selected Papers, LNAI 5269: 1–16. Springer, Berlin, 2009.

R.J. House, P.J. Hanges, M. Javidan, P.W. Dorfman, V. Gupta. Leadership culture and organizations: The GLOBE study of 62 societies. Sage, Thousand Oaks CA, 2004.

C.M. Jonker, S. Meijer, D. Tykhonov, T. Verwaart. Multi-agent Model of Trust in a Human Game. In P. Mathieu, B. Beaufils, O. Brandouy, editors, Artificial Economics. Lecture Notes in Economics and Mathematical Systems 564: 91–102. Springer, Berlin, 2006.

B.R. Kirkman, K.B. Lowe, C.B. Gibson. A quarter century of Culture's Consequences: a review of empirical research incorporating Hofstede's cultural values framework. Journal of International Business Studies, 37: 285–320, 2006.

A. Kirman. Artificial Markets: Rationality and Organisation. In K. Schredelseker, F. Hauser, editors, Complexity and Artificial Markets, Lecture Notes in Economics and Mathematical Systems 614: 195–234. Springer, Berlin, 2008.

I. Kónya. Modeling Cultural Barriers in International Trade. Review of International Economics 14: 494–507, 2006.

S. Meijer, G.J. Hofstede, G. Beers, S.W.F. Omta. Trust and Tracing game: learning about transactions and embeddedness in a trade network. Production Planning and Control 17: 569–583, 2006.

M. Minkov. What makes us different and similar, A new interpretation of the World Values Survey and other cross-cultural data. Klasika i Stil, Sofia, 2007.

U. Schimmack, S. Oishi, E. Diener. Individualism: A Valid and Important Dimension of Cultural Differences Between Nations. Personality and Social Psychology Review, 9(1), 17–31, 2005.

S.H. Schwartz. Beyond individualism / collectivism: new dimensions of values. In U. Kim, H.C. Triandis, C. Kagitçibasi, S.C. Choi, G. Yoon, editors. Individualism and collectivism: theory, application and methods, 85–119. Sage, Thousand Oaks CA, 1994.

P.B. Smith. Culture's consequences: Something old and something new. Human Relations 55(1): 119–135, 2002.

P.B. Smith. When elephants fight, the grass gets trampled: the GLOBE and Hofstede projects. Journal of International Business Studies 37: 915–921, 2006.

P.B. Smith, S. Dugan, F. Trompenaars. National culture and the values of organizational employees: A dimensional analysis across 43 nations. Journal of Cross-Cultural Psychology 27: 231–264, 1996.

M. Sóndergaard. Hofstede's consequences: a study of reviews, citations and replications. Organization Studies 15, 447–456, 1994.

F. Trompenaars and C. Hampden-Turner. Riding the waves of culture: understanding cultural diversity in business, 2nd edition. Economist Books, London, 1993.

G. Weisbuch, A. Kirman, D. Herreiner. Market Organisation and Trading Relationships. Economic Journal 110: 411–436, 2000.

O.E. Williamson. The Economic Institutions of Capitalism. Free Press, New York, 1985.

O.E. Williamson. Transaction Cost Economics: how it works, where it is headed. De Economist 146: 23–58, 1998.

D.S. Wilson. Evolution for Everyone. Delacorte Press, New York, 2007.

Lecture Notes in Economics and Mathematical Systems   631

Founding Editors:

M. Beckmann
H.P. Künzi

Managing Editors:

Prof. Dr. G. Fandel
Fachbereich Wirtschaftswissenschaften
Fernuniversität Hagen
Feithstr. 140/AVZ II, 58084 Hagen, Germany

Prof. Dr. W. Trockel
Institut für Mathematische Wirtschaftsforschung (IMW)
Universität Bielefeld
Universitätsstr. 25, 33615 Bielefeld, Germany

Editorial Board:

A. Basile, H. Dawid, K. Inderfurth, W. Kürsten

For further volumes:
http://www.springer.com/series/300